Postcard Companion

The Collector's Reference

Postcard Companion

The Collector's Reference

Jack H. Smith

Wallace-Homestead Book Company
Radnor, Pennsylvania

Suggestions and comments for future editions or requests for further information
may be addressed to the author: Jack H. Smith, P. O. Box 9185, Cincinnati,
OH 45209.

Copyright © 1989 by Jack H. Smith
All Rights Reserved
Published in Radnor, Pennsylvania 19089, by Wallace-Homestead Book Company

Designed by Anthony Jacobson
Manufactured in the United States of America

Library of Congress Cataloging in Publication Data

Smith, Jack H.
   Postcard companion.
   Bibliography: p.369
   Includes index.
   1. Postcards—Collectors and collecting—United
States.   2. Postcards—Information services.   I. Title.
NC1872.S65   1989   741.68'3   88-51498
ISBN 0-87069-519-3

1 2 3 4 5 6 7 8 9 0   8 7 6 5 4 3 2 1 0 9

Contents

Preface   ix

Acknowledgments   ix

1. Postcard History   3
The Pages of History   3
No Turning Back   6
Shattered Illusions   10
Chronological Table   12

2. Postcard Publishers   17
Publishers and Printers by Location and Types of Postcards   17

3. Postcard Artists   55
Rarity Scale   55
Artists by Types of Cards, Publisher, and Rarity   56

4. Categories and Types of Postcards   137
Types of Cards   137
Novelty Postcards   145
Definitions   147

5. Books About Postcards   211
Postcard Books: Recommended Reading   211
Selected Book Reviews   219

6. Modern Postcard Publishers   257
Listing of Current Publishers   257
Publisher Profiles   259
  Coral Lee (Coralie Dixon Sparre)   259
  Curt Teich   260
  Faga   261
  Molloy Postcard Services   261
  Visual Vacations   262
  Numismatic Card Company   263
  Adfactor   264
  Columbus Street Press   265
  Suzy's Zoo   265

7. Modern Postcard Artists   269
Artist Profiles   269
  Richard Blake   269
  Jean Boccacino   270
  Rick Geary   271
  Fred Gonzales   272
  Patrick Hamm   273
  Sherry Kemp   274
  Marc Lenzi   275

    Daniel Mennebeuf 275
    Ed Pfau 277
    Don Preziosi 278
    Anthony Quartuccio 279
    Ann Rusnak 280
Other Artists 281
    American 281
    British 282
    Canadian 282
    French 282
    Others 282

8. Postcard Publications 297
    Periodicals 297
      Picture Postcard Monthly 297
      Postcard Collector 298
      Barr's Post Card News 300
      A Note About "The Big Three" 301
      Gruss Aus 302
      British Postcard Collector's Magazine 302
      Forum Cartes et Collections 302
      De Prentbriefkaart 303
      La Cartolina 303
      Other Postcard Periodicals 304
      Former Publications 304
    Postcard Price Catalogues/Annuals 306
      I.P.M. Catalogue of Picture Postcards & Year Book 306
      Catalogo delle Cartoline Italiane 307
      Stanley Gibbons Postcard Catalogue 307
      Neudin 307
      Picture Post Card Catalogue, 1870–1945 308
      Other Catalogues 308
    Postcard Auction Catalogues 309
      The Nuhns' Postcard Auction Fair 309
      Sally Carver Auctions 309
      Other American Auction Dealers 309
      Neales of Nottingham 310
      I.P.M. Auctions 310
      Phillips 311
      Acorn Philatelic Auctions 311
      Specialized Postcard Auction 311
      Other British Mail Auction Firms 311
      Helmut Labahn's Auktions 312

9. Postcard Dealers   315

Services Defined   316
Addresses and Services of Postcard Dealers   316
Postcard Supply Dealers   331

Appendix A. Everything You Wanted to Know About Postcards: Questions and Answers   335

Appendix B. Questionnaire Results   341

Dealers' Questionnaire   341
Collectors' Questionnaire   343

Appendix C. Annual Postcard Shows   345

American Shows   345
British Shows   348

Appendix D. Postcard Clubs   349

American Clubs   349
Australian Clubs   352
British Clubs   352
Canadian Clubs   353
French Clubs   353
Norwegian Clubs   353
South African Clubs   353
Analysis of a Few Clubs   353

Appendix E. Publishers' Colophons   357

Glossary of Foreign Terms   368

French   368
German   368
Other Languages   368

Bibliography   369

Index   370

Preface

Picture postcards haven't always been here. In fact, before the 1860s, they weren't here at all. Since then, they have been everywhere, showing us every conceivable side of ourselves. Postcards have recorded our history, shown us an endless stream of pictures about our world, and pictured its people—young, old, rich, royal, or wretched. They have furnished us with glimpses of war and views of popular entertainment.

Postcards have shown, and continue to show, it all. They are social records, political comments, links to the past, parts of the present, and views with claims on the future. Want a picture of the old hometown as it used to be? Want to see a Model T automobile or New York's Coney Island in its heyday or views of the San Francisco earthquake? Perhaps scenes of World War I and II are more to your liking. Picture postcards are willing and eager—and able—to oblige.

Indeed, there is no end to it. Postcards have illuminated human history, displaying it from this angle and that. They are the vehicles we ride as we view the human landscape; they are our camera on the world and on ourselves. In a sense, an unprofound but true sense, this world of ours is a mosaic with each piece of the puzzle having its postcard representation. Whether we may be able to place each postcard in the sort of configuration that furnishes meaning is another question. The postcard merely offers us options and opportunities, some might say. Are they right?

Or does the picture postcard, like the magician, see all and know all? Does it tell all, as well?

At this writing, postcards are the fourth most popular collectible in America and even more popular in many other countries. Considering their relationship to mankind, that of being a mirror image, it might be wondered why they are not higher on the desirability scale. This book is an attempt to examine postcards, to define them and ultimately to instill in the reader an appreciation of them: for what they are is what we are. Nothing more, nothing less.

Want to know why life is an incredible journey? Look at a postcard.

Acknowledgments

It would be all but impossible for anyone to prepare a volume of this nature without receiving considerable assistance from many sources. To merely express my appreciation to all of them with the spoken or written word seems altogether unsatisfactory and clearly insufficient. I am left to hope that each of those listed below will accept this acknowledgment, therefore, as a small token of my gratitude for his or her invaluable contributions.

Helen Ackert (Ackert Enterprises), Diane Allmen, John Alsop, Helen Angell (Cape Cod Postcard Club), Antique Collectors' Club, Paul-Noel Armand, Brian Asquith, Archie Atkinson (Southern Africa Postcard Research Group), Dorothy Baron (Upstate New York Postcard Club), Angela Beadell (Mid-South Postcard Club of Memphis), Jennifer Berman, Big Nickel, Richard Blake, Jean Boccacino, Q. David Bowers, Mrs. Drene Brennan (Post Card Club of Great Britain), Brightwaters Press Inc., Ken Brown, Cameo Creations, Canal Captains Press, Tom Capparelli, Joan Carlson, Sally Carver, Cassel PLC, David Clough (Canal Card Collectors Circle), Bill Cole, Corona Publishing, Michael Cousins (N. S. W. Postcard Collectors Society), Lee Cox, Roy Cox, Jean-Michel Cresto, Pete Davies, De Prentbriefkaart-verzamelaar, P.I.V., E. Demey (Antwerp Post Card Club), Dover Books, Anita Eisenhower, Jane Elwell, Siegfried Feller (*Cartomania* magazine), Filipandre, Forum Cartes et Collections, Ray Franks Publishing, Glen Gardiner (Toronto Post Card Club), Rick Geary, George Gibbs, Godine Publishing, Laura Goldberg (Wolverine Postcard Club), Fred Gonzales, Graphic Arts Center Publishing, J. R. Greene, R. M. H. Greenwall (Southern Africa PC Research Group), Gruss Aus Verlag, Patrick Hamm, Historic Kansas City Foundation, Hobby House Publishers, John Holman (Stanley Gibbons), Tonie and Valmai Holt, Lloyd Hoyoak, M. W. Hudd, Intercard, Irish Books Media, Beverly Jenkins (T Town Postcard Club), Pierre Jeudy, Charles Kay (Wealden Postcard Club),

S. E. Kemp, Joan Klepac, Klutz Press, Austin Knetzger (Gateway Post Card Club), Joanne Krusche, La Cartolina, La Posta Publications, Lake County Museum, Stavrakis Lazarides, Carolyn Lee (Torrance Post Card Club), Marc Lenzi, Jo Long, John Long, Brian and Mary Lund, Harry and Betty McCallion, John McClintock, Pierre Marquer, Evelyn Marshal (Rhode Island Post Card Club), Mary L. Martin, Joseph May (Windy City Postcard Club), Marge Mayes, Fred and Mary Megson, Doris Miller, George Miller, Molloy Postcard Services, Yannick Moure, Tom Mulvaney (Montana Postcard Club), Peggy Nash (San Jose Post Card Club), Neales of Nottingham, Susan Nicholson, Richard Novick, Roy Nuhn, Numismatic Card Co., Hal Ottaway, Parent-Child Press, A. J. Peacock (*Gun Fire* magazine), David Pearlman (*Postcards of Palestine* magazine), Anne Petitjean, Phillips Fine Art Auctioneers, Gilbert Pittman, Don Preziosi, Publishers Group West, Roy Pugh (Queensland Cartophilic Society), Anthony Quartuccio, Etienne Quentin, Paolo Riaro, Rizzoli International, Harvey Roehl (Vestal Press), Ann Rusnak, Nouhad Saleh, Jack Sammons, Del Schuler, David Shannon, Bertran Silman, Jean Claude Sizler, J. H. D. Smith, Societa Internazionale Caroline, J. C. Souyri (International Modern Postcard Club), Suzy Spafford, Coralie Sparre (Coral-Lee), Specialized Postcard Auctions, Kay Stansbury, Steam PR., Taplinger, Taylor Publishing, Albert Thinlot, University of Tennessee, Alfred Van-Der-Mark, Ms. Erella Vent, Tony Wales, Martha Walton, Arretta Wetzel (Black Hawk Post Card Club), Raymond and Maggie Zwolenski (Rhode Island Post Card Club).

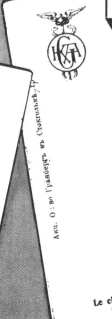

1
Postcard History

1
Postcard History

Few events in human history were met with such instant success and attention as the introduction of the postcard. The date was 1869, and the issuer of this most welcome piece of buff paperboard was the Austrian Postal authority. The following year, the North German Confederation, a geopolitical grouping of Austrians and Germans, followed suit. The records reveal the immediate acceptance of the postcard; within the first month, it is reported that 1.5 million of them, their stark blandness invaded only by the two-kreuzer stamp, were purchased by a ready public. These Correspondenz Kartes were government postals, but it appears that there were private issues even prior to this, for in 1861 John P. Charlton of Philadelphia had requested, and was granted, a copyright on a private postal card. H. L. Lipman accepted a transfer of the copyright and printed his Lipman's Postal Cards, a card with a stamp box and message lines on one side and a blank back, which was frequently used for advertising purposes.

In 1870, Britain and France printed their first government-issued cards to a citizenry that quickly clamored for them. Britain's first-year sales exceeded 75 million, and no one looked backward. The United States did not offer postals until 1873, by which time the postcard had become one of the most popular, if not the standard, means of communication between people everywhere.

Austrian Correspondenz Karte

Early U.S. government postal

The Pages of History

But these are the bare bones. In order to develop an appreciation of the welcome with which the postcard was received, it is necessary to spend a few moments poring over the pages of history. It is a sad fact but true that throughout most of human history the vast majority of the people in any given society were essentially, if not totally, illiterate. Those few who could read and write were routinely afforded positions of respect and authority, a situation thought to befit this cherished ability. It is clear that in the ancient world, the nobility and clergy—the two groups at the top of the social hierarchy—descended by and large from men who possessed this talent. Though in both cases this did not remain the prevailing reality (patronage and heredity took the place of education), the inroads to social standing quite frequently demanded a degree of literacy. In other words, the amelioration of inherited wealth and friendship or kinship with the exalted notwithstanding, a man who had any expectation of reaching his full potential was best advised to acquire an

Karnak - Colonnades

Pioneer Egyptian postcard

Scandanavian postal

A German postal card used in 1890

academic education, one that began with the mastery of the written and spoken word.

With the arrival of the Industrial Revolution, the Factory Act (mandating 2 hours of schooling per day for children under 13 years of age) and Robert Raikes's establishment of the first Sunday school (instituted to teach lower-class children to read and write) the number of those with an opportunity to rise, like cream, to the top increased dramatically. Literacy spread, very slowly at first but with some measure of regularity. Schools appeared, often poorly attended because they were privately financed and not compulsory; then, under the aegis of the state, schools began to flourish. A middle class of prosperous tradesmen and small business owners, many the descendants of opportunistic, hardworking individuals of the type who had existed as far back as the Guild Period of the Middle Ages, was beginning to assert itself. Their ideas were starting to be explored in the universities and in that popular phenomenon, the newspaper. Familiarity with language had made much possible that had been impossible before. Men contemplated concepts such as civil rights, forms of government, economic policies, and foreign relations. Men who could read and write became thinking men who insisted on intimate contact with their government and their society. They agreed with Aristotle that man was a political animal, and they proved it with the formation of societies, political parties, scientific organizations, and the like. Words were tools, and all men, according to their intellect, ambition, and curiosity, made use of them to greater or lesser effect.

In an age before television, movie houses, and the automobile, book reading along with the reading of magazines and daily newspapers became fashionable.

A scarce early Luxembourg postal

1898 postcard authorized by U.S. government for private use

Early Württemburg, Germany, government postal, 1878

This was part of the scenario. Another part was in the fact that people who appreciated the power of language to motivate and to incite one's imagination and encourage the thinking process generally were very often the same people who enjoyed using words to express their opinions. Conversation was becoming a highly developed art form.

In the meantime, the idea of communicating on a one-to-one basis over long or not-so-long distances emerged as a problem that needed to be examined and remedied. Previously, the few postmen who had labored in Europe and elsewhere were the king's couriers and, as such, were not concerned with the dispatch of letters between those of less than noble rank. In fact, in most cases, it was illegal for these early postmen to act on behalf of the common people. In 1450, Louis XI set up in France what is often acknowledged as the precursor of the permanent postal system, with a series of post houses at regular intervals; but it, like

Britain's system of 1523, was reserved for the use of the royal family.

Conditions improved only slightly over the next century, or even over the next, for that matter. The reality was that international communication that was both inexpensive and reliable did not occur until the formation of the Universal Postal Union in 1878. This organization established rates and worked out efficient methods of conveyance, thus correcting the inadequacies of the International Postal Service, which had preceded it. Although people had been sending written correspondence since the 1600s, the affair had always been a precarious one wrought with frequent failure, too much expense, and too little reliability.

What was needed in a rapidly changing world, once the transport and rate difficulties had been erased, was a way to communicate quickly. The time-consuming and cumbersome business of letter writing, which involved stationery and envelope, was tiresome to a generation focusing on the patterns of a changing environment. The agitation for a single piece of card stock on which a hurried message might be written had become keen in many parts of the world. The need for quickly dispatched notes with brief wording has become part of the modern world through everything from interoffice communiqués to international computer correspondence. The beginnings of this mindset, while certainly less acutely experienced and of a slightly different sort, may trace its genesis to this period.

Businesses envisioned the postcard as an excellent, inexpensive vehicle for touting their wares and services. Expanding government bureaucracies welcomed the invention as a convenient way of transmitting small bits of information. The common people saw in it an opportunity to both save money and to extricate themselves from the sometimes worrisome task of composing paragraphs of prose to be placed in an envelope.

But not everybody was happy. Stationers, eager to sell their occasionally elegant writing paper, recognized the threat immediately and managed to provoke the postal authorities, who saw the new card with its imprinted stamp as an opportunity to lighten their load at the expense of the envelope makers and the pretty paper sellers. Still, even the post office was not entirely overjoyed as they had continuously to contend with complaints about busybodied postal employees who might sneak a peek at what was regarded as private correspondence.

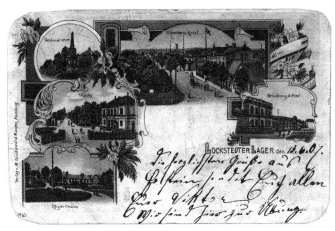

A detailed lithographic multiview

Bavarian postal, 1884

No Turning Back

No matter. Austria had led the way, and there was no turning back. If anything, the postcard may properly be viewed as the world's first attempt at rapid, international communication, and it was successful beyond the wildest dreams of even its promoters. Among the greatest purchasers of these first government postals—beside the letter-writing public itself—were the thousands of businesses whose use for the card has been mentioned earlier. They would buy the cards in bulk and place a printed message about their product or service or they would illustrate, occasionally in color, either the product or the company logo.

These were not the first ''picture'' postcards, however, as this distinction is generally accorded to the postcards produced during the Franco-Prussian War of 1870–71. It may be of interest to note that, like science, the postcard has frequently been used as a tool by the military, usually for purposes of propaganda and patriotism.

This first picture card was offered for sale on September 29, 1870, by the German Army Corps Society. Designated for the wounded, the uncolored card was illustrated with the Red Cross symbol. Signed by the commander of Occupied Headquarters in France and authorized by German Occupation Headquarters, it was released barely more than two months after the war was declared on July 15, 1870. More surprising is the fact that the missive was in circulation so soon after the government postal's invention. It was a large leap made in a short time.

The second group of picture postcards was a series of sketches drawn by M. Leon Besnardeau, a stationer at Sille-le-Guillaume. Their intended use, once the drawings had been reproduced on postcard stock, was for correspondence homeward from the French soldiers then in training at Conlie under Count Keratry. The printing itself was accomplished by the House of Oberthur de Rennes. The first series (November 1870)

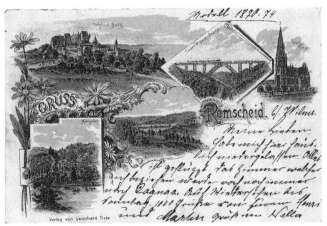

Gruss Aus Verchau: six views

Five early views of Remscheid on one card

Gruss Aus Steinau

by A. Schwartz, a printer from Oldenburg, Germany, to his father-in-law in Magdeburg, the artistic piece of pasteboard depicts a soldier and cannon on the front and has a patriotic poem on the reverse.

Unmentioned thus far is a fourth postcard connected to this war. The "par ballon nom monte" or balloon cards of 1870 were privately produced specimens whose function was to send messages out of Paris by air, this being the only means available since the city was in a state of siege by the Prussian army. Although they are very rare and are in every way to be considered devices for communication, it is equally true that they were not dispatched through the mails and are not, strictly speaking, "post" cards. Interestingly enough, had these cards been postally franked and similarly transported forty years later, they would have been classified as "airmail."

At some point shortly after the Franco-Prussian War, the first "gruss aus" or "greetings from" cards began to appear. Initially presented in brown tone or with blue or green backgrounds, they were essentially local view cards with the Art Nouveau style of embellishments, including intricately flowing vines, flow-

included sketches of cannons, pyramids of shells, and stacked guns. The second series (early 1871) featured outline drawings of cartridges in the center of which the soldier might include such information as military camp, battle units, and the like. Both series were instant successes and required printing in quantity.

A third Franco-Prussian-related card, postmarked July 16, 1870, may be a one-of-a-kind specimen. Sent

Gruss Aus Hall: a German celebration

An elegant Italian postal used in 1899

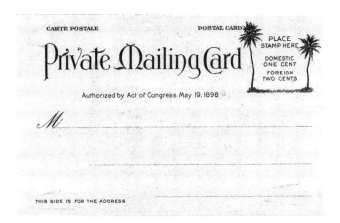

U.S. private mailing card used from 1898 to 1901

Early German advertising card

A simple Italian postal card

Souvenir d' Egypte: a rarely seen early Egyptian card

Un mercado en la calle.

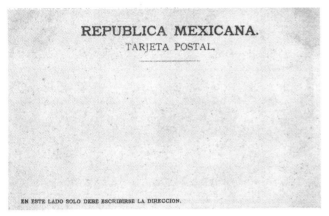

REPUBLICA MEXICANA.

TARJETA POSTAL.

EN ESTE LADO SOLO DEBE ESCRIBIRSE LA DIRECCION.

A pioneer Mexican card

ers, or scrollwork. Toward the end of the 1880s and concluding at a period not later than 1905, these cards were often gorgeously colored lithographs showing village and city views (sometimes military camp settings or special occasion cards carried this same salutation) from locations in Germany, France, Italy, Switzerland, and elsewhere. In 1894, England began producing its own variation with some of their beautiful, privately printed "court cards," which are today eagerly sought. For the most part, however, these views were both colored and produced in Germany where the art of lithography had reached its apogee and where the handsome colored dyes could be found.

America entered the picture postcard scene at an earlier date than many other countries. Their first example was for the Industrial Exposition in Chicago in 1873, and they produced a few other vignettes for other special occasions. Fundamentally regarded as the first U.S. picture postcards by most collectors, who seldom even see illustrations of these earlier issues, are the beautiful sets of cards printed for the 1892–93 Columbian Exposition held in Chicago, a popular place for such events.

By this time, the various world governments had relinquished their monopolies on the exclusive right to print postcards, and private publishers, eventually hundreds of them, offered and promoted their own wares to avid postcard collectors the world over. The figures attest to the popularity: by 1903 even tiny Japan was printing almost 500 million of them annually while the postcard behemoth Germany was churning out nearly 1.2 billion of them every twelve months. Still the rush continued.

Greeting cards, advertising cards, view cards, royalty, animals, political, military, celebrations, and more; it seemed that every human activity along with the entire panorama of nature was captured on the picture postcard. Even staid Queen Victoria was said to have a postcard album maintained for her perusal.

Before the telephone, radio, televison, and computer, the postcard was the chief means of communication. Previous to the invention of the airplane and the widespread use of the private automobile and the railways, most people did little traveling. They did not, therefore, have the opportunity to visit foreign lands or, for that matter, anyplace further than fifty miles or so from where they happened to live. Picture postcards furnished these "common people" a glimpse of strange and exotic places; of different kinds of people; of different types of architecture; of unfamiliar social habits or styles of dress; of events; even some animals and plants heretofore unknown.

Humanity couldn't get enough. From the mid 1890s to 1914, the fascination with picture postcards was unequaled by any wholesale passion that had preceded it. No one had to say, "Wish You Were Here": the postcard images made sure that you were. For those with the money, and that number was rising along with the level of education and the mass production of popular culture, a trip to these new lands could now become a reality. For those who could not go, there were always the postcards sent back to them or the postcards purchased from local sellers of foreign view cards, cards that could be placed into albums that graced the table in the foyer or sitting room. The picture postcard may have done little toward eliminating cultural prejudices, but it assuredly made more people aware of other cultures and, in some instances, explained what may have been inexplicable before.

An interesting Cuban postcard

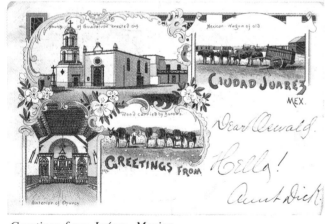

Greetings from Juárez, Mexico

Shattered Illusions

Then the bubble burst. To some, World War I shattered the illusion of a world rolling merrily along. For others,

An undivided-back Russian card

it revealed the tenuous thread of 5,000 years of acquired culture behind which the uncivilized brute in all of mankind resided. Perhaps the cultural trappings were merely a disguise to camouflage the true nature of the human beast. In any event, World War I gave mankind a classic opportunity to live down to his worst instincts. Some found it impossible to resist the primal call; nor was the postcard to escape useful service. Pressed into duty by combatants and neutrals alike, the picture postcard was used as propaganda, as letter home, as devices of patriotism, and as vignettes of reality picturing the battlefields, the machines of combat, the leaders, the dead or dying, and humor in the trenches. Much like the conflict in Vietnam being exposed to the point of distraction on television in the 1960s, so World War I was presented from every conceivable angle and perspective on picture postcards.

Well, perhaps not every angle. A few of the neutral countries (Holland and the United States) were peopled by individual citizens or groups with their own hatreds and agendas, and cards sympathetic to the Allied cause—or uncharitable characterization of the leaders of the Central Powers—were not infrequently produced.

Not one minute too soon, the war ended, though not on the same high note with which it had begun. Expectations were more realistic, more sobering. The Vienna Cafe Society had disappeared beneath the clamor of subject people demanding autonomy. As with Austria and Germany, so with the rest of the world, or at least the European part of it. Monarchy as the politically stable, normative form of government was being trampled into near oblivion under the omnipresent banner of People's Rights while the prewar gaiety of the middle classes was buried along with the bodies of their sons and daughters, their friends and allies.

Souvenir Athenes: a beautiful Greek lithograph

Scenics of Dermbach in the long ago

Souvenir of Zante; another masterpiece of the lithographer's art

of pessimism and introspection offered the postcard scant opportunity for renewal. Yet they did survive through the 1920s, 1930s, and 1940s; not, to be sure, at prewar levels, and they were frequently unnoticed, but the coterie of devotees and aficionados refused to give up on their preoccupation.

The decade of the 1960s witnessed a reemergence of interest in picture postcards, more in the United States than elsewhere, at least in the beginning. Postcard clubs, a few having been active since the 1940s, experienced new growth. A small but significant group of books devoted to studying the postcard were published. These in turn stimulated yet more interest. As was the case with the earlier fascination, the movement soon developed a life-sustaining force of its own; popularity fostered popularity.

Unlike the earlier craze period, however, much of the interest, especially in the older cards, is based on a view of them as a combination of antique and historical artifact. They are both—and more. But the tale has become a broader, more encompassing one, for even the cards that have been published since World War II and cards currently found in the racks or those offered for sale by a new generation of postcard artists have garnered an enthusiastic reception that is still very much in its infancy.

The interest is apparently a widespread one, as shown by the number of publications and periodicals related to the hobby of deltiology, or postcard collecting. A further proof is furnished by the fact that more books either dealing with postcards or that have postcards as their primary means of illustration have been printed in the last ten years than is the case for any other single collectible or antique.

Those who can only see what is going on around them will observe that the picture postcard has truly

In such a world, the wonder and joy created by the picture postcard found infertile soil in which to continue its upward spiral. They were now viewed as frivolous, a part of a lifestyle that, even in retrospect, seemed rather mindless and unstable. The new feelings arrived. Those who know the priceless value and time-less appeal of these picturesque jewels will tell you that they had never left.

Chronological Table

1861 The first copyright for a postcard was issued to John P. Charlton of Philadelphia, Pennsylvania. It was transferred to H. L. Lipman of the same city. Many were used for advertising purposes, but only a few have thus far been recovered.

1869 The Austrian Post Office, acting on the suggestion of Vienna's Dr. Emmanuel Hermann—in addition to several other sectors of various societies that had been championing the need for an inexpensive and quick means of communication—issued the first government postal.

1870 1. The North German Confederation, the Germans, and the French speedily followed the example by printing their own postals, which also were met with immediate success.
2. A. Schwartz, an Oldenburg printer, and M. Leon Besnardeau, a French stationer, produced the first picture postcards. Their separate efforts were related to the Franco-Prussian War of 1870–71. Most of the picture postcards were for the use of the troops in training or otherwise engaged in prosecuting the war.

1873 1. First government postal was issued by the United States on May 13.
2. First exposition card was of the Industrial Exposition in Chicago on a government postal.
3. Industrial Exposition in Providence, Rhode Island, was featured on a government postal.

1874–84 Other U.S. celebrations/expositions on government postals.

1878 Formation of Universal Postal Union.

1889 Public opening of the Eiffel Tower for the French Exposition held in Paris. Cards were franked at the top of the tower.

1880s–1890s Gruss aus types appear; first ones are black on buff or black on blue or brown on green; later many in full colors.

1891 First British pictorial postcards. They were views of the Eddystone Lighthouse designed for the Royal Naval Exhibition.

1893 The Columbian Exposition (sometimes called the Chicago World's Fair) was the occasion for the production of a series of lavish, full-color postcards that were sold as souvenirs to those in attendance at the exposition. They were printed on government postals and are often misidentified as the first U.S. picture postcards.

Turn-of-the-century scenics from Stollberg

Divided back card used in Europe from 1902 and in America from 1907

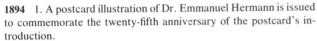

A white-bordered card in use 1916–1930

A linen card used 1930–1945

1894 1. A postcard illustration of Dr. Emmanuel Hermann is issued to commemorate the twenty-fifth anniversary of the postcard's introduction.

2. Introduction of England's "court cards." These were the first British nongovernmental or private postcards. Their name derives from the size (4½" × 3½"), which ensured that many of the illustrations on their fronts were placed up and down rather than side to side (i.e., vertical rather than horizontal).

1898 1. Private printers and publishers in the United States are given permission on May 19, 1898, to produce their own cards. The actual production date was set at July 1, 1898, which represents the end of the Pioneer Era.

2. First U.S. private mailing cards, souvenir cards, patriographics, and early "greetings from" types.

1902 First divided back cards appear in Europe. With the divided back, a message could be added opposite the mailing address. Previously, only the address was permitted on the address side, which accounts for the writing that is often found on the picture side of early cards.

1907 Divided backs in the United States.

1916–1930 White border cards, that is, picture postcards that have about a one-quarter-inch white border around the illustration. Not all the cards produced during this period have the border, but those that do are thus easier to date.

1930–1945 Linen cards used.

1945 Modern Chrome Era begins.

2
Postcard
Publishers

2
Postcard Publishers

There are two groups of people who make the picture postcard a reality: the publishers and the printers. In some instances, both occupations are assumed by the same individual or company, for a publisher is in effect nothing more than a person with a camera or a sketchbook who captures the image that is to be turned into a postcard.

The business of producing the final product is accomplished by the printer. Many of them in turn hired or commissioned photographers and artists to click, paint, or sketch while they took the result and reproduced it on postcard stock. Others were strictly printers for sale, furnishing the publisher with from 500 to 5,000 reproductive pictures of his or her original at the rate of perhaps one-half-cent per card. However, some of the entrepreneurs wore both hats; that is, they accepted orders to provide clients with postcards of their originals while also turning their own creations into material to fill the postcard racks.

The list of those who may be placed in this latter category includes such prestigious names as Curt Teich, J. Beagles, Gustav Liersch. N.P.G., Philco, Photochemie, Bruder Kohn, and a host of others. The problem is that it is sometimes impossible to determine whether these firms were producing their own cards or were performing a printing service for someone else. In some cases, publishers and printers are identified; in some cases, they are not.

This explanation is complicated further when it is understood that a number of the more famous—as well as many not-so-famous—joined their efforts to one another. Thus, one may encounter a photograph by Gustav Liersch produced by N.P.G. or artwork by Asheville Post Card Co. printed by Curt Teich. And so the mysteries continue.

The listing of publishers and printers presented here is not intended to by exhaustive. Rather, it is to be hoped that this large number of names, covering the entire face of the globe may give an idea as to the postcard's universal appeal and worldwide dispersal.

Publishers and Printers by Location and Types of Postcards

Publisher	Location	Types of Cards
A.B. & Co.	Austria	Views, military, political
A.D.M.	Italy	Glamour, views
A.H. Co.	United States	Greetings, humorous, military
A.M.P.	United States	Military
A.N. Co.	United States	Military
A.P.E.	Germany	Royalty, views, political
A.R. & C.i.B.	Germany	Royalty, views
A.S. Co.	United States	Views, military
A.V. et M.	Belgium	Military
Abraham & Sons	England	Views, military
Abrahamson & van Straaten	Amsterdam, Holl.	Views, social customs
M. Abrams	Roxbury, Mass.	Views, famous people
Acacia Card Co.	New York, N.Y.	Views, military

n/a = information not available

Publisher	Location	Types of Cards
F. A. Ackerman	Munich, W. Ger.	Views, advertising, glamour
Acme Photo Co.	Norfolk, Va.	Views
Acme Pub. Co.	England	Military, views
Acmegraph Co.	Chicago, Ill.	Views
John Adams	Belfast, Ire.	Political, views
Adams Specialty Co.	Nashville, Tenn.	Views
C. R. Adamson	Miami, Fla.	Views, sports, social conventions
A. Adlington	England	Views, military
Aero Distributing Co.	Chicago, Ill.	Views, advertising
Alabama Postcard Co.	Bessemer, Ala.	Views
Albany News Co.	Albany, N.Y.	Views, military
Albertype Co.	Brooklyn, N.Y.	Views, famous people, special occasion, military
A. Albonetti	Italy	Advertising, special occasion, glamour
Album Salon	Spain	Special occasion, glamour
Alexander Mfg. Co.	United States	Views, military
T. & G. Allan	England	Views, military
David Allen	England	Theatrical, advertising
Allentown Adpostal Corp.	Allentown, Pa.	Advertising
Alliance Party	Ireland	Political
Allied Printing	St. Louis, Mo.	Special occasion
Alpha	England	Famous people, military
Alpha Pub. Co.	England	Views, advertising
Alphalsa Pub. Co.	London, Eng.	Views, glamour, historical, advertising
Alterocca	Terni, It.	Views, historical, advertising, glamour
F. H. Altman	n/a	Royalty, famous people
American Art Pub. Co.	New York, N.Y.	Views, military
American Colortype Co.	Chicago/New York	Views, sports, animals, military
American Greeting Pub.	Cleveland/Detroit	Greetings, military, views, large letter
American Italian General Relief Committee	United States	Special occasion (disaster)
American News Co.	New York, N.Y.	Views, military
American Postcard & Mfg. Co.	Atlanta, Ga.	Humor
American Postcard Co.	Boston, Mass.	Views, military
American Red Cross	United States	Military
American Souvenir Card Co.	New York, N.Y.	Views, military, patriotic
Americhrome	New York/Leipzig/Berlin	Views
Th. Anderegg	Switzerland	Famous people
Anderson News Co.	Florence, Ala.	Views, large letter
Wesley Andrews	Baker, Oreg.	Views
Angelus Commercial Studio	Portland, Oreg.	Large letter

Publisher	Location	Types of Cards
B. Angerstein	Germany	Royalty, views
Anglo-American Pub. Co.	New York, N.Y.	Views, humorous, military
Anglo-Eastern Pub. Co.	England	Military
T. & R. Annan & Sons	Glasgow, Scot.	Art, historic
Aquarell	Germany	Views
Arden Press	Letchworth, England	Royalty
E. Arenz	Vienna, Aust.	Views, glamour, advertising
Aristophot Co.	London, Eng.	Royalty, famous people, military, social history, special occasion, views, crests, patriotic
Armandi & Testa	Torino, It.	Royalty, military
Armanino	Genoa, It.	Views, advertising, special occasion
Armoricaine	France	Views
Army & Navy Novelty Co.	United States	Military
Art & Humorous Pub. Co.	England	Military, propaganda, humorous
Art & Humour Co.	United States	Propaganda, military
Art Institute of Chicago	Chicago, Ill.	Museum views
Art Mfg. Co.	Amelia, Ohio	Greetings
Art Post Card Co.	New York, N.Y.	Views
Art View Distributors	Camden, N.J.	Views
Artistic Novelty Mfg. Co.	United States	Military
Artistic Photographic Co.	England	Views, art reproductions
Joseph Asher & Co.	Ireland	Political
Asheville Post Card Co.	Asheville, N.C.	Views, military, large letter, Indians, presidential
J. Ashworth	England	Views, military
Astro	Italy	Views, religion
Atelier Muller	Germany	Royalty, views, political, military, special occasion
Atelier Tonka	Zagreb, Yugo.	Royalty, military, political, views
Atkinson Bros.	Toronto, Can.	Views, patriotic
Atlas Society	New York, N.Y.	Views
G. Attanasio	Italy	Views
Auburn Postcard Mfg. Co.	Auburn, Ind.	Views
Augener	England	Children, fantasy
J. I. Austin	Chicago, Ill.	Famous people, blacks, greetings, animals, children, views, royalty
Austin News Co.	Austin, Tex.	Views
W. E. Ayres	Columbus, Ohio	Views, large letter
B. & C.	London, Eng.	Military, famous people
B.H. Pub.	Los Angeles, Calif.	Views, presidential
B.K.M.	Germany	Royalty
Back & Schmitt	Vienna, Aust.	Views, glamour
Jack H. Bain	Canada	Military

Publisher	Location	Types of Cards
W. & G. Baird	Belfast, Ire.	Political
Ballerini & Fratini	Italy	Royalty, military
Bamforth & Co.	New York/England	Humor, military, social conventions, satire, greetings, children
Elizabeth Banks	England	Military
Barber & Thatcher	Gulfport, Miss.	Large letter, views
Barkalow Bros.	Denver/Omaha	Views
L. I. Bartrina	Barcelona, Spa.	Views, glamour, special occasion, art reproductions
Barty Pub. Co.	England	Military
Batchelder Bros.	Croydon, Eng.	Political, views, military
Baudiniere	France	Military
Baxter Lane Co.	Amarillo, Tex.	Humor
Baxtone	Amarillo, Tex.	Humor
Paul Bayer	Dresden, Ger.	Royalty, military, political
Bazar Parisien	France	Views
J. Beagles	London, Eng.	Royalty, views, humor, animals, greetings, famous people, novelty (bas relief)
W. H. Bechtel	United States	Military
Hermann Becker	Germany	Military, children, humorous
Beger & Rockel	Munich, Germany	Royalty, military, political
Richard Behrendt	San Francisco, Calif.	Views
Benjamin's Photo Art Service	Mackinac Island, Mich.	Views
H. H. Bennett	Wisconsin Dells, Wis.	Views, Indians
Benzaquen & Co.	Tanger, Alg.	Military, views
G. Berger	Potsdam, Germany	Royalty, military, special occasion
Rene Berger	Brussels, Bel.	Views
Berger Bros.	Providence, R.I.	Large letter, views
S. Bergman	New York, N.Y.	Greetings, views
Bergstrom & Slattengren Co.	Rock Island, Ill.	Views, sports
Bering	Germany	Military
Morris Berman	New Haven, Conn.	Views
Ch. Bernhoeft	Luxembourg	Royalty, views
Max Berstein	Kansas City, Mo.	Views, military
Leon Besnardeau	France	Military
Bible Institute Colportage Assoc.	Chicago, Ill.	Views
E. Bieber	Berlin/Hamburg	Royalty, military
Julius Bien & Co.	New York, N.Y.	Greetings
Risto Biljanovic	Montenegro	Royalty, political, special occasion
Bill's Gay Nineties	New York, N.Y.	Advertising
Billings News Agency	Billings, Mont.	Views, western studies

Publisher	Location	Types of Cards
Birn Bros.	England	Views, humor, greetings, crests, military, royalty
E. A. Bishop	Racine, Wis.	Views
Edward Bittner & Co.	Berlin, Germany	Royalty, military
A. & C. Black	London, Eng.	Views, military, historical, children
Black & Grant Co.	Zanesville, Ohio	Large letter, views
Blackwell Wielandy	St. Louis, Mo.	Views
Blair Cedar & Novelty Works	Camdenton, Mo.	Humor
Blankvaardt & Schoonhoven	Holland	Royalty, military, views
O. Blaschke	Germany	Royalty, military
Bloc Freres	France	Views
Bluebonnet News Co.	Houston, Tex.	Views
Bluff City News Co.	Memphis, Tenn.	Views
Blum & Degan	London, Eng.	Views
Karl Blumenthal	Germany	Royalty, military
G. Boccolari	Italy	Advertising, views, special occasion
T. B. den Boer	Holland	Views, children
W. den Boer	Holland	Royalty
Bohlgemuth & Lissner	Germany	Military
Jos. Paul Bohm	Munich, W. Ger.	Royalty, military
Jesse Boot ("Boots Cash Chemist")	Nottingham, Eng.	Views, art reproductions
A. C. Bosselman & Co.	New York, N.Y.	Views, patriotic, military
E. T. Bottom	London, Eng.	Views
Boutelle	Toledo, Ohio	Views, transportation
N. W. Bouwes	Edam, Holl.	Views
J. W. Boyd & Co.	Belfast, Ire.	Political
A. Brank	Romania	Royalty, views, famous people
Braun	Paris, Fr.	Royalty, historical
Braun & Cie	Paris, Fr.	Views, famous people
Braun Art Pub. Co.	Cleveland, Ohio	Large letter, views
Brend'amour, Sinhart & Co.	Munich/Düsseldorf	Military, royalty
Bristol Printing & Pub. Co.	England	Views
British Art Co.	London, Eng.	Humorous, historical, views
F. A. Brockhaus	Germany	Military
Bronx Novelty & Post Card Co.	New York, N.Y.	Views
Jas. Brown	Limavady, Ire.	Political
William Brown & Son	Belfast, Ire.	Political
Brown & Calder	England	Military
Brown News Co.	Kansas City, Mo.	Views
H. L. Browning	United States	Military, views
F. Bruchmann	Munich, Germany	Views, special occasion, military

Publisher	Location	Types of Cards
T. Brudmann	Germany	Military
Aug. Bruning	Germany	Royalty, military
Brunner & Co.	Italy	Military, special occasion
AuH Brunotte	Hannover, W. Ger.	Royalty, military, political, special occasion
Bryant Union Pub. Co.	United States	Military
Buchhanduing	Vienna, Aust.	Royalty, military, views
F. Buchmann	Germany	Royalty, military
Buffalo Stationery Co.	Buffalo, N.Y.	Views
Bulletin Newspaper Co.	Australia	Views, humorous, animals
George W. Buohl	Gettysburg. Penn.	Large letter, views, presidential
Burgert Bros.	United States	Views
Burnham News Agency	United States	Military
H. J. Burrowes Co.	Portland, Maine	Famous people
Buss Bros.	Chicago, Ill.	Views
C. & A.G. Lewis	England	Military
C.A.P.	Paris, Fr.	Military
C.D.	Brussels, Bel.	Royalty, military
C.F.	France	Views
C.H.W.	Austria	Royalty
C.T. American Art	Chicago, Ill.	Views, military, transportation, advertising, presidential
Cadbury's	England	Advertising, special occasion, views
G. Cailliau	Brussels, Bel.	Royalty, political, military
Cairo News Co.	Cairo, Ill.	Views
Cairo Postcard Trust	Egypt	Views, military
Caledonia Post Card Co.	England	Special occasion
Cambridge Picture Post Card Co.	Cambridge, Eng.	Humorous, sports, views
Cameo Greeting Cards Inc.	Chicago, Ill.	Views
Canadian Souvenir Post Card Co.	Canada	Views, famous people
Canadian View Card Co.	Toronto, Can.	Views
Harry P. Cann & Bro. Co.	Baltimore, Md.	Views
Canney's Music Store	Portsmouth, N.H.	Views, special occasion, political
Canning	Belfast, Ire.	Political
Esare Capello	Milan, It.	Famous people
Capern's Bird Foods	England	Advertising
Capitol News Agency	Erie, Penn.	Views, large letter
Capitol News Agency	Richmond, Va.	Views, large letter
Capitol News Co.	Nashville, Tenn.	Views, large letter
Capitol Souvenir Co.	United States	Views, military
Arthur Capper	Topeka, Kans.	Views, political
Carbonora Co.	Liverpool, Eng.	Political
Carlton Pub. Co.	London, Eng.	Views, glamour, children, greetings, political

Publisher	Location	Types of Cards
Carnation Milk	United States	Advertising
Carrache	Paris, Fr.	Views
M. Carroll & Co.	London, Eng.	Views
A. J. Carter	Eastbourne, Eng.	Political
H. R. Carter	Belfast, Ire.	Political
Carter's Little Liver Pills	England	Advertising
Carter's News Agency	United States	Military
Cassell	England	Military
Castle Studios	England	Military
Catalonia	Barcelona, Spain	Views
Caterham Fancy Stores	England	Military
Central Art Gallery	England	Military
Central News Co.	Philadelphia/Leipzig/Berlin	Views, large letters
Central Sales Bureau	United States	Royalty, special occasion
Chaffee & Co.	Detroit, Mich.	Views
Champaign & Urbana News Agency	Champaign, Ill.	Views
M. Champenois	France	Views, advertising, glamour
Champion's Vinegar	England	Advertising
F. Chapeau	France	Military, views
Chapin News Agency	United States	Military
E. Chapman	England	Views
E. Chappuis	Bologna, It.	Special occasion
Charles & Russell	Belfast, Ire.	Political
Charleston News Co.	Charleston, S.C.	Views
E. P. Charlton & Co.	Montreal, Can.	Views, political, patriotic
Chessler Co.	United States	Military
Chiattone	Milan, It.	Views, military
Chicago Daily News/Kavanaugh War Postals	Chicago, Ill.	Military
Chicago Roller Skate Co.	Chicago, Ill.	Advertising
Chicago Sunday American	United States	Military
Chisholm Bros	Portland, Maine	Views
A. Christensen	French	Military
A. Christie	England	Views
Chronicle Co.	England	Views, political
Cies Des Arts Photomecaniques	Strasbourg, Fr.	Views
Cincinnati News Co.	Cincinnati, Ohio	Views
Cinema Art	England	Royalty
G. Citterio	Milan, It.	Glamous, advertising
City News Agency	South Bend, Ind.	Views, large letter
City Post Card Co.	London, Eng.	Humorous, military, views
Clark	Stillwell, Okla.	Real photo odd & curious, real photo exaggeration
Clarke & Sherwell	England	Royalty, historical

Publisher	Location	Types of Cards
Joseph Clarkson	Manchester, England	Views, military
Clearwater News Co.	Clearwater, Fla.	Views
John Cleland & Son	Belfast, Ire.	Political
Wm. W. Cleland	Belfast, Ire.	Political
W. M. Cline	Chattanooga, Tenn.	Views
Coastal News Co.	Savannah, Ga.	Views
Cochran News Agency	United States	Military
Coe Collotype Co.	Yorkshire, Eng.	Humorous
E. W. Cole	Australia	Views, greetings
Coleby-Clarke	England	Military
Collector's Pub. Co.	London, Eng.	Military, views
Collins Bros & Co.	Australia	Views, greetings, humorous, children, famous people
Collotype	United States	Military
Colman-Levy	France	Famous people
Colonial Art Pub. Co.	New York, N.Y.	Views, romantic, transportation
Color	France	Military, glamour
Colourpicture	Boston, Mass.	Views, large letter, ships, humor
L. Comerio	Italy	Royalty
A. G. Comings & Son	Oberlin, Ohio	Famous people
Commercial Colortype Co.	Chicago, Ill.	Views, patriotic
Continental Post Card Co.	Manchester, Eng.	Humorous, views, special occasion
L. R. Conwell	New York, N.Y.	Views, greetings
H. T. Cook	United States	Military
L. L. Cook Co.	Milwaukee, Wisc.	Views
A. H. Cooper	Toronto, Can.	Views
Frank E. Cooper	New York, N.Y.	Special occasion
Coopers News Agency	United States	Views, military
Corona Pub. Co.	Blackpool, Eng.	Views, famous people, political, greetings
Corwin News Agency	Jefferson City, Mo.	Views, large letter
H. Courtney	Belfast, Ire.	Political
M. M. Couvee	Holland	Royalty, political, views
Alex Cowan & Sons	Australia	Views, animals
C. Cozens	England	Military
Stephen Cribb	England	Military
H. S. Crocker	Oklahoma City, Okla.	Views, large letter
H. S. Crocker	San Francisco, Calif.	Views, special occasion
Crown Studios	Australia	Views, children, animal studies
Samuel Cupples Envelope Co.	St. Louis, Mo.	Special occasion, novelty (e.g., hold-to-light transparencies)
J. Cussac	Paris, Fr.	Art, military
Cynicus Pub. Co.	England/Scotland	Humorous, views
D. & G. Enterprises	Emblem, Wyo.	Views

Publisher	Location	Types of Cards
D.G.M.	Italy	Glamour
D.R. & Co.	Vienna, Italy	Military
Dade County News Dealer Supply Co.	Miami and Tampa Fla.	Views, military, animals
A. Daehler	Germany	Military
Harry L. Daily	Parkersburg W. Va.	Views, military
Daily Mail	England	Military, political, social conventions
Daily Mirror	Canada	Royalty, military, political
Daily Sketch	England	Military, political
Dallas Post Card Co.	Dallas, Tex.	Views, animals
Davidson Bros.	London/New York	Royalty, humorous, famous people, animals, special occasion, greetings
A. M. Davis & Co.	England	Blacks, views, fantasy, animals
George Davis	Oxford, Eng.	Views
George J. Davis	United States	Military
John Davis Pub.	London, Eng.	Views
Davis, Allen & Sons	England	Military
Norman Davy	England	Advertising
W. de Haan	Utrech, Holl.	Royalty, military, historical, views, art, glamour
De Ryker	Brussels, Bel.	Views, special occasion
De Wolf News Co.	Indianapolis, Ind.	Views, sports
H. C. J. Deeks	Paterson, N.J.	Novelty, royalty
E. Deffrene	French	Views, military
P. Degrave	n/a	Views
J. Deil	Austria	Royalty, military
Del Mar News Agency	Wilmington, Del.	Views, large letter
Marcel Delboy	n/a	Views
E. Le Deley	Paris, Fr.	Royalty, military, historical
Delittle, Fenwick & Co.	York, Eng.	Views, political, humorous
Dell'Anna e Gasperini	Milan, It.	Views, political, military, glamour
Dells Photo Service	Wisconsin Dells, Wis.	Views, military
Delta Fine Art Co.	England	Military
Aug. Denk	Vienna, Aust.	Royalty, military
E. T. W. Dennis & Sons	Scarborough, Eng.	Views, novelty, animals, humorous
Deseret News Co.	Salt Lake City, Utah	Views, large letter, novelty
Detroit Photographic Co.	Detroit, Mich.	Views, historical, Indians
Detroit Pub. Co.	Detroit, Mich.	Views, Indians, blacks, historical, famous people, special occasion, children, fantasy, glamour
H. Deutmann	The Netherlands	Royalty, military, political
Dexter Press	Pearl River, N.Y.	Views, humorous, sports, Indians, animals

Publisher	Location	Types of Cards
Deyhle & Wagner	Germany	Military, royalty
Diamond News Co.	Havana, Cuba	Views
Dickson's Ulster Series	Ireland	Views
Dietrich & Cie	Brussels, Bel.	Glamour, sports, views, fantasy, animals, ships
District News Co.	Washington, D.C.	Views, large letter
Dixie News Co.	Charlotte, N.C.	Views, large letter
Dobbs, Kidd & Co.	England	Royalty
H. M. Dobrecourt	Brussels, Bel.	Royalty, military
Dobson, Molle & Co.	London, Eng.	Views, military
H. C. Dollison	United States	Military, propaganda
Thomas Domby	London, Eng.	Views
Doring & Huning	Germany	Military
Doubleday-Heuther	United States	Views, military
W. & D. Downey	England	Royalty, famous people, special occasion
Dricot & Cie	France	Advertising
Driscoll Vendors	Davenport, Iowa	Views
Hermes Druckerel	Austria	Military
Druco-Optus Drug Stores	Philadelphia, Pa.	Views
Dungannon Club	Belfast, Ire.	Political
Dunlap	United States	Military
Dunlap-Henline Pub.	North Platte, Nebr.	Views
Dunlop Tires	England	Advertising
Ralph Dunn & Co.	London, Eng.	Views, sports, famous people, political
L. Dupont	Paris, Fr.	Views
Glenn Durham Printing	Harlan, Ky.	Views
Durie Brown & Co.	Edinburgh, Scot.	Views, special occasion
Dutta	Kashmir, India	Royalty, famous people
E. P. Dutton & Co.	New York, N.Y.	Greetings, views
Duval News Co.	Jacksonville, Fla.	Views, large letter
E. & S.	Dublin, Ire.	Views
E.B. & C.	England	Royalty
E.F.A.	England	Military, large letter
E.F.A. Military Series	England	Military
E.L.	Vienna, Aust.	Royalty, military
E.P. & Co.	Germany	Military, royalty
Earle	Bromley, Eng.	Views, famous people
Earnheart's Studio	Idabel, Okla.	Views
Eastern Illustrating	Tenants Harbor, Maine	Views, large letter
Eastern News Co.	Portland, Maine	Views, large letter
Josef Eberle	Germany	Military
Ebers-White	United States	Military

Publisher	Location	Types of Cards
Edward News Co.	Port Arthur/Beaumont Tex.	Views
A. R. Edwards & Sons	Selkirk, Scot.	Views, famous people
Edwards Press	Rochester, N.Y.	Views, large letter
Ehler S. News Co.	Birmingham, Ala.	Views, large letter
Egyptian Gazette	Cairo, Egy.	Views, character studies
Joseph Eilen	n/a	Military
Axel Eliassons	Stockholm, Swed.	Royalty, political, military, views
Eliotipia Molfese	Italy	Royalty, military, political
Elliot & Fry	England	Royalty, military, views, famous people
Otto Elsner	Germany	Military, royalty
Empire Novelty Co.	Chippawa, Ont., Can.	Views
Emporium	San Francisco, Calif.	Large letter
Eneret	Sweden	Royalty
Adolph Engel	Berlin, E. Ger.	Military, royalty
Emil Engel	Vienna, Aust.	Royalty, military
English Fine Art Co.	England	Views, humorous
English Pharmacy	Khartoum, Egy.	Military, views
Frank G. Ennis Paper Co.	Norfolk, Va.	Views
I. L. Eno	n/a	Military
Epko Film Service	Fargo, N.D.	Views
W. L. Erwin	United States	Military
F. Esch.	Germany	Royalty
Max Ettlinger & Co.	London, Eng.	Views, military, greetings, art reproductions
Excelsior Fine Art Pub. Co.	London, Eng.	Views, animals, crests, famous people, art reproductions, humorous
Exchange Pub. Co.	Belfast, Ire.	Political
Exposition Souvenir Corp.	New York, N.Y.	Special occasion
Eyre & Spottiswoode	London, Eng.	Views, famous people, military, art reproductions, animals
Dr. Eysler & Co.	Berlin, E. Ger.	Military, royalty, propaganda
F.H. & S.W.	Germany	Royalty, military, political
M. Fackler	Germany	Views, royalty, military
Fairman Co.	Cincinnati/New York	Views, humorous
P. Falk & Co.	Australia	Views
Famous Artists Syndicate	United States	Military, humorous
Fatherland Magazine	United States	Military, ships, special occasion
C. W. Faulkner	London, Eng.	Royalty, fantasy, special occasion, animals, political, views, crests, advertising, military, children, art
Feige & Parreyss	Vienna, Aust.	Military, royalty
N. Ferrell	United States	Military

Publisher	Location	Types of Cards
W. A. Field	London, Eng.	Views
Fine Arts Pub.	England	Military
Albert Fink	Germany	Royalty, military
Finke	Wilhelmshaven, W. Ger.	Views, royalty, military
Paul Finkenrath of Berlin (PFB)	Berlin, E. Ger.	Fantasy, babies, beautiful women, novelty (metamorphics), greetings, views, animals, political, humorous, political
M. Fischer	Berlin, E. Ger.	Glamour, fantasy
Fischer & Kramer	Germany	Views, royalty
Fischer & Uninger	Germany	Military
Fischgrund	United States/Mexico	Views, royalty, animals, sports, children, famous people
Flag of Peace Co.	United States	Military, propaganda
P. J. Flion	Brussels, Bel.	Views
Florida Natural Color	Miami, Fla.	Humorous, views
Forbes Lithograph Mfg. Co.	United States	Military, views
Fordham & Co.	England	Military
Forson Bros.	United States	Military
Foster & Reynolds	Washington, D.C.	Views
F. Frankel	London, Eng.	Humorous
Robert Frante	Germany	Military
v. Lorenz Franzl	Munich, Germany	Royalty
Frascati's	London, Eng.	Advertising
Frey Wholesale Post Card Co.	Dallas, Tex.	Views
Friends of the Army Museum	France	Military
Frisch (Albert)	Germany	Royalty, military
F. Frith & Co.	Reigate, Eng.	Views
Wilhelm Fulle	Germany	Views, greetings
Fuller & Richard	London, Eng.	Fantasy, views
I. A. Fulp & Co.	Sapulpa, Okla.	Views
Fulton Distributing Co.	Goddard, Kans.	Views
Oscar Furstenau	Leipzig, E. Ger.	Views
G.D. & D.L. (Gottschalk, Dreyfuss & Davis)	London, Eng.	Royalty, special occasion, views
G.G.A.M.	Italy	Fantasy, social conventions, satire
G.G.W.	Austria	Military, royalty
G.H.Z.	Germany	Royalty
G.M.K.	Germany	Famous people, views
Gale & Polden	Aldershot/London/Portsmouth, Eng.	Military, historical, views
P. J. Gallais et Cie	Paris, Fr.	Glamour, children, military, special occasion, views, art reproductions, political

Publisher	Location	Types of Cards
Galveston Wholesale News Co.	Galveston, Tex.	Views, military
W. H. Gannet	Augusta, Maine	Greetings
Gardner-Thompson Co.	Los Angeles, Calif.	Views, large letter
Frederick Garnett	England	Military
Garrison Toy & Novelty Co.	Washington, D.C.	Views
Gebruber Dietrich	Germany	Military
W. Geiger & Co.	London, Eng.	Views
General Distributing Co.	Omaha, Nebr.	Views, large letter
Luca Gentile & Co.	Naples, It.	Art reproductions
Henri Georges	Brussels, Bel.	Views
Gerlach & Schenk	Germany	Greetings, views
Gerson Bros.	Chicago, Ill.	Views, special occasion
Geschwister Moos	Karlsruhe	Royalty, views, military
Gibson Art. Co.	Cincinnati, Ohio	Views, greetings
Adolf Gierster	Munich, W. Ger.	Views, glamour, advertising
Giesen Bros. & Co.	London, Eng.	Political, greetings, famous people, children, transportation, animals
Carl Giessel	Germany	Views
Gilbert Post Card Co.	United States	Military, views
Louis Glazer	Leipzig, E. Ger.	Views, greetings, ships
Glen Photography	Dundalk, Ire.	Political
Glockner-Blattman	Switzerland	Views
J. Goffin	Brussels, Bel.	Views, political
Adolf Gohring	Germany	Military, political, royalty
D. Goldberg	United States	Military
Golden Gift Shop	United States	Military
J. Goldiner	England	Royalty
A. C. Gomes & Son	Zanzibar	Royalty
J. A. Goossens	Belgium	Military
Gottschalk, Dreyfuss & Davis	England	Humorous, views
Grafos	Madrid, Spa.	Royalty, views
Glen Graham	Leeds, Eng.	Political
Graham & Heslip	Belfast, Ire.	Political
Gramatan Art Co.	Mount Vernon, N.Y.	Views
W. H. Grant	England	Novelty (woven silk)
Graphic Facts of America	Alamogordo, N.M.	Views
Graphic Post Card Co.	New York, N.Y.	Views, famous people
F. Lli Grassi	Italy	Views
Gray & Thompson	Chapel Hill, N.C.	Views
Graycraft Card Co.	Danville, Va.	Military, views
Greaves & Co.	England	Views, greetings
E. R. Green & Co.	England	Humorous
Greningaire	Paris, Fr.	Glamour, advertising

Publisher	Location	Types of Cards
Grinnel Litho Co.	New York, N.Y.	Special occasion, views
Friedrich Grober	Germany	Royalty, military
A. Grubicy	Milan, It.	Views, special occasion
Fedor Grunthal	Berlin, Ger.	Views
H. M. Guest	n/a	Military
H. Guggenheim & Co.	Zurich, Switz.	Royalty, views
Guigoni & Bossi	Italy	Royalty, views, political, military
Guiness	England	Advertising, historical, fantasy
Gulf Coast News Service	Gulfport, Miss.	Views
Gulf Stream Card & Distrubuting Co.	Miami, Fla.	Views, large letter
Gussoni	Milan, It.	Views, special occasion, advertising
L. Gutierrez	Veracruz, Mex.	Views
H.H.I.W.	Austria	Military
H.H.T.	United States	Views
H.S.B.	United States	Views, western studies
Hackley News	Des Moines, Iowa	Views
Hagedorn Studio	Sister Bay, Wis.	Views
Wolff Hagelberg	Berlin, Germany	Views, novelty (hold-to-light)
K. Hagen	Offenbach, W. Ger.	Views
Harry H. Hamm	Erie, Penn.	Views, transportation
V. O. Hammon Pub. Co.	Chicago, Ill.	Military, views, humorous
Hancock's Variety Store	Warm Springs, Ga.	Views
Handleman Co.	Chicago, Ill.	Views
Handler News Agency	Grand Island, Nebr.	Views, large letter
Hannaford & Nasser	United States	Military
Wilhelm Hannemann	Germany	Military, political
Hannibal News Co.	Hannibal, Mo.	Views, famous people
Karl Harbauer	Germany	Military
Harding & Billings	Sydney, Aust.	Views, large letter, glamour, military, humorous, novelty
W. E. Hardison	United States	Military
J. Harrap	London, Eng.	Views
W. S. Harriman	Columbus, Ohio	Views
W. J. Harris	United States	Military
Harris Bros	Cuba	Views, military
Harris News Agency	Baton Rouge, La.	Views
Harrop's	Liverpool, Eng.	Views
Hart Pub.	London, Eng.	Views, greetings, special occasion
Hartman Litho Sales Co.	Largo, Fla.	Views
Hartman News Agency	Peoria, Ill.	Views, large letter

Publisher	Location	Types of Cards
F. Hartmann	Germany	Views, pretty women, novelty (hold-to-light), sports, children, humorous, animals, military, royalty, trains
J. G. Hatton	Mexico	Views, sports (bullfighting)
Hauser & Menet	Germany	Royalty
Hawaii & South Seas Curio Co.	Honolulu, Hawaii	Royalty, views, social conventions
Franz Hayer	Munich, W. Ger.	Views
Haynes Studios	Bozeman, Mont.	Views
Paul Hechscher	Germany	Royalty, military
F. M. Heck	United States	Views
Frank E. Hecox	El Paso, Texas	Military
P. Hiejloo	Holland	Views
Max Heimbrecht	Germany	Novelty (coin cards)
Percy Hein	Munich, W. Ger.	Royalty, military, political
Henry Heininger	United States	Military
Heinz Ocean Pier	Atlantic City, N.J.	Views, advertising
Hemine	France	Military
James Henderson & Sons	London, Eng.	Views, humorous, glamour, animals, greetings, military, fantasy
Henderson's	Newtownstewart, Ire.	Political
Hendrickson Post Cards	Poplar Bluff, Mo.	Views, large letter
Edwin Henel	Munich, Germany	Advertising, special occasion
Hennessy	United States	Military
Hermann-Martin	Nuremberg, W. Ger.	Views
Martin Herpich	Munich, Germany	Royalty, military
Gebr. Herz	Altona, Germany	Views
Herz Post Cards	San Diego, Calif.	Views, animals
Max Herzig & Co.	Vienna, Aust.	Glamour, advertising
Fritz Heuchkel	Germany	Royalty, military
Heverin News Co.	Louisville, Ky.	Views
E. J. Hey & Co.	London, Eng.	Military
Hickey Bros.	Davenport, Iowa	Views
Hilburn	United States	Military, views
A. Hildebrandt	Berlin, Germany	Military, royalty, political
S. Hildesheimer	London, Eng.	Views, humorous, animals, glamour, greetings, historical, art reproductions
Hillsboro News Co.	Tampa, Fla.	Views
D. Hilson	United States	Social conventions, political
A. Hirschwitz	New Orleans, La.	Views

Publisher	Location	Types of Cards
G. Hirth	Munich, W. Ger.	Advertising, glamour
Historic Event Series	Ireland	Political
Hochstetter & Vischer	Stuttgart, W. Ger.	Royalty, military
Hodder & Stoughton	England	Military, animals
Roberto Hoesch	n/a	Views, religious
D. W. Hoffman	Germany	Military
Heinrich Hoffman	Germany	Military, political, special occasion
J. B. Hoffmann	United States	Military
Hoke Drug Co.	United States	Military
H. A. Hollander Drug Co.	Cincinnati, Ohio	Views
Holloway's Pills & Ointment	England	Royalty
Eskil Holm	Stockholm, Swed.	Views, greetings, special occasion
C. Holmes	Centerville, Ind.	Views, sports
W. Holmes	Glasgow, Scot.	Humorous, views
H. Homann	Darmstadt, W. Ger.	Views
Suzanne Homann	Darmstadt, Germany	Royalty, military
Hong Kong Pictorial Postcard Co.	Hong Kong	Views, military
W. H. Horne Co.	El Paso, Tex.	Views, military
Hornick Hess & More	Sioux City, Iowa	Views
Horrocks & Co.	England	Views, advertising
A. L. Hoste	France	Military
Franz Josef Huber	Munich, W. Ger.	Military, royalty
Menke Huber	Germany	Royalty, military
Hudson River Day Lane	United States	Military
C. W. Hughes & Co.	United States	Views, presidential
Hughes & Mullins	Ryde, Isle of Wight	Royalty
Franz Huld	New York, N.Y.	Views, military, special occasion, novelty, greetings, blacks, Indians
Franz Hummel	Augsburg, W. Ger.	Royalty, military
Hungerford-Holbrook Co.	United States	Military
Barral Huros	Barcelona, Spain	Views, advertising
Hurst & Co.	Belfast, Ire.	Political
Husnik & Hausler	Hungary and Yugoslavia	Military
Hutson Bros.	London, Eng.	Military, humorous
L. Hyman's News & Book Store	Des Moines, Iowa	Military, views
I.F.S.	United States	Military
Illustrated Post Card Co.	Montreal, Can.	Patriotic, views, crests, special occasion, Indians
Illustrated Postal Card Co.	New York/Leipzig	Views, historical, royalty, greetings, military
Imberg & Lefson	Berlin, E. Ger.	Military
Imperial Cigar & Tobacco Co.	United States	Military, advertising
Imperial Greeting Card Co.	United States	Military, greetings, views

Publisher	Location	Types of Cards
Imperial War Museum	London, Eng.	Military, political
Independent Labour	Ireland	Political, propaganda
Independent News Agency	Fargo, N.D.	Views
Indianapolis Motor Speedway Corp.	Indianapolis, Ind.	Views, famous people, sports
Inter Art (International Art Co.)	England	Views, humorous, children, greetings, animals, military, novelty, glamour, art
Inter City News Co.	United States	Military, views
International Art. Pub. Co.	New York/Berlin	Greetings
International Film Service	United States	Views, military
International Fine Art Co.	Montreal, Can.	Views
International News Service	United States	Views, military
International Post Card Co.	New York, N.Y.	Views, presidential, greetings
International Post Card Co.	St. Louis, Mo.	Views, greetings
Interstate Co.	United States	Military
Irish Pictorial Post Card Co.	Cork, Ire.	Views, humorous
Island Curio Store	Honolulu, Hawaii	Views, royalty, animals
Italian Aeronautical Command	Italy	Military
Izdanje ''Rubens''	Zagreb, Yugo.	Royalty
J.M.P.	United States	Military
J.S.M. & Co.	Germany	Military
Ja Ja (Stoddart & Co.)	England	Crests, views, tartans
Jamaica News & Post Card Supplier	Kingston, Jamaica	Views
Jane & Gentry	England	Military
A. L. Jansson	Holland	Military, novelty
Jarrold & Sons	Norwich, Eng.	Views, crests, military, floral, political, heraldic
Jeffers Postcard Pub.	Ireland	Political
Jobber Bradford News Co.	Bradford, Penn.	Views, famous people
Tom B. Johnson	United States	Military
James Johnston	Belfast, Ire.	Political
W. & A. K. Johnston	England	Heraldic, views, famous people, royalty, military
Johnston's Art Stores	United States	Military
Robert Jolley	Australia	Views, royalty, special occasion, greetings, shipping
G. W. Jones	England	Military
Tom Jones	Cincinnati, Ohio	Views
A. V. N. Jones & Co.	London, Eng.	Royalty
Jones & Gullen	United States	Military
Jones Sewing Machine	England	Military, advertising
Joplin News Co.	Joplin, Mo.	Views, large letter

Publisher	Location	Types of Cards
C. Jordi	Havanna, Cuba	Views
Judd	United States	Military
Judges	Hastings, Eng.	Views, animals, military
Jullien Bros.	n/a	Military
Th. Jurgensen	Kiel, W. Ger.	Royalty, military
K.B. & Co.	Germany	Military
K.G.H.	Germany	Military
K.M. & Co.	Hong Kong	Views, social history
M. Kaineder's Nachf.	Vienna, Aust.	Royalty, military
A. Karcher Candy Co.	Little Rock, Ark.	Views
Robert Kashower	Los Angeles, Calif.	Views
A. H. Katz	n/a	Military
Louis Kaufman & Sons	United States	Military
Kaufmann & Strauss	United States	Views, humorous, animals
Kawin & Co.	United States	Military
Keliher	England	Military
Frank D. Kelley	United States	Military
G. Kennedy	Belfast, Ire.	Political
Kerry & Co.	Australia	Views, children, animals, greetings
Kester & Co.	Munich, Germany	Royalty, military
John J. Keyes	United States	Military
F. Killinger	Zurich, Swit.	Views
Kilo Post Card Co.	London, Eng.	Postcard importer
Kilophot	Vienna, Aust.	Views, royalty, military, special occasion
F. M. Kirby & Co.	United States	Views
George R. Klein News Co.	Cleveland, Ohio	Views, large letter
Wilhelm Kleinschmidt	Germany	Military
Paul Klemann	Hannover, Germany	Views, famous people
L. Klement	Frankfurt, Germany	Royalty, military, political, history
Klinghardt & Eyssen	Dresden, Germany	Royalty, military
Knackstedt & Co.	Germany	Royalty, military
Gebr. Knauss	Germany	Advertising, views, glamour
Knight Bros.	London, Eng.	Views, military, greetings, famous people, children, animals
Knight Series (Bros.)	England	Political, views
Knowles & Co.	London, Eng.	Views, patriotic
S. H. Knox & Co.	New York, N.Y.	Views, greetings
Rudolf Knuffman	Germany	Novelty (woven silk)
Kobert Color Pub.	Doniphan, Mo.	Views
Koch News Co.	United States	Military

Publisher	Location	Types of Cards
Koch & Werner	Austria	Royalty, military
J. Koehler	United States	Military, greetings, special occasion, royalty
Koelling & Klappenback	Chicago, Ill.	Views, royalty
Hubert Kohler	Munich, Germany	Views, fantasy, royalty
Bruder Kohn	Vienna, Aust.	Royalty, military, political
J. C. Konig & Ebhardt	Hannover, Germany	Views, royalty, special occasion
Koppel Color Cards	Hawthorne, N.J.	Views
Korsand & Co.	Frankfurt, Germany	Glamour, views
H. C. Kosel	Austria	Royalty, military
Kraemer Art. Co.	Cincinnati, Ohio	Views, special occasion
S. H. Kress & Co.	United States	Views
Krieger	Germany	Novelty (silk)
Kriegskarten Verlag ("War Card Pub.")	United States	Military
E. C. Kropp	Milwaukee, Wis.	Views, military, humor, sports, presidential
Chr. Kufner	Bayreuth, Germany	Royalty
W. J. Kuh	Frankfort, Ky.	Views, historical
Edward Kutter	Luxembourg	Views, royalty
Kyle Co.	Louisville, Ky.	Views, sports
L. & P.	Germany	Royalty
L.H.	Paris, Fr.	Famous people
L.L. (Levy et Fils & Levy Fils et Cie)	Paris, Fr.	Views, military, royalty, art reproductions, special occasion, historical
L.W. Co.	Chicago, Ill.	Views, military
La Tradotta	Italy	Views, military
F. Ladendorf	Germany	Military, political
Lakehead Wholesaler	Port Arthur, Ont., Can.	Views
Lancashire & Yorkshire Railway Co.	England	Trains, special occasion, views
Landeker & Brown	London, Eng.	Views
Lange & Schwalback	United States	Military
A. Langen	Munich, Germany	Views, satire
Langley & Sons	n/a	Views
S. Langsdorf	New York, N.Y.	Views, military, novelty, greetings
Langsdorff & Co.	London, Eng.	Views, children, humorous
I. Lapina	Paris, Fr.	Views, fantasy, glamour, advertising, military
L. H. ("Dude") Larson	Phoenix, Ariz.	Western studies (Indians, cowboys, western views, rodeos)
W. T. Lattig & Co.	n/a	Military

Publisher	Location	Types of Cards
Laureys	France	Military
Lautz & Isenbeck	Darmstadt, Germany	Royalty
W. Lawrence	Dublin, Ire.	Views, sports, humorous, transportation
Lawrence & Jellicoe	London, Eng.	Military, humorous, royalty
Lawrence Pub.	Dublin, Ire.	Political, views
Bruder Lazar	Vienna, Aust.	Royalty
Le Journal	France	Advertising
Le Rire	France	Royalty, political
League of Nations	Geneve, Swit.	League of Nations views, royalty
A. Leconte	n/a	Views, military
P. Ledermann	Vienna, Aust.	Royalty, military
Leeds Postcards	Leeds, Eng.	Views, political
Th. Lehmstedt	Germany	Royalty, military
H. C. Leighton	Portland, Maine	Views, military, special occasion
Leighton & Valentine Co.	United States	Military
E. Lerch	Vienna, Aust.	Royalty, military
F. H. Leslie	Niagara Falls, N.Y.	Views, historical
Lester Book & Stationery Co.	Atlanta, Ga.	Presidential
Levin Bros.	Terre Haute, Ind.	Views
Chas. Levy Circulating Co.	Chicago, Ill.	Views
F. & H. Levy Mfg. Co.	New York, N.Y.	Views, romantic
Levy News Agency	La Crosse, Wis.	Views, large letter
Librarie de l' Estampe	Paris, Fr.	Views, glamour, advertising
Lichtenstern & Harrari	Cairo, Egy.	Views
Gustav Liersch	Berlin, E. Ger.	Royalty, military, political
Life Pub. Co.	United States	Military
O. K. Liga	Vienna, Aust.	Royalty, military
Lincoln's New Salem Enterprises	Petersburg, Ill.	Views
W. M. Linnand Sons	Columbus, Ohio	Presidential, animals
Little	London, Eng.	Political
Arthur Livingston	New York, N.Y.	Military, views, humor, special occasion, ships
Locomotive Pub. Co.	London, Eng.	Railway, advertising, views
Lollesgard	Tucson, Ariz.	Views, large letter, western studies
London Stereoscopic Co.	London, Eng.	Views, royalty
Longbranch News Agency	Fremont, Ohio	Views, large letter
Longshaw Card Co.	Los Angeles, Calif.	Views, famous people
D. Longo	Italy	Views, fantasy
Louisiana News Co.	New Orleans, La.	Views
Fred Lounsbury	United States	Greetings, patriotic, children
Lowman & Hanford Co.	Seattle, Wash.	Views
Loyalist Coalition	Ireland	Political

Publisher	Location	Types of Cards
Ludlow & Sons	England	Advertising, views
O. Ludwig	Peking, China	Royalty
Peter Luhn	Germany	Military
Lychgate	England	Children
William Lyon	Glasgow, Scot.	Views, humorous, special occasion
R. Clements Lyttle	Belfast, Ire.	Political
M.B. & C.	Italy	Views
M.M. & F.	Belgium	Military
M.M.S.	Vienna, Aust.	Royalty, military
M.W.M.	Aurora, Mo.	Views, military, humor
Stevenson McCaw	Ireland	Political
McCaw, Stevenson & Orr	Belfast, Ire.	Views, children, advertising, sports
McClenathan Printery	Dunkirk, N.Y.	Views, large letter, trains
McCormick Co.	Amarillo, Tex.	Views
L. T. McDaniel	United States	Military
Frank McDougal	Sacramento, Calif.	Views
W. & G. Macfarlane	Buffalo/Toronto	Views, greetings
Macfarlane, Lang & Co.	England	Advertising
William Mackenzie & Co.	London, England	Views, humorous, greetings, political
McLagan & Cumming	England	Military
McLaughlin & Barnhart	Omaha, Nebr.	Views
W. E. Mack	London, Eng.	Political, military, greetings, humorous, transportation
I. L. Maduro Jr.	Panama	Views
Maggi	England	Advertising
P. Mahler	Stuttgart, W. Ger.	Royalty, military
Alfred Mainzer	New York, N.Y.	Views, large letter, animals (cats)
Majestic Pub. Co.	United States	Children
E. Malcuit	France	Views
Malik	Germany	Political, military
Manhattan Post Card Pub. Co.	New York, N.Y.	Views, large letter, special occasion, military, character studies, animals, glamour, children
A. Vivian Mansell	London, Eng.	Views
Manson News Agency	Rochester, N.Y.	Views
H. Manuel	Paris, Fr.	Views, patriotic
Marion Candy & Cigar Co.	Marion, Ohio	Views, large letter
Marken & Bielfeld	Frederick, Md.	Views, historical
Alex. F. Martignoni	New York, N.Y.	Views
Harry Martin	Asheville, N.C.	Views, Indians

Publisher	Location	Types of Cards
Hermann Martin	Nuremberg, W. Ger.	Famous people
Martin & Murtry	Belfast, Ire.	Political
Martin Post Card Co.	United States	Exaggerations
C. A. Maschke	Dresden. E. Ger.	Military, royalty
Mastercraft Pictures	United States	Military
Mastercraft Printers	Dayton, Ohio	Views, transportation (airplane)
J. Mat.	Belgium	Military
Mather Book Stores	Alton, Ill.	Views, large letter, military
May & Co.	England	Military
Mayer Post Card Co.	Roanoke, Va.	Views, historical
Mebane Greeting Card Co.	Wilkes-Barre, Penn.	Views, large letter
Medici Society	London, Eng.	Royalty, art reproductions, children, famous people
A. S. Meeker	New York, N.Y.	Greetings
Ezra Meeker	Seattle, Wash.	Views, famous people, special occasion
Meissner & Buch	London, Eng.	Greetings, children, glamour, views
Memphis Paper	Memphis, Tenn.	Views
Merval Corp.	United States	Military
Meta & Lautz	Darmstadt, W. Ger.	Views, royalty, military
Methodist Pub. House	United States	Famous people
Metrocraft	Everett, Mass.	Views
Metropolitan	New York, N.Y.	Views, military, presidential
Metropolitan News Co.	Boston/Germany	Views
Frank C. Meyer	United States	Military
Mid Continent News Co.	Oklahoma City, Okla.	Views
Midland Railway Co.	England	Advertising
J. Miesler	United States	Military
L. Miguel	Cuba	Special occasion
Humphrey Milford	England	Fantasy, animals, children
Millar & Lang	Glasgow, Scot./London, Eng.	Views, homorous, greetings, military, novelty, political, special occasion, famous people, social history, children, heraldic
Miller Art Co.	Brooklyn, N.Y.	Special occasion
Walter H. Miller & Co.	Williamsburg, Va.	Views
E. Milner	England	Military
Milton Candy & Tobacco Co.	Cleveland, Ohio	Views, large letter
Franz Milz	Germany	Views
H. W. Minett	Birmingham, Eng.	Royalty
Minsky Bros. & Co. Pub. Div.	Pittsburgh, Penn.	Views, large letter, special occasion

Publisher	Location	Types of Cards
Misch & Co.	London, Eng.	Views, glamour, greetings, humorous, transportation, art
Misch & Stock	England	Fantasy, views, greetings
Mission News Co.	San Francisco, Calif.	Views
Edward H. Mitchell	San Francisco, Calif.	Views, Indians, famous people, special occasion
Model Variety Store	Nowata, Okla.	Views
Modena & Co.	London, Eng.	Military, views
Moffat, Yard & Co.	New York, N.Y.	Views, glamour
Eliotipia Molfese	Italy	Royalty, military, political
Hans Moller	Munich, W. Ger.	Royalty, military
Charles M. Monroe Co.	United States	Views, ships
Paul Monroe Co.	St. Louis, Mo.	Views
Otto Moore & Son	Texarkana, Texas	Views
A. Morgagni	Italy	Advertising, glamour
Morgan Station Co.	Cincinnati, Ohio	Views
C. W. Morris	United States	Military
Joseph F. Morsello	United States	Military
H. Moss & Co.	London, Eng.	Glamour, fantasy, views, animals, famous people, advertising
J. Lewis Motz News Co.	Cincinnati, Ohio	Views
Walter Muller	Germany	Military
von C. Muller	Oldenburg, W. Ger.	Views, historical, famous people, greetings
M. Munk	Vienna, Aust.	Glamour, views, royalty, military, political
Murray, Richardson & Co.	Dungannon, Ire.	Political
Muskogee Indian Trading Co.	Muskogee, Okla.	Views
Mutoscope	United States	Military
N.P.G. (Neve Photographische Gesselschaft)	Germany	Military, royalty, political (German cards imported into England)
N.R.M.	Italy	Royalty, military
Nash, Adrienne	England	Military, children, humorous
National Art Co.	New York, N.Y.	Greetings, patriotic
National Art Views Co.	United States	Military
National Council for Prevention of War	United States	Military
National Fund for Welsh Troops	London, Eng.	Military
National Portrait Gallery, Trustees	England	Military
National Post Card Co.	New York, N.Y.	Views
National Unionist	Ireland	Political

Publisher	Location	Types of Cards
Ed Neli	n/a	Royalty
Eric Nelson News Co.	Omaha, Nebr.	Views
Nestor Gianaclis	India	Military
Neurdein Freres	Paris, Fr.	Royalty, views, political, novelty (woven silk)
New Haven Illustrating Co.	United States	Views, royalty, military
New South Wales Bookstall Co.	Australia	Views, historical, large letter, sports, famous people
New York Central Lines	United States	Military
New York Zoological Society	New York, N.Y.	Animals, Views
S. Newcomb & Co.	n/a	Royalty
News Shop	Delaware, Ohio	Views, large letter
Newspapers Illustrations	England	Military, political
Niagara Envelope Co.	Buffalo, N.Y.	Special occasion, views
John Nicholson	Belfast, Ire.	Political
Niedersedlitz	Germany	Military, royalty
Niles Office Supply	Niles, Mich.	Views
Buck Nimy	Lovelock, Nev.	Western studies (cowboys, Indians, bronc busting)
Ernest Nister	England/Nuremberg, Germany	Greetings, famous people, fantasy, children, animals, novelty, art reproductions, humorous, religious, historical, views
Cecil C. Nixon	United States	Military
Noble	United States	Humorous
Nodher	Germany	Military
Noever & Co.	Germany	Military
Heinrich Nord	Wiesbaden, W. Ger.	Views
North American Post Card Co.	Kansas City, Mo.	Exaggerations
North British Railway Co.	England	Railway-related, views
North Texas Stamp Co.	Dallas, Tex.	Advertising
Northern Ireland Labour Party	Ireland	Political
Northern Minnesota Novelties	Crosslake, Minn.	Views
Northwest Curio & Post Card Co.	Boise, Idaho	Views
Norton News Agency	Dubuque, Iowa	Views
Norwood Souvenir Co.	Cincinnati, Ohio	Views
Nossi Lespinne	France	Military
Novelti-Craft Co.	Miami, Fla.	Views
Novelty Co.	Rhode Island	Animals
Novelty Post Card Co.	England	Views, famous people, greetings
A Noyer (A. N.)	Paris, Fr.	Military, royalty, historical, art reproductions
O.K.W.	Austria	Royalty, military
Ocean Comfort Co.	Bremen, Germany	Views, ships

Publisher	Location	Types of Cards
Oceanic Stamp & Post Card Co.	Australia	Views, animals, humorous, novelty (embossed stamp cards)
Odhams	England	Military
Official Unionist Party	Ireland	Political
Official War Committee	United States	Military
Ogden News Co.	Ogden, Utah	Military
Oklahoma News Co.	Tulsa, Okla.	Views, humorous, famous people
O. H. Oldroyd	Washington, D.C.	Presidential
H. A. Olsen Specialty Co.	St. Paul, Minn.	Views
Olson News Co.	Sioux City, Iowa	Views, large letter
Opal Drake Photoprint Co.	Oklahoma City, Okla.	Views
Osboldstone & Co.	Australia	Views, animals, famous people, greetings, military, children
Cal Osborn	United States	Military
Ostdick	United States	Military
E. F. Otis	United States	Military
I. & M. Ottenheimer	Baltimore, Md.	Views, famous people, ships
Wilhelm Otto	Düsseldorf, Germany	Views, special occasion
Ozark Post Card Pub.	Monett, Mo.	Views, large letter
P. & C.	Athens, Greece	Views
P.M. & Co.	London, Eng.	Views, military
Pacific Novelty Co.	San Francisco, Calif.	Views
Pacific Pub. Co.	Vancouver, Can.	Views, patriotic
John Paddington	England	Military
Pahl & Co.	Germany	Military
L. Paller	Belgrade, Yugo.	Royalty, military
Pallis & Cotzias	Greece	Views
Palmer Pub. Co.	United States	Military
A. Papeghin	Germany	Royalty
Partridge & Love	Bristol, Eng.	Advertising
Pascalis, Moss & Co.	London, Eng.	Views, sports, glamour, humorous
W. T. Pater	Australia	Views, humorous, children, glamour
R. Paterson & Co.	Glasgow, Scot.	Advertising, views
Patriotic Pictorial Postcard Co.	England	Military, propaganda
D. A. Patterson	Abingdon, Va.	Views
W. J. Patton	Belfast, Ire.	Political
Patton Post Card Co.	Salem, Oreg.	Views
Paula Co.	Cincinnati, Ohio	Humorous
T. H. Payne Co.	Chattanooga, Tenn.	Views
A. Pearson	United States	Military
Robert Peel	England	Views, heraldic
Penn Pub. Co.	United States	Military
Pennsylvania Academy of Fine Arts	United States	Famous people

Publisher	Location	Types of Cards
Pepsi Cola	United States	Military, advertising
W. B. Perkins	Lead, S.D.	Views, famous people
Hans Pernat	Germany	Special occasion, advertising, military
Peterborough Post Card Co.	Peterborough, Can.	Views
Philadelphia Post Card Co.	Philadelphia, Penn.	Views, famous people, humorous
Philco Pub. Co.	London, Eng.	Views, royalty, famous people, large letter, novelty (portrait relief)
Philippine Education Co.	Manila, Philip.	Views
R. P. Phillimore & Co.	Berwick, Eng.	Views
Phillip & Kramer	Vienna, Aust.	Views, glamour, advertising, special occasion
N. D. Phot	Paris, Fr.	Royalty, military, special occasion, art reproductions, views
Photo Arts	Winnsboro, S.C.	Views, military, large letter
Photo Roto	United States	Military
Photochrom Co.	London/Turnbridge Wells, Eng.	Royalty, ships, political, famous people, military
Photochromie	Germany	Royalty, military, political
Photohaus "Lange"	Braunschweig, Germany	Royalty, military
Pictorial Stationery Co.	London, Eng.	Views, historical, political
Picture Postcard Co.	England	Military
Picture Postcard Co.	Ottawa, Can.	Views, greetings
Piek	Potsdam, Germany	Royalty
C. Pietsch	Austria	Royalty, military
C. Pietzner	Vienna, Aust.	Royalty, military
Pifer Printing Co.	Winchester, Va.	Views
Stanley A. Piltz Co.	San Francisco, Calif.	Views, special occasion
Joh. Pilz	Austria	Royalty, military
George E. Pinard	Dominica	Views
C. A. Pini	Bologna, It.	Special occasion
Emil Pinkau & Co.	Leipzig, E. Ger.	Views
G. Pipbot	France	Royalty
Pitman's	London, Eng.	Views, advertising
P. J. Plant	United States	Military
Plastichrome of Texas	San Antonio, Tex.	Views, special occasion
F. Polenghi & Co.	Turin, It.	Views, glamour, advertising
Lucien Pollet	United States	Views
C. Porter & Co.	Belfast, Ire.	Political
Portland News Co.	Portland, Maine	Views, famous people
Portland Post Card Co.	Portland, Oreg.	Views
Post Card Specialties	Metarie, La.	Views
Post Card Union of America	Philadelphia, Penn.	Views, humorous

Publisher	Location	Types of Cards
Post Exchange, U.S. Soldier's Home	Washington, D.C.	Military
Post Fund, Soldier's Home	California	Military
Post Office News Shop	Fort Worth, Tex.	Views
Postal Card & Novelty Co.	England	Military
Louis Prang & Co.	Boston, Mass.	Views, children, art, greetings
A. Prantl	Munich, Germany	Views
T. Presser Co.	Philadelphia, Penn.	Views, famous people
Printeries	Manchester, Eng.	Political
Printline	United States	Military
Printing Corp.	San Francisco, Calif.	Views
Prosdocimi	Rome, It.	Views, special occasion, advertising
Prudential Insurance Co.	United States	Military, advertising
George Pulman & Sons	England	Military
Purcell & Co.	Cork, Ire.	Views, special occasion
Purger & Co.	Munich, Germany	Historical, royalty, greetings
R. & C.	Naples, It.	Views, special occasion, advertising
R. & Cie	Paris, Fr.	Glamour, advertising
R. & K.L.	Germany	Military
R. & R. News	Atlanta, Ga.	Views, large letter, military
Radermacher, Aldous & Co.	England	Military
Raffailli	Italy	Military
E. Ragozino	Naple, It.	Views
Rapid Photo Printing Co.	London, Eng.	Royalty, famous people, greeting cards, children, animals, views, heraldic
H. Rathjen	Germany	Military
Ratto-Magana & Fils	France	Views
R. C. Reaves	Indianapolis, Ind.	Views, sports
Red Cross	Various Countries	Military
Red River News Co.	United States	Military
Red Star Line	Antwerp/New York/Belgium	Ships, advertising
Regal Art Pub.	London, Eng.	Views, glamorous, famous people
Regal Post Card Co.	Australia	Views
Regent Pub. Co.	London, Eng.	Military, famous people, children
Arthur Rehn & Co.	Berlin, E. Ger.	Royalty, military
Reichard & Lindner	Berlin, E. Ger.	Royalty, military
Henry Reichert	Poughkeepsie, N.Y.	Views
Reichner Bros.	United States	Views, presidential
M. Reider	Los Angeles, Calif.	Views, humor
Reifter's Sohne	Vienna, Aust.	Views, glamour

Publisher	Location	Types of Cards
O. T. Reilly	United States	Military
Reinhardt	Germany	Military
Reinthal & Newman	New York, N.Y.	Art, glamour, greetings, military, blacks, children
Christoph Reisser's Sohne	Vienna, Aust.	Royalty, military
Ernst Rennert	Germany	Military
Republican Clubs	Ireland	Political
Republican Movement	Dublin, Ire.	Political
Review Miner	Lovelock, Nev.	Western studies
B. S. Reynolds Co.	Washington, D.C.	Views, military, political, historical
Reynolds & Branson	England	Military
Rhode Island News Co.	Providence, R.I.	Views
Arthur H. Richards	Watkins Glen, N.Y.	Views, military
Richmond News Co.	Richmond, Va.	Views, military
Ricordi	Italy	Special occasion, glamour, military, historical
Max Rigot Selling Co.	Chicago, Ill.	Views, special occasion, transportation, military
R. Ringoet	Brusssels, Bel.	Famous people
William Ritchie & Sons	London, Eng.	Views, humorous, political
H. Robbins	Boston, Mass.	Views, humorous, greetings, blacks, children, animals, fantasy
Pilade Rocco	Milan, It.	Glamour, advertising, political
Rochester News Co.	Rochester, N.Y.	Views, military
C. G. Roder	Germany	Military
Rome Souvenir Card Co.	Rome, N.Y.	Views
Rommiler & Jonas	Dresden, E. Ger.	Views, art reproductions
Ronchi & Roncoroni	Italy	Special occasion, fantasy, views
Rood Bros.	England	Military
Rose News Co.	Lansing, Mich.	Views, large letter, sports
Rose Stenographic Co.	Australia	Views
Rosin & Co.	United States	Military
Rossi-Lespinne	France	Military
H. A. Rost Printing & Pub. Co.	New York, N.Y.	Views, military, famous people, special occasion
Rotary Photographic Co.	London, Eng.	Views, royalty, famous people, political, children, greetings, art reproductions, military
Rotograph	New York, N.Y.	Views, presidential, famous people, military, views, large letter, greetings, children
Rotophot	Berlin, E. Ger./London, Eng.	Royalty, military, famous people
Roukens & Erhart	Baarn, Holl.	Glamour, fantasy, views

Publisher	Location	Types of Cards
R. Roveri	Bologna, It.	Views, special occasion
Roycroft Shop	East Aurora, N.Y.	Views, famous people
Phillip Rubel	Austria	Military
Ruben Pub. Co.	Newburgh, N.Y.	Views
J. W. Ruddock & Sons	Lincoln, Eng.	Views, transportation
Rudolph Bros.	Philadelphia, Penn.	Animals, presidential
Ruitenbeek	Doorn, Nether.	Royalty
Rushmore News	Rapid City, S.D.	Views
Ruskin Studio Art Press	London, Eng.	Views, floral
J. Russell & Sons	London, Eng.	Royalty, military, famous people, special occasion
Rutledge Curio Co.	Mexico	Views, transportation
S.	Paris, Fr.	Views, sports, humorous
Dr. S. & Co.	Germany	Military
S. & G.S.	Berlin, E. Ger.	Royalty, military
S.I.P.	Paris, Fr.	Historical, royalty, military, art reproductions
S.L. & Co.	United States	Views, firefighting
S.P. Co.	United States	Greetings
S.T.A.	Italy	Views
S.V.D.	Austria	Royalty, military, political
Sabold-Herb Co.	United States	Military
Sackett & Wilhelms Corp.	Brooklyn, N.Y.	Views, military
St. Joseph Calendar & Novelty Co.	St. Joseph, Mo.	Views
St. Louis Greeting Card Co.	St. Louis, Mo.	Views, greetings
St. Louis Souvenir Card Co.	St. Louis, Mo.	Views, special occasion
St. Marie's Gopher News Co.	Milwaukee, Wis.	Views, sports
St. Paul News Agency	St. Paul, Minn.	Views
J. Salmon	Sevenoaks, Eng.	Views, patriotic, royalty, animals, children, military, fantasy
J. J. Samuels	London, Eng.	Royalty, military
San Antonio Card Co.	San Antonio, Tex.	Views
Sanborn Souvenir Co.	Denver, Colo.	Views, famous people, western studies
P. Sander	Philadelphia, Pa.	Humorous, views, famous people
Sandoval News Service	El Paso, Tex.	Views, large letters
Santway Photocraft Co.	Watertown, N.Y.	Views, military
Sapirstein Greeting Card Co.	Cleveland, Ohio	Views, large letter
S. & G. Saulsohn	Germany	Military
G. Savigny	Paris, Fr.	Military, views
E. W. Savory	England	Animals, views, sports, historical, fantasy

Publisher	Location	Types of Cards
E. Sborgi	Florence, It.	Religious, historical, art reproductions
Scenic Color Card Co.	Oklahoma City, Okla.	Views
Scenic South Card Co.	Bessemer, Ala.	Presidential, views
Scenic View Card Co.	San Francisco, Calif.	Views
J. H. Schaefers	n/a	Military
Louis Scheiner	Portland, Oreg.	Views
Scherer, Nabholz & Co.	Germany	Military
August Scherl	Germany	Military, royalty
Scheuber Drug Co.	Livingston, Mont.	Views
Schlesinger Bros.	New York, N.Y.	Views, greetings, humor
Edgar Schmidt	Germany	Military
Schmidt, Rickar & Co.	Hannover, Germany	Royalty, military
Franz Schneider	Vienna, Aust.	Famous people, historical
F. Schnell & Co.	Nuremberg, Germany	Views, special occasion
J. Schober	Karlsruhe, Germany	Views, special occasion
Hermann Schott	Germany	Royalty, military
J. F. Schreiber	Esslingen, Germany	Advertising, glamour
Alfred Schulze	Berlin, Germany	Royalty, special occasion
Arthur Schurer	Austria	Views, social history
Emil Schwalb	Berlin, Germany	Historical
A. Schwartz	Germany	Military
A. Schweitzer	Hamburg, Germany	Glamour, views
E. A. Schwerdtfeger & Co.	London/Berlin	Royalty, military, greetings, political, art reproductions
Scopes & Co.	London, Eng.	Royalty, novelty, (bas relief)
Scott Photo Co.	Massachusetts	Views, military, political
Scranton News Co.	Scranton, Penn.	Views
Seagrams	United States	Military, advertising
Eric J. Search Co.	Salt Lake City, Utah	Views
Seawall Specialty Co.	Houston/Galveston	Views
M. Seeger	Germany	Military
E. A. Seeman	Germany	Military
Hermann Seibt	Meissen, Germany	Views
A. Selige	St. Louis/Leipzig	Military, greetings, views, animals
Marshall Semmelman	United States	Military
R. Sennecke	Germany	Military
Service News Co.	Macon, Ga.	Views
C. Sfetea	Romania	Royalty, political, military
Shannon	n/a	Views
W. N. Sharpe	England	Royalty, advertising, famous people, novelty (fab patchwork)
Shaw News Agency	Grand Rapids, Mich.	Views

Publisher	Location	Types of Cards
M. T. Sheahan	Boston, Mass.	Views, political, greetings, animals, presidential, famous people
Shredded Wheat	Niagara Falls, N.Y.	Advertising
Shreveport News Agency	Shreveport, La.	Views, military
Shurrey's Pub.	England	Views
A. Sibbons	Belfast, Ire.	Political
Signal Corps (Army)	United States	Military
S. K. Simon	New York, N.Y.	Views
A. L. Simpson	United States	Military
Max Sinz	Dresden, E. Ger.	Royalty, military
Smiling Scat	Columbus, Ohio	Views
L. E. Smith	Gettysburg, Pa.	Presidential
W. H. Smith & Co.	England	Military
Smith News Co.	San Francisco, Calif.	Views
R. Snakenbroek	Brussels, Bel.	Royalty, military
Social Democrat & Labour Party	Ireland	Political
Socialists Unlimited	London/Ireland	Political
A. Sockyl	Vienna, Aust.	Glamour, views, advertising
Solarfilma	Iceland	Famous people
Sonora News Co.	Mexico	Views, military, famous people
A. Sorocchi	Italy	Views
Southern Card & Novelty Co.	Holly Hill, Fla.	Views
Southern Card Co.	San Antonio, Tex.	Views, humor, famous people
Southern Post Card Co.	Asheville, N.C.	Views
South-West Co.	Kansas City, Mo.	Views
Southwest Post Card Co.	Albuquerque, N.M.	Views
Souvenir Post Card Co.	New York, N.Y.	Views, advertising
Spagna	United States	Military
Spangenthal's Wholesale	United States	Military
W. C. Spangler News Agency	Sacramento, Calif.	Views
H. S. Speelman	The Netherlands	Royalty
H. W. Speyer	n/a	Military
Frederick Spies	Germany	Military
Springfield News Co.	Springfield, Mass.	Views
Squires, Bingham & Co.	Manila, Philip.	Views, military
Gerhard Stalling	Oldenburg, W. Ger.	Military
Standard News Agency	Knoxville, Tenn.	Views, large letter
Standard Sales Co.	Indianapolis, Ind.	Views, sports
Stanton's Novelty Co.	Lake Ozark, Mo.	Views
Stecher Lithographing Co.	New York, N.Y.	Greetings, fantasy, children
Steiff Co.	United States	Animals (bears)
Ewald Steiger	Germany	Royalty, military

Publisher	Location	Types of Cards
Max Stein	Chicago, Ill.	Views, military
Stengel & Co.	Dresden, E. Ger.	Royalty, historical, military, views, sports, art reproductions
Thomas Stevens	Coventry, Eng.	Novelty (woven silk)
George Stewart & Co.	Edinburgh, Scot.	Views, military, historical, special occasion
Steward & Woolf	London, Eng.	Views, military, animals, children, historical
W. H. Stockbridge	United States	Military
Stoddard	England	Heraldic
Theo. Stoefer	Nuremberg, W. Ger.	Views, glamour
J. O. Stoll	Chicago, Ill.	Views, large letter
E. Storch	Vienna, Aust.	Views, advertising, glamour
William Strain & Son	Belfast, Ire.	Political
H. H. Stratton	Chattanooga, Tenn.	Views, military
Arthur Strauss	New York, N.Y.	Views, military, famous people
W. S. Stuart	England	Royalty, military
Sun News Co.	St. Petersburg, Fla.	Views
Svenska Americanaren	United States	Royalty, views
T. P. & Co.	New York, N.Y.	Views, military
T.W.A. (Trans World Airlines)	United States	Advertising, patriotic
Taber Bas Relief	England	Novelty, royalty, military, famous people
M. W. Taggart	New York, N.Y.	Greetings
A. Talbot & Co.	London, Eng.	Views, crests, patriotic
H. H. Tammen	Denver, Colo.	Views, Indians
C. A. Tanner Co.	Wichita, Kans.	Views
Dora Tarnke	Braunschweig, Germany	Royalty, military
A. & G. Taylor	London, Eng.	Views, famous people, royalty
Tecraft Co.	Tenafly, N.J.	Views
Curt Teich	Chicago, Ill.	Views, advertising, transportation, animals, western studies, humorous, military, famous people, political, greetings
A. Ternois	Paris, Fr.	Views, military
Tester, Massy & Co.	London, Eng.	Views
J. E. Tetirick	Kansas City, Mo.	Views
B. G. Teuber	Leipzig, Germany	Views
Texas Co.	United States	Views, advertising
Becky Thatcher Book Shop	Hannibal, Mo.	Famous people
Frank S. Thayer	United States	Humorous
Thayer Pub.	Denver, Colo.	Views
Theochrom	n/a	Military
Hugo J. Thiede	United States	Military

Publisher	Location	Types of Cards
Ern. Thill	Brussels, Bel.	Royalty, military, views
J. Thomas	United States	Views, humorous, romance
G. L. Thompson	New York, N.Y.	Views, military
W. R. Thompson	Richmond, Va.	Military
Tichnor Art. Co.	Chicago, Ill.	Views, advertising, military
Tichnor Bros.(See Curt Teich & Tichnor Art Co.)		
Tichnor Quality Views (See Curt Teich.)		
Tilley & Son	Ledbury, Eng.	Views, military
Times Press	Bombay, India	Military, views
Timmermans & Co.	Dordrecht, Holl.	Views
H. Tobben	Holland	Views
Tokyo Printing Co.	Tokyo, Japan	Military, royalty
Tolmers Square Co-op	London, Eng.	Political
Tomlin Art. Co.	United States	Military
Town Topics	Belfast, Ire.	Political
A. Traldi	Italy	Royalty, military, views
Trau & Schwab	Germany	Military
Dr. Trenkler Co.	Leipzig, E. Ger.	Views, royalty, military, greetings
E. Trim & Co.	Wimbleton, Eng.	Sports
Paul E. Trouche	Charleston, S.C.	Views
Raphael Tuck	London/Berlin/New York	Views, military, royalty, art reproductions, political, trains, greetings, heraldic, children, special occasion, animals, famous people, blacks, novelty, advertising, humor, transportation
Tucson News Agency	Tucson, Ariz.	Views
Tulate	n/a	Royalty
U.S.O.	United States	Military
Uitgave Nijgh & Van Ditman	The Netherlands	Royalty, Military
Ullman Mfg. Co.	New York, N.Y.	Views, greetings, children, blacks, patriotic, humorous
Underwood & Underwood	New York, N.Y.	Views, military, royalty
Union News Co.	Cincinnati, Ohio	Views
Union Oil Co. of California	San Francisco, Calif.	Views, advertising, special occasion
Union Pacific Co.	Omaha, Nebr.	Views, military, advertising
United News Co.	Detroit, Mich.	Views
U.S. Army	United States	Military
U.S. Army Signal Corps	United States	Military
U.S. Army Y.M.C.A.	United States	Military
U.S. Navy	United States	Military
U.S. Treasury	United States	Views, military
Universal Postal Card Co.	New York, N.Y.	Views, military

Publisher	Location	Types of Cards
Universal Postal Union	Canada	Views
Universal Postcard & Picture Co.	Shanghai, China	Views
Uris Sales Corp.	New York, N.Y.	Views, military
A. Utrillo & Co.	Spain	Views, glamour, advertising
V.K.K.W.	Germany	Military
Valentine's & Sons	England/United States/Scotland/Ireland/Canada	Views, special occasion, ships, heraldic, military, royalty, children, advertising, art reproductions, political
Van Ornum Colorprint Co.	United States	Military
C. F. Van Steijn Jr.	The Netherlands	Royalty, political, military
Vaugirard	France	Military
J. Velten	Germany	Views, special occasion
Vercasson & Cie	Paris, Fr.	Advertising, glamour
Victoria Stamp Market	Australia	Views
Villardi	Milan, It.	Advertising, glamour
Virtuani	Milan, It.	Military
Vise	France	Military, views, art reproductions
E. Voghera	Rome, It.	Views, special occasion, advertising
T. H. Voigt	Bad Hamburg/Frankfurt	Royalty, military
Charles Voisey	England	Humorous, views
P. F. Volland & Co.	n/a	Military
Paul Vondrann	Germany	Military
D. J. Voorhees	United States	Military
Voss News Co.	Iowa City, Iowa	Views, large letter
Voyle News Agency	Richmond, Ind.	Views
W.R. & S.	England	Views
W.R.B. & Co.	Vienna, Aust.	Royalty, military
Wall, Nichols & Co.	Honolulu, Hawaii	Royalty, views
Wallace	United States	Military
J. P. Walmer	United States	Military
F. Walschaerts	Brussels, Bel.	Views
John E. Walsh	Quebec, Can.	Views
W. E. Walton	Belfast, Ire.	Political
John Wanamaker	Philadelphia, Pa.	Views, famous people
War Cartoon Studios	England	Military
Warwick Bros. & Rutter	Toronto, Can.	Views, large letter, Indians, crests, ships, military, famous people, greetings, novelty (bas relief)
Wasatch News Service	Salt Lake City, Utah	Famous people, views
Washington News Co.	Washington, D.C.	Views, large letter, presidential, military

Publisher	Location	Types of Cards
Washington Novelty	Washington, D.C.	Presidential
Washington Souvenir Co.	Washington, D.C.	Views
W. Wasserman	Basel, Swit.	Views, special occasion
Watford Engraving Co.	England	Royalty, novelty
Wayne Calendar & Novelty Co.	Fort Wayne, Ind.	Views, large letter
Wayne Paper Box & Printing Co.	Fort Wayne, Ind.	Views
Webbs	Cincinnati, Ohio	Views
Weenenk & Snel	The Netherlands	Royalty, views
Weiner News Co.	San Antonio, Calif.	Views, large letter, military
Wm. Weiss & Co.	Bermuda	Military
Weiss-Reinschmidt	Germany	Military
J. Welch & Sons	Portsmouth, Eng.	Views, art reproductions
Welstadt	Berlin, E. Ger.	Views
Wenk e Figli	Bologna, It.	Views, advertising, special occasion
Wesley Advertising Co.	Chicago, Ill.	Advertising
H. Wessler	New York, N.Y.	Views, greetings, fantasy, glamour
Thomas R. West	Miami, Fla.	Views, large letter
Westermann	Braunschweig, Germany	Royalty, military
Western News Co.	Chicago, Ill.	Views
Western Pub.	United States	Military
Western Pub. & Novelty Co.	Los Angeles, Calif.	Views, large letter
Western Resort Pub.	Santa Ana, Calif.	Views
Wezel & Naumann	Leipzig, Germany	Military
C. E. Wheelock & Co.	Peoria, Ill./Leipzig	Views
B. W. White	Monterey, Calif.	Views
White Co.	Columbus, Ga.	Military
Wholesale Post Card Co.	Dallas, Tex.	Views
Johannes Wieland	Berlin, E. Ger.	Royalty, military
Wiener Rotophot	Vienna, Aust.	Royalty, military
Wiese Gravure	St. Louis, Mo.	Views
Wildt & Kray	London, Eng.	Views, political, trains, animals
Wilke & Sons, Tourist Agents	Cork, Ire.	Views, advertising
Bryant Williams Pub.	New York, N.Y.	Views
C. U. Williams	Bloomington, Ill.	Views, military
Charles F. Williams	Philadelphia, Pa.	Views, large letter
Williams Photo Co.	Hastings, Neb.	Views
Williamsburg Art. Co.	New York, N.Y.	Views, greetings
Williamsburg Post Card Co.	United States	Military
Wilson's Book & Stationery Store	Paducah, Ky.	Views, large letter
Josef Windhager	Munich, W. Ger.	Royalty, military
Windsor News Co.	Windsor, Can.	Views, transportation
John Winsch	United States	Greetings

Publisher	Location	Types of Cards
Wirth & Co.	England	Military
Wittenborg Toy Co.	Cincinnati, Ohio	Views
Wolf Co.	Philadelphia, Pa.	Greetings
J. E. Wolfensberger	Zurich, Swit.	Military, historical, views, special occasion
F. Wolff	Brussels, Bel.	Views, advertising, glamour, fantasy
Hermann Wolff	Berlin, Germany	Royalty, military
Wolfrum & Hauptmann	Nuremberg, Germany	Glamour, views
C. Woll & Son	Munich, Germany	Military, propaganda
J. Wollstein	Berlin, Germany	Royalty, military
Woodcock Mfg. Co.	Hot Springs, Ark.	Views, large letter
Woodgifts	United States	Military
Woodland Card Co.	England	Military
Woolstone Bros.	London, Eng.	Political, views, greetings, propaganda
Charles Worcester	Bristol, Eng.	Views
World Post Card Co.	Philadelphia, Pa.	Views
Worth & Co.	England	Historical, famous people, views
Wreck	South Africa	Military
J. E. Wrench	London, Eng.	Views, animals, art reproductions
Wright Library	New York, N.Y.	Views
Wurthle & Sohn	Vienna, Aust.	Royalty, military
Young Bros.	Toronto, Can.	Views, Indians, historical
Zibart Bros.	Nashville, Tenn.	Views
Ottmar Zieher	Munich, W. Ger.	Novelty (embossed stamp cards), views, art reproductions

3
Postcard Artists

3
Postcard Artists

Among the more ecstatic moments for both novice and experienced postcard collectors are those times when he or she finds yet another card drawn by an artist who has attracted the collector's attention. The habit of gathering specimens by artist has a long and venerable tradition, especially when the painter or sketcher in question is a well-recognized figure in the art world. Alphonse Mucha, Harrison Fisher, Howard Chandler Christy, Charles Dana Gibson, and many more better-known artists either executed original work for postcards or saw their drawings reproduced on them, often in limited numbers.

But this, as the old saying would assure us, is merely the iceberg's tip relative to this fascinating business because for every Fisher or Gibson whose signatures appear on these rectangular pieces of paperboard there are hundreds of lesser-known talents who also enriched and graced the lowly postcard with their renditions. Though not all are collected with equal relish—indeed, many languish in obscurity for want of a little attention—those that are accumulated so lovingly are purchased with pleasure and exhibited with pride.

The listing of postcard artists offered here does not pretend to be all-inclusive. In fact, several thousand more names would be necessary to complete it. However, those that are placed here are among the most popular and more frequently encountered artists at postcard shows and in auctions. First, though, is a discussion of the postcard's rarity scale.

Rarity Scale

With the sophistication that is now an integral part of the collecting world has come an insistence that the information about any given collectible be as detailed as possible. People willing to spend what sometimes amounts to lavish sums of money want as much knowledge about their potential purchases as they may obtain. This is increasingly becoming the case and the prevailing attitude in a climate where one extra bit of information or one small upward—or downward—move

on the grading or rarity scale may translate into vast sums of money.

For this reason, among others, the following rarity scale has been devised. It is not, however, to be used strictly as a tool to aid in purchasing but rather as an assistant in the business of appraising and appreciating. The difference in these terms may seem to be a small one, but it is of utmost significance. Rarity relates to precisely that and often has little or no bearing on prices, which are generally slaves to the whims and caprices of popularity and faddism. The aim of this scale is to furnish some idea as to the relative ease or difficulty with which a collector may encounter specific postcards.

As with all such scales, a certain amount of arbitrariness will find its way into the calculations. There will undoubtedly be those who will disagree with this or that assessment. The author agrees that all have the right to dissent and will only say in his defense that these figures have been arrived at through many years of study, of collecting, and of association with dealers and collectors the world over. Each of the books that will be reviewed later in this volume (see Chapter 5) was also helpful, as was examination of prices realized after auctions, conversations with dealers at postcard and antique shows, and ongoing correspondence with fellow researchers.

Finally, it should be borne in mind that this rarity scale refers to material in very good or better condition. Tears, delaminations, bends, cracks, dirt, and other disfigurement greatly reduce the value of the cards.

R1: Material commonly and frequently encountered that often has little appeal.
R2: Material that is easy to obtain but is seen with somewhat less frequency than R1 postcards.
R3: Material in this range varies from that which is seen often to that which is not encountered on a regular or routine basis. R3 postcards are of the type that one sees offered on a regular basis in auctions.
R4: Scarce material of the sort seen more often among better auction listings than encountered at many postcard shows.
R5: Very rare postcards seldom seen and rarely offered for sale.

Artists by Types of Cards, Publisher, and Rarity

Artist	Types of Cards	Publisher	Rarity
S. E. A.	Views	Tuck	R3
Louise Abbema (1858–1927)	Famous people, views	n/a	R3–R4
Jack Abeille (French)	Special occasion, satire, glamour	n/a	R3–R4
George Abraham (British; 1872–1965)	Views	n/a	R2–R3
C. Acoppola	Views	Tuck	R2–R3
Frank Adams (British)	Views	William Collins & Sons	R2–R3
J. T. Adams (British)	Views	Tuck	R2–R3
William Addison (British)	Views	Tuck	R2–R3
S. Aellet	Views	Tuck	R3
C. Agazzi (Italian)	Military, views	n/a	R2–R3
Anne Ainsley (British)	Animals, special occasion, greetings	Regent Pub. Co.	R2–R3
Aisen (Italian)	Military, views	n/a	R2–R3
Alacchiati (Italian)	Satire, views	n/a	R2–R3
Joseph Alanen (1885–1920)	Military	B.K.W.I. (Bruder Kohn)	R3–R4
Albano (Italian)	Military	n/a	R3
Martha Alber	Fantasy, views	Wiener Werkstatte	R4
Alberts	Humorous, satire, views	n/a	R2–R3
Albrecht (German)	Military	n/a	R3
Cecil Aldin (British; 1870–1935)	Animals, humorous, advertising	Tuck; Valentines; Lawrence & Jellicoe	R3
Aleinmuller	Greetings, children	International Art (Inter-Art)	R3–R4
Alessandri (Italian)	Military, famous people	n/a	R3
James Alfred (American)	Glamour	Gray Lithographic Co.	R3
Andrew Allan (British)	Views	Millar & Lang	R3

R. Allmann

n/a = information not available

Artist	Types of Cards	Publisher	Rarity
Daphne Allen	Children	n/a	R4
S. Allen	Views	n/a	R2–R3
Stuart Allen (Australian)	Advertising, humorous	Hollander & Govett	R3–R4
William Allen	Views	n/a	R2
R. Allmann (German)	Royalty	n/a	R3
Robert Allouin	Animals	n/a	R3
M. Alys	Children	n/a	R3
J. Alzarion	Views	Tuck	R3
Edmond Aman (French)	Views, glamour	G. Hirth	R4–R5
Edmond Aman-Jean	Views	n/a	R2–R3
C. Ambler	Animals, views	n/a	R3
Amerio (Italian)	Military	n/a	R4–R5
A. Amorico (Italian)	Military, satire	n/a	R3–R4
Amorozo (Italian)	Views, military	n/a	R3
G. D. Amour (British)	Military	n/a	R3
Anatas	Military	n/a	R3
O. Anders (British)	Animals	n/a	R3
Martin Anderson (Scottish; 1854–1932)	Satire, humorous, views	Cynicus Pub. Co.; Tuck	R2
Victor C. Anderson (American; 1882–1937)	Children, humorous, views, nostalgia	Reinthal & Newman; Wildt & Kray	R2–R3
Claire Angell (British)	Military, views	Bamforth	R2–R3
Ezio Anichini (Italian)	Military, political, views	n/a	R2–R3
G. Anichini (Italian)	Art, glamour	n/a	R3
F. Anivetti (Italian)	Views	A. Scrocchi	R3
Hans Anker (German; 1873–1950)	Glamour	Etzold v. Kiessling	R5
B. Appleby	Humorous	n/a	R2–R3
Edward Ardizzone	Military	n/a	R3

Amorozo

Artist	Types of Cards	Publisher	Rarity
Ernest Aris	Humorous	Tuck	R3
Arlent (French)	Military	n/a	R3
William Armitage (British; 1856–1941)	Military, views	Boots	R3
William Armstrong (British)	Military	Boots	R3
Raoul Arus (French)	Military	n/a	R3–R4
Alf Ashley (Australian)	Floral, views	Robert Jolley; Victoria Stamp Market; Oceanic Stamp & Post Card Co.	R2–R3
C. C. Ashwell	Views	n/a	R2
Angelo Asti (Italian; 1847–1903)	Glamour	n/a	R2–R3
Anton Asti	Glamour	Tuck; Max Ettlinger	R2–R3
Attilio (Italian)	Military, political	n/a	R3
Mabel Lucie Attwell (British; 1876–1964)	Children, patriotic, humorous	Tuck; Valentines; Bamforth	R2–R3
Norman Ault (British)	Views	n/a	R3
Georges Auriol (French; 1863–1938)	Views, fantasy	Greningaire	R4
E. Austerlitz	Humorous	n/a	R3
Alex Austin (British)	Views	n/a	R3
E. Austin	Animals, children, views	n/a	R3
Winifred Austin (British)	Animals	Mansell	R3
Charles Auty (British)	Views	Mansell	R3
F. Aveline (British)	Glamour	J. Henderson & Sons	R3–R4
Joyce Averill (British)	Views, floral, children, military	n/a	R2–R3
Axster-Heudtlass (German)	Military	n/a	R3–R4

Artist	Types of Cards	Publisher	Rarity
C. B. (German)	Military	n/a	R3
E. B. (British)	Animals	n/a	R2
J. V. B. (Irish)	Political	J. Johnson	R4
D. Baccarini (Italian; 1883–1907)	Views	Pilade Rocco	R4–R5
Ferdinand Bach (German; 1859–1952)	Glamour, royalty, views, historical	n/a	R4
Bachtiger (Swiss)	Views, greetings	Fretz	R4–R5
F. S. Backus	Humorous	n/a	R3
Baertsoen	Military	n/a	R3
O. Bafeni (Italian)	Special occasion, views	n/a	R2–R3
Bruce Bairnsfather (British; 1887–1959)	Military	Bystander; Tuck; Beagles; David Allen	R2–R3
Bernard Baker (British)	Military	Tuck	R3
Granville Baker	Military	n/a	R3
L. Bakst (Russian; 1886–1924)	Views, art, famous people	n/a	R3–R4
G. Balata	Military	n/a	R3
Baldelio (Italian)	Humorous, military	n/a	R2–R3
A. Baldinelli (Italian)	Military	n/a	R3
Frederick Ball (British)	Children	Frith	R3
G. Balla (Italian)	Advertising, satire	n/a	R3–R4
O. Ballerio (Italian; 1870–1942)	Special occasion, military, royalty, views, advertising	n/a	R3–R4
Ballester	Military	n/a	R3
E. C. Banks (American)	Glamour	n/a	R3
M. Banks	Greetings, children	Tuck	R3–R4
Alexander Bannerman	Military	Stewart & Co.	R4
Bannister	Military	Salmon	R3

C. B.

Bruce Bairnsfather

Paul Barbier

Artist	Types of Cards	Publisher	Rarity
C. Barber	Glamour	Carlton Pub. Co.	R3
M. Barberis (Italian)	Military, political	n/a	R3–R4
Court Barbier	Glamour	Carlton Pub. Co.; R.H.B.	R3
Paul Barbier (French)	Military	P.C.	R4
Rene Barbier	Glamour, military	n/a	R3
Barday	Views	n/a	R2
Sybil Barham (British)	Children	C. W. Faulkner	R3
Guiseppe Barison (Italian)	Views	n/a	R2–R3
Barlog (German)	Military, humorous	n/a	R3
F. Barnard (British; 1846–1896)	Historical	n/a	R3–R4
A. Barnes (British)	Animals	n/a	R2
George Barratt (British)	Humorous	J. Henderson & Sons	R3
R. Barratt (British)	Views	Medici	R3
A. Barraud (British)	Views, military	Tuck	R2
Adrien Barrere (French; 1877–1931)	Advertising, views	n/a	R4
L. Barribal (Italian)	Glamour, children, advertising	Valentines; Inter-Art; J. Henderson & Sons	R3

ARTILLERIE—ARMEE BELGE. *Par A. Bastien.*

A. Bastien

COMMANDING OFFICER'S QUARTERS
JEFFERSON BARRACKS, MO.

Robert Batey

Artist	Types of Cards	Publisher	Rarity
W. Barribal	Glamour, military, children, advertising	Inter-Art; David Allen	R3
W. E. Bart	Humorous	n/a	R2
P. Barthel	Views	Tuck	R3
S. Bartoli (Italian)	Military	F. Duval	R3–R4
Bartos	Military	n/a	R3
Alfredo Baruffi (Italian; 1873–1948)	Special occasion, views, military	Chappuis; Dr. Trenkler & Co.	R4
Arpad Basch (Hungarian; 1873–1944)	Glamour, views	n/a	R3–R4
Bass-Smith (British)	Views	Tuck	R2
A. Bastien (Belgian)	Views, military	n/a	R3

C. Becker

Artist	Types of Cards	Publisher	Rarity
H. M. Bateman (British)	Satire, humorous	n/a	R3
Marjorie Bates (British; 1883–1962)	Views	n/a	R3
Lt. Robert Batey	Military	n/a	R4
Karl Bauer (German)	Royalty, military	n/a	R3
Lewis Baumer	Humorous	Tuck	R3
Baumgarten (German)	Military	n/a	R3
L. M. Bayle (French)	Military	Moullet-Marseille	R4
Sarah Beale (British)	Views	Tuck	R3
Beaty (American)	Social history, views	n/a	R3
C. A. Beaty	Humorous	Mather	R3
R. Beaudouin	Satire, humorous, famous people	n/a	R2–R3
C. Becker	Military, children	F. Hartmann	R3
P. A. Becker (German)	Military	n/a	R3
Herbert Beecroft (Australian; 1864–1951)	Views, famous people, religious, humorous	New South Wales Bookstall Co.	R3–R4
Albert Beerts	Military	A. H. Katz	R3–R4
S. Begg	Military	n/a	R3–R4
Beggarstaff Bros.	Special occasion	Tuck	R4
Peter Behrens (German; 1868–1940)	Special occasion	Georg Stilke	R4–R5

Artist	Types of Cards	Publisher	Rarity
F. O. Beirne (British)	Military	Blum & Degen	R4
C. Belcher	Humorous	Tuck	R2–R3
George Belcher (British)	Humorous, advertising	Tuck	R3–R4
A. Belinbau	Views	Savory	R2
Alfred Bell	Glamour	Valentines	R3
Hilda Bell (British)	Views	n/a	R2
Henri Bellery-Desfontaines (French; 1867–1910)	Special occasion	Charles Verneau	R4–R5
D. Bellini (Italian)	Military, political	n/a	R3
Achille Beltrame (Italian; 1871–1945)	Military, special occasion, advertising	Ricordi	R4
Giovanni Beltrami (Italian; 1860–1926)	Advertising, views	n/a	R4
Georg Belwe (German; 1878–1954)	Views	n/a	R4
Paul Bender	Views	n/a	R2
C. Benesch (German)	Military, royalty	n/a	R3
Godwin Bennett	Views	n/a	R3
Alexandre Benois (1870–1960)	Views	n/a	R5
N. Beraud	Military	Tuck	R3
Berdenier (French)	Military	n/a	R3
Claus Bergen (German)	Military	n/a	R3–R4
Fritzi Berger	Glamour, decorative	Wiener Werkstatte	R5
Georg Berger	Views, humorous	n/a	R3
Stanley Berkeley (British; 1855–1909)	Animals	Hildesheimer	R3–R4
Edouard Bernard	Advertising, satire	P. Freres; Wiener Werkstatte	R4
Berndsen (Dutch)	Military	n/a	R3
Max Bernuth (German)	Views	n/a	R5

Georg Berger

A. Bertiglia

Artist	Types of Cards	Publisher	Rarity
Berthelet (Italian)	Military	V. E. Boeri	R3–R4
Paul Berthon (French; 1872–1909)	Advertising, views, satire	n/a	R4
A. Bertiglia (Italian)	Children, special occasion, military, propaganda, famous people	n/a	R3–R4
Giulio Bertoletti (Italian)	Military	n/a	R4
Betanzos (Mexican)	Children	Ammex Asociados	R2
Anna Betts (American)	Romance, views, nostalgia	M. Munk	R4
Ethel F. Betts (American)	Romance, views, nostalgia	M. Munk	R4
S. E. Beurmann (German)	Military	n/a	R3

Artist	Types of Cards	Publisher	Rarity
Otto Beyer (Polish)	Fantasy, special occasion	n/a	R5
Alberto Bianchi (Italian; 1882–1969)	Military, special occasion, satire	n/a	R4
B. Bieber (German)	Royalty, military	n/a	R3
Ernest Bieler (1863–1943)	Special occasion, views	Sauberun & Pfeiffer	R5
J. L. Biggar (British)	Military, romantic, views	E. T. W. Dennis & Sons; T. & G. Allan; Brown & Calder	R2
Vespasiano Bignami (Italian; 1841–1929)	Special occasion, military, advertising	n/a	R4
Ivan Bilibine (Russian; 1876–1942)	Views, historical, famous people	A. Li'ina	R4
M. Billing (British)	Views, art	Tuck; Nister; Hildesheimer	R2
Armand Biquard	Military	Picture Postcard Co.	R4–R5
Nora Birch	Children	William Ritchie & Sons	R3
Cyril Bird (British)	Military, social history	n/a	R3–R4
H. Bird (British)	Animals	F. C. Southwood	R3
C. Bishop (American)	Children, greetings, humorous	A.H. & Co.	R3
F. V. Bisson	Views, art	Tuck	R3
Bizuth (Belgian)	Military	L.E.L.	R4
Algernon Black (British)	Military	Photochrom	R3
W. Black (British)	Views, humorous	n/a	R2
W. G. Blackall (British)	Views	A. & C. Black	R3
A. Blair	Views	Tuck	R2
Clifford Blampied	Views	J. Salmon	R2
Rivo Blass	Military	n/a	R3–R4
Rudolf Blind	Views	Langsdorff	R3

Betanzos

Ernest Bieber

Artist	Types of Cards	Publisher	Rarity
Marcel Bloch	Military	A. Noyer	R3
Bertha Blodgett (American)	Greetings, children	Edward Gross; Kaplan	R3
V. A. Blomstedt (Finnish)	Greetings, views	n/a	R4
Karl Blossfeld (German)	Military	Red Cross	R3
Leslie Board (Australian; 1883–1935)	Glamour, historical, advertising	New South Wales Bookstall Co.	R3
Boccasile (Italian)	Military	Acta	R3–R4
Umberto Boccioni (Italian; 1882–1916)	Special occasion	Chiattone	R5
Hans Bohler (Austrian; 1884–1961)	Views, famous people	Wiener Werkstatte	R4
Adolf Bohm (Austrian; 1861–1927)	Special occasion, views	Gerlach & Shenk	R5
Hans Bohrdt (German)	Military	n/a	R3
Philip Boileau (Canadian; 1864–1917)	Glamour, children, advertising, military	Reinthal & Newman; Tuck; Wildt & Kray; Charles Hauff & Co.; National Art	R3
John Bolton (British)	Views	W. H. Smith & Sons; Water Colour Post Card Co.	R3
Luigi Bompard (Italian; 1879–1953)	Glamour, fantasy, art	Ricordi; Minarelli; G. Mengoli; Chappuis	R3–R4
S. Bompard (Italian)	Special occasion, advertising, glamour	Art & Humour Pub. Co.	R3
Bob Bondart	Military	n/a	R3
Sir Muirhead Bone (British; 1876–1953)	Special occasion, military	n/a	R3
Gigi Bonfigliori	Special occasion	n/a	R5
G. W. Bonte (American)	Humorous	n/a	R2

Phillip Boileau

Artist	Types of Cards	Publisher	Rarity
Aroldo Bonzagni (Italian; 1887–1918)	Military, glamour, propaganda	Pilade Rocco; A. Marzi	R3–R4
Booth (American)	Humorous, greetings	Drawing Board Greeting Cards	R2
Fred Booty (Australian)	Humorous	Oceanic Stamp & Post Card Co.	R2–R3
Zoe Borelli	Glamour, views	n/a	R3
Mario Borgoni (Italian)	Special occasion, advertising, military	Italian government issues	R4
Margaret Boriss	Children	n/a	R3
Len Borkowski (American)	Military	n/a	R3
William H. Borrow (British)	Views	Tuck; Water Colour Post Card Co.; B. & W.	R2–R3
Fritz Boscovits (Swiss)	Special occasion	Red Cross	R4
W. Bothams (British)	Views	Tuck	R2
George Bottomley	Glamour	n/a	R3
J. F. Boucher	Military	n/a	R3
Maurice Boulanger (French)	Animals (cats, rabbits, pigs)	Tuck	R3
Henri Boutet (French; 1851–1919)	Advertising, views, glamour	Motot; Southwood	R3–R4
Doris Bowden	Children	C. W. Faulkner	R3
E. B. Bowden (British)	Views	J. Salmon	R2
Maurice Bower (American; 1889–1980)	Historical, nostalgia	n/a	R3–R4
Albert Bowers (British)	Views	Tuck	R2
May Bowley (British)	Children, animals	Tuck; Valentines; J. Salmon	R2–R3
W. J. Boyd	Humorous	n/a	R2–R3
Tom Boyne	Views	J. W. Ruddock & Sons	R3
Will H. Bradley (American; 1868–1962)	Views, art	La Critique	R3–R4–R5
Percy Bradshaw (British)	Humorous, satire	Tuck; Misch & Co.; H. Moss & Co.	R2–R3

J. F. Boucher

PRIVATE BREGER
By Sgt. Dave Breger

"Sorry, Sir, he didn't have time to shave for this inspection!"

Dave Breger

Artist	Types of Cards	Publisher	Rarity
Dorothy Braham (British)	Children	Tuck	R2
Paul Bransom (American; 1885–1979)	Animals, humorous	n/a	R3
W. Braun	Glamour	n/a	R3
Fritz Brauner (German)	Military	n/a	R3–R4
Sgt. Dave Breger (American)	Military	n/a	R3
Ambrose Breininger (British)	Humorous	Inter-Art	R2
F. M. Brent	Military	n/a	R3
Harold Matthews Brett (American; 1880–1955)	Historical, famous people, views	n/a	R3–R4
Molly Brett (British)	Fantasy, views, animals	C. W. Faulkner; J. Salmon; Valentines	R2–R3
Arthur Bridgeman (British)	Views	Tuck	R2
Barbara Briggs	Animal studies	Humphrey Milford	R3
George Brill	Humorous	n/a	R2–R3
E. C. Brinsley	Military, glamour, children	Vivian Mansell	R3
Jack Broadrick (British)	Humorous	n/a	R3
Charles Brock (British; 1870–1938)	Views, art	Tuck	R2–R3
Oscar Brock (Australian)	Glamour, military, patriotic	L. Garling	R3–R4
Dorothy Brown (British)	Views	J. Salmon	R2
Francis Brown (British)	Military	A. M. Davis	R3
Maynard Brown	Advertising, glamour	n/a	R3
P. Brown (British)	Humor	Technical Art Co.	R3
Gordon Browne (British)	Humor	John Walker & Co.	R3
John Browne (British)	Famous people	n/a	R3

Tom Browne

Francis Brundage

Artist	Types of Cards	Publisher	Rarity
Tom Browne (British; 1870–1910)	Humorous, children, advertising, sports, military, satire	Tuck; Valentines; Davidson Bros.; Wrench	R2–R3
O. Bruch (German)	Royalty, military	Christoph Reisser Sohne	R3
Bruncher	Royalty, military	n/a	R3
Frances Brundage (American; 1854–1937)	Children, greetings	Tuck; Gabriel	R3
Umberto Brunelleschi (Italian; 1886–1949)	Military, propaganda, fantasy, political	Ricordi	R4
Herbert Bryant (British)	Views, military	Tuck	R2–R3
Fred Buchanan (British; 1879–1941)	Humor, views	Tuck; Woolstone Bros.	R2–R3

Erzherzog Eugen
k. u. k. General der Kavallerie
Hoch- und Deutschmeister

O. Bruch

Artist	Types of Cards	Publisher	Rarity
Arthur Buckland	Views	E. W. Savoy	R2
O. Budd	Animals	Charles Voisey	R3
Giovanni Buffa (1871–1964)	Views, special occasion	Chiattone	R3
René Bull (Irish)	Humorous, satire, romance	Davidson Bros.; C. W. Faulkner; Voisey	R3
C. Bunnel	Greetings, views	Sander	R2–R3
Paul Burck (German; 1878–1947)	Special occasion	n/a	R5
R. Burger (British)	Views	n/a	R2
W. F. Burger	Military	n/a	R3
Arthur Burgess (1879–1956)	Ships, views	n/a	R3–R4
Victor Burnand (1868–1940)	Views	A. G. Curtis	R3
C. C. Burnard	Views	Tuck	R2
E. Burner (French)	Military	n/a	R4
Jean-Leonce Burret (French; 1866–1915)	Views, special occasion	Greningaire	R5
F. W. Burton (British)	Views	J. Salmon	R2–R3
T. Bushby	Views	E. T. W. Dennis & Sons	R2–R3
Adolfo Busi (Italian; 1891–1977)	Advertising, satire, views	Ricordi; C.A.B.	R4
William Busk	Views	Tuck	R3
Gaston Bussiere (French; 1862–1929)	Famous people, decorative, views	n/a	R5
Arthur Butcher (British)	Glamour, military, greetings, humor, animals (cats)	Inter-Art; E. Mack	R3
Charles Butler	Views	Mansell	R2
Dudley Buxton (British)	Humorous, military, children	Inter-Art; Charles Voisey	R2
Percy Buzzard (British)	Views	n/a	R2–R3
C. Byrnes	Children, greetings, views	Gibson Art Co.	R2–R3

Artist	Types of Cards	Publisher	Rarity
A. E. C. (British)	Military	Regent Pub. Co.	R2
Cadore	Military	n/a	R3
William Caffyn (British)	Advertising	Bird's Custard	R4
Randolph Caldecott (British; 1846–1886)	Children, fantasy, social history	Frederick Warne & Co.	R4
C. Calderara (Italian)	Glamour, greetings, military	D.G.M.; Ars Parva	R4
Captain Ben Caldwell	Military	n/a	R4
Achille Calzi (Italian; 1873–1919)	Advertising, special occasion	A. Morgagni; A. Albonetti	R4
D. Cambellotti (Italian; 1876–1960)	Special occasion, military, historical	E. Chappuis; Alterocca	R3
Glauco Cambon (Italian; 1875–1930)	Special occasion, military	n/a	R3–R4
I. Camelli (Italian; 1876–1939)	Glamour, fantasy	n/a	R4
Alexander Cameron (British)	Views	J. Salmon	R2–R3
John Campbell (British)	Military	W. & A. K. Johnston	R3
John Campbell (Irish; 1883–1962)	Political	Dungannon Club	R3
Percy Campbell (Australian)	Views	New South Wales Bookstall Co.	R3
K. E. Canderay (British)	Views	Tuck	R3
H. Canivet	Military	Dobson; Molle & Co.	R2–R3
Walter Cannon (British)	Views	J. Salmon	R3
J. M. Cantle (Australian; 1849–1919)	Animals (birds), views	New South Wales Bookstall Co.	R3
Leonetto Cappiello (Italian; 1875–1942)	Advertising, military	Ricordi; Greningaire; Vercasson & Cie; Le Rive	R3–R4

P. Carcedo

Artist	Types of Cards	Publisher	Rarity
V. Cappieri	Views	Tuck	R3
Caputi	Advertising	n/a	R3–R4
Ramon Carbo (Spanish; 1866–1932)	Advertising, glamour, transportation	Catalonia; Miro	R3–R4
P. Carcedo (Spanish)	Royalty	n/a	R4
Emil Cardinaux (1877–1936)	Special occasion	J. E. Wolfensberger	R5
J. W. Carey (Irish; 1859–1937)	Military, views, political, historical	Dungannon Club; Charles L. Reis	R3–R4
John Carey (Irish; brother of J. W.)	Views, political	Valentines; Woolstone Bros.; Baird	R3–R4
Charles Carlegne	Advertising	n/a	R5
Charles Carlin (British)	Views	Photochrom	R2–R3
George Carlin (British; 1855–1920)	Views	n/a	R2–R3
Carmichael (American)	Humorous	T.P. & Co.; S.B.	R3
Albert Carnell	Children	Valentines	R2
Giovanni Carpanetto (Italian; 1863–1928)	Special occasion, military, transportation	n/a	R4
Gene Carr (American; 1881–1959)	Children, greetings, views, humorous	n/a	R2–R3
Leslie Carr (British)	Military	n/a	R3
Salvador Carreno (Mexican)	Bullfighting, views	n/a	R2
Ouillon Carrere (French)	Military	n/a	R3–R4
Carrey	Military	Laureys	R3
W. Carruthers (British)	Views	J. Salmon	R2
D. Broadfoot Carter (British)	Views	William Lyon	R3
Reginald Carter (British; 1886–1950)	Humorous, military, political, sports	Tuck; Valentines; Wildt & Kray; Millar & Lang; J. Salmon; E. Mack; Max Ettlinger	R2

R. Cavi

A. Cenni

Artist	Types of Cards	Publisher	Rarity
Sydney Carter (British; 1874–1945)	Children, fantasy, views, historical	Tuck; Birn Bros.; Hildesheimer	R3
T. Cartiel (French)	Military	n/a	R3–R4
Basilio Cascella (Italian; 1860–1950)	Glamour, children, special occasion, fantasy, views	G. Citterio; C. C. M.; Pilade Rocco	R3–R4
Walter Caspari (German; 1869–1913)	Advertising, glamour	G. Hirth	R4
Cass (French)	Military	n/a	R3
Henri Cassiers (Belgian; 1858–1954)	Views, special occasion, ships, advertising	W. de Haan; Red Star Line; Dietrich & Cie; F. C. Southwood; Rycker	R3–R4
V. Castelli (Italian)	Children, animals	n/a	R2–R3

Chapman

Artist	Types of Cards	Publisher	Rarity
J. R. Cattley	Military	n/a	R3–R4
Paul Cauchie (Belgian; 1875–1952)	Advertising	Dricot & Cie	R4
W. Cauer (German)	Military	n/a	R3–R4
Leon Cauvy (French)	Greetings, glamour, advertising	Stengeí & Co.	R4
Ludovico Cavaleri (Italian; 1867–1942)	Special occasion	n/a	R4
E. Cavi (Italian)	Special occasion, religious	L. Salomone	R3
R. Cavi (Italian)	Religious	L. Salomone	R3
Fritz Cawood (American)	Humorous	Cawood Comic Card Co.	R3
Neville Cayley (British; 1853–1903)	Animals (birds)	New South Wales Bookstall Co.	R2–R3
A. Cenni (Italian)	Military	n/a	R3–R4
Paul Chabas (French)	Character studies, views	n/a	R3
Chabaud	Military	n/a	R3
Stanley Chaplin	Fantasy	n/a	R3
Chapman (American)	Greetings, historical, famous people	n/a	R2–R3
J. Charmer	Military	n/a	R4
F. Chatterton (British)	Animals	Tuck	R3
Gladeys Checkley (British)	Fantasy	Valentines	R3
Jules Cheret (French; 1836–1932)	Advertising, glamour, views, special occasion	Greningaire; Tuck	R4–R5
Cheveral (French)	Military	n/a	R3
Lilian Cheviot (British)	Animals	Wildt & Kray	R3
A. Chidley (British)	Military	Gale & Polden	R3
Galileo Chini (Italian; 1843–1956)	Special occasion, advertising	n/a	R3–R4

Ellen Clapsaddle

Artist	Types of Cards	Publisher	Rarity
Carlo Chiostri (Italian; 1863–1939)	Humorous, floral	Ballerini & Fratini	R3–R4
Sofia Chiostri (Italian)	Fantasy	n/a	R3–R4
Hans Christiansen (German; 1886–1945)	Glamour, views	Gebr. Herz; G. Hirth; Wolfrum & Hauptmann	R3–R4
George Fyffe Christie (British)	Views, special occasion, military, humorous	Photochrom; J. Wrench; Misch & Co.	R2–R3
F. Earl Christy (American)	Glamour	Illustrated Postal Card Co.; Souvenir Post Card Co.; Stecher Lithographic Co.; Julius Bien	R3–R4
Howard Chandler Christy (American; 1873–1952)	Glamour, military	Moffat; Yard & Co.	R3–R4
Bernard Church (British)	Transportation (aviation), military	J. Salmon	R3–R4
Averardo Circello (Italian)	Military	V. E. Boeri	R3
Guilio Cisari (Italian)	Satire, views	G. Ricordi & Co.	R3
Ellen Clapsaddle (American; 1865–1934)	Children, greetings	Inter-Art; Wolfe Co.; Philco; Kopal	R3
Charles A. Clark	Humorous	n/a	R2
Christopher Clark (British)	Views	n/a	R3

F. Earl Christy

Artist	Types of Cards	Publisher	Rarity
J. Clayton Clark (British)	Historical	Tuck; C. W. Faulkner	R2–R3
Scotson Clark	Views	C. W. Faulkner	R2
Joseph C. Clarke (aka Kyd) (British)	Historical, humorous, satire	J. Wrench; Hildesheimer; C. W. Faulkner	R2–R3
Robert Clarkson	Views	n/a	R2
John Cecil Clay (American)	Glamour	Rotograph	R4
Henry Clayton	Views	n/a	R3
Ralph Cleaver (Irish)	Political	Davis Allen & Sons	R5
Erich Cleff (German)	Military	n/a	R4
John Clegg	Views	n/a	R3
Clarice Cliff	Glamour, romance	n/a	R3–R4
Rene Cloke (British)	Children, fantasy	Valentines; C. W. Faulkner	R2–R3
Lucy Cluff	Views	n/a	R3
A. Coates (British)	Views	n/a	R2–R3
H. Bernard Cobbe	Animals, views	Tuck	R2–R3
Cockrell	Blacks	n/a	R3
Plinio Codognato (Italian; 1878–1940)	Special occasion, military, advertising, glamour	Chappuis; Pilade Rocco	R3–R4
Haskell Coffin (American)	Military	n/a	R3
Lawrence Colborne (British)	Military	J. Salmon	R3
Vincent Colby (American)	Children, animals, historical	n/a	R2–R3
Edwin Cole	Views	n/a	R2
William Coleman	Views	Tuck	R3
Hilda May Coley (British)	Floral, views	Medici Society	R2–R3
Nathan Collier (American)	Humorous	n/a	R2
G. T. Collins (British)	Glamour	Regal Art Pub.	R3
J. Collins	Military	n/a	R3
Harry Colls (British)	Views	n/a	R2–R3
Colombo	Children	n/a	R3

Artist	Types of Cards	Publisher	Rarity
Pierre Comba (French)	Military	n/a	R3
Gizbert Combaz (Dutch; 1869–1941)	Fantasy, animals, views, shipping	Dietrich & Co.	R4–R5
"Comicus" (Harry Partlett) (British)	Children, humorous	Tuck; A. & G. Taylor	R2–R3
L. Connell	Glamour	n/a	R3
William Conor (Irish; 1881–1968)	Military	David Allen & Sons; Headquarters Council, Ulster Volunteer Force	R3–R4
B. Conti	Military	n/a	R3–R4
C. K. Cook (British)	Humorous	Valentines	R2
W. Jeffrey Cook (British)	Views	n/a	R3
Hubert Coop	Views	n/a	R2–R3
Cooper (American)	Humorous	Cooper's Photo	R2
Alfred Cooper (British)	Views	n/a	R2–R3
Phyllis Cooper (British)	Children, greetings, advertising	n/a	R3–R4
Reginald Cooper (British)	Humorous	n/a	R2–R3
Harold Copping (British; 1863–1932)	Historical, religious	Tuck	R3
Tito Corbella (Italian; 1885–1966)	Children, military, glamour	n/a	R3–R4
Bertha Corbett (American)	Children (Sunbonnet Kids), greetings, views	n/a	R2–R3
G. Cordingly (British)	Views	Tuck	R2–R3
C. Essenhigh Corke (British)	Views	Tuck	R2–R3
Salvator Correno (Mexican)	Bullfighting, views	Publicaciones Barrera	R1–R2
Thomas Cossins (British)	Special occasion, views	n/a	R4

Artist	Types of Cards	Publisher	Rarity
A. J. Couch (British)	Views	n/a	R3
Hilda Cowham (British)	Children, advertising, humorous	Valentines; Inter-Art	R2–R3
Aurelio Craffonara (Italian; 1875–1945)	Glamour, military	n/a	R4
Reginald Crail (British)	Political	n/a	R4
Rie Cramer	Glamour, art	W. de Haan	R3–R4
M. Crete	Military	n/a	R3–R4
S. Crite	Humorous, animals ("Billy Possum")	Amp Co.	R3–R4
Anne Croft (British)	Views	Vivian Mansell	R3
Charles M. Crombie (British)	Satire, humorous	Valentines	R2–R3
J. Cross (British)	Views	Tuck	R3
Norman Cross (British)	Advertising	E. T. W. Dennis & Sons	R3–R4
Alfred Crowquill (British)	Famous people, views, historical	Stewart & Woolf	R3
William Croxford (British)	Views	J. Salmon	R2–R3
George Cruikshank (British)	Views	n/a	R3
Edith Cubitt (American)	Children, greetings	E. P. Dutton & Co.; Ernest Nister	R2–R3
Hadfield Cubley (British)	Views	Tuck	R2–R3
Henry Cubley (British)	Views	n/a	R3
Neville Cumming (British)	Military	n/a	R3
Cyrus Cuneo	Military	n/a	R3
E. Curtis	Children	Tuck	R3
Carl Czeschka (Austrian; 1878–1960)	Military, greetings, glamour	Gerlach & Schenk; Bruder Kohn	R3–R4

Artist	Types of Cards	Publisher	Rarity
Caran D'Ache (French; 1852–1909)	Advertising, political	Greningaire; Le Journal	R4–R5
Frederic-Hugo d'Alesi	Views	n/a	R4–R5
Mary Daniell	Special occasion	Tuck	R4
Dauber	Humorous	n/a	R2
R. A. Davenport (American)	Views	G. C. Mather	R2–R3
George Davey (British)	Political, humorous	Valentines; Misch & Stock	R2–R3
L. H. Davey	Views	Boldstone & Attkins; W. T. Pater	R3
Arthur Davis	Animals	Tuck	R4
Marshall Davis (American)	Military	Marshall Davis	R3
F. T. Daws	Animals	n/a	R2–R3
Lucy Dawson (British)	Animals	Valentines	R3
A. De Breanski (1877–1945)	Views	J. Salmon; C. W. Faulkner	R2–R3
De Camara	Views, political, humorous	n/a	R3
Leal De Camara (Spanish; 1877–1948)	Military, political, transportation	P. Lamm; F. Jackl; B.C.I.	R3–R4
Adolfo De Carolis (Italian; 1874–1928)	Special occasion, military, fantasy, historical	Alterocca	R3–R4
E. T. ("Tiger") De Closay (French; 1859–1928)	Famous people, fantasy, glamour, views	New South Wales Bookstall Co.; Harding & Billings	R3–R4
Bryan de Grineau	Military	Valentines	R2
F. de Haenen	Views, military	A. & C. Black	R3–R4
Paul de Longpre (American)	Views, floral	n/a	R2–R3
Walter De Maris	Children, military	n/a	R2–R3
Crosby De Moss (American)	Animals, humorous	Dexter Press	R1–R2
Alexandre De Riquer (Spanish; 1856–1920)	Glamour, advertising, special occasion	L. I. Bartrina	R4

Paul de Longpre

Artist	Types of Cards	Publisher	Rarity
Henri de Toulouse Lautrec (French)	Advertising, glamour	n/a	R5
Bazil Dean (American)	Humorous	n/a	R1–R2
Debarre	Military	n/a	R3
S. Debernardi (Italian)	Fantasy	n/a	R4
Eugene Deblaas (Italian)	Character studies	Hildesheimer	R3
Frank Dech	Views	n/a	R3–R4
Balho Del Vella	Glamour	n/a	R3
H. Delalain (French)	Military	n/a	R3
F. K. Delavilla (Austrian; 1884–1967)	Greetings	Wiener Werkstatte	R4
Maurice Denis (1870–1943)	Advertising	n/a	R4
Depiere	Military	n/a	R3–R4
M. D'ercoli	Military	V. E. Boeri	R3
Oscar Detering	Views, humorous, greetings	n/a	R3
Ethel Dewees	Children, greetings	A.P.M. Co.	R2–R3
Alfred Dewey (American)	Romantic, views	n/a	R2–R3
Marjorie Dexter (British)	Children	Valentines	R2–R3
Dhuzmer (French)	Military	n/a	R3–R4
F. C. Dickinson (British)	Military	George Pulman & Sons	R3
Carl Diehl (German)	Military	n/a	R2–R3
Michael Diemer (British)	Views, military	Wrench	R2–R3
Julius Diez (German; 1870–1957)	Special occasion, fantasy	Herst. v. Vertr.; Wiener Werkstatte	R4
Dinah (British)	Children, military	Tuck	R2
Josef Diveky (Hungarian; 1887–1951)	Special occasion, views, children, greetings, fantasy	Wiener Werkstatte	R3–R4
Dorothy Dixon	Children	Ernest Nister	R3
Francis Dodd	Military	n/a	R3

GENERALS OF THE BRITISH ARMY. *Portraits by Francis Dodd.*

General SIR H. C. O. PLUMER,
G.C.M.G., G.C.V.O., K.C.B., A.D.C.
who commanded the Army which captured the highly fortified Wytschaete-Messines ridge in June, 1917, taking 7,000 German prisoners. In command of the British forces in Italy, November, 1917.

Francis Dodd

An Bord des Dampfers „Borussia"   Oberwesel

Osc. Detering

Artist	Types of Cards	Publisher	Rarity
Dohnalek	Military	n/a	R3–R4
Donadini	Humorous, satire	n/a	R3
B. Dondorf (German)	Military	n/a	R2–R3
D'Ostoya	Military	n/a	R3–R4
T. Dreger	Royalty	n/a	R3
Drieux	Military	n/a	R3
J. Nelson Drummond (British)	Views	n/a	R3
Norah Drummond	Views, animals	n/a	R2–R3
Josephine Duddle (British)	Children	Regent	R3
Jessie Dudley	Views	E. T. W. Dennis & Sons	R3
Marcello Dudovich (Italian; 1878–1962)	Advertising, special occasion, military	Chappuis	R3–R4
M. Dulk (American)	Views, children	n/a	R2–R3
J. Dulst	Royalty	n/a	R4
Frederick Duncan	Romance, views	Reinthal & Newman	R3
James Duncan (aka Hamish) (British)	Humorous, views	Tuck; Davidson Bros.	R2–R3
Louis Dunki (Swiss)	Special occasion	J. E. Wolkensberger	R5
Emile Dupuis (French)	Military, glamour	Vise	R3
Edward Dussek	Royalty	n/a	R4

T. Dreger

81

Artist	Types of Cards	Publisher	Rarity
Clare Dwiggins (American; 1873–1958)	Humorous, children, greetings	Tuck; Charles Rose; Vincent Cardinell	R3
W. H. Dyer (British)	Views	J. Salmon	R2–R3
Maud Earl (British)	Animals	E. W. Savory	R3
Harold Earnshaw (British)	Children, humorous	J. Henderson & Sons; George Pulman & Sons; Valentines; G.D. & D.L.	R2–R3
Pauli Ebner (Italian)	Children, greetings, military	August Rold; M. Munk; A. Pokl; Dondorf	R3
Otto Eckmann (German; 1865–1902)	Advertising	G. Hirth	R4
V. Edel	Military	n/a	R3
Albert Edelfelt (Finnish; 1854–1905)	Historical, views	n/a	R4
Linda Edgerton (British)	Children	Vivian Mansell	R3
Mabelle Edmonds (Australian)	Glamour, large letter, children	Harding & Billings	R3–R4
George Edwards (British)	Views	n/a	R2–R3
H. Edwards (EDY; American)	Children, military	n/a	R2–R3
Franz Eichorst (German)	Military	n/a	R4
Helmuth Eichrodt (German)	Advertising, glamour	Gebr; Knauss	R4
Ernst Eigener (Germany)	Military	n/a	R3
Oscar Elenius (Finnish; 1885–1965)	Social customs/conventions, views	n/a	R4
Harry Eliott (British)	Views, sports, humorous	n/a	R4
William Ellam (British)	Animals (cats, teddy bears), famous people, humorous, royalty	Hildesheimer; C. W. Faulkner	R2–R3
Ellem	Military	Photochrom	R3
Kathryn Elliott (American)	Greetings, children, glamour	Gibson Art Co.	R2–R3

Artist	Types of Cards	Publisher	Rarity
Arthur Elsley	Views, animals	Tuck; Hildesheimer	R2–R3
Marc Ely (French)	Satire	n/a	R3
Frank Emanuel (British; 1865–1948)	Views	Tuck	R2
Sidney Endacott (British; 1873–1918)	Famous people, views, religious	Worth & Co.; Frith	R2–R3
P. O. Engelhard (P. O. E.) (German)	Military, children	n/a	R3
Robert Engels (German; 1866–1926)	Glamour, fantasy	G. Hirth	R4
Albert English (A. E.) (British)	Military, children, humorous	Wildt & Kray; Mitchell & Watkins; William Ritchie & Sons; Thridgould & Co.	R2–R3
Archibald English (A. E.) (British)	Humorous, views	William Ritchie & Sons; Wildt & Kray	R2–R3
Fritz Erler (German; 1868–1940)	Fantasy, military	G. Hirth; C. Woll & Son	R4
Felix Erlich	Royalty	n/a	R3
Harry Evans	Transportation	n/a	R4
Willy Exner (German)	Military	n/a	R3
Eysler	Military	n/a	R4
A. F.	Military	n/a	R3–R4
T. F.	Advertising	Ludlow & Sons	R4
Fabio Fabbi (Italian; 1861–1946)	Special occasion, fantasy	Alterocca	R4
Fabien Fabiano (French)	Glamour, advertising	n/a	R3–R4
Fahringer	Military	n/a	R3
Jules Faiure (French; 1867–1945)	Advertising, military	n/a	R4
Jacques Faizant (French)	Military	n/a	R3–R4
A. Farcy (French)	Advertising	n/a	R4

Sidney Endacott

Artist	Types of Cards	Publisher	Rarity
May L. Farini (American)	Views, greetings	n/a	R2–R3
Theo. Fasche	Royalty, military	M. Munk	R3
Alexander Federley (Finnish; 1864–1932)	Political/propaganda	n/a	R5
H. Feiertag	Children, views	n/a	R3
R. Feld (German)	Military	n/a	R3
Frank Feller	Military	Tuck	R3–R4
Fercham	Military	n/a	R3
F. Ferlberg (German)	Views	n/a	R2
F. Fernand (French)	Transportation, political, satire	n/a	R3–R5
Fernand Fernel	Advertising, humorous	Greningaire	R4
Ferrari (Italian)	Military	V. E. Boeri	R3
Arthur Ferraris	Royalty, military	n/a	R3–R4
Alice Leulla Fidler (American)	Glamour	n/a	R3–R4
Fidus (Hugo Hoppener) (German; 1868–1948)	Fantasy, romance, advertising, animals, children	G. Hirth	R4
G. Filoginno (Italian)	Military	Arti Grafiche	R3–R4
Joseph Finnemore (British; 1860–1939)	Views	Tuck	R2–R4
V. Finozzi (Italian)	Military	n/a	R3
Walter Firle	Royalty	n/a	R4
Art Fischer	Royalty, military	n/a	R4
Harrison Fisher (American; 1875–1934)	Glamour, character studies	Reinthal & Newman; Detroit Pub. Co.	R3
Florence Fitzgerald (British)	Views	C. W. Faulkner	R3
Dennis Fitzsimmons (British)	Advertising	David Allen	R4
James	Military, glamour,	Jack Dempsey	R3–R4

Harrison Fisher

Craig Fox

Artist	Types of Cards	Publisher	Rarity
Montgomery Flagg (American; 1877–1960)	character studies, satire	Restaurant	
Otto Flechiner (German)	Military	n/a	R3–R4
P. Fletcher-Watson (British)	Views	Tuck	R3
Herman Fleury	Transportation (trains), humorous	Misch & Co.; G.D. & D.L. (Gottschalk, Dreyfuss & Davis, London)	R3–R4
Margaret Flockton (Australian)	Floral	New South Wales Bookstall Co.	R3
Charles Flower (British; 1871–1951)	Religious, views	Tuck	R2–R3
Folexondy	Military	n/a	R3–R4
Charles Folkard (British; 1878–1963)	Fantasy, children	A. & C. Black	R3–R4
Leo Fontan (French)	Glamour, military	n/a	R3
Edmondo Fontana (Italian; 1861–1929)	Special occasion, fantasy, military	n/a	R3–R4
Jean-Louis Forain (French; 1852–1931)	Military	n/a	R4
Amedee Forestier (French; 1854–1930)	Military, views	Tuck; Picture Postcard Co.; A. & C. Black	R3–R4

B. V. Francken

Artist	Types of Cards	Publisher	Rarity
Kit Forres (British)	Children, humorous	Regent Pub. Co.	R2
E. Forster	Royalty	n/a	R3
Gilbert Foster (British)	Views	Tuck	R2–R3
C. Fouqueray	Military	n/a	R3
Craig Fox (American)	Humorous	Tichnor Bros.	R2
G. Fraipont	Advertising	Maggi	R4
B. V. Francken (German)	Military, royalty	n/a	R2–R3
Roberto Franzoni (Italian; 1882–1960)	Advertising, special occasion	A. Pini	R4
L. Frassini (Italian)	Military	n/a	R3
Ernest Frater	Military	Hildesheimer	R4
J. Freixas	Greetings	Winsch	R3
Paul Frenzeny (French; 1840–1902)	Military	Picture Postcard Co.	R4
Mitzi Friedmann-Otten (Italian; 1884–1955)	Fantasy, greetings	Wiener Werkstatte; Bruder Kohn	R4
Frohlich (German)	Military	n/a	R3–R4
John Fry (British)	Ships	J. Salmon	R3
R. Fuchs (German)	Glamour	n/a	R3–R4
Edmund Fuller (British)	Views	Stewart & Woolf; Davidson Bros.; Moss; Henry & Co,; Tuck	R2–R3
John Fulleylove (British; 1847–1908)	Views	Tuck; Regal Art	R3
A. Fullwood (Australian)	Views	Tuck	R2–R3
Harry Furniss (British)	Political, humorous	Studio Art	R3
J. P. G. (Irish)	Political	Ulster Pub. Co.	R4
M. P. G. (American)	Children, humor	Majestic Pub. Co.	R2–R3

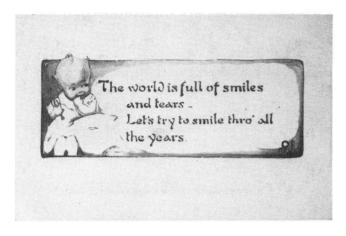

M. P. G.

I. A. Gerstenhauer

Artist	Types of Cards	Publisher	Rarity
Gabard (French)	Military	n/a	R3–R4
R. Gallon (British)	Views	Hildesheimer	R2
Sidney Gardner (British)	Views	Tuck	R3
F. Gareis	Romance, satire	n/a	R3
Katherine Gassaway (American)	Children, greetings	Tuck; Rotograph; Ullman; National Art Co.	R3
Gassner	Military	n/a	R3
Cherry Gay	Children	n/a	R3
Mabel Gear	Animals	Valentines	R3
R. Geiger (French)	Glamour	Pascalis; Moss & Co.	R4
Genni (Italian)	Military	n/a	R3–R4
Lemon George (Irish)	Political	J. Johnson	R4

Artist	Types of Cards	Publisher	Rarity
Mary E. George	Children, satire	Ernest Nister	R3
Vesper George (American)	Military	n/a	R3
Guy Georget (French)	Military	Mercure Publicite	R4
W. Georgi	Military	n/a	R3
Henri Gerbault (French; 1863–1930)	Glamour, political	Tuck; Greningaire; R. & Cie	R4
I. A. Gerstenhauer	Views	W. de Haan	R3
H. Gervese	Military	Raffaelli	R3
Gesner (American)	Political views	n/a	R3
Remigius Geyling (Austrian; 1878–1974)	Special occasion, glamour	n/a	R3–R4
Taylor Ghee (Australian; 1872–1951)	Views, social customs	Tuck	R3
May Gibbs (British; 1877–1969)	Children, greetings, views	Osboldstone & Co.	R2–R3
Charles Dana Gibson (American; 1867–1944)	Glamour, satire	J. Henderson & Sons; A. Schweizer	R3–R4
A. Gieste	Floral	n/a	R3
C. A. Gilbert (American)	Glamour	J. Henderson & Sons	R4
John Gilbert (Irish)	Special occasion	Purcell & Co.	R3–R4
Arthur Gill (British)	Humorous, views	Tuck	R3
T. Gilson (British)	Military, humorous	E. J. Hay & Co.; J. Salmon	R2
Adolphe-Paul Giraldon (French; 1855–1933)	Advertising	Greningaire	R4
May Gladwin	Children, views	Tuck	R3
Glanville (British)	Military, humorous	Millar & Lang	R3
Ceasare Gobbo (Italian)	Special occasion	n/a	R3–R4
Godia	Military	n/a	R3–R4
V. Goland	Military	n/a	R3

Artist	Types of Cards	Publisher	Rarity
Mary Golary (American)	Views, greetings	n/a	R1–R2
Rube Goldberg	Satire, humorous, views	n/a	R3
Golia (Italian; 1885–1967)	Advertising, military	n/a	R3–R4
Maud Goodman (American)	Children	Tuck; Hildesheimer	R3
Gray Gordon	Animal studies (horses)	J. Henderson & Sons	R3
Xavier Gose (1876–1915)	Advertising, glamour	Greningaire	R4
Gossett	Political	n/a	R3
F. Gothard (British)	Humorous	E. Mack; Tuck; J. Salmon	R3
Gotschke (German)	Military	Greishaber & Sauberlich	R3–R4
Lilian Govey (British)	Children	Wildt & Kray; Humphrey Milford	R3–R4
Marte Graf	Silhouettes, views	n/a	R3–R4
Duncan Grahm (British)	Humorous	Cynicus Pub. Co.	R3
Gordon Hope Grant (American; 1875–1962)	Shipping, views, military	n/a	R3
Eugene Grasset	Advertising, glamour, historical	Tuck; Greningaire	R4
Vittorio Grassi (Italian; 1878–1958)	Advertising, military	Bestetti e Tumminelli	R4
Kate Greenaway (British; 1846–1901)	Children	n/a	R4
A. Greer (Irish)	Political	J. W. Patton	R3
Magnus Greiner (American)	Glamour, children, blacks, teddy bears	Inter-Art; Ullman	R2–R3
Bernard Gribble (British)	Military	n/a	R3
H. B. Griggs (American)	Greetings, children, views	L. & E.	R2–R3
Leslie Grimes (British)	Military	Tuck	R3

H. B. Griggs

H. H.

Artist	Types of Cards	Publisher	Rarity
H. Gross (German)	Military	J. Thordsen	R3
Manni Grosze	Silhouettes	n/a	R3
Jules A. Grun (French; 1868–1934)	Advertising, political, glamour	Tuck; Greningaire	R4
Giovanni Guerrini (Italian)	Special occasion	n/a	R3–R4
Albert Guillaume (French; 1873–1942)	Advertising, military, glamour	Greningaire	R4
A. Guillome	Glamour	n/a	R3
Archie Gunn (American)	Glamour, military	National Art Co.	R3
Bill Gunn (Irish)	Social history	Ulster Pub. Co.	R4
Gurnsev	Military, royalty	n/a	R3
T. Guy	Views	E. T. W. Dennis & Sons	R2–R3
H. H. (American)	Military, greetings	Ullman	R3
P. H.	Views, humorous, military	n/a	R2–R3
Arthur Hacker (British; 1858–1919)	Glamour	C. W. Faulkner	R3
F. J. Haffner	Humorous, children	n/a	R3
Nini Hager	Glamour	n/a	R3–R4
C. A. Hall	Views	A. & C. Black	R3
A. Halle	Military	n/a	R3

Artist	Types of Cards	Publisher	Rarity
A. Halmi (Hungarian; 1866–1939)	Advertising, glamour	G. Hirth	R4
Max Halverson (American)	Military	n/a	R3–R4
E. Hamilton (British)	Advertising, ships	n/a	R4
T. M. Hamilton	Humorous	n/a	R3
J. Hammick	Glamour	Photochrom	R3
Charles Hammond (1870–1953)	Animals (horses), views	Osboldstone & Attkins	R3
Walter Hampel (Austrian; 1868–1949)	Glamour, advertising	Gerlach & Schenk; G. Hirth; Phillip & Kramer	R4
Hanitzsch (German)	Children	Hanitzsch Karte	R2
Charles Hannaford (1863–1955)	Views	E. T. W. Dennis & Sons	R2–R3
Hansi (J. J. Waltz) (French; 1873–1951)	Military, children	P. J. Gallais et Cie	R3–R4
A. Hansteen	Animals	Tuck	R3
Jennie Harbour	Views, glamour	Tuck	R3
Dudley Hardy (British; 1867–1922)	Humorous, advertising, military, children	Tuck; Valentines; C. W. Faulkner; Davidson Bros.	R2–R3
Florence Hardy (British)	Children	C. W. Faulkner	R3
Heywood Hardy (British; 1842–1933)	Sports, animals	Langsdorff & Co.	R3
Paul Hardy (British)	Views, historical, sports	Tuck	R3
J. Knowles Hare (American)	Glamour	Saturday Evening Post; National Art Co.	R3–R4
Harlitzsch (Austrian)	Royalty	M. Kaineder	R4
H. Harmony (American)	Children, views	n/a	R3
W. Hartman (German)	Military	n/a	R3
John Hassall (British; 1868–1948)	Humorous, advertising, greetings	Tuck; Valentines; C. W. Faulkner; David Allen	R2–R3

Kid, in all the West,
You for mine.
The pick of the best,
My Valentine.

P. H.

John Hassell

Artist	Types of Cards	Publisher	Rarity
Hassenkamp (German)	Military	n/a	R3
Paul Haustein (German; 1880–1944)	Special occasion	M. Fischer	R5
Georges Hautot (French)	Military	n/a	R3
Bill Haverstein (American)	Military	n/a	R3
A. E. Hayden	Children, humorous	n/a	R3
Frederick W. Hayes (British; 1848–1918)	Views, greetings	Inter-Art; Tuck; Meissner & Buck	R3
M. G. Hayes (American)	Children	Ernest Nister	R2–R3
Sydney Hayes (British)	Animals	Tuck	R2–R3
Arthur Head	Views	Tester; Massy & Co.	R3–R4
John Heartfield (Helmut Herzfelde) (German; 1891–1968)	Political, military	Malik	R3–R4
William Heath-Robinson (British; 1872–1944)	Humorous, satire	Valentines; Harrap	R3
Sidney Hebbletwaite (British)	Humorous	Tuck	R3
Dora Heckel	Military	n/a	R2–R3

Artist	Types of Cards	Publisher	Rarity
Thomas Heine (German; 1867–1948)	Glamour, advertising	M. Fischer; Hans Pernat	R4
Paul Helleu (French; 1859–1927)	Glamour	n/a	R4–R5
Joseph Hemard (French; 1880–1961)	Advertising, special occasion, military	Edwin Henel	R4
Carl Henckle	Military	n/a	R3–R4
P. Henn	Military	n/a	R3
Henry	Military	Colorprint	R3
A. Hensel (German)	Military	n/a	R3
Rene Hermann-Paul (French; 1864–1940)	Military, political	Greningaire	R4
Herouard (French)	Military	n/a	R3
Herve	Glamour	n/a	R3
Hesse (German)	Military	n/a	R3–R4
Ludwig Hesshaimer (German)	Special occasion	n/a	R4
Axster Heudtlass (German)	Military	n/a	R3–R4
Paul Hey (German; 1867–1952)	Views, children, social conventions	Hubert Kohler; Bruckmann	R4
Jean Heyermans (Belgian)	Views	Tuck	R2–R3
Heyman (American)	Greetings	n/a	R2
A. Hildesheimer (British)	Special occasion, advertising	Tuck	R4
D. Hillson (American)	Views, greetings	n/a	R2–R3
Alfred Hilton (British)	Military	Modena & Co.	R4
Frederick Hines	Views	Ernest Nister	R3
Hirlemann	Military	n/a	R3
W. Hoeck (German)	Military	n/a	R3
A. Hofer	Military	A.T.	R3
R. J. Hoffman (German)	Military	n/a	R3

Anton Hoffmann

Edgar A. Holloway

Artist	Types of Cards	Publisher	Rarity
Anton Hoffman	Military, royalty, views	n/a	R3
Josef Hoffmann (Austrian; 1870–1956)	Glamour, fantasy, advertising, special occasion	Gerlach & Schenk; Phillip & Kramer; Bruder Kohn	R3–R4
Adolfo Hohenstein (German)	Special occasion, fantasy	Ricordi	R4–R5
Ludwig Hohlwein (German; 1874–1949)	Political, special occasion, military, advertising	C. Wolf	R4
F. Hollart	Military	n/a	R3–R4
Edgar A. Holloway (British)	Military, royalty	Gale & Polden	R3
Eva Hollyer	Children	Birn Bros.; Langsdorff & Co.	R4
Conrad Hommel (German)	Military	n/a	R3
Honer	Military	n/a	R3–R4
Eileen Hood (British)	Animals	Humphrey Milford	R3–R4
Livingstone Hopkins (American; 1846–1927)	Satire, views	Bulletin Newspaper Co.	R3
E. Hoppe (Austrian; 1876–1957)	Views	Wiener Werkstatte	R4
H. Horina (American)	Humorous, greetings, children	J. I. Austen	R2–R3
Hornert	Military	n/a	R3
Charles Horrell	Glamour	J. Henderson & Sons	R3
Mary Horsfall (British)	Glamour, political, children	Tuck; William Ritchie & Sons	R3–R4
Charles Howard (British)	Views, military	Salmon; Photochrom	R3–R4
Fred Howard	Humorous, sports, firefighting	Pictorial Stationery Co.; Misch & Co.	R3
Theodor Hoytema (Dutch; 1863–1917)	Advertising	n/a	R4–R5
G. Huber	Humorous	n/a	R3

Ernest Ibbetson

Artist	Types of Cards	Publisher	Rarity
Peter Hubner (British)	Children	Inter-Art	R3
Isabel Hudson (British)	Children	Inter-Art	R3
H. Huesser (German)	Military	n/a	R3–R4
Maud Humphrey (American)	Children, glamour, greetings	L. R. Conwell; Tuck; Gray Lithographic Co.	R4
Lynn Bogue Hunt (American; 1878–1960)	Animal studies	n/a	R3–R4
Hal Hurst (American)	Military	n/a	R4
August Hutaf (American)	Humorous, children, greetings	n/a	R2
J. Hutchings (Australian)	Historical, views	New South Wales Bookstall Co.	R3
Frances Hutchinson	Views	J. W. Ruddock	R3
H. H. Hutson (American)	Humorous	M.W.M.	R2
Henry Hutt (American)	Glamour	Detroit Pub. Co.	R4
Graham Hyde	Blacks, humorous	Tuck	R3
Ernest Ibbetson (British)	Military, humorous	Gale & Polden; C. W. Faulkner	R3
Ibels	Military	n/a	R3
Leslie Illingworth	Military	Daily Mail	R2–R3
Inguar (Danish)	Military	Stenders Forlag	R4

Artist	Types of Cards	Publisher	Rarity
John Innes (Canadian; 1864–1941)	Views, character studies	W. G. MacFarlane	R2–R3
I. M. J.	Children	C. W. Faulkner	R3
Helen Jackson (American)	Children	n/a	R3–R4
Bruno Jacobs (German)	Military	n/a	R3
Helen Jacobs (British; 1888–1970)	Children, fantasy	C. W. Faulkner	R2–R3
G. L. Jaderholm (aka Snellman) (Finnish; 1894–1973)	Glamour, greetings	n/a	R4
A. Jaegy	Military	n/a	R3
Ivy Millicent James (British; 1879–1965)	Children, greetings	C. W. Faulkner; Tuck; M. Munk	R3
Angelo Jank (German; 1868–1940)	Political, special occasion	G. Hirth	R4
Urban Janke (Austrian; 1887–1914)	Views, greetings	Wiener Werkstatte	R4
A. Jarach	Military	n/a	R3
A. P. Jarry (French)	Military	n/a	R3–R4
J. Jaunbersin (Austrian)	Military, royalty	n/a	R3
G. H. Jenkins	Views	Tuck	R2
J. Johnson	Children, greetings	Gabriel; Tuck	R3
Karl Joseph	Military	n/a	R4
Karoly Jozsa (Hungarian)	Glamour	n/a	R4–R5
Jung (German)	Military	n/a	R3
J. Jungers (German)	Royalty	n/a	R3–R4
Gaspar Junyent (Spanish; 1875–1942)	Special occasion, advertising	Album Salon; L. Miguel	R3–R4
A. Jusmet (American)	Military	n/a	R3

Kaskeline

Artist	Types of Cards	Publisher	Rarity
A. K. (Austrian)	Royalty	Bruder Kohn	R3–R4
C. K. (Austrian)	Military	n/a	R3–R4
Leo Kainradl (German; 1872–1943)	Advertising, glamour	J. F. Schreiber; Phillip & Kramer	R4
Kaklo	Military	n/a	R3
Gustav Kalhammer (Austrian)	Views, advertising	Wiener Werkstatte	R4
Hans Kalmsteiner	Special occasion, fantasy, children	Wiener Werkstatte; A. Berger	R4
J. Kalous	Military	n/a	R3
Rudolf Kalvach (Austrian; 1883–1932)	Fantasy, greetings	Wiener Werkstatte	R4
R. Kammerer	Views	Tuck	R3
Kargl	Military	n/a	R3
A. H. Karlinsky	Military	n/a	R3–R4
Kaskeline (German)	Military, royalty	Bruder Kohn	R3
Kit Kat (British)	Humorous	Inter-Art	R2–R3
Elmer Keene (British)	Views	Tuck; C. W. Faulkner; E. T. W. Dennis & Sons	R2
Frank Keene	Sports, humorous	Cambridge Postcard Co.	R3

A. K.

Don Keller

Generalissimo Chiany Kai-shek

Morris Kellern

Artist	Types of Cards	Publisher	Rarity
Don Keller (American)	Views	E. C. Kropp	R2
Morris Kellern	Famous people, military	Photochrom; Graphic Post Card Co.	R3
Robert Kelly (British; 1861–1934)	Views	Tuck	R3
E. B. Kemble (American)	Views, greetings	n/a	R2–R3
A. E. Kennedy	Humorous, animals	C. W. Faulkner	R3
E. H. Kiefer	Romance	n/a	R3
Georgio Kienerk (Italian; 1869–1948)	Advertising, historical	Alterocca	R4
Alonzo Kimball (American; 1874–1923)	Glamour	Reinthal & Newman	R3
A. Price King	Views	Tuck	R3
Gunning King (British; 1859–1940)	Floral	Tuck; Hildesheimer	R2–R3
Hamilton King (American)	Glamour, advertising	Coca Cola Co.; J. T. Wilcox	R3–R4
Jessie M. King (Scottish; 1876–1949)	Children	Millar & Lang	R4
John W. King	Special occasion	Tuck	R3
Edward Kinsella (Irish)	Children, advertising	Langsdorff & Co.; David Allen	R3–R4

Artist	Types of Cards	Publisher	Rarity
Raphael Kirchner (Austrian; 1876–1917)	Glamour, advertising, greetings	Tuck; Meissner & Buch; Phillip & Kramer; A. Sockl; S. Hildesheimer	R4
Ida Kirkpatrick	Views, floral	C. W. Faulkner	R2–R3
Klaber	Military	n/a	R3
Hofrat Klamroth	Royalty	Von Friedrich Grober	R3
Catherine Klein (American)	Greetings, fantasy, views, large letter	Meissner & Buch; Stehli	R2–R3
Christina Klein (German)	Floral, animals	Tuck; C. W. Faulkner; Inter-Art	R2–R3
Gottfried Klein (German)	Military	n/a	R3–R4
Richard Klein (German)	Military, political	n/a	R3
Kletschman (German)	Military	n/a	R4
Julius Klinger (Austrian; 1876–1950)	Views, special occasion	J. F. Schreiber	R4–R5
Ludwig Koch (Austrian)	Animals, special occasion	Bruder Kohn	R3–R4
Mela Kohler (Austrian; 1885–1960)	Advertising, glamour, fantasy, children	Wiener Werkstatte; Bruder Kohn; M. Munk	R4
Oskar Kokoschka (1886–1980)	Fantasy, greetings, views	Wiener Werkstatte	R4
W. Kossaka (Polish)	Military	n/a	R4–R5
Rie Kramer	Glamour, fantasy	W. de Haan; Roukens & Erhart	R4
W. Kramer	Views	Tuck	R3
Walter Krane (British; 1845–1915)	Fantasy, children	n/a	R5
R. K. Kratki	Greetings	n/a	R2–R3
Kraus-Wichmann (German)	Military	n/a	R3–R4
Ernst Kreidolf	Religious, military, children	O. G. Melin; G. D. W. Callwey	R4–R5
Kristen	Military	n/a	R3

Ferdinand Kruis

Artist	Types of Cards	Publisher	Rarity
Ferdinand Kruis (Austrian; 1869–1944)	Glamour, royalty	F. A. Ackerman; Phillips & Kramer	R3–R4
F. Kudherna (Austrian)	Military	n/a	R3–R4
Franz Kuhn (Austrian; 1889–1952)	Views, greetings	Wiener Werkstatte	R4
Carl Kunst (1884–1912)	Views, special occasion, advertising	n/a	R4
H. W. Kuntz	Military	n/a	R4
F. Kupka (Austrian; 1871–1957)	Advertising, military, political	Le Rire	R4–R5
M. Kurzweil (Austrian; 1867–1916)	Glamour, advertising	Phillip & Kramer	R5
D. L.	Fantasy	n/a	R4
E. L.	Glamour, fantasy	J.K.	R3
R. B. L. (German)	Military	n/a	R3
La Monaca (Italian)	Military	V. E. Boeri	R3
Ch. Laborde	Military	n/a	R4
Lafayette	Royalty	n/a	R3
Lalia (Italian)	Military	I.G.A.P.	R3–R4
Percy Lancaster (British; 1878–1951)	Humorous	n/a	R3
H. Landgrebe (German)	Military	Doring & Huning	R3–R4
R. Langer (German)	Military	n/a	R3
L. H. ("Dude") Larsen	Views, Western studies	L. H. Larsen	R2–R3
Hans Larwin (Austrian)	Military	n/a	R3
Jean Lasalle	Views	Tuck	R2–R3
Franz Laskoff	Advertising, glamour, special occasion	Ricordi	R4
Lassar	Military	n/a	R3–R4
N. Laurenti (Italian)	Special occasion	n/a	R4
Le Clerc	Military	n/a	R3–R4

L. H. ("Dude") Larsen

Artist	Types of Cards	Publisher	Rarity
Henriette Le Mair (Dutch; 1889–1966)	Children, fantasy	Augener	R3
Pearle Le Munyan	Glamour	E. Gross	R3
Charles Leandre	Royalty, political, advertising, military	Le Rire; Greningaire	R4–R5
Leon Lebegue (French; 1863–1944)	Glamour	Greningaire	R4
Franz Lebisch (Austrian; 1881–1965)	Views, greetings	Wiener Werkstatte	R4
C. P. Legget (British)	Humorous	n/a	R2
P. Lehmann (German)	Advertising	n/a	R4
Frederick Leighton (British)	Crests/heraldic	C. W. Faulkner	R3–R4
Leopold Lelee (1872–1947)	Glamour, views	Greningaire	R4
Pearle Fidler Lemunyan	Glamour	Edward Gross	R3–R4
Otto Lendecke (Polish; 1886–1918)	Glamour, greetings	Wiener Werkstatte	R5
Lenhard	Military	Kilophot	R4
Maximilian Lenz (Austrian; 1860–1948)	Military, fantasy, sports	A. Berger; Phillip & Kramer	R4
Leo	Glamour, fantasy	n/a	R3–R4
G. Leonnec	Military	L.E.	R3

Artist	Types of Cards	Publisher	Rarity
Leroy	Military	n/a	R3
Ernest Lessieusx (French; 1848–1925)	Fantasy, advertising, glamour	Theo Stoefer	R4
Frederick G. Lewin (British)	Humorous, greetings, Blacks, children, military	Inter-Art; J. Salmon; Bamforth; M. Munk	R2–R3
Joseph C. Leyendecker (German-American; 1874–1951)	Advertising, military	n/a	R4
Ernst Liebermann (German)	Views	Hubert Kohler; H. Hohmann	R4
Lienz (Austrian)	Military	n/a	R3–R4
Maria Likarz-Strauss (Austrian)	Glamour	Wiener Werkstatte	R4–R5
E. M. Lilien (1874–1925)	Views, fantasy	G. Hirth	R5
R. Lillo (American)	Humorous	P. Sander	R3
William Limpart (German)	Military	n/a	R4
Norman Lindsay (Australian; 1879–1969)	Views	Bulletin Newspaper Co.; New South Wales Bookstall Co.; National Art Gallery	R4
Norman Lindsey (Australian)	Views	n/a	R3
L. Lindsell	Views	Tuck	R3
R. Lipus (German)	Military	n/a	R3–R4
H. Liska	Military	n/a	R3–R4
Privat Livemont (1861–1936)	Advertising, special occasion	n/a	R4–R5
T. Ivester Lloyd (British)	Military	W. N. Sharpe	R3–R4
B. Loffler (Austrian; 1874–1960)	Fantasy, historical, special occasion	Wiener Werkstatte; A. Berger	R3–R4

Artist	Types of Cards	Publisher	Rarity
F. Lohmann	Floral	n/a	R3
B. F. Long (American)	Military	n/a	R3
F. G. Long (American)	Greetings, children, blacks	n/a	R2–R3
Wilf Long	Military, humorous	Photogelatine Engraving Co.	R3
Wilhelm Long	Military	n/a	R3
Edgar Longstraffe	Views	Tuck; Hildesheimer	R2–R3
Lopit (Mexican)	Bullfighting, views	n/a	R1–R2
R. H. Lord (American)	Greetings	R. H. Lord	R3
E. C. Lounsbury (American)	Greetings, views	n/a	R2–R3
Montague Love	Military	Blum & Degen	R3–R4
F. Low-Lazar (1891–1975)	Glamour, greetings	Wiener Werkstatte	R4
Tex Lowell (American)	Humorous	Baxtone	R1
Ludgate (British)	Military	n/a	R2–R3
Anthony Ludovici	Humorous, political, views	Davidson Bros.; Valentines	R2–R3
S. Lumley (British)	Military	Gale & Polden	R3–R4
Peter Lutz	Military	n/a	R3
A. F. Lyndon (British)	Animals	n/a	R3
Amedee Lynen (Belgian; 1852–1938)	Views, advertising, military	Malvauz	R4
E. M.	Fantasy	n/a	R3
L. MacBean	Humor	Photochrom	R2
Winsor McCay (1869–1934)	Greetings, cartoon characters	Tuck	R4
A. McCormick (1860–1943)	Views	Tuck	R3
John McCutheon (American; 1870–1949)	Humor, satire, historical, children, military	n/a	R3–R4
A. K. MacDonald	Special occasion	Valentines	R3–R4

F. Mackain

Artist	Types of Cards	Publisher	Rarity
Donald McGill (British; 1875–1962)	Humorous, military, political	Inter-Art; Birn Bros.; Woolstone Bros.; Eyre & Spottiswoode	R2
R. F. McIntyre (British)	Views	Tuck	R2
F. Mackain (British)	Military, humor	G. Savigny	R2–R3
George McManus (American; 1884–1954)	Humorous (cartoon characters)	Star Co.; North American	R3
J. McNeill (British)	Military	n/a	R2–R3
Harry Maden (British)	Military	n/a	R2–R3
Adolfo Magrini (Italian; 1876–1957)	Special occasion, historical	Alterocca	R4
Bertha Maguire	Views	Tuck	R3
Frank Mahoney	Views, historical	Bulletin Newspaper Co.	R4
R. Mailick (German)	Greetings, fantasy, military, views	Giesen Bros.	R3–R4
A. Majani (1867–1959)	Special occasion, satire, advertising, military	Menolia	R4
Beatrice Mallett (British)	Children, advertising	Goosens; Tuck	R3–R4
Burkhard Mangold (Swiss; 1873–1950)	Military, special occasion	J. E. Wolfensberger; W. Wasserman	R4

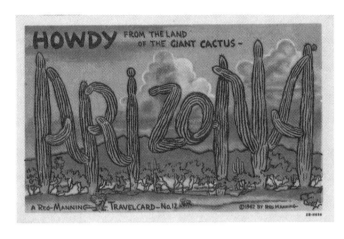

Reg Manning

Artist	Types of Cards	Publisher	Rarity
Reg Manning (American)	Views, large letters	Curt Teich	R2
M. Marco	Glamour	n/a	R3
San Marcos	Glamour	n/a	R3–R4
Marienrux (French)	Military	n/a	R3
William Marquis (French)	Whimsical, character studies, views	n/a	R3
G. Marr (Austrian)	Military	n/a	R3–R4
Irene Marsallus	Greetings	Ernest Nister	R3
Marschall	Views	Herman Rutz	R2–R3
Abe Martin (American)	Views, satire	n/a	R3
Phil Martin (British)	Humor	Inter-Art	R3
Alberto Martini (Italian; 1876–1954)	Military, glamour, historical, advertising, special occasion	Alterocca; D. Longo	R4
Marussig (Austrian)	Military	n/a	R3
A. Sternberg Masolle (Swedish)	Greetings	Eskil Holm	R4
Massonet	Military	Belgian Red Cross	R3–R4
Mastroianni (Italian)	Military	n/a	R3

Mater

Artist	Types of Cards	Publisher	Rarity
Giovanni Mataloni (Italian; 1869–1944)	Glamour, fantasy, historical, military, special occasion, political, advertising	Alterocca; Ricordi	R4
F. Matania (Italian; 1881–1963)	Military, royalty, advertising	n/a	R3
Theo. Matejko	Military	n/a	R3–R4
Mater (American)	Greetings	n/a	R3
William Matthison (British)	Views	Tuck; A. & C. Black	R2–R3
Reginald Maurice (British)	Humorous, military	Regent Pub.	R2–R3
L. Mauzan (Italian)	Military, glamour, advertising	Ricordi; Chiattone	R3
Phil May (British; 1864–1903)	Humorous, advertising, satire	Tuck; Valentines; Wrench; Davidson Bros.	R3
Henry Mayer	Humorous	Ernest Nister	R2–R3
Aldo Mazza (Italian; 1880–1964)	Advertising, military, special occasion	Ricordi	R3–R4
A. S. Meeker (American)	Satire, views	n/a	R2
Lon Megargee (American)	American western studies	Lollesgard Specialty Co.	R2–R3
Melville (American)	Views, greetings	n/a	R2–R3
Mortimer Menpes (Australian; 1860–1938)	Views, military, children	Tuck; Wrench; A. & C. Black	R3
Joyce Mercer (British; 1896–1965)	Children, fantasy	C. W. Faulkner	R3
I. Mermagen (German)	Military	Peter Luhn	R3–R4
K. Merten	Military	n/a	R3
G. Meschine (Italian)	Military	n/a	R3
L. Metivet (French; 1863–1932)	Advertising, military, royalty, historical	Greningaire	R4–R5

"HOME ON THE RANGE"

Lon Megargee

Artist	Types of Cards	Publisher	Rarity
Leopoldo Metlicovitz (Italian; 1868–1944)	Military, glamour, views, advertising	Ricordi	R3–R4
G. Metz	Military	n/a	R3
Henri Meunier (Belgian; 1873–1922)	Glamour, fantasy, advertising	F. Wolff; Dietrich & Cie; Stroefer	R4
Suzanne Meunier (French)	Military, glamour	n/a	R3
Lou Meyer (American)	Humor	n/a	R2–R3
Victor Mignot (Belgian; 1872–1944)	Sports	Dietrich & Cie	R3–R4
Hilda Miller	Fantasy	n/a	R3
Marion Miller (American)	Greetings, views	n/a	R2–R3
R. C. Miller (British)	Military	n/a	R3
Maurice Milliere (French)	Glamour	M. Munk	R4
Mirko (Italian)	Political	n/a	R3–R4
Georges Monbard (French; 1841–1905)	Military	Picture Postcard Co.	R4
Maggy Monier	Military, glamour	n/a	R3
M. Monteduro (Italian)	Glamour	n/a	R4
W. Moore (British)	Views	Tuck	R2–R3

Artist	Types of Cards	Publisher	Rarity
Willy Moralt (German)	Military	n/a	R3
Arthur Moreland (British)	Humorous, political	C. W. Faulkner	R3
Fred Morgan	Humor	n/a	R2
Val Morgan (British)	Humor	Inter-Art	R2–R3
W. Morgan (American)	Military	A. D. Steinbeck & Sons	R2–R3
M. Morris (British)	Humorous, views (nautical)	n/a	R2
Albert Morrow (British)	Advertising	n/a	R4
George Morrow (Irish; 1870–1955)	Political	n/a	R4–R5
Jack Morrow (Irish; 1872–1926)	Political	Dungannon Club	R4
Norman Morrow (Irish; 1879–1927)	Political	Dungannon Club	R4
M. Mortimer (British; 1860–1938)	Special occasion, children	J. Wrench	R3–R4
Koloman Moser (Austrian; 1868–1918)	Glamour, special occasion, fantasy	Phillip & Kramer; J. F. Schreiber; Gerlach & Schenk; Wiener Werkstatte	R4–R5
Leslie Mosley	Animal studies	Alpha	R3
Marjorie Mostyn (British)	Glamour	Tuck	R2–R3
Alphonse Mucha (Czech; 1860–1939)	Advertising, glamour, historical, fantasy, special occasion	Greningaire; F. Champenois	R4–R5
Augustus Muller (German)	Animals, views	Hildesheimer	R3
E. Muller	Military	n/a	R3
V. Mundorff (German)	Military	n/a	R4
Walt Munson (American)	Humorous, military, blacks	Tichnor Bros.	R1–R2
J. N. (British)	History, views	H. & K.	R2
Giovanni Nanni (Italian; 1888–1969)	Glamour, military, advertising	n/a	R3–R4

GIVING A FLAT TIRE THE AIR

60311

Walt Munson

Artist	Types of Cards	Publisher	Rarity
Adrienne Nash	Children, military	Inter-Art	R2–R3
Nashnyekov	Glamour, Art Deco	n/a	R4
G. Nasi (American)	Military, romantic	H. T. Cooke Co.	R3
Thomas Nast (American; 1840–1902)	Military, political, satire	n/a	R5
Arnold Nechansky (Austrian; 1888–1938)	Glamour, greetings	Wiener Werkstatte	R4–R5
Nerino (Italian)	Special occasion	n/a	R3
Ernst Neumann (German; 1871–1954)	Advertising, views	G. Hirth	R4
Henry Newbolt (British)	Military	Tuck	R2
Walter Newman (American)	Satire, humor, views	n/a	R2–R3
G. E. Newton (British)	Views	n/a	R2
Ney	Glamour	Editions Delta	R3
Muriel Nicholls (British)	Children	New South Wales Bookstall Co.	R3
Buck Nimy (American)	American West, cowboys, animals	Buck Nimy	R2–R3
Kathleen Nixon	Fantasy, animals	C. W. Faulkner	R3
Ernest Noble	Humor	n/a	R3
F. Nockher (German)	Military	n/a	R3–R4
G. Nogel	Military	n/a	R3

Buck Nimy

E. H. Nunes

Artist	Types of Cards	Publisher	Rarity
Emil Nolde (German; 1867–1956)	Views, fantasy	A. Prantl; F. Killinger	R3–R4
P. Nomellini (Italian; 1866–1943)	Special occasion, military	Ricordi	R4
Francesco Nonni (Italian; 1885–1976)	Glamour, special occasion, advertising	n/a	R3–R4
Val Norman (British)	Views	J. Salmon	R3
A. Harding Norwood (British)	Military	J. Salmon	R2–R3
Robert Nosak (Austrian)	Military	n/a	R3–R4
H. E. Nosworthy	Children, fantasy	F. A. Owen Co.	R3
Gaston Noury (French)	Glamour, fantasy, advertising, historical	n/a	R4

The U.S.O. Buddies' Club, Boston, Mass.

E. M. Orr

Artist	Types of Cards	Publisher	Rarity
E. H. Nunes	Military	n/a	R3–R4
Charles Nuttall (Australian)	Glamour, historical, views, humor	Oceanic Stamp & Post Card Co.; J. Collis; W. T. Pater; Osboldstone & Attkins	R2–R3
Jenny Nystrom (Swedish; 1854–1946)	Views, children, greetings, glamour	Eneret; Axel Eliassons	R2–R3–R4
O. H. O. (German)	Humor	August Lengauer	R2
F. O'Beirne	Military	n/a	R3
Willy Oertel (German)	Greetings, views	Stengel & Co.	R4
E. Offel (Belgian; 1871–1959)	Advertising	n/a	R5
Joseph Olbrich (Austrian; 1867–1908)	Special occasion, views	Gerlach & Schenk; A. Berger	R4
Rose O'Neill (American; 1874–1944)	Children, greetings, political	Gibson Art Co.; Campbell Art Co.; Tuck	R3–R4
A. Operti	Views	Tuck	R2
Frederick Opper (American; 1857–1937)	Greetings, humor, children	Tuck; Kaufman & Strauss	R3
Denizard Orens (French)	Political, military, royalty	n/a	R4–R5
Emil Orlik (Austrian; 1870–1932)	Views, fantasy	B. G. Teuber	R4
E. M. Orr	Views, humorous, animals	n/a	R2–R3

Richard F. Outcault

A. Pallolio

Artist	Types of Cards	Publisher	Rarity
Alfred Ost (Belgian; 1884–1945)	Animals, military, satire	J. Goffin	R3
Edmund H. Osthaus	Animals, advertising	n/a	R5
Richard F. Outcault (American)	Children, animals, humorous	Kaufmann & Strauss; American Journal Examiner	R3
I. Outhwaite (Australian; 1889–1961)	Children, animals, fantasy	A. & C. Black; Robert Jolley; M. L. Hutchinson	R3–R4
Will Owen (British; 1869–1957)	Humorous, advertising	Tuck; Wrench; David Allen; Davidson Bros.	R3
C. P. (German)	Views	Carl Giessel	R2–R3
Paco	Military	n/a	R3–R4
Paul Padua (German)	Military	n/a	R3–R4

Artist	Types of Cards	Publisher	Rarity
Alexander Paischeff (Finnish; 1894–1937)	Views	n/a	R4
G. Palanti (Italian; 1881–1946)	Special occasion, military	Ricordi	R4
A. Palliolio	Views, humorous, children, animals	n/a	R2–R3
Harry Palmer (1854–1933)	Views	Tuck; A. & C. Black	R2–R3
Sutton Palmer	Views	J. Henderson & Sons	R3
R. Pannett	Views, greetings	J. Henderson & Sons	R3–R4
Rudolfo Paoletti (Italian)	Advertising, special occasion, views	Villardi	R4
Wilhelm Pape	Royalty	n/a	R3
F. G. Parbury (British)	Views	Tuck	R2
Paris (American)	Military	n/a	R3
Ethel Parkinson	Children	C. W. Faulkner; M. Munk	R3
Maxfield Parrish (American; 1870–1966)	Fantasy, children, advertising	n/a	R3–R4
Norman Parsons	Views	n/a	R3
Harry Partlett (aka "Comicus")	Humorous, views	Tuck; A. & G. Taylor; Gottschalk	R2–R3
Bernard Partridge (British)	Political	Wrench	R3
Emile Pastien	Military	n/a	R2–R3
B. Patella	Glamour	E.P.	R4
Vera Paterson (British)	Humorous, children, military	Regent Pub. Co.	R3
Bruno Paul (German; 1874–1968)	Special occasion, advertising, fantasy	G. Hirth; E.M.	R4
Arthur Payne (British; 1856–1933)	Views, military	Tuck; Hildesheimer	R3
G. M. Payne (British)	Humor	Gale & Polden	R3

THE TRIUMPH OF "CULTURE."

NO. 12.   (Reproduced by special permission of the proprietors of "Punch")

Bernard Partridge

Harry Payne

Alfred Pearse

Artist	Types of Cards	Publisher	Rarity
Harry Payne (British; 1858–1927)	Military	Tuck; Gale & Polden; Hildesheimer	R3–R4
Rene-Louis Pean (French)	Advertising, views, historical	Greningaire	R4
Alfred Pearse (1854–1933)	Military	Tuck; War Photogravure	R3
Bessie Pease (also B. P. Gutmann) (American)	Children	Reinthal & Newman	R3
D. Peche (Austrian; 1887–1923)	Views	Wiener Werstatte	R5
L. Peltier	Military	n/a	R3–R4
Edwin Penley (British)	Views	Tuck	R2
A. Penot (French)	Glamour	n/a	R3–R4
Floriano Pepe (Italian)	Military	V. E. Boeri	R3
Maurice Pepin (French)	Military	S. Herbert	R3
Pergine (Italian)	Military	n/a	R3
F. Perlberg (German)	Views	C. A. & Co.	R2–R3
Alice Person	Glamour	n/a	R3
L. Peterson (American)	Indians	Tammen Postcard Co.	R4
Bob Petley (American)	Humor	Petley Laff Card	R1–R2
A. Petroni (Italian)	Military, special occasion	n/a	R3–R4
Valerie Petter-Zeis (Austrian; 1881–1963)	Greetings, views	Wiener Werkstatte	R3–R4
Reginald Phillimore (British; 1855–1941)	Views	Reginald Phillimore	R2–R3
Coles Phillips (American; 1880–1927)	Glamour, Art Deco	Edward Grosse; Life Pub. Co.	R4
J. Picot	Military	n/a	R3
C. Pietzner	Royalty	Red Cross	R3–R4
Harold Piffard (British)	Military	Gale & Polden	R3

A. Prosdocimi

Artist	Types of Cards	Publisher	Rarity
James E. Pitts (American)	Glamour, animals, views, art	Strecher Lithographic Co.	R4
Dorothy Travers Pope (British)	Animals	Misch & Co.	R3
A. Porni (Italian)	Military	n/a	R3
F. Poulbot (French)	Military, advertising, political	n/a	R2–R3
Lyman C. Powell (American)	Glamour, children	n/a	R3
H. Praetorius	Views, advertising, special occasion, animals	Victoria Stamp Market; Oceanic Stamp & Post Card Co.; Osboldstone & Co.	R3–R4
Maria Pranke (Hungarian)	Views	Wiener Werkstatte	R4
A. L. Pressland (British)	Views	n/a	R2
Chloe Preston (British)	Children, novelty	Valentines; Humphrey Milford	R3
F. Corbyn Price	Greetings	Winsch	R3
Paul Prien (German)	Military	n/a	R3
A. Prosdocimi (Italian)	Views	n/a	R2
V. Pryani (Italian)	Military	n/a	R3
William Quartermain (British)	Views	J. Salmon	R3

Poulbot

115

INDIA FOR THE KING!

NO. 3. *Reproduced by special permission of the Proprietors of "Punch."*

Leonard Ravenhill

O. H. Renatus

Artist	Types of Cards	Publisher	Rarity
Alfred Quinton (British; 1853–1934)	Views	Tuck; C. W. Faulkner; J. Salmon	R2–R3
Max Rabes	Military	n/a	R3
M. Radiguet	Military	n/a	R3–R4
Louis Raemaekers (Dutch; 1868–1956)	Military, political, satire	George Pulman & Sons	R3
Ramberg (German)	Military	n/a	R3–R4
R. Rampling (British)	Views	J. W. Ruddock	R3
George Ramsey (British)	Views	n/a	R2
George Rankin	Animals	n/a	R2
Joe Rankin	Military	n/a	R3
Ranzenhofer (Austrian)	Military	n/a	R3
Rappini	Glamour	n/a	R3
Leonard Ravenhill (British; 1876–1942)	Military, political	Wrench	R3
L. Ravenny	Military	n/a	R3
J. L. Rawboh	Views	Tuck	R3
Georges Redon (French)	Advertising, special occasion	n/a	R4
Regamey (French)	Military	n/a	R3–R4
Frederic Regamez	Military	E. Le Demey	R2
Fritz Rehm (German; 1871–1928)	Advertising	Adolf Gierster	R4–R5
C. Reichert	Animals	Tuck	R3
Georges Remi (Belgian; 1907–1983)	Children, Indians	n/a	R3
Frederick S. Remington (American; 1861–1909)	Cowboys, Indians, American West	n/a	R4
Otto Renatus (German)	Military, royalty	n/a	R3–R4
Virgilio Retrosi (Italian)	Military	n/a	R3
Reynolds (American)	Greetings, views	n/a	R3
Frank Reynolds (British)	Humor	Tuck	R2

Artist	Types of Cards	Publisher	Rarity
L. R. Rhiptchu (Austrian)	Royalty, military	Bruder Lazar	R4
Federico Ribas	Military	n/a	R3
Agnes Richardson (British; 1884–1951)	Children, military	Tuck; Birn Bros.; C. W. Faulkner; Inter-Art	R2–R3
Cecil T. Rigby (British)	Humorous, military	n/a	R2–R3
Right (British)	Military	n/a	R3
Violet Roberts (British)	Animals	n/a	R2–R3
Robinson (*not* Robert) (American)	Military	n/a	R3–R4
Florence Robinson	Views	Tuck	R3
H. Robinson (British)	Satire, views	n/a	R3
Robert Robinson (American; 1886–1952)	Views	Edward Gross	R4
Wallace Robinson (American)	Military	Henry Heininger	R3
Norman Rockwell (American; 1894–1978)	Military, character studies, nostalgia	Whitney; Knights of Columbus; Life Pub. Co.	R3–R4
Roessler	Military	n/a	R3
Freda Mabel Rose	Children	n/a	R2–R3
Rostro	Royalty	n/a	R4–R5
Auguste Roubelle (French; 1872–1955)	Royalty, political, military	Le Rire; Greningaire; Tuck	R4
Frank Rouse	Views	Tuck	R2–R3–R4
L. L. Roush (American)	Children	Harding & Billings	R4
Mario Roverini (Italian)	Military, political	n/a	R3
Harry Rowntree (British)	Humor	n/a	R3
Tony Roy (American)	Humor	Dexter Press	R1–R2
Antonio Rubino (Italian; 1880–1964)	Advertising	n/a	R3
Santiago Rusinol i Prats	Views, art	Ll. Bartrina	R4

Hat auch viel tausendfaches Weh geraubt
Den Kranz des Glückes seinem teuren Haupt,
Der Kaiser trug es, stark und gottergeben. —
Doch als die letzte Nachricht kam, erschüttert
Sprach er, das Herz vom tiefsten Schmerz durchzittert:
«So bleibt mir nichts erspart in meinem Leben».
Das eigne Leid er im Gebet bezwang. —
Zu Gottes Thron des Kaisers Bitte drang:
«Nur meinem Reiche, Herr, sei Heil gegeben».   O. H.

L. R. Rhiptchu

117

Tony Roy

G. E. S.

Artist	Types of Cards	Publisher	Rarity
Charles Marion Russell (American; 1865–1926)	Indians, American West, cowboys, character studies	Charles E. Morris; Trail's End Pub. Co.; Ridgley Calendar Co.	R4
E. Ryan (American)	Humor, greetings, glamour	J. I. Austen; Reinthal & Newman; Art Mfg. Co.	R2–R3
Henry Ryland (British; 1856–1924)	Glamour	Tuck; M. Munk	R4
F. S. (British)	Humorous	n/a	R2
G. E. S. (American)	Views, humorous	n/a	R2
R. L. S. (American)	Humor	Baxtone	R1–R2

St. John

R. L. S.

Artist	Types of Cards	Publisher	Rarity
Enrico Sacchetti (Italian; 1877–1967)	Advertising, military, royalty	F. Polenghi & Co.; George Pulman	R3
Xavier Sager (French)	Glamour, military, children	A. Noyer	R3–R4
St. John (American)	Views, humor, glamour	Western News Co.	R2–R3
A. Sala (Italian)	Special occasion	n/a	R4
R. Salles	Military	n/a	R3–R4
Tito Sanbidet (French)	Military, glamour	P. J. Gallais et Cie	R3–R4
F. Sancha	Military, fantasy	Tuck	R3–R4
A. E. Sanders (British)	Views	Tuck; C. W. Faulkner	R2–R3
H. Sanford	Children	n/a	R3
A. G. Santagata (Italian)	Military	n/a	R3
N. V. Santho	Royalty, military	Hermann Wolff	R3
Saroukhan	Military	Eastern Pub. Co.	R3–R4
Robert Sauber (1865–1936)	Views, satire	Tuck; Pictorial Stationery Co.	R3
Tito Saubidet	Military	n/a	R3–R4
Sauter (German)	Military	n/a	R3–R4
Filiberto Scarpelli (Italian)	Military, advertising	n/a	R3–R4
L. Sch. (Austrian)	Military	n/a	R3
Richard Schaupp (Swiss)	Special occasion	J. E. Wolfensberger	R3–R4

Willi Schever-Mann

Artist	Types of Cards	Publisher	Rarity
Willi Schever-Mann	Views, military, animals, humorous	n/a	R3
Schickardt (German)	Military	n/a	R4
Ed. Schicki (Austrian)	Military	n/a	R3–R4
F. Schiegel (German)	Military	n/a	R3–R4
Egon Schiele (Austrian; 1890–1918)	Glamour	Wiener Werkstatte	R4–R5
Erich Schmal (Austrian; 1886–1964)	Views	Wiener Werkstatte	R4
C. Schmidt (German)	Views	Ernest Nister	R2–R3
Samuel Schmucker (American)	Glamour, greetings, fantasy	Winsch; Detroit Pub. Co.	R3
Jean Schnebelen (French)	Military	n/a	R4
Hermann Schneider (German)	Military	Erich Gutjahr	R3
Rudolf Schneider	Royalty, military	n/a	R3
Leo Schnug (German; 1878–1933)	Greetings	Phillip & Kramer	R4–R5
W. Schodde	Royalty	n/a	R4
Fritz Schonpflug (Austrian; 1873–1951)	Glamour, military	Bruder Kohn; M. Munk; K.W.H.W.	R3–R4
Rich Schreiber (German)	Military	n/a	R3–R4
Karl Schulpig (German; 1884–1948)	Views, royalty	J. C. Konig & Ebhardt	R4–R5
Johann Schult (German)	Military	n/a	R3–R4
Curt Schulz (German)	Military	n/a	R3
Hans Rudolf Schulze (German)	Military	n/a	R3–R4
Karl Schwetz (Austrian; 1888–1965)	Views	Kilophot; Wiener Werkstatte	R5

Felix Schwormstadt

R. Searle

Artist	Types of Cards	Publisher	Rarity
Felix Schwormstadt (German)	Royalty, military	n/a	R4
Scolik (Austrian)	Fantasy	n/a	R3
Charles Scoliksen	Royalty	B.K.W.I. (Bruder Kohn)	R4
Georges Scott	Military	A. Noyer	R3
R. Searle (American)	Humor	Baxtone	R1
Ule Seidl. (Austrian)	Special occasion	J. Weiner	R4
Raoul Serres (French)	Military	Societe Philatelique De Bayeux	R3–R4
Walter Severin	Views	Tuck	R3–R4
Augusto Sezanne (Italian; 1856–1935)	Special occasion	n/a	R4
C. E. Shand	Glamour, Art Deco	n/a	R3

Shearer

Slimgo

Artist	Types of Cards	Publisher	Rarity
Stocker Shaw (British)	Military, humor	W.B.	R3
W. Shaw (British)	Views, humorous	Woolstone Bros.; A. M. Davis	R2–R3
Shearer	Animals, humorous, views	n/a	R3–R4
Shearey (British)	Animals (bears), humor	n/a	R3
A. Shearme	Views	Salmon	R3
Charles Sheldon (American; 1866–1928)	Military	Picture Postcard Co.	R4
Sidney Shelton (British)	Views	Tuck	R3
George Shepheard (British)	Famous people, historical, Blacks	Tuck; C. W. Faulkner	R2–R3
Sherie	Military	n/a	R3
Cobb Shinn (American; 1887–1951)	Humorous, military, children, glamour, famous people, historical	Commercial Colortype Co.; T.P. & Co.; E. B. Scofield; C.W.P.	R2–R3
E. F. Skinner (British)	Occupation-related views	n/a	R2–R3
Slimgo	Military	n/a	R3–R4
David Small	Views	Tuck	R2–R3
Smeele (Dutch)	Military	Colorprint	R3
F. V. Smith (American)	Greetings	Walkover Shoes	R3
Harvey Partridge Smith (American)	Views	Harvey Partridge Smith	R2
Howard Smith (American)	Military	n/a	R3

F. V. Smith

Harvey Partridge Smith

Artist	Types of Cards	Publisher	Rarity
Jesse Wilcox Smith (American; 1863–1935)	Children	Reinthal & Newman	R3
Larry Smith (American)	Humor	Graycroft Card Co.	R2
Robert Smith	Military	n/a	R3
Roland Smith	Animals	n/a	R2–R3
Smits	Military	n/a	R3–R4
I. Snowman	Royalty	J. Beagles	R3
Snyder (American)	Military	n/a	R3
Soldatini (Italian)	Military	n/a	R3
Serge Solomko (Russian)	Glamour, fantasy	I. Lapina; Theo Stroefer	R4–R5
D. H. Souter (Scottish; 1862–1935)	Military	Harding & Billings; Bulletin Newspaper Co.	R3

Larry Smith

William Standing

Artist	Types of Cards	Publisher	Rarity
Millicent Sowerby (British; 1878–1967)	Children, fantasy	C. W. Faulkner; Misch & Co.; J. Salmon; Reinthal & Newman	R2–R3
Spear	Military	n/a	R3
Percy Spence (Australian; 1868–1933)	Views, glamour, famous people	Tuck; A. & C. Black; New South Wales Bookstall Co.	R3
Ferdinand Spiegel (German; 1879–1950)	Views, art	H. Kohler; F. Bruckman	R4
F. Spoltora (Italian)	Military	n/a	R2–R3
Fred Spurgin (British; 1882–1968)	Military, children, political, humorous	Inter-Art; Tuck; Bamforth; Wildt & Kray	R2–R3
G. L. Stampa	Military	Fine Arts Pub.	R3
William Standing (American)	Humor	Western Stationery Co.; Dennis Delger	R2

Artist	Types of Cards	Publisher	Rarity
Henry Stannard (British; 1870–1951)	Views	Tuck	R2
Franz Stassen	Military	n/a	R3
Steen (Dutch)	Military	n/a	R3–R4
Cesare Stefanini (Italian)	Military	V. E. Boeri	R3
Alexandre Steinlen (French; 1859–1923)	Views, advertising, military	Greningaire	R4
V. W. Sternberg (British)	Humorous	Valentines; J. Henderson & Sons	R3
Stewart (British)	Military	n/a	R2–R3
Eduard Stieffel (Swiss)	Special occasion	Gebr. Fretz	R4–R5
Stimson (American)	American western studies	Union Pacific	R3
Stockwell (American)	Military	n/a	R3
W. Stower (German)	Military	n/a	R3
George Studdy (British; 1878–1948)	Animals (''Bonzo''), humor, children, military, advertising	Inter-Art; Vivian Mansell; Valentines; Photochrom	R2–R3
Chris A. Suchel	Advertising	n/a	R4
Jarko Sumavsky (Czech)	Military	n/a	R4–R5
Arthur Szyx (Polish/American)	Military	Esquire Magazine	R4–R5
Clementine Tafuri (Italian)	Military, special occasion	n/a	R3–R4
R. Tafuri (Italian; 1857–1929)	Glamour, views, greetings	n/a	R4
Hector Talvart	Military	n/a	R3–R4
Jean Tam	Military	n/a	R3–R4
Georg Tappert (German; 1880–1957)	Special occasion	J. Schober	R5
Margaret Tarrant (British; 1888–1959)	Children, floral, views	C. W. Faulkner; Medici Society	R2–R3

Stimson

D. Tempest

Tex

Artist	Types of Cards	Publisher	Rarity
Tato (Italian)	Military, special occasion	n/a	R3–R4
Louis Tauzin (French)	Military	F. Braun	R3
Laurie Tayler (Australian)	Humorous, military	Tuck	R3
Arnold Taylor	Humorous, children	Bamforth	R2
George Taylor (Australia; 1872–1928)	Views, political, humor, sports	Pictorial Post Card Co.; Collins Bros.	R3
Laurie Taylor (British)	Military	n/a	R3
William Ladd Taylor (American; 1854–1926)	Views, historical	n/a	R4
Teller	Military	n/a	R4
Douglas Tempest (British)	Children, humorous, military, saline	Bamforth	R2–R3

Artist	Types of Cards	Publisher	Rarity
Margaret Tempest (British)	Animals	Medici Society	R2
Alcardo Terzi (Italian; 1870–1943)	Advertising, special occasion, glamour, military	E. Voghera; Ricordi; Gussoni	R4
Tex (American)	Humorous	n/a	R1–R2
Lance Thackeray (British)	Humorous, military, greetings, sports, views, satire, theatrical	Tuck; C. W. Faulkner; A. & C. Black; David Allen	R2–R4
Arthur Thiele (German)	Animals, fantasy, military, sports, greetings	Tuck; C. W. Faulkner; Stoeffer; Dietrich	R3–R4
J. Thiriar	Military	n/a	R3–R4
Bert Thomas (British)	Military, humor	Tuck; Gale & Polden	R2–R3
Barney Tobey (American)	Military	Stage Door Canteen	R3
A. Torello	Military	n/a	R3
H. Torggler	Military, children, views	Hermes-Druckerel	R3–R4
Fernand Toussaint (Belgium; 1873–1955)	Glamour, special occasion	Dietrich & Cie; De Rycker	R4
Maurice Toussaint (French)	Military	n/a	R3–R4
Dorothy Travers (British)	Animals	n/a	R2–R3
Treiber (German)	Military	n/a	R3–R4
Joseph Triado i Mayol (Spanish; 1870–1929)	Advertising, special occasion, fantasy	n/a	R4
Karl Truppe (German)	Military	n/a	R3–R4
Will Tschech (German)	Military	n/a	R3–R4
George Turner (American)	Character studies, views	Baxtone	R2
J. Turner (British)	Military, views, social customs	Osboldstone & Attkins; Robert Jolley; Tuck	R3

H. Torggler

E. R. Tyrrell

Hugo Voigt

Artist	Types of Cards	Publisher	Rarity
Charles Twelvetrees (American)	Children, humorous, animals, military, greetings	Reinthal & Newman; Alpha; Edward Gross; Illustrated Postal Card Co.	R2–R3
E. R. Tyrrell (American)	Greetings, humor	A. H. Co.	R3
Otto Ubbelohde (German)	Views, special occasion	n/a	R4
H. Ulmer	Royalty	M.L.M.	R4
Clarence Underwood (American)	Glamour	F.A.S.; Reinthal & Newman; National Art Co.; M. Munk	R3
Clare Ungel (British)	Military	n/a	R3
Florence Upton (American; 1873–1922)	Children (Golliwogs), greetings	Tuck; M. Munk; Dondorf	R3–R4
Usabal	Glamour, military	n/a	R3
Lotte Usabal	Glamour, greetings	Erkal; P.F.B.	R3–R4
Antoni Utrillo i Viadera (Spanish)	Glamour, advertising	A. Utrillo & Co.	R4
Felix Vallatton (Swiss; 1865–1925)	Military, advertising	n/a	R4
Joan Vallhonrati i Sadurni (Spanish; 1874–1937)	Advertising	Barral Huros	R4
Florence Valter (British)	Animals, greetings	Inter-Art; C. W. Faulkner	R2–R3
Piet Van Der Hem	Military, royalty	n/a	R3
Van Hier	Views	Tuck; C. W. Faulkner	R2
Eugene Charles Vavasseur (French)	Advertising, special occasion	Tuck	R4–R5
F. Vecchi (Italian)	Military, children, glamour	n/a	R3
A. Ventiorini (Italian)	Military	n/a	R3

Artist	Types of Cards	Publisher	Rarity
Ventura	Military	n/a	R3–R4
Pierre Vibert (Swiss; 1875–1937)	Famous people, special occasion	n/a	R4
P. A. Vicary (British)	Military	n/a	R3
A. Villa (Italian; 1865–1906)	Advertising	Ricordi	R4–R5
Jacques Villon (French; 1875–1963)	Glamour, historical, famous people	Le Rire; Greningaire	R4–R5
A. Vimaz	Fantasy, views	n/a	R4
Rene Vincent	Military	n/a	R3
Vleck	Military	n/a	R4
Heinrich Vogeler (German; 1872–1942)	Historical, military	n/a	R4–R5
Hugo Voigt (German)	Military	n/a	R3
Franz von Bayros (Austrian; 1866–1924)	Glamour	M. Victor	R4
Alois Von Lowenthal (Austrian)	Views	Wiener Werkstatte	R5
Ferdinand von Reznicek (Austrian; 1868–1909)	Views, satire	G. Hirth; A. Langen	R4
Rud. von Schneider	Views, military, royalty, satire, famous people	n/a	R3–R4
R. Von Wichera (German)	Military	n/a	R3–R4
H. W.	Royalty	A. Hildebrandt	R3–R4
Richard Wagner (German)	Views	n/a	R1–R2
Louis Wain (British; 1860–1939)	Animals, sports	Tuck; Beagles; Millar & Lang; C. W. Faulkner; J. Salmon	R3–R4
Louis Wain (British; 1872–1956)	Animals (cats), humor	Tuck; Philco; Beagles; J. Salmon; F. Hartmann; C. W. Faulkner; Davis & Co.	R3–R4

Rud. von Schneider

H. W.

B. Wall

Artist	Types of Cards	Publisher	Rarity
Winifred Walker	Floral, views	n/a	R2–R3
Bernhardt Wall (American; 1872–1956)	Children (Sunbonnet), greetings, animals (bears), views, humorous	Ullman Co.; Gibson Post Card Co.; Illustrated Postal Card Co.; Valentines	R2–R3
R. Wallace	Animals	n/a	R2–R3
J. J. Waltz (aka Hansi)	Military	n/a	R4
A. Wanke (Austrian; 1873–1936)	Children	M. Munk	R3
Dudley Ward (British)	Humor	n/a	R2
Herbert Ward	Military	C. W. Faulkner	R4
Arthur Wardle	Animals	J. Henderson & Sons	R2–R3
Jack Watson (American)	Military	n/a	R3
William Watson (Irish)	Political, views	H. Courtney; Ulster Pub. Co.; J. Johnson; W. & G. Baird	R3
Albert Weisberger (German; 1878–1915)	Special occasion, advertising	F. Schnell & Co.	R4
V. Weisberger (American)	Views	Tichnor Bros.	R2
Weiss (German)	Military	n/a	R3
Walter Wellman	Views, satire, animals, character studies	n/a	R3

Walter Wellman

H. Wessler

Artist	Types of Cards	Publisher	Rarity
Jacques Wely	Historical, views	Greningaire	R4–R5
Brynolf Wennerburg (1866–1950)	Military, glamour, sports	A. Langen; Meissner & Buch; Dr. Eysler & Co.	R3–R4
W. W. Werestchaguine	Military	n/a	R3–R4
H. Wessler	Greetings	n/a	R2–R3
Harry Weston (Australian)	Military, views, advertising	Bulletin Newspaper Co.	R3
Dorothy Wheeler (British; 1891–1966)	Children	A. & C. Black; J. Salmon	R3
Brian White (British)	Children	Valentines	R3
Flora White (British)	Children, fantasy	Photochrom; J. Salmon	R2–R3
Raimund Wichera (Austrian)	Military, glamour	M. Munk	R4
Otto Wiedemann (German)	Royalty, military	Gustav Liersch	R4
Grace (Drayton) Wiedersheim (American)	Children (Campbell Kids), advertising	Rose Co.; Reinthal & Newman; Alfred Schweizer; Tuck; Joseph Campbell Co.	R3–R4
Hans Wieland	Special occasion	Ricordi; J. E. Wolfensberger	R4
Manuel Wielandt (German; 1863–1922)	Views, special occasion	J. Velten; Moser; Ernest Nister	R2–R3–R4

J. R. Willis

Witt

P. A. Wolfe

Artist	Types of Cards	Publisher	Rarity
Adolf Wiesner (Austrian; 1871–1942)	Children, fantasy	Augener; A. & C. Black	R3–R4
L. Wilbur	Military	n/a	R3
H. G. Wilda	Royalty	n/a	R3
K. A. Wilke (Austrian)	Military	n/a	R3–R4

Artist	Types of Cards	Publisher	Rarity
Bob Wilkin (British)	Military	n/a	R3
Gilbert Wilkinson (British)	Military	Tuck	R2
Adolphe Willette (French; 1857–1926)	Royalty, military, views	Greningaire	R4–R5
George Willis	Humorous	Valentines	R3
J. R. Willis (American)	American western studies	J. R. Willis	R2
W. Willrich (German)	Military	n/a	R3
Oscar Wilson (British)	Military	Inter-Art	R3
Henry Wimbush (British)	Views	A. & C. Black	R2–R3
Witenski	Military	n/a	R3–R4
Witt (American)	Military, children, greetings, humor	A.P.C. Co.	R3
P. A. Wolfe (American)	Views	Florida Souvenir Co.	R2
Kurt Wolfram (German)	Military	n/a	R4
Lawson Wood (British; 1878–1957)	Children, animals, military, humor	Inter-Art; J. Salmon; Valentines; Davidson Bros.; Dobson; Molle & Co.	R2–R3
Stanley Wood (British; 1866–1928)	Military	n/a	R3
Richard Caton Woodville (British; 1856–1927)	Military	Picture Postcard Co.; Fred Hartmann; Collectors' Pub. Co.; Valentines	R4–R5
Julia Woodworth (American)	Children, greetings	n/a	R3–R4
Wolf Woolrich (German)	Military, political	n/a	R3–R4
Sikko Woude (Dutch)	Military	n/a	R3
Gilbert Wright	Animals	J. Henderson & Sons	R3
Henry C. Wright (British; 1849–1937)	Military	Picture Postcard Co.	R4–R5

Zimmerman

Artist	Types of Cards	Publisher	Rarity
W. Wylie	Views	Tuck	R2–R3
S. H. Y. (Irish)	Political	Valentines	R4
Alexander Young	Views	Tuck; C. W. Faulkner	R3
Charles Young	Views	W. T. Pater	R3
Walter Hayward Young ("Jotter"; British; 1868–1920)	Humorous, military, views, railways, advertising	Tuck; Photochrom; F. Hartmann; Woolstone Bros.; Jarrolds; Durley Dene Hotel	R2–R3
Zandrino	Glamour	n/a	R3
E. Mazzoni Zarini	Military	n/a	R2
Gyula Zilzer (French)	Military	n/a	R3
Zimmer	Humorous, animals, views	n/a	R2–R3
Zimmerman (German)	Military, views, historical	n/a	R2–R3
K. Zinn	Military	n/a	R3
C. Zirka	Glamour	n/a	R3–R4

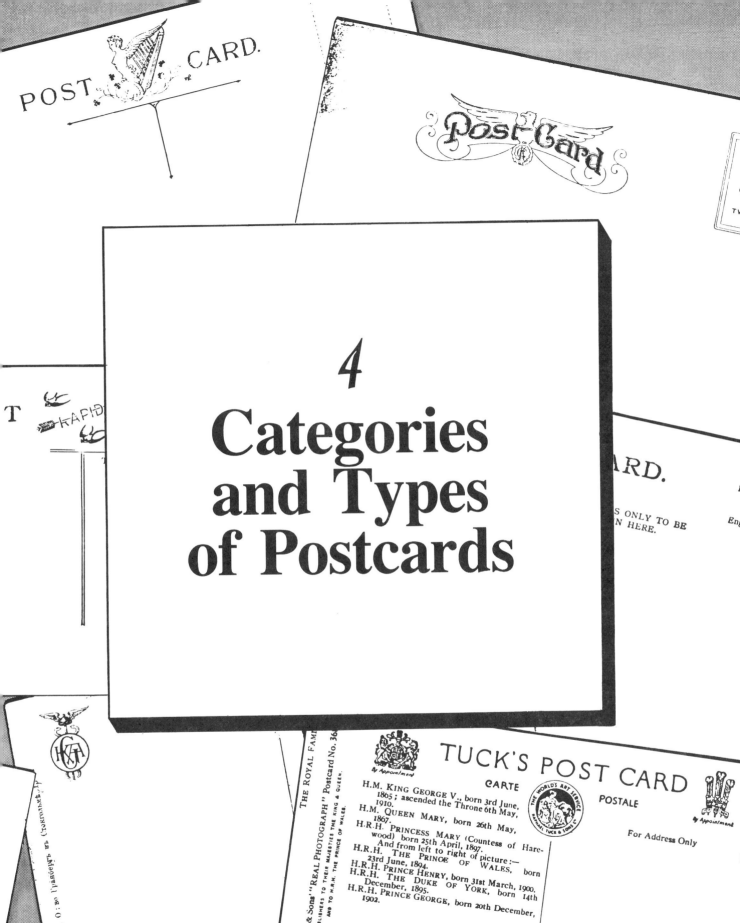

4
Categories
and Types
of Postcards

4
Categories and Types of Postcards

To report that picture postcard producers took the entire realm of human experience and also that of natural phenomena as their province is no misstatement of fact. As a goal, they may have fallen a little short—but not by much. The first list that is presented below only skims the surface of the incredible multiplicity of offerings but should be sufficient proof of the postcard's ubiquitous character. In addition, a second list featuring novelty postcards is offered, followed by a glossary of novelty postcard definitions. Wherever action took place; whenever state of being was the impassive situation or state of affairs; wherever rain fell and wind blew, the artists and photographers who peddled their wares to the printers were in attendance.

North, south, east, or west. Brown skin, yellow skin, red, or white. Rich, poor. Laborer, president, king, Bedouin tribesman. Sunshine, snow, hurricane, volcanic activity. Beaches, palaces, grass huts. Politics, wars, social history. Holidays and humor. Street scenes and pastures. And always, always more.

Take a look.

Types of Cards

Abbeys (R1–R2)
Accidents (R2–R4)
Advertising
    East European/Asian (R4–R5)
    Famous poster type (R4–R5)
    Famous products (R3–R4)
    Modern (R1–R2)
    On government postals, black and white (R2–R3)
    On government postals, color (R3–R4–R5)
    Pre-1898 (R4–R5)
    Pre-1905 (R4–R5)

Airplanes, civilian
    Modern (R1)
    Post-1920 (R2–R3)
    Pre-1920 (R3–R4)
Airports
    Modern (R1)
    Pre-1950 (R2)
Alcohol-related (R2–R3)
Alphabet-related (R2–R3)
Ambulances (R3–R4)
American Girl (R3–R4)
American West (R1–R2)
Amusement parks
    Modern (R1)
    Post-1920 (R2)
    Pre-1920 (R2–R3)
Angels (R2–R3)
Animals
    Cats
        Maurice Boulanger (R2–R3)
        Reg Carter (R2–R3)
        W. H. Ellam (R2–R3)
        Modern cards (R1–R2)
        Other artists (R2–R4)
        Real photo (R2–R3)
        Arthur Thiele (R3–R4)
        Louis Wain (R3–R4)
    Dogs
        Norah Drummond (R2–R3)
        Modern cards (R1–R3)
        Other artists (R2–R3–R4)
        Real photo (R2–R3–R4)
        George Studdy, "Bonzo" (R2–R3)
        Maud Watson (R3)
    Other animals
        Alligators (R1–R2)
        Birds (R2–R3)
        Desert (R1–R2)
        Exotic (R2–R3)
        Farm (R2)
        Fish (R1–R2)

Horses (R2–R3)
Other (R2–R4)
Teddy bears (R2–R4)
Zoo (R1–R2)
Announcement cards (R2–R3)
Anti-Semitic (R3–R5)
Antiquity
  Ruins/sites (R2–R3)
  Museum relics (R2–R3)
Aqueducts (R2–R3)
Arcades (R2–R3)
Archaeology (R3)
Architecture (R2–R3)
Art Deco
  Common designs (R2)
  Famous artists (R3)
  Less-well-known artists (R4)
  Poster style (R3)
Art Nouveau
  Common designs (R2–R3)
  Famous artists (R3–R4)
  Less-well-known artists (R4–R5)
  Poster style (R3–R4–R5)
Artist signed
  Advertising (R2–R3–R4)
  Animals (R2–R3–R4)
  Art Deco (R2–R3)
  Art Nouveau (R4–R5)
  Common views (R1–R2)
  Famous people (R2–R3–R4)
  Famous posters (R3–R4)
  Fantasy (R2–R3–R4)
  Floral (R1–R2)
  Glamour (R3–R4)
  Historical (R2–R3)
  Humor (R1–R2)
  Military (R2–R3–R4)
  Other transportation (R2–R3–R4)
  Pastoral scenes (R1–R2)
  Political (R2–R4)
  Royalty (R2–R3–R4)
  Satire (R2–R3–R4)
  Ships (R2–R3–R4)
  Street scenes (R2–R3)
Astrology/zodiac (R3)
Astronomy (R2–R3)
Autograph cards
  Real autographs (R3–R4–R5)
  Reproductions (R2–R3)

B

Babies (R2–R3)
Ballet (R2–R3)
Balloons, aviation (R2–R4)
Ballrooms (R2)
Banks (R1–R2–R3)
Bathing beauties (R1–R2–R3)
Bazaars (R2)
Beefeaters (R1–R2)
Before/after cards (R2–R3)
Bells (R1–R2)
Bibles (R3)
Bioscopes (R3–R4)
Bird's-eye views (R2)
  Modern (R1)
Birthplaces/gravesites of famous people (R1–R2)
Bizarre (R2–R3)
Blacks
  Other (R2–R3)
  Pre-1905 (R3–R4)
Boardwalks (R2–R3)
Boats (R1–R2)
Book-related (R2–R3)
Bottles (R2–R3)
Boy Scouts (R2–R3–R4)
Bridges (R1–R2)
  Covered (R2–R3)
Broadcasters (R3)
Bus depots (R2–R3)
Buses (R2–R3)
Business interiors
  Close up (R2–R3)
  Close up, real photo (R3–R4)
Business views/locations (R1–R2)

C

Calendars (R2–R3)
Camping (R1–R2–R3)
Canals (R2–R3–R4)
Canoeing (R2–R3)
Carnivals
  Pre-1920 (R3–R4)
  Post-1920 (R1–R2)
Cathedrals (R1–R2)
Caves (R1–R2)

Cemeteries (R2)
Chain letters (R3)
Children
    Artist-drawn (R2–R3–R4)
        Billikens (R4)
        Campbell Kids (R3)
        Golliwoggs (R4)
        Kewpies (R3)
        Kornelia Kinks (R3)
        Others (R2–R3)
        Sunbonnets (R3)
    Modern cards (R1–R2)
    Real photo (R2–R3–R4)
Churches (R1–R2)
Circus-related (R2–R3–R4)
City halls/municipal buildings
    Modern (R1)
    Post-1920 (R2)
    Pre-1920 (R2–R3)
City skylines (R2)
    Modern (R1)
Clay and wax model figures on cards (R3)
Clocks (R2–R3)
Clothing fashions (R2–R3)
Clowns (R2–R3)
Coast Guard (R2–R3)
Coca-Cola-related (R2–R3–R4)
College girls (R3)
Colleges/universities (R2–R3)
Comic strip characters (R3)
Commemoratives
    Government postals (R3–R4–R5)
    Others (R2–R3–R4–R5)
Construction work (R2–R3)
Contests/competitions (R2–R3)
Continuing-story cards (R2)
Convents (R2–R3)
Corkscrews (R3–R4)
Correspondence-related (R2–R3)
Country clubs (R2)
Court houses
    Modern (R1)
    Post-1920 (R2)
    Pre-1920 (R2–R3)
Cowboys (R2–R3)
Crests/coat of arms/heraldic (R2–R3)
Curiosities (R2–R3–R4)

D

D.A.R.-related (R3)
Dairy-related (R2)
Dams and reservoirs (R2)
Dancing (R2–R3)
Days of the week (R2–R3)
Death/funeral-related (R2–R3)
Dentistry (R2–R3)
Devils (R2–R3)
Dikes (R1–R2)
Diners (R1–R2)
Disasters
    Airplane crashes (R2–R3)
    Car wrecks (R2–R3)
    Earthquakes (R3–R4)
    Fires (R3)
    Floods (R3–R4)
    Hurricanes (R3–R4)
    Others: droughts, duststorms, plagues, explosions
        (R4)
    Shipwrecks (R3–R4)
    Tornadoes (R3–R4)
    Train wrecks (R3–R4)
    Tram/bus wrecks (R3–R4)
    Volcanic eruptions (R2–R3)
    Zeppelin/dirigible crashes/explosions (R4)
Diseases (R3–R4–R5)
Disney-related (R1–R2)
Distilleries (R2)
Document reproductions (R2)
Dog carts (R2–R3)
Doll cards (R2–R3)
Dreyfuss Affair (R4)
Drunks and drinking (R1–R2)
Dwarfs (R3–R4)

E

Economic upheavals (depressions) (R3–R4)
Elks lodges (R2)
Elves (R2–R3)
English court cards (R4–R5)
Esperanto (R2–R3)
Executions (R3–R4)

Expeditions (R3–R4–R5)
Explosions (R2–R3)
Expositions and fairs
    Modern (R1–R2)
    Post-1920 (R2–R3)
    Pre-1900 (R4–R5)
    Pre-1920 (R2–R3–R4)

F

Facisms (R2–R3)
Factories (R1–R2)
Fairies (R2–R3)
Famous buildings (R1–R2)
Famous landmarks/locations
    Eiffel Tower, Stone Mountain, Niagara Falls,
        London Bridge, Leaning Tower of Pisa, Ro-
        man Colosseum, Arch de Triomphe (Paris),
        Tower of London, The Alamo, Statue of
        Liberty, others (R1–R2)
Famous people
    Entertainers, miscellaneous (R1–R2)
    Explorers (R2–R3)
    Famous historical figures (R1–R2–R3)
    Inventors, poets, composers, authors, playwrights
        (R2–R3)
    Movie stars
      American (R2–R3)
      British (R2–R3)
      German (R3–R4)
      Modern (R1–R2–R3)
      Other (R3–R4)
    Presidential (R3–R4–R5)
    Royalty
      Modern (R1–R2)
      Other (R1–R2–R3)
      Pre-1898 (R4–R5)
      Seldom seen (R3–R4–R5)
      Special occasion (R3–R4–R5)
    Sports stars (R2–R3)
    Stage stars
      American (R2–R3)
      British (R2–R3)
      German (R3)
      Other (R3–R4)
    Television stars
      American (R2–R3)
      British (R2–R3)
      German (R3–R4)
      Modern (R1–R2)

Other (R3–R4)
    World leaders (R2–R3)
      Modern (R1–R2)
Famous people residences (R1–R2)
Famous quotations (R1)
Fantasy (R2–R3–R4)
Farms and farming (R1–R2)
Federal buildings (R1)
Ferries (R2–R3)
Fetes (R2–R3–R4)
Firefighting (R3)
Fishing (R1–R2)
Flags (R1–R2)
Fleas, spiders, other insects (R2–R3)
Flora, plants (R1–R2)
Flowers (R1–R2)
Folklore (R2–R3)
Food-related (R1–R2)
Foreign dignitaries' residences (R2)
Founder's Day cards (R3)
Fountains (R2)
Four seasons (R2–R3)
Fraternal (R2)
Friezes (R1–R2)
Frogs (R2–R3–R4)
Fruit (R1–R2)
Furniture (R2–R3)
Futurism (R2)

G

G.A.R.-related, Grand Army of the Republic (R3)
Gambling (R2–R3)
Games (R1–R2–R3)
Gems (R2–R3)
Geneology (R3)
Geysers (R1–R2)
Ghosts (R3)
Giants (R3)
Gibson Girls (R3)
Girl Scouts (R3)
Glamour (R2–R4–R5)
Golf courses (R2)
Governmental departments (R2)
Governors' mansions (R1–R2)
Gramophones (R3)
Grand openings (R2–R3)
Great exploits/feats (R2–R3)
Greetings
    April Fool's Day (R3)

Arbor Day (R3)

Aunts, uncles, husbands, wives, sweethearts, brothers, sisters (R2–R3)

Birthday (R1–R2)

Christmas
Common cards (R1)
Fantasy issues (R2–R3)
Santa, common cards (R1–R2)
Santa, silk-suited (R3–R4)

Columbus Day (R3)

Easter
Common cards (R1)
Fancy issues (R2–R3)

Father's Day (R3–R4)

Flag Day (R3)

Good-luck types (R1–R2)

Guy Faulke's Day (R3)

Halloween
Common (R2)
Fancy issues (R3)

Independence Day
July 4 (R2–R3)
July 14 (R3)

Invitations (R2–R3)

Lincoln's Birthday
Common (R1–R2)
Fancy issues (R2–R3)

Maundy Thursday (R4)

May Day (R3–R4)

Memorial/Decoration Day (R3–R4)

Mother's Day (R3)

Mourning/condolences (R2–R3)

New Year's Day
Common cards (R1)
Fancy issues (R2)

Penecost (R4)

Rally Day (R2–R3)

St. Patrick's Day
Common cards (R1)
Fancy issues (R2)

Thanksgiving
Common (R1)
Fancy issues (R2)

Valentine's Day
Common (R1)
Fancy issues (R2)

Washington's Birthday
Common (R1)
Fancy issue (R2–R3)

Grotesque (R3)

Gruss aus
Pre-1898 (R4)
Later issues (R3)

Gypsies (R3)

H

Halley's Comet (R3)

Handmade cards (R2–R3)

Harbors (R1–R2)

Headwear (R2)

Hermits (R3)

High schools (R2–R3)

Highways/country roads (R1–R2)

Historical events (R2–R3)

Hobby/craft-related (R2–R3)

Hospitals (R1–R2)

Hotels (R2–R3)
Modern (R1)

Houseboats (R2–R3)

Humorous (R1–R2–R3)
Modern (R1–R2)

Hunting (R1–R2)

I

Indian Territory (R4)

Indians
Famous chiefs (R3–R4)
Modern (R1)
Post-1905 (R2–R3)
Pre-1905 (R3)
Real photo (R3–R4)

Industrial (R2–R3)

Information cards (R1–R2)

Insane asylums (R3)

Insect cards, royalty, political (R3–R4)

Insurance-related (R2–R3)

J

Jails (R2–R3)

Jewish/Judaica (R3–R4)

K

Krampus (European version of Satan) (R4)

141

L

Labor
   Other union activity (R2–R3–R4)
   Protests/demonstrations (R3–R4)
   Riots/strikes (R3–R4)
Lakes (R2)
Landscapes (R1–R2)
Language cards (R2–R3)
Large letters
   Post-1920 (R1–R2)
   Pre-1920 (R2–R3)
Legends (R2–R3)
Libraries (R2)
Lighthouses (R2)
Limericks (R1–R2)
Literary (R2–R3–R4)
Local customs (R2–R3)
Local events (R2–R3–R4–R5)
Lorries (R2–R3–R4–R5)
Lumbering industry (R2)

M

Macabre (R3–R4)
Magazine-related (R2–R3)
Mail coaches (R4)
   Modern (R2)
Map cards (R1–R2–R3)
Markets, open (R1–R2)
Masonic-related (R2)
Medal reproductions (R3–R4)
Medicine-related (R2–R3)
Menu cards (R2)
Midgets (R3–R4)
Military
   Balkan Wars (R4–R5)
   Boer War (R4–R5)
   Cards related to pre-1870 (R2–R3)
   Franco-Prussian War (R3–R4–R5)
   Inter War cards (R2–R3–R4–R5)
   Mexican Revolution (R3–R4–R5)
   Other wars (R4–R5)
   Russian Revolution (R4)
   Russo-Japanese War (R3–R4–R5)
   Spanish-American War (R4–R5)
   World War I
      Common types (R1–R2)
      Others (R2–R3–R4–R5)
   World War II
      Comic (R2–R3)
      Other (R2–R3–R4–R5)

Milk carts (R3)
Minerals (R2–R3)
Mines (R2–R3)
Months of the year (R3)
Monuments (R1–R2)
Motels (R1–R2)
Multiviews
   Alligator border (R3)
   Butterfly types (R3–R4)
   Four-leaf clover types (R3–R4)
   Regular types (R2–R3)
Municipal elections, mayor, sheriff, (R2–R3–R4)
Museums (R1–R2)
Musical groups and music halls, (R2–R3–R4)
Musical instruments (R2)
Musicians (R2–R3)
Mythology (R2–R3)

N

Names (R2–R3)
National Guard armories (R2)
National parks (R1–R2)
Native costumes (R2)
Native customs (R2–R3)
Newspaper reproductions (R2–R3)
Nonsense cards, rebus type, (R2–R3)
Nudes (R2–R3)
Nurseries (R3)
Nursery rhymes (R2–R3)
Nursing-related (R2–R3)

O

Occupation-related (R1–R3)
Odd and unusual (R2–R3)
Oil wells (R1–R2)
Oiletes, Tuck (R2–R3)
Old folk's homes (R2)
Opera (R2–R3)
Orchestras (R3)
Organizational meetings (R2–R3)
Outhouses (R1–R2)

P

Pagodas (R2)
Parades (R2–R3–R4)
Parks, city (R1–R2)
Passion plays (R3–R4)

Patriographics (R4)
Patriotic
    All others (R2–R3–R4–R5)
    Pre-World War I (R3–R4–R5)
    World War I
        All others (R4–R5)
        American (R2–R3)
        British (R2–R3)
        French (R2–R3)
        German (R2–R3–R4)
        Russian (R4–R5)
    World War II
        All others (R2–R3)
        British (R3)
        German (R3)
Pianos (R2–R3)
Pinups (R3)
Pioneer postcards
    All others (R3–R4–R5)
    Government postals, plain (R3–R4–R5)
Pirates (R2–R3)
Playing cards (R3–R4)
Poem cards (R1–R2)
Police (R3)
Political
    Campaigns/election-related (R3–R4)
    Caricatures
        Modern (R1–R2)
        Post-1905 (R3–R4)
        Pre-1905 (R4–R5)
    Communist-related (R2–R3–R4)
    Politicians touring/at events (R2–R3–R4)
    Political figures (R2–R3–R4)
    Rebellions/uprisings (R3–R4)
    Socialist-related (R2–R3–R4)
    Suffragettes (R3–R4)
Posed silliness cards (R2)
Post offices
    Modern (R1)
    Post-1920 (R2)
    Pre-1920 (R2–R3)
Postcards on postcards (R3)
Postmen (R3)
Prehistoric sites (R2)
Pretty women
    Common cards (R2)
    Famous artists (R3)
Prisons (R2–R3–R4)
Prohibition (R2–R3–R4)
Promotion types (R2)
Propaganda, military/political (R2–R3–R4–R5)
Public squares (R1–R2–R3)
Punch cartoons (R2–R3)

R

Radios (R2)
Railroad stations (R2–R3)
Railway commemoratives (R2–R3–R4–R5)
Real photo, studio types and local (R1–R2–R3)
Recreation-related (R1–R2)
Religious (R2–R3)
    Modern (R1)
Religious leaders (R2–R3)
Resort areas (R1–R2)
Restaurants (R1–R2)
Reward cards, given to school children (R3)
Rickshaws (R3)
Risque (R3)
Romance/lovers (R2)

S

Salvation Army (R2–R3)
Sanitoriums (R3)
School-related or teacher-related (R2–R3)
Scottish rite-related (R3)
Seas, oceans (R2)
Seasides and beaches (R1–R2)
Sentimentals (R1–R2)
Sequence, cards in (R2–R3)
Service stations (R2–R3–R4)
Sharks (R2–R3)
Ships (R1–R2–R3)
Shrines (R1–R2)
Silhouettes (R2–R3)
Smoking, cigarettes, cigars, pipes (R2–R3)
Snowmen (R1–R2)
Social history (R2–R3–R4–R5)
Song cards (R2–R3)
Souvenir folders (R1–R2–R3)
Space (R2–R3)
Sports
    Archery (R3–R4)
    Automobile racing (R1–R2–R3)
    Badminton (R3)
    Baseball (R1–R2–R3)
    Basketball (R3)
    Billiards/pool (R2–R3)
    Boating/yachting (R2–R3)
    Body building/weightlifting (R3–R4)
    Boxing (R2–R3)
    Bullfighting (R1–R2–R3)
    Bicycling (R2–R3)
    Cock fighting (R2–R3)
    Cricket (R2–R3–R4)

Dog racing (R2–R3)
Equestrian events (R1–R2–R3)
Fencing (R3)
Football (R2–R3)
Handball (R3–R4)
Hockey (R2–R3–R4)
Horse racing (R1–R2–R3)
Ice skating (R1–R2–R3)
Marbles (R3)
Olympics-related (R1–R2–R3–R4)
Ostrich racing (R3)
Polo (R3)
Roller skating (R3)
Rugby (R2–R3–R4)
Skiing (R1–R2–R3)
Swimming (R3)
Tennis (R1–R2–R3)
Wrestling (R2–R3)
State capitols (R2–R3)
    Modern (R1)
State fairs (R3–R4)
    Modern (R1–R2)
Statuary (R1)
Street scenes
    Modern (R1–R2)
    Post-1905
        Larger cities (R2–R3)
        Real photo (R2–R3–R4)
        Small towns/villages (R2–R3–R4)
    Pre-1905
        Larger cities (R2–R3)
        Real photo (R3–R4–R5)
        Small towns/villages (R3–R4)
Sunday school-related (R1–R3)
    Special commemoratives (R3–R4–R5)
Superlatives, largest, smallest, oldest, best, worst
        (R1–R2–R3)
Swastika-related (R2–R3)
Swimming pools (R1–R2)
Swimsuits
    Modern (R1–R2)
    Pre-1920 (R3)

T

Tall Tale (R2–R3)
Tartans (R3)
Telephone-related (R2–R3)
Television/movie house-related (R2–R3)
Temperance (R3–R4)
Territorial (R4–R5)
Thimbles (R3)

Titanic-related (R3–R4)
Tools (R2–R3)
Toys (R2–R3–R4)
Trains
    Modern (R1–R2)
    Post-1920 (R2–R3)
    Pre-1920 (R3–R4–R5)
Trains, railroad stations
    Modern (R1)
    Post-1920 (R2)
    Pre-1920 (R2–R3)
Transportation
    Cable cars (R2)
        Close-up (R3–R4)
    Cars (R2)
        Close-up (R3–R4–R5)
    Farm vehicles (R2)
        Close-up (R3–R4–R5)
    Horse drawn (R2–R3)
        Close-up (R3–R4)
    Lorries (R2)
        Close-up (R3–R4–R5)
    Odd transportation (R2–R3)
    Street/trolley cars (R2)
        Close-up (R3–R4–R5)
    Trams (R2–R3)
        Close-up (R3–R4–R5)
    Trucks, other buses (R2)
        Close-up (R3–R4–R5)
Trees (R1)
Types of people
    Nationalities, Laplanders, Eskimos (R2–R3)
Typewriters (R3)

U

UFOs (R3)
Unique types of cards, "Miss Post Card" (R3–R4)
Unusual cards, mailgrams (R2–R3)
Unusual people (R3)

V

V.F.W.-related (R2–R3)
Vacation-related (R1–R2)
Veteran's Day (R3–R4)
Viaducts (R2–R3)

"Wanted" poster types, criminals (R4)
Waterfalls (R2)
Weddings (R2–R3)
Whales (R2–R3)
Wiener Werkstatte artist cards (R4–R5)
Windmills (R1–R2–R3)
Witches (R3)
"Write Away" types (R2–R3)

Y.M.C.A. (R1–R2–R3)
Y.W.C.A. (R2–R3)

Zeppelins, nonmilitary (R3–R4)
Zodiac (R2–R3)

Novelty Postcards

Airbrush (R2–R3)
Aluminum (R4)
Applique
    Glitter added (R2)
    Attachments added, miscellaneous (R2–R3)
    Other, real hair, real feathers, beaded (R2–R3)

Bas relief (R2–R3)
Bookmarks (R3)
Braille (R4)

Celluloid (R3–R4)
Cloth cards (R3–R4)
Coin cards, embossed (R3)
Composites
    Each installment cards (R3)
    As a set (R5)
Copper (R4)
Cork (R3)

Easel cards, stand-ups (R3)
Embossed, common types (R1–R2)
Embroidered (R3)
Exaggerations (R2–R3)

Fab patchwork (R4)
Fluorescent cards (R3)
Folded/outsized (R2–R3)

Gelatine (R3)
Gramophone record cards (R4)

Hand-painted (R2–R3)
Hidden door (R3–R4)
Hold-to-lights
    Others (R4–R5)
    Transparencies (R4)

Irish peat (R2–R3)
Iron-on (R3–R4)

Lacquer (R3)
Large/small cards (R2–R3)
Leather (R2–R3)

Macerated money (R3–R4)
Match cards (R3–R4)
Maximum (R2–R3)
Mechanicals (R4–R5)
Metamorphics (R3–R4)
Mirror type (R3)
Mosaics (R3)
Moving eyes (R3–R4)

Pennants, added on (R2–R3)
Pincushion (R3)
Proof cards (R5)
Puzzle cards (R3–R4)

Revolving disc (R4–R5)

Salt bag cards (R2–R3)
Samuel Cupples silvers (R3)
Scented cards (R3–R4)
Silk screen (R2–R3)
Squeakers (R3)
Stamp cards, embossed (R3–R4)

Unusual shapes (R3–R4)

Wood (R2–R3)
Woven silk (R3–R4)

Definitions

Airbrush: Cards onto which colors have been painted by using air compression or cards having this effect.

Aluminum: Cards made out of aluminum.

Applique: A postcard onto which something has been added or applied, hence the designation. The most frequently encountered items are real hair, real feathers, bits of wood or metal, and beads. Faddish postcards, their popularity increases or diminishes according to the dictates of geography (they may be desirable in one place but not in another at any given time) and momentary fashion.

Bas Relief: Postcards, often portraits of famous people (royalty, military, political, stage stars) in which the portrait has been elevated or raised from the card's surface, thereby creating a three-dimensional effect. The characters on the cards thus have a more realistic appearance.

Bookmarks: Postcards in the oblong shape of a bookmark. Such cards may have several different lengths but are generally not in excess of two inches wide.

Braille: Postcards that illustrate examples of the language utilized by people who are blind.

Celluloid: A postcard with the addition of a specially designed, often decorative, piece of celluloid.

Cloth Cards: Cards made out of cloth that has been stiffened.

Coin Cards: Embossed (or flat) coin replicas of various countries. Perfect representations even as to size and color.

Copper: Cards made out of copper.

Cork: Cards made out of cork.

Easel Cards: Postcards with an attachment that allows them to stand, easel-style.

Embossed: Common types are postcards that have some or all of the design or wording raised from the card's surface.

Embroidered: Postcards onto which decorative cloth has been stitched or embroidered. The designs may be simple wording or a detailed picture or portrait. Themes range from greetings to military motifs (man-made during World War I).

Exaggerations: This designation usually refers to real photos of gigantic fruits, animals, or plants.

Fab Patchwork: Cards with a patch of decorative, colored cloth, usually portraits of royalty, famous people, or some other motif.

Face Mask Postcards: Postcards that may double as a mask. They have cutouts for the eyes and strings with which they may be tied to the head.

Foldups: Postcards that are folded. Each fold may be standard postcard size (3-1/2 × 5-1/2″) although they are sometimes either larger or smaller. Among subjects to be thus treated are royalty, city views, geographical locations, and exaggerations of a nonreal photo type.

Gelatine: A card upon which a gelatine finish has been applied to create a brilliant shine. Unfortunately, many of these cards were subject to cracking and peeling.

Hand Painted: Self-descriptive. Depending on the effort or the painter, these were sometimes among the most beautiful of cards.

Hidden Door (Concertina): Cards with folded-up paper views under a latch door or flap on the card's face. Sometimes called pullouts.

Hold-to-Light (HTL): Cards that must be held against a light to reveal what would not otherwise be seen. The basic types include cutouts (dozens of small cutout windows) that reveal different colored lights shining through; silvers (sometimes placed in a separate category) made by Samuel Cupples for the St. Louis World's Fair in 1904, which show orange/yellow details against a silver background; florescent cards that have been painted with a substance that reflects light, especially in the dark (in effect, these are the opposite of cards that must be held to the light, but they have always been categorized with HTLs); metamorphics (not to be confused with the other type of metamorphic, which will be described later) that, when held to the light, reveal an entirely different picture than what is first encountered upon observing the card.

Installments/Composites: Six to twelve cards that are placed side by side or atop one another to form a portrait or scenic. Each card may or may not be viewed as a picture separate unto itself. These cards are generally found as individual specimens rather than all together as a set. Favorite topics are military and royalty figures surrounded by the glorious deeds or occurances in their lives.

Irish Peat: A card that is reputed to be composed of Irish peat or from the soil of Ireland. Such claims may or may not be accurate.

Lacquer (or frosted lacquer): Self-descriptive except to note that the chalky finish of these cards makes them either prized or ignored.

Large Cards/Small Cards: Self-explanatory. The large cards (sometimes called jumbos) may be up to a foot wide while the small postcards are as little as two inches (sometimes called miniatures).

Large Letter: This designation covers a variety of types, including: a) large letters of people's names, sometimes intertwined in a floral design (these are mainly earlier cards); b) large letters that comprise the names of geographical locations (for example, Ireland, Spain, or San Francisco) and have either views of the area or famous people from the location (also earlier cards, for the most part); c) large letters of cities, states, military bases, and other locations, most of the type with views inside the letters (generally linen era cards).

Leather: Cards that have been made of leather. This type of card has been made since the early days of the twentieth century. Some of the designs on them are crude while others are more detailed, even including the addition of color.

Macerated Money: For centuries, the shredding of paper currency into very small bits of colored paper has been one of the accepted ways of withdrawing unusable or out-of-style money from circulation. At some point, an individual thought of the novel idea of placing some of the shreds in containers for paperweights and clear pencil tube attachments. An extension of the idea reached what many would call its logical conclusion of recycling the paper bits into reusable paper, especially for postcards. These cards are frequently—though not always—identified as containing a specified amount of money ("This card is worth . . .").

Magic Cards: Postcards that have been treated with a chemical to reveal a picture when they are held next to heat.

Man-made: These are either blank government postals or individual paperboard cut to postal specification (3-1/2 × 5-1/2") that have special artistic renditions or designs on them. Some of these designs and renditions were quite ingenious, and a few of them are very well executed. Everything from add-ons (including some real photos of the sender) to collages to stamp pieces arranged in mosaic style to form characters are among the offerings. Usually these cards were of greetings, but not infrequently a military, political, social, or other motif sought expression in this manner of presentation.

Match Cards: A metal type that has a strip of added metallic material making it possible to ignite a match by running it along the surface of the metal.

Maximum: The best definition of a maximum card is the one given by Ms. Jo Long, editor of *Maximaphily*, the quarterly journal of the Maximum Card Study Unit. She states that there are three ingredients essential to a true maximum card. They are 1) a postcard that matches the stamp design; 2) the stamp being in accordance with the stamp design; and 3) the cancellation being in concordance with both the postcard and the stamp. Long further states, "Maxi cards produced by the U.S. [Postal System] and other post offices in other countries are not considered 'true' maximum cards because they are merely reproductions of the stamps."

Mechanicals: Essentially, these are cards with moving parts that either alter the illustration or design already on the postcard or add to it. Revolving discs, which are wheels that reveal different personalities, family members, or stages in the life or career of the principal figure on the card when turned, is another type of mechanical. Kaleidoscopes also use a revolving disc to showcase various colors when the wheel is turned. Tab pulls are still another type.

Metamorphics: The term itself merely implies an alteration or change, a moving from one stage or position to another, or simply a type of transformation. In America, a metamorphic card is recognized as one in which the faces of famous royal or military figures, such as Napoléon, Bismarck, Wilhelm II, or Abdülhamīd, are composed of nude women or military figures and equipment.

Mirror Type: A type of add-on in which a square of polished material resembles a mirror effect.

Mosaics: Various types of material—or merely pictures of material—are added to form a montage of a person or a scene. One of the classic types are the ones where bits of stamp illustrations are made to resemble a person; the Dutch firm of A. W. Jannsen is one of the more popular publishers of this type. The difference between stamp mosaics and man-made types is that the man-made cards use real stamps rather than stamp illustrations.

Moving Eyes: Generally, these are animal cards with plastic "bubbles" surrounding the eyes. Under the bubbles are beads or discs that move when the card is handled or shaken.

Pennants: Another add-on, in this instance of a felt-like pennant flag with the name of a town, a state, a person, or a greeting.

Phonograph: A postcard that has been specially treated in such a way that it may be played on a phonograph. The most popular variety has a picture of a composer with one of his or her songs on the special coating.

Pincushion: An add-on card that has a square of puffed-up cloth on which a colored picture or design appears. These are not nearly as popular as the fab patchwork cards even though the appearance is quite similar.

Proof Cards: These are prototypes or samples for what is supposed to become a postcard. In most instances, these proofs were later accepted as the model and post-cards were produced from them. Each is obviously one of a kind.

Puzzle Cards: Cards that, when turned from one side to another, reveal a second personality or view. A look at one side might reveal the German Kaiser while a flick of the wrist might show his wife. Many of these cards were published by the H. C. J. Deeks Company.

Salt Bag Cards: Cards with a small sack of salt attached to the card. Nevada and Utah appear to be favored locations for the publishing of these cards. Often a desert view—of Las Vegas or Salt Lake City—dominates the face of the card.

Scented Cards: Sometimes called perfumed sachet cards, they are treated with perfume or powder and an illustration that may or may not correspond to the scent.

Silk Screen: A card made by a similar process to that employed in the making of silk-screen cloth. In fact, silk cloth is used in an intertwining fashion. One of the more noteworthy sets are the "Original Serigraphs," which show historical motifs and famous people.

Squeakers: Cards that emit a sound when the elevated center that contains a whistle gadget inside the card is pressed. The sound escapes through a small hole on the card's back. The illustration on the card is generally of an animal, the cat being a favored topic.

Stamp Cards: Most of these, like most of the coin cards, are embossed. Also like the coin cards, these are accurate stamp representations both as to color and to size.

Unusual Shapes: Including round shape cards as well as oblong, triangular, and square ones.

Wood: All wood or wood veneer cards.

Woven Silk: Beautiful embossed squares made of silk that have a picture of royalty or a military figure as their main theme. These much-sought-after cards were manufactured by the British firms of W. H. Grant and Thomas Stevens, among others.

The Healing Cup, thought to be made from the wood of the Holy Cross (religious). Galloway

Oberammergauer Passion Play (religious). Anonymous

25th anniversary (1882–1907) Philander Smith Biblical Institute, Japan (religious/special occasion). Anonymous

149

Lewis and Clark Exposition, 1905 (special occasion). Allied Printing

New York World's Fair, 1939 (special occasion). Miller Art Co.

Texas Centennial Celebration, 1945. (special occasion). C. T. Art

Franco-British Exhibition, 1908 (special occasion). Valentine's

Pan Pacific Exposition, 1915 (special occasion). Pacific Novelty Co.

Century of Progress, Chicago, 1933 (special occasion). Gerson Bros.

St. Louis World's Fair, 1904 (silver hold-to-light; special occasion/novelty). Samuel Cupples Envelope Co.

225th anniversary, Founder's Week, Philadelphia, 1908 (special occasion). T. R. G.

12th Annual Founder's Day Celebration, Lawton, Oklahoma, 1912 (special occasion; real photo)

Post Office, Centerville, Iowa (post offices post-1920). Curt Teich

Boardwalk Front, Atlantic City, New Jersey, 1930s (street scene). Tichnor

Times Square, New York, 1950s (street scene). Acacia Card Co.

Business District, De Queen, Arkansas, 1950s (street scene). Curt Teich

Main Street Looking South, Tulsa, Oklahoma, 1940s (street scene). E. C. Kropp

Main Street, Niles, Michigan, 1940s (street scene). Niles Office Supply

Hollywood and Vine, Hollywood, California, 1940s (street scene). Western Publishing & Novelty Co.

Main Street, Salt Lake City, Utah, pre-1920 (street scene). Edward H. Mitchell

Main Street, Greenville, South Carolina, 1920s (street scene).
Southern Post Card Co.

Business Section, Sarasota, Florida, 1940s (street scene).
Curteich

Paix Street, Paris, France, pre-1920, (street scene). L. L.

The Royal Exchange, London, pre-1920 (street scene). Anonymous

Patrick Street, Cork, Ireland, pre-1920 (street scene). Lawrence

Cockington Village, Torquay, pre 1920 (street scene). F. Frith

Scene at Venice, Italy, pre-1920 (street scene). A. C. Bosselman & Co.

Berlin, Germany, pre-1920 (street scene). Weltstadt

San Refael Street, Havana, Cuba, pre-1920 (street scene). Jordi

Ludgate Circus, London, pre-1920 (street scene). Anonymous

Rotten Row, London, pre-1920 (street scene). Anonymous

The Drapery, Northampton, pre-1920 (street scene). Surrey Publications

Bird's-eye View of Moscow, Russia, pre-1920 (bird's-eye views). Anonymous

Cheapside, London, pre-1920 (street scene). Anonymous

Brooklyn Bridge, New York City (bridges). Frank E. Cooper

Westminster Bridge, London (bridges). Valentine's

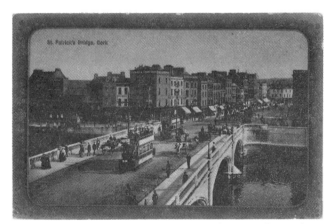

St. Patrick's Bridge, Cork, Ireland (bridges). Valentine's

London Bridge, London (bridges). Anonymous

Golden Gate Bridge, San Francisco (bridges). Scenic View Card Co.

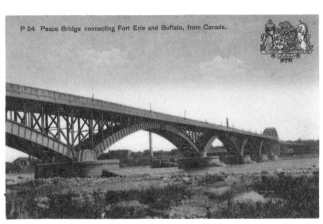

Peace Bridge connecting Fort Erie and Buffalo from Canada (bridges), F. H. Leslie

George Washington Bridge, New York City (bridges). Frank E. Cooper

New York City (postcards on postcards). Anonymous

J. B. Pound Hotels (multi-views/advertising). C. T. Art

Greetings from Akron, Ohio (large letter post-1920). C. T. Art

Greetings from Oklahoma (large letter post-1920). Mid-Continent News Co.

Greetings from Indian Country (large letter post-1920). J. R. Willis

University of Notre Dame (large letter post-1920). City News Agency

Grown in Stillwell, Oklahoma (exaggerations). P. G. Clark

Harvesting Onions (exaggerations). North American Post Card Co.

Missouri Cabbages (exaggerations). North American Post Card Co.

A Load of Missouri Apples (exaggerations). North American Post Card Co.

Raised in Missouri between two corn rows (exaggeration). North American Post Card Co.

First Presbyterian Church, Enid, Oklahoma (churches). C. T. Art

Catholic Church, Kingston, Jamaica (churches). Jamaica News & Post Card Supplies

Moses Tabernacle in the Wilderness (churches). C. T. Art

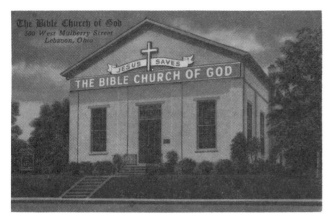

The Bible Church of God, Lebanon, Ohio (churches). Tichnor Bros.

Safford Memorial Library, Cairo, Illinois (libraries). E. C. Kropp Co.

Chicago Public Libraries (libraries/multiviews). J. O. Stoll Co.

Armenian girls made orphans through genocide (disaster). Anonymous

Boston Avenue Methodist Church, Tulsa, Oklahoma (churches). Oklahoma News Co.

The Norwich Flood (disasters). Valentine's Series

159

Flood in Nuremberg, Germany, 1909 (disasters). Anonymous

Earthquake and fire, San Francisco, 1906 (disasters). American News Co.

Cooking on the streets after San Francisco Earthquake, 1906 (disasters) Richard Behrendt

Tornado, Cincinnati, Ohio, July, 1915 (disasters). George Harriman

Results of Great Flood, Hamilton, Ohio, 1913 (disasters). Kraemer Art Co.

Circus train wreck, 1915 (disasters). Anonymous

160

Another view of circus train wreck, 1915 (disasters). Anonymous

Apache Ghost Dancers (Indians). C. T. Art

Chief Iron Tail, the Indian on the Nickel (Indians). Cunningham Post Card

Oklahoma Indians in Stilwell (Indians). Anonymous

Acoma Indian Brave (Indians). Frashers

Hiawatha and Minnehaha, Minneapolis, Minnesota (Indians). Gopher News Co.

When Dreams Come True (glamour). Anonymous

Misplaced ethnic humor (blacks). C. T. Art

Cherokee Indians doing Corn Dance, North Carolina (Indians) Asheville Post Card Co.

A Negro School (blacks). Franz Huld

Black children working in the field (blacks). C. T. Art

162

Topping the Turnips in Ireland (occupation-related). Wilkie & Son

Making Appalachian handicrafts (occupation-related). Asheville Post Card Co.

Seining for Salmon, Columbia River, Oregon (occupation-related). Edward Mitchell

Loading Anthracite Coal, Pennsylvania (occupation-related). Scranton News Co.

Chrysler plant and workers (occupation-related). Chaffee & Co.

Weighing Sugar, Barbados (occupation-related). Anonymous

Picking Cotton in Oklahoma (occupation-related). S. H. Kress Co.

Going to Market, Vicksburg, Mississippi (occupation-related). International Post Card Co.

Ferdinand De Lesseps (famous people). Riccardi

Sir Walter Raleigh (famous people). Worth & Co.

Pope Leo X. (famous people/ religious leader). Stengel & Co.

Georges Ohnet, famous writer (famous people). Anonymous

Austria's murdered chancellor, Doll-fuss (famous people). RUWA

Memorial card to Will Rogers (famous people). C. T. American Art

Albert Lebrun, French President in the 1930s (famous people). Braun & Cie.

Playwright Henrik Ibsen (famous people). Anonymous

Knute Rockne, the legendary football coach (famous people). Dunlap Henline Distributors

Sir Humphrey Gilbert (famous people). Worth & Co.

Dr. McCleery and his famed Wolf Pack (famous people). Jobber-Bradford News Co.

Huey P. ''Catfish'' Long (famous people). Harris News Agency

Mark Twain (famous people). Hannibal News Co.

Brigham Young, larger-than-life Mormon leader (famous people/religious leader). Wasatch News Service

Sir Francis Drake (famous people). Worth & Co.

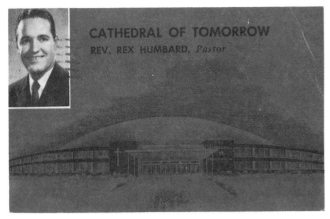

Rex Humbard, renowned evangelist (famous people /religious leader). Anonymous

Paul De Longpre (famous people). Van Ornum Colorprint Co.

Franz von Liszt, great musical composer (famous people). T. Presser

Richard's Restaurant, Aberdeen, Maryland (advertising). Dexter Press

The Cavern Cafe, Nogales, Mexico (advertising). C. T. Art

Bill's Gay Nineties (advertising). Bill's Gay Nineties

Morning Call, New Orleans (advertising). E. C. Kropp

Shredded Wheat Plant, Niagara Falls, New York (advertising). Shredded Wheat

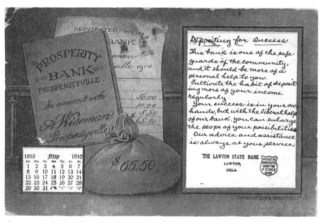

Lawton State Bank, Lawton, Oklahoma (advertising). Wesley Advertising Co., Chicago

Hotel Metropole, Brussels, Belgium (advertising). G. Marci

Hotel George Washington, Jacksonville, Florida (advertising). E. C. Kropp

The Free (advertising). The Free

St. Ermins Hotel, London (advertising). St. Ermins

First Avenue Hotel, London (advertising). First Avenue Hotel

Sanders Court and Cafe (of Colonel Sanders chicken fame), Corbin, Kentucky (advertising). Cline Photo Co.

Ann Hathaway's Cottage (famous people's residences). Pictorial Stationery Co.

Betsy Ross House, Philadephia (famous people's residences). Art View Card Distributors

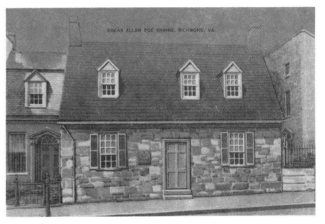

Edgar Allan Poe Shrine, Richmond, Virginia (famous people's residences). Richmond News Co.

Richard Wagner Theater, Bavaria (famous buildings). Von Carl Giessel

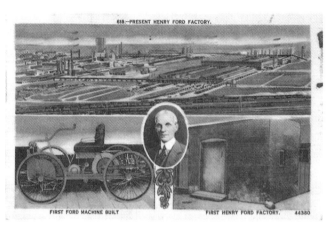

Henry Ford Factory (famous locations). Metrocraft

Pony Express Barn, St. Joseph, Missouri (famous buildings). Woodgifts

Wellington Hippodrome (famous locations). Ern Thill

Cleopatra's Needle, New York City (famous locations). Curt Teich

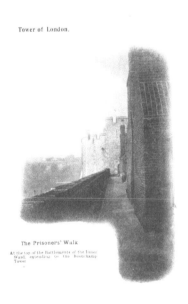

The Prisoner's Walk, Tower of London (famous locations). Gale & Polden

Old Slave Market, Charleston, South Carolina (famous locations). Paul E. Trouche

Wonder House, Bartow, Florida (Famous buildings). Lakeland News Co.

Charles Darwin's House, Downe (famous people's residences). Earle

Gunn Carriage, Tower of London (famous locations). Gale & Polden

Blair House, President Truman's temporary residence (famous buildings). Washington News Co.

The Opera, Paris (famous buildings). Anonymous

White House of the Confederacy, Richmond, Virginia (famous buildings). Richmond News Co.

The place where Jesus was said to be baptized. (famous locations). Anonymous

Temple of Theseus, Athens (antiquity, ruins). Anonymous Greek publisher

The Parthenon, Athens (antiquity, ruins). A Pallis & Cie.

Romance; Anonymous

Romance; J. Thomas

Romance; Anonymous

Utah State Capitol at Night (state capitols). Deseret Book Co.

Liars License (fill in the blank; humorous). T. C. G.

Alfred E. Newman and sister (?) (humorous). Anonymous

Permit to Use the Phone (Oh, if only!) (humorous). T. C. G.

Romance; Anonymous

The most well known of postcard messages (humorous). Curt Teich

Royal Poinciana Tree, Florida (trees). G. W. Romer

The Sausage Tree, Miami, Florida (trees). Novelti-Craft Co.

Joshua Trees in the desert. (trees). Western Publishing & Novelty Co.

The Four Horsemen. (plants). Sandoval News Service

Varieties of Texas Cactus (plants). San Antonio Card Co.

Tree growing out of solid rock (trees). Sandborn Souvenir Co.

Billy the Kid. (cowboys). H. S. B.

A Range Rider, Billings, Montana (cowboy). Billings News Agency

Post Card Storiettes (cowboy-related) Lollesgard Specialty Co.

Birthday Greetings (Art Deco). Anonymous

Tourist activity (Art Nouveau). Anonymous

A Holdup on the Road (transportation/romance). Anonymous

Double Deck Buses in Chicago. (transportation). Max Rigot

Intra Mural Bus, Chicago World's Fair (transportation/special occasion). Max Rigot

Bus in London with multiadvertising messages (transportation/advertising). Eyre & Spottiswoode

An elegant open air touring coach (transportation). Anonymous

Delivery Wagon in Havana, Cuba (transportation). Anonymous

Train coach from El Paso, Texas, to Juarez, Mexico (transportation/bridges). H. S. B.

Double Deck tram on Lord Street, Liverpool (transportation/ street scenes). Harrop's

A Crowded Street, Cheapside, London (transportation). Raphael Tuck

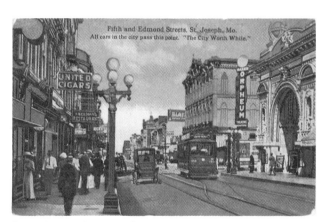

Busy Scene, St. Joseph, Missouri (transportation). St. Joseph Calendar & Novelty Co.

Oxford Circus, London (transportation). Anonymous

Traffic in Paris (transportation). L. L.

177

A riding buggy, Quebec, Canada (transportation). Warwick Bros. & Rutter

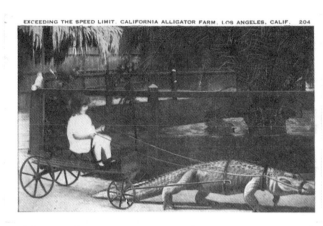

California Alligator Farm (unusual transportation). Pacific Novelty Co.

The good life in Portugal (unusual transportation). Anonymous

An interesting method of transport (unusual transportation). Anonymous

"Nubie," famous riding bird, Los Angeles Ostrich Farm (unusual transportation). Anonymous

The Three Rogues (animals, cats). M. T. Sheahan

Funeral car in Havana, Cuba (unusual transportation).
Anonymous

Athletic felines (animals, cats). Max Kunzli

Man of War, the Wonder Horse (animals, horses). Kyle Co.

A girl and her pet (animals, dogs). Anonymous

A Texas Longhorn, width of horns 9 feet, 6 inches (Animals,
farm animals). Dallas Post Card Co.

Who Whistled? (animals, dogs). Anonymous

Flying Fish, Catalina Island (animals, fish). Adolph Selige Publishing Co.

Native Arizona Buffalo (animals). Lollesgard Specialty Co.

A Lonely Tabby (animals, cats). Anonymous

A busy railroad system (trains). Curt Teich

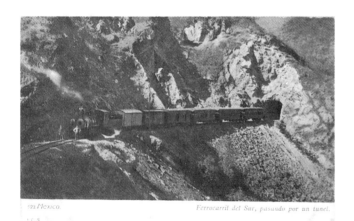

In the Mexican mountains (trains). Anonymous

A locomotive riding high (trains/bridges). Anonymous

Doctor Laird's Private Car (trains). Anonymous

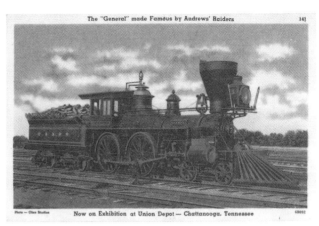

The ''General'' made famous by Andrew's Raiders (trains). W. M. Cline

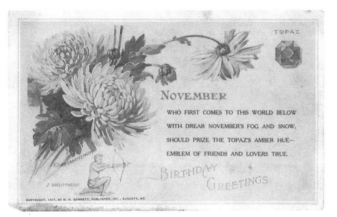

Birthday card with horoscope connections (greetings/zodiac). W. H. Gannett

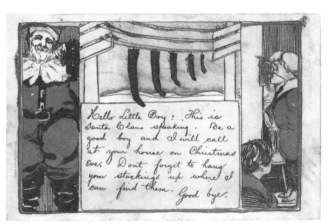

Letter from Santa (greetings). W. G. MacFarlane

Thanksgiving transitions (greetings). Anonymous

Thanksgiving wishes (greetings). Anonymous.

Anticipation: the night before Christmas (greetings). Anonymous

Christmas beginnings, the true message (greetings). Anonymous

A scarce Leap Year postcard (greetings). S. Bergman

Father Time with the New Year babe (greetings). Gibson Art Co.

A forceful yet simple proclamation of the Easter message (greetings). Anonymous

Year Date (greetings). Anonymous

A rarely seen type of greeting card (greetings). Anonymous

A combination card: Year Date/New Year's (greetings). United Art Publishing Co.

An unusual Halloween card (greetings). S. Bergman

Halloween black cats in black hats (greetings/cats). Anonymous

Halloween with symbols abounding (greetings). Anonymous

A proper Valentine question (greetings). Anonymous

A rare Mother's Day card (greetings). Anonymous

Cupid at work (greetings). Anonymous

Valentine's universal message (greetings). Anonymous

A scarce real photo Valentine's card (greetings). Anonymous

American Independence Day (greetings). Anonymous

Rare Veteran's Day card (greetings). Anonymous

Leprechaun or lad? (greetings). S. Bergman

An unmistakable message (greetings).
Anonymous

A young Irishman (greetings). Anonymous

A card sent to those at home (posed silliness). Anonymous

A Child Being Nursed with Goat's Milk (posed silliness).
Anonymous

The Yankee Clipper (airplanes). Tourist Development Bureau

Lost, Strayed, or Stolen (posed silliness). Anonymous

185

Pan American Airways "China Clipper" (airplanes). Stanley A. Piltz

Municipal Airport, Kansas City, Missouri; Fairfax Airport, Kansas City, Kansas (airports). Max Bernstein

Holman Municipal Airport, St. Paul, Minnesota (airports). H. A. Olson

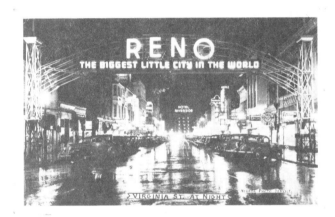

Reno, Nevada: Biggest Little City in the World (superlatives). Anonymous

First House Built in Utah (superlatives) Deseret Book Co.

"So Big" Texas (superlatives). J. R. Willis

Oldest Schoolhouse, St. Augustine, Florida (superlatives). Duval News Co.

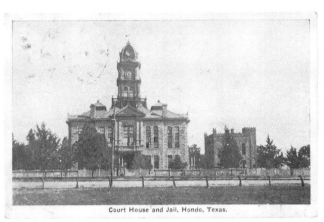

Courthouse and Jail, Hondo, Texas (courthouses/jails). Auburn Post Card Manufacturing Co.

A well-known flag (patriotic). Raphael Tuck

Allegheny County Courthouse, Pittsburgh, Pennsylvania. (courthouses). Minsky Bros. & Co.

German and Austrian emperors, World War I (patriotic). Anonymous

What all armies seek (patriotic). Tichnor Bros.

America's National Birds (patriotic). Anonymous

United in a Great Cause (patriotic). Anonymous

Wrigley Field, Chicago (sports). C. T. Art

Race between the "Natchez" and the "Robert E. Lee," St. Louis, Missouri (sports). E. C. Kropp Co.

Indianapolis Speedway, Indianapolis, Indiana (sports). Standard Sales Co.

Bonneville Salt Flats, World's Fastest Speedway (sports/ superlatives). Deseret Book Co.

Judge's Stand, Hollywood Dog Track, Hollywood, Florida (sports) C. R. Adamson

Dusquesne University, Pittsburgh, Pennsylvania (universities). Minsky Bros. & Co.

Carnegie Institute of Technology, Pittsburgh, Pennsylvania (colleges). Minsky Bros. & Co.

Bradley Polytechnic Institute, Peoria, Illinois (colleges). Hartmann Bros.

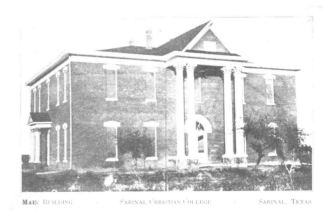

Sabinal Christian College, Sabinal, Texas (colleges). Anonymous

189

State Normal School (Teacher's College), Kirksville, Missouri (colleges). Curt Teich

Dutch Windmill, Golden Gate Park, San Francisco (windmills). Stanley A. Piltz Co.

Old Dutch Mill, Des Moines, Iowa (windmills). Hackley News.

Windmill, Holland, Michigan (windmills). Shaw News Agency

Windmill, Mooi, Holland, (windmills). Anonymous

Dutch Windmill, Rotterdam, Holland, (windmills). Anonymous

Dutch Mill Village, Glasglow, Kentucky (windmills). C. T. Art

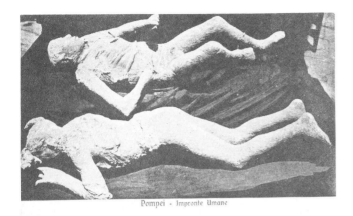

Petrified bodies from Pompei. (bizarre). Anonymous

Franklin Roosevelt at dedication of Smokey Mountains Park (presidential). Asheville Post Card Co.

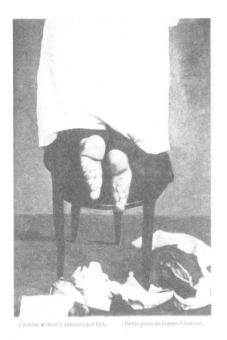

Chinese woman's unbandaged feet (bizarre). Anonymous

Abraham Lincoln (presidential). Scenic South Card Co.

President James Monroe (presidential). Raphael Tuck

President and Mrs. Richard Nixon (presidential). Washington Novelty

President Theodore Roosevelt and Family (presidential). Rotograph Co.

Welsh Woman at Arthog (local costumes/bizarre). Valentine's XL Series

Greetings from Stilwell, Oklahoma (animals/bizarre). Anonymous

Carpenter's Hall, Philadelphia, Pennsylvania (famous buildings). Tichnor Bros.

Women's Building, Moody Bible Institute, Chicago (famous buildings). Bible Institute Colportage Association.

Washington Taking Oath of Office (presidential/Washington). Anonymous

George Washington with facsimile signature (presidential/Washington). Eastern National Park & Monument Association

Washington Mansion (presidential/Washington/famous buildings). B. S. Reynolds

High School, Twin Falls, Idaho (high schools). Wesley Andrews

Central High School, Omaha, Nebraska (high schools). McLaughlin & Barkhart

Union Pacific Station, Cheyenne, Wyoming (railroad stations). Barkalow Bros.

Canadian Pacific Railway Station, Montreal, Canada (railroad stations). E. P. Charlton & Co.

Union Station, Nashville, Tennessee (railroad stations). Capitol News Co.

Pennsylvania Railroad Station, Pittsburgh, Pennsylvania (railroad stations). Minsky Bros.

Union Station, Galveston, Texas (railroad stations). Galveston Wholesale News Co.

Union Depot, Los Angeles, California (railroad stations). Western Publishing & Novelty Co.

Union Station and Post Office, St. Louis, Missouri (railroad stations/post offices). Blackwell Wielandy

Union Station at Night, St. Louis, Missouri (railroad stations). E. C. Kropp

Union Station and Sky Line, Kansas City, Missouri (railroad stations). Max Berstein

City Hall, Independence, Missouri (city halls). Curt Teich

City Hall and Fire Department, Marysville, California (city halls/firefighting-related). Pacific Novelty Co.

City Hall, Salina, Kansas (city halls). Anonymous

City Hall, Toronto, Canada (city halls). Valentine-Black Co.

City Hall, Philadelphia, Pennsylvania (city halls). Druco-Optus Drug Stores

City Hall, Mitchell, South Dakota (city halls). J. S. Broadbent & Co.

A Swiss pleasure ship (ships). Louis Glaser

Baltimore's excursion steamer ''Tolchester'' (ships). I. & M. Ottenheimer

North German Lloyd Bremen, the ''George Washington'' (ships). Ocean Comfort Co.

Steamboat near St. Louis (ships). Charles M. Monroe Co.

Coronation of Queen Elizabeth, 1953 (royalty). Raphael Tuck

Albert I of Belguim, c. 1910 (royalty). Rotary

Dutch Royal Family, 1909 (royalty). J. H. Schaefers

George VI and Queen Elizabeth in coronation robes, 1937 (royalty). Valentine's

Marriage commemorative of Kaiser Wilhelm II's only daughter, 1913 (royalty). Gustav Liersch

Italy's diminutive king, Victor Emmanuel III, c. 1910 (royalty). J. Beagles & Co.

Mary, Princess of Wales, with children, 1904 (royalty). J. Beagles & Co.

Queen Victoria with prince consort Albert, c. 1840 (royalty). Rotary

King Carlos and Queen Amalia of Portugal, c. 1906 (royalty). Rotary

Queen Alexandra of England, Bas Relief (royalty/novelty). J. Beagles & Co.

Austria's emperor Franz Joseph, 1914 (royalty/military). Christoph Reisser's Sohne

Last Austrian emperor, Karl I, 1916 (royalty/military). S. V. D.

Kaiser Wilhelm II in exile, 1920s (royalty). Piek

Germany's Prince Max (royalty/military). Bruder Kohn (B. K. W. I.)

Prussia's Queen Louise (royalty). Bru-der Kohn.

Queen Charlotte of Württemberg, Ger-many (royalty). Hochstetter & Vischer

Kaiser Wilhelm II and Kaiserin "Dona" (royalty). Reichard & Lindner

Austria's ill-fated crown prince Franz Ferdinand and Sophie Chotek (roy-alty). Anonymous

Empress Zita of Austria-Hungary while still a princess, c. 1915 (royalty) Ho-fatelier Kosel

Kaiser Franz Joseph with grandchil-dren (royalty). Bruder Kohn

199

Unfavorable characterization of Kaiser Wilhelm II (military/royalty). Anonymous

German infantry after battle, World War II (military). Erich Gutjahr

Holland's Queen Wilhelmina and prince consort in riding habit (royalty). Anonymous

Hero of the American South, Robert E. Lee (military). Haydon Ord Merrill

German General von Haesler, World War I's oldest soldier (military). Gustav Liersch

The Constitution "Old Ironsides" (ships/military). Reichner Bros.

British field marshal Earl Roberts, Boer War (military). Raphael Tuck

Wilhelm II as an acquisitive warlord. (military/royalty). Anonymous

The German architect, Count von Bismarck. (military/royalty). Anonymous

Emperor Napoleon I. (royalty). S. I. P.

Commodore Perry at the Battle of Lake Erie (military). Anonymous

General Kuroki inspecting the captured Russian guns, Russo-Japanese War (military). A. J. Young

Napoléon's metamorphic (military/royalty/novelty). E. L. D.

General Francisco "Pancho" Villa (military). Anonymous

Lord Kitchener, Great Britain's war chief during World War I (military). Photochrom Co.

Russo-Japanese peace treaty drama (military). Rotograph Co.

Flag card; anonymous

Flag card; Anonymous

Lily Brayton and Oscar Ashe (stage stars). J. Beagles & Co.

Miss Edna May (stage stars). J. Beagles & Co.

Miss Camille Clifford (stage stars). J. Beagles & Co.

Judy Garland and residence (movie star). Longshaw Card Co.

Clark Gable and residence (movie star). Longshaw Card Co.

Miss Phyllis Dare (stage stars). J. Beagles & Co.

Death condolence (greetings). Photocelere

Arab women (native costumes). L. L.

Charles Chaplin (stage star/movie star). Essanay

Laplanders (native costumes). Anonymous

Charles Dickens' Old Curiosity Shop (famous locations). Anonymous

Gasparilla carnival, Tampa, Florida (carnivals). Hillsboro News Co.

Swastika, good luck symbol (greetings). Anonymous

The Jail, Juárez, Mexico (jails). Sandoval News Service

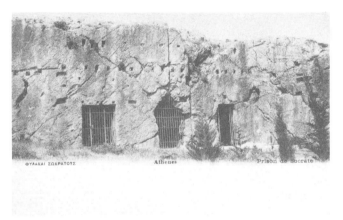

Prison of Socrates, Athens (prisons). Pallis & Cotzias

Union Bus Station, Jacksonville, Florida (bus depots). Duval News Agency

Mailing a postcard "To Me Pal" (correspondence-related). Anonymous

$2 million banyon tree, Fort Lauderdale, Florida (trees). C. R. Adamson

The ultimate in fashion (?) (headgear). Anonymous

Joaquin Miller "Poet of the Sierras," Oakland, California (famous people). Edward Mitchell

John Hopkins Hospital, Baltimore, Maryland (hospitals). I. & M. Ottenheimer

City Hall, St. Louis (city halls/novelty—hold-to-light). Anonymous

Kissing the Blarney Stone, County Cork, Ireland (curiosities). Lawrence.

Busy Bears (bears/humorous). J. I. Austen

National costume/dancing/novelty (embroidered). Anonymous

Hotel Stockton, Stockton, California (hotels). Curteich

New York World's Fair, 1939 (special occasion). Miller Art Co.

Golden Gate International Exposition, San Francisco (special occasion). H. S. Crocker

Administration building, Oklahoma College for Women, Chickasha, Oklahoma (colleges). E. C. Kropp

Home of William Penn, Philadelphia (famous people residence). P. Sander

Fort Reno, El Reno, Oklahoma (military). Curt Teich

5
Books About Postcards

5
Books About Postcards

As exhaustive as the following list of postcard books may seem to be, it is far from complete. (Selected books are reviewed following the postcard book bibliography.) The growth of interest in postcard collecting during the past decade has increased scholarship, which in turn has led to more book titles from an increasingly sophisticated group of collectors.

The European Library in Zaltbommel, the Netherlands, is currently producing a series of books on European towns and cities using postcards to show how these areas looked during Victorian and Edwardian years. A quote from their literature gives some idea of the ambitious scope of this undertaking. In 1987, the European Library reported:

> A book about virtually every town in the United Kingdom is to be published in this series (. . . IN OLD PICTURE POST-CARDS). By the end of this year about 300 different volumes will have appeared. 1500 books have already been published devoted to the Netherlands with the title IN OUDE ANSICHTEN. In Germany, Austria and Switzerland 650, 100 and 25 books have been published as IN ALTEN ANSICHTEN; in France by the name EN CARTES POSTALES ANCIENNES and in Belgium as IN OUDE PRENTKAARTEN and/or EN CARTES POSTALES ANCIENNES, 400 volumes have been published.

Undoubtedly, there are a lot of books available, and the end is nowhere in sight. It might prove helpful for readers in the United States to know that Andreas Brown, the owner of New York City's Gotham Book Mart, stocks and offers a brochure of books on postcards (Gotham Book Mart & Gallery, 41 West 47th Street, New York, New York 10036). A collector of long standing and high repute, Brown has been at the forefront of promoting deltiology. Readers in Europe may be interested to learn that Reflections of a Bygone Age stocks many titles (15 Debdale Lane, Keyworth, Nottingham, NG12 5HT, England). As with all such communications, a thoughtful policy is to include a large self-addressed, stamped envelope with sufficient postage to cover the price of sending you their brochures.

Postcard Books: Recommended Reading

Ackert, Helen O. *A Collector's Resource Through Post Cards of Our Antique Dolls* (hardbound). De Kalb, Ill.: Ackert Enterprises, 1976.

Alderson, F. *The Comic Postcard in English Life.* U.K.: David & Charles, 1969.

Aldrich, Lanny (ed.). *Postcard Art of San Francisco Circa 1910.* U.S.A.: Hidden House/Flash Books, 1976.

Alfred, Van Der Marck. *Varga, The Esquire Years.* Toronto: St. James Press, 1987.

Alloula, Malek. *The Colonial Harem* (hardbound). Godzich, Myrna & Godzich, 1986.

———. *The Colonial Harem* (paperback). University of Minnesota Press.

Alsop, John. *The Official Railway Postcard Book* (paperback). Bedford, Eng.: John Alsop, 1987.

Anderson, Allen, and Betty Tomlinson. *Greetings from Canada.* 1978.

Andrews, Barbara. *A Directory of Postcards, Artists, Publishers and Trademarks.* Irving, Tex.: Little Red Caboose, 1975.

Anonymous. *Ivy Millicent James: A Children's Postcard Artist.* U.K.: 1980.

Applegate, Ray (ed.). *Trolley & Streetcars on American Picture Postcards* (detachable cards; paperback). Mineola, N.Y.: Dover Publications.

———. *Trolleys and Streetcars on American Picture Postcards.* New York, 1979.

Armand, Paul Noel. *Historique de la Cartes Postale* (paperback). Herblay, Fr.: Cartes Postales et Collection, 1987.

Arrasich, Furio. *La Cartolina Militari 1900* (paperback). Rome: La Cartolina.

———. *Catalogue of Italian Postcards.* Rome: 1984.

Asher-Gallant. *The National Directory of Postcard Deck Media* (paperback). Asher-Gallant, 1987.

Astolat, John. *Phillimore: The Postcard Art of R. P. Phillimore* (hardbound). London: Greenfriar Press, 1985.

Austin, Elisabeth. *Checklist of H. B. Griggs Signed Post Cards* (paperback). Pawcatuck, Conn.: Elisabeth Austin, 1972.

———. *Ellen H. Clapsaddle* (paperback). Pawcatuck, Conn.: Elisabeth Austin, 1967.

Baeder, John. *Gas, Food & Lodging* (paperback). New York, 1986.

Banneck, Janet. *Rose O'Neil a Post Card Checklist* (paperback). California, 1979.

Barbier, George. *Post Cards of the Elegant Twenties* (detachable cards). New York, 1985.

Barilli, Renato. *Art Nouveau*. London, Eng.: Cassell Pub., 1984.

Barker, Ronnie. *Book of Bathing Beauties*. U.K. 1974.

———. *Book of Boudoir Beauties*. U.K.: Hodder & Stroughton, 1976.

———. *Gentleman's Wish*. U.K., 1979.

———. *Suace!* U.K.: Hodder & Stroughton, 1978.

Baudet, A., and F. Baudet. *L'Encyclopedie Internationale de la Carte Postale*. Paris, 1978.

Beachboard, J. H. (ed.). *United States Postal Card Catalogue*. U.S. Postal Stationery Society, 1980.

Beltrametti, Franco. *Airmail Postcards*. Vehicle Editions, 1979.

Bernhard, Martin. *Motor Cars Special Catalogue, 1895–1975* (hardbound). Germany.

Bernhard, Martin. *Picture Postcards of Germany 1870–1986*. Germany: Bernhard, 1986.

Bernhard, Willi. *Picture Postcard Catalogue, 1870–1945 (Bildpostkartenkatalog)* (paperback). Hamburg: Willi Bernhard, 1972.

———. *Special Picture Postcard Catalogue: National Socialism, 1933–1945* (hardbound). 1975.

Berthier, A. *La Carte Postale Photographique et les Procedes D'Amateur*. Paris: C. Mendel, 1904.

Bloodgood, Dorothy. *A Post Card Portrait: The Queen of the Catskills Grand Hotel Era, 1883–1942*. Bogota, N.J.: Dorothy Bloodgood, 1986.

———. *A Post Card Portrait with Memorabilia of John Burroughs, Literary Naturalist*. Bogota, N.J.: Dorothy Bloodgood, 1983.

Bosker, Gideon, and Jonathan Nicholas. *Greetings from Oregon* (hardbound). Portland: Graphic Arts Center Publishing Co., 1987.

Bossert, Jill. *Santa Claus: Forty Antique Post Cards* (detachable cards; paperback). New York: Madison Square Press, 1986.

Bourgeron, J. P. and P. J. Balboa. *Nude 1900: Classic French Postcards*. 1980.

———. *Nude Nineteen Twenty-Five*. 1978.

Bower, Alan. *Chesterfield and North-East Derbyshire on Old Postcards*. U.K.

Bowers, Q. David. *Nickelodeon Theatres and Their Music* (paperback). Vestal, N.Y.: Vestal Press, 1986.

Bowers, Q. David, and Christine Bowers. *Robert Robinson: American Illustrator* (paperback). Vestal, N.Y.: Vestal Press, 1981.

Bowers, Q. David, and Mary L. Martin. *The Postcards of Alphonse Mucha* (paperback). Vestal, N.Y.: Vestal Press, 1980.

Bowers, Q. David, George M. Budd, and Ellen H. Budd. *Harrison Fisher* (paperback). Iola, Wis.: Q. David Bowers, 1984.

Bozarth, Theodore. *Preliminary Listing of Titles of Post Cards Published by Arthur Strauss* (paperback). Pennsylvania: Washington Crossing Card Collectors Club, 1981.

Bray, Maurice. *Railway Picture Postcards* (hardbound). U.K.: Moorland Publishers.

Brewster, Harding. *Roadside New England, 1900–1955*. Maine.

Brooks, Andrew, Fred Fletcher, and Brian Lund. *What the Postman Saw* (paperback). Nottingham, Eng.: Reflections of a Bygone Age, 1982.

Brown, Andreas. *L'Amerique au Fil des Jours: Cartes Postales Photographiques, 1900–1920*. Paris, 1983.

Brown, Robert C. *Greetings from Norwich*. Connecticut: 1979.

Buchholz, Shirley. *Victorian Children Postcards* (detachable cards). Cumberland, Md.: Hobby House Press, 1985.

Buckland, Elfreda, and M. Tickner. *The World of Donald McGill* (hardbound). Dorset, Eng.: Blandford Press Poole, 1984.

Buday, George. *The History of the Christmas Card*. Rockcliff, Eng.: 1954.

———. *The Story of the Christmas Card*. England: Odhams Press, 1951.

Burdick, J. R. *Directory of Jeff R. Burdick Collection of Postcards* (paperback). New York: Metropolitan Museum of Art, 1970.

———. *The Handbook of Detroit Publishing Company* (paperback). 1954.

———. *Pioneer Postcards* (paperback). Franklin Square, N.Y.: Nostalgia Press, 1957.

Butland, A. J. and E. A. Westwood. *Picture Postcards and All About Them*. Teddington, Eng., 1959.

Byatt, Anthony. *Collecting Picture Postcards: An Introduction*. Malvern, Eng., 1982.

———. *Picture Postcards and Their Publishers* (hardbound). Malvern, Eng.: Golden Age Postcard Books, 1978.

Calder-Marshall, Arthur. *Wish You Were Here*. Hutchinson, 1966.

Caley, George. *Postcards of Yesteryear, 1893–1926: Delaware and Elsewhere*. Delaware: George Caley, 1973.

Cane, Michael, and R. G. Harris. *For Queen & Country: The Career of Harry Payne*. U.K., 1978.

Capparelli, Tom. *The Military Postcards of the Third Reich*. Villa Park, Ill.: Tom Capparelli.

Carline, Richard. *Pictures in the Post: The Story of the Picture Postcard*. Ridley Park, Penn.: Deltiologists of America.

Carreras, F. *Las Tarjetas Postales in Espana*. Barcelona: F. Altes, 1903.

Carter, Elizabeth. *Sydney Carter*. U.K., 1948.

Carver, Sally S. *The American Postcard Guide to Tuck* (paperback). Brookline, Mass.: Carver Cards, 1976.

Chapman, Alberta, and Marge Rosecrans. *The Corn Palace Postcard Year Identifier and Checklist* (paperback). New Jersey: Alberta Chapman, 1983.

Chase, E. Dudley. *The Romance of Greeting Cards*. Boston, 1926.

Chesney, Allen (ed.). *Chattanooga Album: Thirty-Two Historic Postcards* (detachable cards). Knoxville: University of Tennessee Press, 1983.

Chivat, Armande, and Jean-Claude Souyri. *Ier Catalogue Cartes Postales Contemporaines, 1975–80* (paperback). France, 1982.

Chronicle Books. *Modern Postcards: Postcard Reproductions from the Permanent Collection of the San Francisco Museum of Modern Art* (detachable cards). San Francisco, Calif.: Chronicle Books, 1984.

Cirker, Hayward. *Thirty-two Postcards of Old New York* (detachable cards). New York, 1976.

——— (ed.). *Twenty-four Art Nouveau Postcards in Full Colors: From Classic Posters* (detachable cards). Mineola, N.Y.: Dover Publications, 1983.

Cook, David. *Picture Postcards in Australia, 1898–1920* (hardbound). Victoria, Aust.: Pioneer Design Studio, 1986.

Cope, Dawn, and Peter Cope. *Illustrators of Postcards from the Nursery* (paperback). Salem House Publishers, 1983.

Corning Museum of Glass. *Paperweights from the Corning Museum of Glass* (detachable cards). Corning, N.Y.: Corning Museum of Glass, 1987.

———. *Roman Glass in the Corning Museum of Glass* (detachable cards). Corning, N.Y.: Corning Museum of Glass, 1987.

Corona Publishing. *An Album of Old Time Postcards from Houston & Galveston* (detachable cards). San Antonio, Tex.: Corona Publishing, 1979.

———. *An Album of Old Time Texas Postcards* (detachable cards). San Antonio, Tex.: Corona Publishing, 1979.

Corson, Walter E. *Publishers' Trademarks Identified* (paperback). Pennsylvania: 1962.

Cox, Roy. *How to Price and Sell Old Picture Postcards* (paperback). Baltimore, Md.: Roy Cox, 1986.

Coysh, A. W. *The Dictionary of Picture Postcards in Britain, 1894–1939* (paperback). Woodbridge, Suffolk, Eng.: Antique Collectors' Club, 1984.

Crawford, Charles (ed.). *Memphis Memories: Thirty-two Historic Postcards* (detachable cards). Knoxville: University of Tennessee Press, 1983.

Critchfield, Arthur R. *John F. Kennedy Postcard List & Associated Postcards* (paperback). Hazel Park, Mich.: Arthur Critchfield.

Crown Publishers. *Official John Travolta Postcard Book* (detachable cards). Crown Publications, 1985.

Cuppleditch, David. *The John Hassal Lifestyle*. U.K., 1980.

———. *The London Sketch Club*. U.K., 1978.

Dale, Rodney. *Louis Wain: The Man Who Drew Cats*. 1970.

Darrah. *Cartes de Viste in 19th Century Photography* (hardbound).

Davies, Pete. *Collect Modern Postcards* (paperback). Nottingham, Eng.: Reflections of a Bygone Age, 1987.

Davis, Bertha. *The Postcards of Bucks County as Printed by the Arnold Brothers* (paperbound). Washington Crossing, Penn.: Washington Crossing Post Card Club, 1980.

Davis, Mary. *Thirty-two Postcards of Old New Orleans* (detachable cards). New York, 1979.

Delulio, Cynthia. *Especially Cats: Louis Wain's Humorous Postcards*. U.S., 1985.

Dichand, Hans. *Jugendstilpostkarten*. Germany, 1978.

Downer, William (compiler). *Complete Works of Faga* (paperback). Brookhill, Eng.: Reprographics, 1985.

Drayton, Grace. *Dolly Dingle Playtime Post Cards* (detachable cards).

Droscher, Elke. *The Victorian Sticker Postcard Book* (detachable cards). Philadelphia: Running Press.

———. *The World of Dolls: A Postcard Book* (detachable cards). Philadelphia: Running Press, 1985.

Duval, William, and Valerie Monahan. *Collecting Postcards in Colour, 1894–1914* (hardbound). Poole, Dorset, Eng.: Blandford Press, 1978.

Edwards, Jim, Mitchell Oliphant, and Hal Ottaway. *The Vanished Splendor: Postcard Views of Early Oklahoma City* (hardbound). Oklahoma City: Abalache Bookshop, 1982.

———. *The Vanished Splendor II: A Postcard Album of Oklahoma City* (hardbound). Oklahoma City: Abalache Bookshop, 1983.

———. *The Vanished Splendor III: A Postcard Album of Oklahoma City* (hardbound). Oklahoma City: Abalache Bookshop, 1985.

Eisenhauer, Anita, and Gigi Starnes. *Corpus Christi, Texas: A Picture Postcard History* (hardbound). Corpus Christi, Tex.: Anita's Antiques, 1987.

Ellis, Norman. *Trams on Old Picture Postcards* (paperback). Nottingham, Eng.: Reflections of a Bygone Age, 1986.

Embree Press. *Profitable Color Postcard Photography* (paperback). U.S.A.: Embree Press.

Ettlinger, L. D., and R. G. Holloway. *Compliments of the Season*. U.S.A.: Penguin Books, 1947.

Evans, Eric J., and Jeffrey Richards. *A Social History of Britain in Postcards, 1870–1930*. U.S.A.: Longman, 1980.

Evans, Jane. *Ivy Millicent James, 1879–1965*. Weston-super-Mare, Eng.: Woodspring Museum, 1980.

Evans, William K. *Princeton University & Princeton in Postcards* (paperback). Almar.

Fanelli, Giovanni, and Ezio Godoli. *Art Nouveau Postcards* (hardbound). New York, N.Y.: Rizzoli International Publications, 1987.

Federico, Bartoli, and Ivo Mataloni. *Cartoline D'Epoca e Gli Illustratori*. Rome: 1979.

Ferris, J. L. *Early American Postcards*. Ridley Park, Penn.: Deltiologists of America.

Filey, Mike. *Wish You Were Here: Great Postcards of Early Toronto* (detachable cards). Toronto: 1977.

Fisher, Janet, and Derek Fisher. *Bristol on Old Picture Postcards.* U.K.

———. *Bristol on Old Picture Postcards, Volume II.* U.K.

Fletcher, F. A., and A. D. Brooks. *British Exhibitions & Their Postcards, Part I: 1900–1914.* London, 1979.

———. *British Exhibitions & Their Postcards, Part II: 1915–1979.* London, 1980.

Forissier, Beatrix. *Les Belles Annes du Cinema a Travers la Carte Postale, 1895–1935.* France, 1979.

———. *Les Belles Annes du Cinema a Travers la Carte Postale, 1935–60.* France, 1981.

———. *25 Ans D'Actualities a Travers la Carte Postale, 1899–1914.* France, 1977.

———. *30 Annes D'Elegance a Travers la Carte Postale, 1900–1930.* France, 1978.

Forster, Michael J. *Sweet Land of Liberty.* U.S.A.: Michael Forster.

Foster, Louise F. *Thirty Two Picture Postcards of Old St. Louis* (detachable cards). New York, 1979.

Franks, Ray, and Jay Ketelle. *Amarillo, Texas, The First Hundred Years* (hardbound). Amarillo, Tex.: Ray Franks Publishing Ranch, 1986.

———. *Amarillo, Texas II, The First Hundred Years* (hardbound). Amarillo, Tex.: Ray Franks Publishing Ranch, 1987.

Freeman, Larry (ed.). *A Centennial Guide to Postcard Collecting* (paperback). U.S.A.: American Life Foundation, 1976.

French, Earl A. (ed.). *Eminent Victorian Americans: 32 Portrait Postcards* (detachable cards). Hartford, Conn.: 1977.

Freund, David (ed.). *Photographic Post Cards of Central New York: 1905–1920.* Syracuse, N.Y.: Penny Publishing, 1984.

Fricke, Charles. *Centennial Handbook of the First Issue Postal Card, 1873–1973.* Philadelphia, 1973.

Fricke, Charles A. (ed.). *A Contemporary Account of the First United States Postal Card, 1870–1875.* U.S.A., 1973.

Gabe, Joseph, et al. *The Ann Scales Postcards* (paperback). Printed Matter, 1977.

Garnier, Michael, and Francois Lluck. *Post Card Illustrators: A Dictionary of Signatures and Monograms.* France, 1984.

Garper, Helen. *Postcards from Surfers* (paperback). Penguin Books, 1986.

Gart, Galen (ed.). *R & B Stars of 1953: Thirty Six Authentic Looking Postcards in Glorious Full Color* (detachable cards). Big Nickel, 1987.

Gent, John B. (ed.). *Croydon Between the Wars* (paperback). Surrey, Eng.: Croydon Natural History and Scientific Society, 1988.

Gibbs, George C. *The Topographical Locator for Picture Postcard Collectors* (paperback). Syracuse, N.Y.: George C. Gibbs.

Giscombe, C. S. *Postcards* (paperback). Greenfield, Rev. Pr., 1977.

Gladwin, David. *Steam Transport on the Roads* (hardbound). Batsford, Eng.: 1988.

Gowrie, Grey. *Postcard from Don Giovanni* (paperback). Oxford University Press, 1972.

Green, Benny. *I've Lost My Little Willie.* U.K.: Elm Tree/Arrow Books, 1976.

Greene, J. R. *Calvin Coolidge, A Biography in Picture Postcards* (paperback). Athol, Mass.: J. R. Greene, 1987.

Greenhalgh, Paul. *Ephemeral Vistas: The Expositions Universelles, Great Exhibitions and World's Fairs, 1851–1939* (hardbound). Manchester, Eng.: Manchester University Press, 1988.

Greenhouse, Bernard L. *Political Post Cards, 1900–1980.* Syracuse, N.Y. 1984.

Gutzman, W. L. *The Canadian Patriotic Post Card Handbook: 1900–1914* (paperback). Toronto: Unitrade Press, 1985.

———. *The Canadian Picture Post Card Catalogue 1988* (paperback). Toronto: Unitrade Press, 1987.

Guyonnet, Georges. *La Carte Postales Illustree.* Paris: 1947.

Hadjipanayis, Anthony. *Cyprus Through Postcards, 1895–1930* (paperback). Larnace, Cyprus: Collectors House, 1988.

Harding, R. *Greetings from Maine: Turn of the Century Views of America's Pine Tree State as Recorded by Portland's Picture Postcard Pioneers.* Portland, Maine: 1975.

———. *Roadside New England, 1900–1955.* Portland, Maine, 1982.

Harrison, Wilfred. *Postcards Please.* New Playwrights Network, State Mutual Books, 1984.

Hartley, Marie, and Joan Ingilby. *Yorkshire Album: Photographs of Everyday Life, 1900–1950* (hardbound). Dent, Eng.: 1988.

Hay, Peter. *Steaming Through West Sussex* (hardbound). West Sussex, Eng.: Middleton Press, 1987.

Heimann, Jim. *Hooray for Hollywood: A Postcard Tour of Hollywood's Golden Era* (detachable cards). San Francisco, Calif.: Chronicle Books, 1983.

Helbock, Richard W. *Postmarks on Postcards* (paperback). Lake Oswego, Oreg.: La Posta Publications, 1987.

Herbert, Ernest. *Greetings from New England* (hardbound). Portland, Oreg.: Graphic Arts Publishing Co., 1988.

Heyburn, Henry, and Frances Heyburn. *Post Cards of the Falkland Islands: A Catalogue: 1900–1950.* Louisville, Ky.: 1985.

Highland, Monica. *Greetings from Southern California* (hardcover). Portland, Oreg.: Graphic Arts Center Publishing Co., 1988.

Hill, C. W. *Discovering Picture Postcards.* U.K.: Shire Publications, 1970.

———. *Edwardian Entertainments.* U.K.: 1978.

Holt, Tonie, and Valmai Holt. *Best of Fragments from France.* U.K.

———. *I'll Be Seeing You: Picture Postcards of World War II* (hardbound). Derbyshire, Eng.: Moorland Publishing Co., 1987.

———. *Picture Postcard Artists: Landscapes Animals & Characters.* U.K.

———. *Picture Postcards of the Golden Age: A Collector's Guide* (paperback). U.K.: MacGibbon & Kee, 1978.

———. *Till the Boys Come Home* (hardbound). Ridley Park, Penn.: Deltiologists of America, 1978.

Hoobler, James A. (ed.). *Nashville Memories: Thirty Two Historic Postcards* (detachable cards). Knoxville: University of Tennessee Press, 1982.

Howell, Georgina. *The Penguin Book of Naughty Postcards.* Penguin Books, 1977.

James, H. A. *The Price Guide to Photographic Cards* (paperback). Bishopsgate Press, 1985.

Jenkins, Mrs. Jack L. *The Narrow Chocolate Hershey Post Cards: A Check List* (paperback). Ill.: Mrs. Jack Jenkins, 1983.

Jenkinson, D. *Mitchell Check List (of D & T Numbers)* (paperback). New Haven, Conn.: D. Jenkinson.

Jennings, Grenville. *Cricket on Old Picture Postcards* (paperback). Nottingham, Eng.: Reflections of a Bygone Age, 1985.

———. *Nottingham and South Notts on Old Postcards* (paperback). Nottingham, Eng.: Reflections of a Bygone Age.

Johanson, Erik. *Picture Postcards of Finland.* Finland: 1981.

Kaduck, John. *Mail Memories: Pictorial Guide to Postcard Collecting* (paperback). Des Moines, Iowa: Wallace-Homestead, 1975.

———. *Patriotic Postcards* (paperback). Des Moines, Iowa: Wallace-Homestead.

———. *Rare and Expensive Postcards, Book I* (paperback). Lombard, Ill.: Wallace-Homestead, 1982.

———. *Rare and Expensive Postcards, Book II* (paperback). Des Moines, Iowa: Wallace-Homestead, 1985.

———. *Transportation Postcards* (paperback). Des Moines, Iowa: Wallace-Homestead, 1976.

Keetz, Frank. *Baseball Comic Postcards.* New York: 1983.

Kelbaugh, Jack. *Wish You Were Here, Postcard Remembrances of a Bygone Day* (paperback). 1984.

Killen, John. *John Bull's Famous Circus* (hardbound). Dublin, Ire.: O'Brien Press, 1985.

Klamkin, Marian. *Picture Postcards* (hardbound). New York: Dodd, Mead and Co. 1974.

Klein, Norma. *French Postcards* (paperback). Fawcett, 1979.

Klutz Press. *The World's Tackiest Postcards* (detachable cards). Palo Alto, Calif.: Klutz Press, 1987.

Kornan. *Australian Post Card Catalogue 1984.* Australia: Kornan, 1983.

Krieger, Eric. *Good Old Soccer: The Golden Age of Football Picture Postcards.* U.S.A.: Longman Group, 1983.

Kyrou, A. *L'age d'or de la Carte Postale.* Paris: A. Ballard, 1966.

LaBelle, Susan. *Peter Rabbit Postcards in Full Color* (detachable cards). Dover Books, 1984.

Lackey, B. B. *Handbook for Issues of Edward H. Mitchell, Publisher* (paperback). North Springfield, Va.

Langstroth, Theodore. *French Lithographs.* (Postcards mounted in loose-leaf album and published this way.) France: 1963.

———. *Hand Painted French Cards Collected in France.* U.S.A.: 1961.

Lanz, Phillis. *More Old New Jersey Postcards* (detachable cards). New Brunswick: 1978.

———. *Old New Jersey Postcards* (detachable cards). New Brunswick: 1977.

Lauterbach, Carl. *Picture Postcard Album, A Mirror of the Times.* London: Thames & Hudson, 1961.

Lawson, Ken, and Tony Warr. *Lance Thackeray (Checklist).* U.K.: 1978.

———. *Tom Browne (Checklist)* (paperback). U.K.

Lazarides, Stavros. *Picture Postcards of Cyprus 1899–1930.* Cyprus: Stavros Lazarides, 1987.

Lee, Ruth Webb. *A History of Valentines.* England: A. F. Batsford, 1953.

Leler, Hazel. *Hallowe'en Post Cards Published by John Winsch* (paperback). Houston, Tex.: Hazel Leler, 1983.

———. *Stecher Hallowe'en Post Card Check List.* Houston, Tex.: Hazel Leler, 1986.

Lemaire, Rene, and E. Simon. *Aeronautic Postcards Before 1914.* France: 1979.

Lent, Joy. *Houston's Heritage* (paperback). Houston, Tex.: 1983.

LeRoque, Roger, and Nick Farago. *L. H. "Dude" Larsen Checklist and Guide* (paperback). Temple City, Calif.: Roger LeRoque and Nick Farago, 1979.

Lewis, Betty. *Highlights in History, Watsonville, California* (paperback). California: Betty Lewis, 1975.

———. *Monterey Bay Yesterday* (paperback). Fresno, Calif.: 1977.

Lindsay, Maurice, and David Bruce. *Edinburgh Then and Now* (hardbound). Batsford, U.K.: 1988.

Lista, Giovanni. *The Art of Futurist Postcards.* France, 1979.

Looney, Robert. *Thirty Two Picture Postcards of Old Philadelphia* (detachable cards). New York: 1977.

Lowe, David. *Thirty Two Postcards of Old Boston* (detachable cards). New York: 1977.

Emily Lowe Gallery (organizer). *Wish You Were Here (A History of the Picture Postcard).* U.S.A.: Hofstra University, 1975.

Lowe, James. *George Washington Postcard Catalog.*

———. *Lincoln Postcard Catalog* (hardbound).

———. *The Standard Post Card Catalog.*

———. *Walden's Post Card Enthusiast Revisited* (paperback).

Lowe, James, and Ben Papell. *Detroit Publishing Company Collectors' Guide* (paperback). New York: 1975.

Luff, Moe. *United States Postal Slogan Cancel Catalog* (paperback). Spring Valley, New York: 1975.

Lund, Brian. *Postcard Collecting, A Beginner's Guide* (paperback). Nottingham, Eng.: Reflections of a Bygone Age, 1985.

———. *Railways in Britain on Old Picture Postcards* (paperback). Nottingham, Eng.: Reflections of a Bygone Age.

Lyons, Forrest D. *The Artist Signed Postcard* (hardbound). Gas City, Ind.: L. W. Promotions, 1975.

McAllister, Ed. *Paul Finkenrath Berlin (Checklist)*. U.S.A.: Ed McAllister.

MacArthur, William J. *Old Knoxville: 32 Historic Postcards* (detachable cards). Knoxville: University of Tennessee Press, 1982.

Maccaro, James A. *American Postcard Publishers, 1895–1945*. Bibliographic Press, 1986.

McCoy, Jack (ed.). *The Winding Roads: Poems & Postcards of Country Down*. Blackstaff Press, 1980.

McCulloch, Lou. *Card Photographs, A Guide to Their History and Value*. Exton, Penn.: 1981.

McLean, Mary, and Colin McLean. *Congleton and District: A Portrait in Old Picture Postcards* (paperback). U.K.: Brampton Publications, 1988.

Margolies, John. *The End of the Road* (paperback). New York, 1981.

Marks, John. *Birmingham on Old Postcards*. U.K.

Marvel Comics. *Marvel Comics Postcard Book* (detachable cards). Franklin Square, N.Y.: Nostalgia, 1978.

Megson, Fred, and Mary Megson. *Sets and Series of American Advertising Postcards*. Martinsville, N.J.: 1985.

Miller, Bonnie. *All About Dwig (Checklist)* Palm Bay, Fla.: 1976.

Miller, George. *A Pennsylvania Album: Picture Postcards 1900–1930* (paperback). University Park, Pa.: Pennsylvania State University, 1979.

Mills, Derek. *The Fishing Here is Great*. Salem House Publishers, 1986.

Mobbs, Anne M. *The Cat Fancier: A Guide to Catland Postcards*. U.S.A.: Longman Group, 1983.

Monahan, Valerie. *An American Postcard Collector's Guide* (hardbound). Poole, Dorset, Eng.: Blandford Press, 1983.

———. *Collecting Postcards in Color, 1914–1930* (paperback). Poole, Dorset, Eng.: Blandford Press.

Morgan, H. *Big Time: American Tall Tale Postcards* (paperback). New York: 1981.

Morgan, Hal. *Wish I Were Here: Eighteen Vintage Tourist Postcards for the Armchair Traveller* (detachable cards). Watertown, Mass.: Steam Press, 1984.

Morgan, Hal, and Andreas Brown. *Prairie Fires and Paper Moons: The American Photographic Postcard, 1902–1920* (hardbound). Boston: David R. Godine, 1981.

———. *Stars & Garters: Twenty Extraordinary Vintage American Postcards* (detachable cards). Watertown, Mass.: Steam Press, 1983.

Morgan, Lane. *Greetings from Washington* (hardcover). Portland, Oreg.: Graphic Arts Center Publishing, 1988.

Mrazek, Wilhelm. *Kunstlerpostkarten aus der Wiener Werkstatte, 1908–1915*. Germany: 1977.

Murphy, Bob. *Large Letter Postcard Catalog* (paperback). Webster, Tex.: Bob Murphy, 1987.

Museum of Fine Arts. *The Museum of Fine Arts Postcard Book: Thirty Two American Impressionistic Paintings in Color* (detachable cards). Boston, Mass.: Museum of Fine Arts, 1985.

Negri, A. *Le Cartoline della Nonna*. Florence, Italy: 1973.

Newman, Melissa (ed.). *Hunks Postcard Book* (paperback). Ritter, Geller Communications, 1984.

Nicholson, Susan Brown. *Teddy Bears on Paper* (hardbound). Dallas, Tex.: Taylor Publishing Co., 1985.

Norgaard, Erik. *With Love—The Erotic Postcard*. 1969.

O'Connor, David. *Old Chenango County in Postcards* (paperback). Molly Yes, 1983.

———. *Old Delaware County in Postcards* (paperback). Molly Yes, 1984.

———. *Old Ostego County in Postcards*. Molly Yes.

Oppitz, Leslie. *Surrey Railways Remembered* (hardbound). U.K.: Countryside Books, 1988.

Osborne, Charles. *The Opera House Album* (hardbound). New York, N.Y.: Taplinger Publishing Co., 1979.

Ouellette, William. *Fantasy Postcards* (hardbound). Garden City, N.Y.: Doubleday & Co., 1975.

Ouellette, William, and Barbara Jones. *Les Cartes Postales Erotiques (The Erotic Postcard)*. Paris: Humanoides Associes, 1977; London, 1977.

Parkin, Markin. *Louis Wain's Cats* (hardbound). U.K.

Paul, Wendell, Mrs. *About Antique Postcards*. Grinnel, Iowa: 1974.

Pearson, George. *Special Event Postmarks of the United Kingdom*. U.K.: 1963.

Peebles, Douglas (photographer). *Landmark Hawaii, Favorite Postcard Views of the Islands* (hardbound). Mutual Publishing of Honolulu, 1986.

Philippen, J. *Historie et Charme de la Carte Postale Illustree*. Europa: Diest, 1977.

Piggot, B. *Ilford Old and New, Volume 3* (paperback). Ilford, Eng.: B. Piggot, 1988.

Pittman, Gilbert, and Roberta Greiner. *World War II Military Comics* (paperback). Wichita, Kans.: Gilbert Pittman, 1988.

Poole, Ray. *Leek* (hardbound). Buckingham, Eng.: Barracuda Books, 1988.

Port, Beverly. *Antique Santa Post Cards* (detachable cards). Cumberland, Md.: Hobby House Press, 1985.

———. *Antique Teddy Bear Post Cards* (detachable cards). Cumberland, Md.: Hobby House Press, 1985.

Pound, Reginald. *Maypole in the Strand*. U.K.: Ernest Benn, 1948.

Radley, C. *Collecting Silk Postcards*. U.K.: 1976.

———. *The Embroidered Silk Postcard*. U.K.: 1977.

———. *History of Silk Postcards*. U.K.: 1975.

———. *The Woven Silk Postcard*. U.K.: 1978.

Raine, Craig. *A Martian Sends a Postcard Home* (paperback). Oxford University Press, 1979.

Random House. *The Sesame Street Postcard Book* (paperback). New York: Random House, 1976.

Range, Thomas E. *Book of Postcard Collecting*. U.S.A.: Dutton, 1980.

Raskin, Arlene. *All in a Day's Work* (paperback). Pennsylvania: American Deltiological Research Society, 1984.

Ray, Sam, Mrs. *Postcards from Old Kansas City* (paperback). Kansas City, Mo.: Historic Kansas City Foundation, 1980.

———. *Postcards from Old Kansas City II* (paperback). Kansas City, Mo.: Historic Kansas City Foundation, 1987.

Reed, Robert. *32 Postcards of Old Washington, D.C.* (detachable cards). U.S.A.: 1977.

Reed, Walt (ed.). *A Book of Post Cards from a Century of Illustration* (detachable cards). New York, N.Y.: Madison Square Press, 1986.

Riehm, Kay, et al. *A Checklist of Frederick L. Cavally* (paperback). U.S.A.: Garden State Postcard Club, 1980.

Rinker, Harry. *The Old Raging Erie, A Postcard History of the Erie and Other New York State Canals, 1895–1915* (paperback). Berkeley Heights, N.J.: Canal Captain's Press, 1984.

Robinson, David. *Historic Hurstpierpoint in Picture Postcards* (hardbound). Hurstpierpoint, West Sussex, Eng.: David Robinson.

Roehl, Harvey. *Cornell & Ithaca in Postcards* (paperback). Vestal, N.Y.: Vestal Press, 1986.

Rosencrans, Marguerite. *Chrome Post Card Collecting*. Wenonah, N.J.: 1980.

Ross, Hal, Hal Ottaway, and Jack Stewart. *Peerless Princess of the Plains, Postcard Views of Early Wichita* (hardbound). Wichita, Kans.: Two Rivers Publishing Co., 1976.

Rouse, Michael. *Cambridgeshire in Early Postcards* (paperback). Oleander Press, 1978.

Running Press. *American Folk Art Postcard Book* (paperback; detachable cards). Philadelphia: Running Press, 1986.

———. *The Audubon Postcard Folio* (paperback; detachable cards). Philadelphia: Running Press, 1986.

———. *Currier & Ives Postcard Book* (paperback; detachable cards). Philadelphia: Running Press, 1987.

———. *The Dinosaur Postcard Book* (detachable cards). Philadelphia: Running Press, 1987.

———. *Norman Rockwell Postcard Book* (paperback; detachable cards). Philadelphia: Running Press, 1987.

———. *The Teddy Bear Postcard Book* (paperback; detachable cards). Philadelphia: Running Press, 1985.

———. *Unicorn Postcard Book* (paperback; detachable cards). Philadelphia: Running Press, 1986.

Ryan, Dorothy. *Philip Boileau: Painter of Fair Women*. New York: 1981.

———. *Picture Postcards in the United States, 1893–1918* (paperback). New York, N.Y.: Clarkson Potter, 1982.

St. James Press. *Varga, The Esquire Years* (hardbound). Toronto: St. James Press, 1987.

Scherer, Robert W. *The Scherer-Silman Bamforth Postcard Catalog* (paperback). Birmingham, Ala.: Bertram Silman, 1981.

Schiefler, von Gustav. *Postkarten an Gustav Schiefler*. Germany: Gustav Schiefler, 1976.

Schnessel, S. M. *Jessie Wilcox Smith*. New York: Thomas Crowell.

Schoonmaker, Patricia. *Old Teddy Bear Post Cards* (detachable cards). Cumberland, Md.: Hobby House Press, 1985.

Schweiger, W. J. *Wiener Werkstatte: Kunst and Handwerk, 1903–1932*. Vienna, Aust.: Christian Brandstatter, 1982.

Scott, W. J. *All About Postcards*. Leeds, Eng.: Scott & Wilson, 1903.

Shannon, David. *Horatio Nelson: A Catalogue of Picture Postcards 1758–1805* (paperback). U.K.: Nelson Society, 1987.

Shomer, Enid. *Florida Postcards* (detachable cards). Florida: Jubilee Press.

Silvain, Gerard. *Jewish Images and Traditions* (hardbound). France: 1984.

———. *The Two Destinies of the Jewish People: 1897–1947, 50 Years of Jewish Memories Told with 1,000 Post Cards* (hardbound). Paris: 1984.

Silvester, John, and Anne Mobbs. *The Cat Fancier: A Guide to Catland Postcards*. U.K.: 1982.

Silvester, Reginald. *Railway Postcards of the British Isles*. London: 1978.

Simmons, Roger. *Kidsgrove, Talke and Mow Cop: A Portrait in Old Picture Postcards* (paperback). Salop, Eng.: Brampton Publications, 1987.

Smith, Jack. *Military Postcards*. Lombard, Ill.: Wallace-Homestead, 1988.

———. *Royal Postcards* (paperback). Lombard, Ill.: Wallace-Homestead, 1987.

Snow, Richard. *Coney Island: A Postcard Journey to the City of Fire* (hardbound). New York, N.Y.: Brightwaters Press, 1984.

Spina, Marie C. (ed.). *Picture Post Cards of Old Brooklyn: 24 Ready to Mail Views* (detachable cards). New York: 1983.

Sprague, Marshall. *Greetings from Colorado* (hardcover). Portland, Oreg.: Graphic Arts Center Publishing, 1988.

Stadtmiller, Bernard. *Postcard Collecting: A Fun Investment*. Palm Bay, Fla.: Bernard Stadtmiller, 1973.

Staff, Frank. *The Picture Postcard and Its Origins* (hardbound). London: Lutterworth Press, 1966.

———. *Picture Postcards and Travel*. U.K.: 1979.

Stansbury, Kay. *Ryan II and Horina, Too* (paperback). Mulhall, Okla.: Kay Stansbury, 1982.

Steinhart, Allen. *The Postal History of the Post Card in Canada: 1871–1911*. Toronto: 1980.

Stenlake, Richard. *Motherwell* (paperback). Glasgow, Scot.: Stenlake & McCourt, 1988.

Stieve, Jeanette. *By the Big Blue Water: Postcards of the Past from South Haven, Michigan*. U.S.A.: 1977.

Sturani, E. *The New Postcard*. Italy: 1981.

Sugar, Bert. *Great Baseball Players of the Past* (detachable cards). New York: 1978.

Thing, Robert. *Sports Postcards*. New York: 1977.

Tucker, Kerry. *Greetings from Los Angeles: A Visit to the City of Angels in Postcards* (paperback). U.S.A.: Steam Press.

———. *Greetings from New York: A Visit to Mahattan in Postcards* (paperback). U.S.A.: Delilah Books, 1981.

Van Boltenstein, W. *Hundred Years of the Postcard*. Los Angeles: 1970.

Vanderwood, Paul J., and Frank N. Samponaro. *Border Fury: A Picture Postcard Record of Mexico's Revolution and U.S. War Preparedness, 1900–1917* (hardbound). Albuquerque, N.M.: University of New Mexico Press, 1988.

Vestal Press. *Picture Postcard History of New York's Broome County Area* (paperback). Vestal, N.Y.: Vestal Press, 1985.

Vucovick, Nick. *Collecting Australian Postcards, A Guide to Values*. Australia: 1983.

Walden, Orville. *The Postcard Enthusiast, 1950–1956*. Ridley Park, Pa.: 1982.

Wales, Tony. *Horsham in Old Picture Postcards*. Zaltbommel, Netherlands: European Library, 1987.

Wallace, Charles. *The Catalogue of Poly Chrome Postcards*. Morongo Valley, Calif.: 1980.

Warr, Tony, and Ken Lawson (eds.). *Postcards for Pleasure*. U.S.A.: 1978.

Watford Museum. *Views of Old Watford—No. 1 Street Scenes*. Hertfordshire, Eng.: Watford Museum.

Webb, J. F. *Canada & Newfoundland Postal Stationery Catalogue*. Ontario, Canada: 1983.

Weill, Alain. *Alphonse Mucha: All the Postcards*. Uppsala, Swed.: 1983.

———. *Art Nouveau Postcards*. New York: 1977.

Weiner, Alfred. *New York's Elmira and Corning Area: A Picture Postcard History*. Binghamton, N.Y.: Almar Press.

Welnetz, Bob. *Ships of the Great Lakes on Postcards* (paperback). Manitowec, Wis.

———. *Ships of the Great Lakes on Postcards, Volume II* (paperback). Manitowec, Wis.

Welsch, Roger. *Tall Tale Postcards: A Pictorial History* (hardbound). U.S.A.: A. S. Barnes.

Welz, Friedrich. *Oskar Kokoschka Fruhe Drickgraphik, 1906–1912*. Germany: 1977.

Whitney, J. T. *Collect British Postmarks*. Longman, 1983.

Wolf, Aline D. *Mommy, It's a Renoir* (paperback). Altoona, Penn.: Parent Child Press, 1984.

Wolff, Chris. *The Delaware and Raritan Canal on Post Cards* (paperback). New Jersey: 1978.

———. *Down by the Depot: New Jersey Railroad Stations on Post Cards* (paperback). New Jersey: 1979.

———. *Fire Post Cards of New Jersey* (paperback). New Jersey: 1981.

———. *The Great Ice House Fire and Other New Jersey Disasters* (paperback). New Jersey: 1985.

———. *The Military Installations of New Jersey on Post Cards* (paperback). New Jersey Chris Wolff, 1986.

———. *The Morris Canal on Postcards* (paperback). Summit, N.J.: 1975.

———. *New Jersey Celebrates! A Checklist of Post Cards of New Jersey Celebrations* (paperback). New Jersey: 1984.

———. *Post Cards of New Jersey Court Houses* (paperback). Summit, N.J.: 1983.

———. *Post Cards of New Jersey Post Offices* (paperback). New Jersey: 1982.

Wolstenholme, George. *A B C of Postcard Collecting: Peeps into the Postcard Past* (paperback). Yorkshire, Eng.: George Wolstenholme, 1973.

———. *Over 900 Things to Know about Postcard Collecting* (paperback). U.K.: George Wolstenholme.

———. *Peeps into the Postcard Past* (paperback). Yorkshire, Eng.: George Wolstenholme, 1974.

Wood, Jane. *Collector's Guide to Postcards*. Paducah, Ky.: Collector's Books, 1983.

Wykes, Alan. *Saucy Seaside Postcards*. U.K.: Jupiter, 1977.

Selected Book Reviews

The following postcard book reviews are in alphabetical order by author. When available, an address is provided at the end of the review.

A Collector's Resource through Post Cards of Our Antique Dolls
Helen O. Ackert

Helen Ackert and her husband, Max, became known some years ago as "the doll people." Max set up a doll hospital in Chicago, where he repaired and rebuilt what he lovingly referred to as "sick and injured" dolls, but the Ackerts' desire to share was unbounding and was not restricted to these gestures.

In 1970, they began photocopying and publishing representations of their dolls in picturesque settings on postcards. By the time they were through, there were sixty-four doll cards and four advertising cards. The first fifty-six are illustrated in color in full size in this book. Both front and back views of the cards are provided, which is most useful as the backs give detailed descriptions.

The illustrations, like the dolls that they reproduce, are fantastic, and this is accentuated even more by the fine, glossy art paper the book uses. Many of the dolls are incredibly lifelike, and the aforementioned settings into which they are placed only add to this effect; so also do the intricately designed costumes.

A Collector's Resource has already become a classic for some good, solid reasons. The wonder is that there are still copies for sale.

Available from:

Helen O. Ackert
Ackert Enterprises
521 South Seventh Street
De Kalb, Illinois 60115

The Official Railway Postcard Book
John Alsop

What a book.

Besides the fact that there are four hundred pages of excellent research, this tome is amply supplied with postcard illustrations. They are black and white, and there can be no denying that this is a disappointment, but it does not detract appreciably from the worth and quality of the book.

The author freely admits that more than twenty years of work went into the preparation of the lists. The first few pages are for purposes of explanation, and they should be read as a guide before plunging forward into page after page of sets and series. A handy numbering system is utilized, and large print separates the hundreds of individual designations. British railroading is obviously a serious business.

Advertising cards, topographicals, ships, and, of course, trains themselves are among the cards pictured. This book deserves a first look and a second. And a third. And . . .

Available from:

John Alsop
Lawrence Close, High Street
Paverham, Bedford MK43 7NU
England

Historique de la Cartes Postale
Paul Noel Armand

They say that dynamite comes in small packages. After examining this book, you'll really be able to appreciate that statement. A slim sixty-six-page paperback, *Historique de la Cartes Postale* is nothing less than what it says it is: a history of the early French postcards. There are cards from other countries—most notably those of Germany—and there is some accompanying text relative to them, but the bulk of the material is French.

Actually, this should not be surprising since the French have a proud early postcard tradition. The debate about which country produced the first picture postcards is not to be taken up here, but it is beyond doubt that France produced more than its share of pre-1895 material. Paul Armand illustrates a number of the cards, and they are, each of them, historical items of merit. Much more could be said, but the reader's time would be better served by viewing the book itself.

Available from:

Paul Noel Armand
BP15–F 95220
Herblay
France

La Cartolina Militari 1900
Furio Arrasich

You don't have to be a collector of militaria to like this book, but you need to be one to fully appreciate it.

Sitting down, putting the feet up, and flipping through the pages will bring enjoyment to almost anybody. Can't read Italian, you say. It doesn't make any difference. In this little volume, the postcard pictures will speak to you. They will tell you about regimental camaraderie, about dignity, about Italian national pride. They also depict the glory of battle or what passes for the glory of battle. Whether there is actually any glory—or honor—in the business of relieving someone of his life before he relieves you of yours is the subject for another debate.

What is unassailable is the fact that Furio Arrasich has prepared a fine book here. Concerning itself, as it so often does, with the visual delights of military uniforms and military gatherings, the book fulfills its primary objective. Some of the postcards are even in color, another concession to the reader's pleasure.

Available from:

Furio Arrasich
Via A. G. Barrili, 35
00152 Rome
Italy

Phillimore: The Postcard Art of R. P. Phillimore
John Astolat

There have been quite a number of books written about artists, including several about postcard artists. All of them, without exception, are said to have made a valuable contribution to the knowledge of that artist. This may be true—it probably is—but few of them went about the business of describing a more intriguing artist than R. P. Phillimore (1855–1941).

John Astolat states that "it is no exaggeration to say that during his peak period there must have been approximately one million Phillimore postcards, paintings, etchings, prints, books, guide books and calendars in circulation." Not a poor number considering that the years in question would have been pre-1920 and that the average printing then for a postcard was one thousand.

His choice of themes showed Phillimore to be an individual of simple, if multifaceted, tastes. His postcard offerings were primarily topographical (or view) cards and included churches, pastoral scenes, castles, theaters, hostels, and cottages. He thus represented the high and the low of society with his artwork and has become the most popularly collected artist in his native England.

The author tells us that Phillimore not only drew and published the approximately 670 known postcards that have been attributed to him but that he also took an active part in selling them as well. In short, Phillimore was more than an artist and an individual of keen discernment and sensitivity. He was also a man who lived his life full measure and shared his perceptions with both his generation and with all of posterity.

Available from:

The Greenfriar Press
28 Manville Road
London SW17 8JN
England

Art Nouveau
Renato Barilli

Although *Art Nouveau* is not, strictly speaking, a "postcard" book, it is a volume that will prove of interest to collectors of Art Nouveau postcards. This style, which permeated European architecture, painting, sculpture, and even furniture, jewelry, and household accessories from the late 19th century, is well represented here.

Colorful paintings, beautiful vases with flowing designs, ornate and finely patterned jewelry, building facades, building interiors, and twisting, curling furniture are among the items illustrated herein. The accompanying text is most instructive as is the list of artists and designers of the pictured material. Each is given a brief sketch related either to the artist or the artwork or both.

Anyone who collects Art Nouveau postcards will want this book. It reveals, among other things, the variety of types within the style.

Available from:

Cassell Publishing
Artillery House, Artillery Row
London SW1P 1RT
England

Greetings from Oregon
Gideon Bosker and Jonathan Nicholas

If you haven't been to Astoria
You owe yourself a trip
Up the Oregon foothills
To view the face of God

In all He's wrought
The language Mother Nature knows
The mountains green
The valley streams
Gold, waiting to be gleaned

At the age of nineteen, in the year of our Lord nineteen hundred and sixty-six, an Oklahoma farmboy, the hayseed still stuck firmly in his hair, journeyed to Oregon. What he found there opened his eyes, and opened wide they needed to be to take in all the beauty of what lay before him. From agricultural farmland in the south, mountains in the north, and ocean to the west, Oregon was—and is—a veritable treat for all the senses. If the rest of America is the main course, Oregon must surely be the dessert.

What this young "Okie" saw was seen many years before him by multiple producers of picture postcards. In fact, they saw it in even more pristine fashion, having preceded him on the world's stage by fifty years and more. Men and women with a keen eye for what would appeal, and ultimately sell, commissioned artists and photographers to paint and click to their heart's content while they, ever conscious of public taste, transformed these photographic and painted treasures into thousands of postcards. Like most such pieces of pasteboard, they were purchased and posted from various ports of call. It may have seemed strange to see view cards of Oregon outside of the state, but there they were, trapped in racks from Yakima, Washington, to Miami, Florida, silent testimony to their popularity.

And now. Now we have them to ogle and cherish all over again, for Gideon Bosker and Jonathan Nicholas, two men who care about both beauty and Oregon—although not necessarily in that order—have created this book of former views. *Greetings from Oregon* is the appropriate title, and in it the viewer is treated to magnificent pictures. The postcards date from 1900 to 1950 and show an Oregon fully in the twentieth century, with tall buildings, gasoline engines, and all of that.

Yet many of the cards are quietly reminiscent of simpler times and more majestic sites of the sort that may have captivated the young Oklahoman. There to be seen are the grandiloquent hotels, the skyscrapers, the busy street scenes, but alongside these views are

scenics of rustic farm life, old ships churning the waters of the once-peaceful Williamette River, lumberjacks pursuing their hardy occupation, the vanishing faces of the Indians native to Oregon. All this is a symphony played against the backdrop of snowcapped mountains, gorgeous azure lakes, breathtaking waterfalls, and lush forests. More than three hundred vintage postcards, most in vibrant color and most reproduced full size, grace the book and provide a sensual feast for the eyes. Oregon is, indeed, a wonderland, winter and summer. The full truth demands a further statement: In a sometime plastic world, Oregon is for real.

We may be sufficiently thankful to the authors of *Greetings from Oregon* to acknowledge our appreciation for the gift of such magically wondrous pictures as these. Perhaps we may even appreciate the expressed sentiments of our would-be Oklahoma poet, who ended his tribute this way:

I went there once, then went away
Angry, chagrined at life
But not the sea
But not the scenery

Available from:

Graphic Arts Center Publishing Company
P.O. Box 10306
Portland, Oregon 97210

Nickelodeon Theatres and Their Music
Q. David Bowers

The author tells us that the term nickelodeon is derived from nickel, the price of admission, and odeon, the French word for theater. Actually, odeon is the Greek word for theater. No matter. Whatever the origin, it is clearly indicated that Q. David Bowers knows his subject well.

Many black-and-white illustrations and 203 pages of text contribute to an authoritative volume on this topic. Anyone wanting to know more about nickelodeons than what is presented here probably wants to know too much and is altogether too hard to please.

Bowers has done his best with this book, and as we have discovered with his other books, Bowers's best is considerable. Some of the illustrations are postcards although others are not, but all of them are of the type that one would expect to find on postcards. More to the point, *Nickelodeon Theatres* demonstrates with crystal clarity both how postcards may aid the cause of scholarship and also the tie-in between postcards and other objects, such as pictures, artwork, statuary, and other collectibles.

In the same sense, this book offers scholarship, visual delight, and social history—and all at one price.

Not a bad package, this.

Available from:

Q. David Bowers
Box 1224
Wolfeboro, New Hampshire 03894

Robert Robinson: American Illustrator
Q. David Bowers and Christine Bowers

This book is an absolute joy for the viewer. Robert Robinson (1886–1952) was as proverbially American as apple pie, baseball games, Sunday picnics, and Norman Rockwell. In fact, Robinson's technique and subject matter were similar to Rockwell's; it remains to be proven that Robinson's work suffers by comparison with Rockwell.

Even a cursory look at the thirty-two color postcards and the other black-and-white illustrations will confirm his mastery of the illustrator's art. Country America, America coming of age, and America with a backward glance are the motifs, and Robinson does justice to them. His paintings make one want to step back, adjust the eye focus, and examine the moments and quintessential events he has frozen in time and space.

Q. David and Christine Bowers have found something worth sharing and worth preserving, and *Robert Robinson* is the vehicle they have chosen to achieve both aims. Only caring people could offer a book like this.

It is a work of love.

Available from:

Q. David Bowers
Box 1224
Wolfeboro, New Hampshire 03894

The Postcards of Alphonse Mucha
Q. David Bowers and Mary L. Martin

Q. David Bowers burst full blown onto the coin collecting scene in the early 1970s. He was one of a select group sometimes referred to as the "Young Turks" because of their ingenuity, dedication to research, and ability to promote.

Comes now the 1980s and Bower has assumed something of the same role with antique postcards, especially with regard to the business of research. Alphonse Mucha, as postcard collectors and devotees of art are well aware, was one of the chief exponents of the style that came to be known as Art Nouveau. This style represented a reaching out, a flowing of graceful lines, an undulation toward the visually pleasing. In a few instances, as with some items of furniture, some architecture, and some pieces of bric-a-brac, Art Nouveau may have been said to go too far as it approached the rococo, the elaborate, the unusual.

Mucha never went to these extremes. What he offered instead were alluringly beautiful maidens garlanded and festooned, surrounded by and intertwined with gorgeously flowering plants or vines in a colorful yet always tasteful and enticing backdrop.

Bowers's book is a first-class piece of scholarship replete with an information-packed text, a most welcome rarity scale into which he has inserted numbers of known postcard specimens, and a price listing in two grades—fine and mint—for each illustration. Unfortunately, only the paperback covers are in color, and this is a disappointment. To be fully appreciated, Mucha's material must be seen with the vibrancy of colors he so wisely employed.

Still, Bowers and Mary L. Martin have presented the postcard world with a well-written and nicely researched volume. Whether one is a generalist or a specialist in the field of deltiology, he or she should find use and location for a book this articulately prepared.

Available from:

Q. David Bowers
Box 1224
Wolfeboro, New Hampshire 03894

Harrison Fisher
Q. David Bowers, George M. Budd, and Ellen H. Budd

Q. David Bowers and friends—in this case, George and Ellen Budd—have done it again, and this time with even more panache. This book on American artist Harrison Fisher is both a must read and a must examine.

The facts: many interesting details about Fisher's life, including lengthy excerpts from magazine articles and other sources, are gleaned and set to type. Complementing them are multiple photographs of Fisher in various settings—Fisher in his studio or at the office, with family and friends, character studies of Fisher the man.

As is typical of author Bowers, each of the black-and-white illustrations of Fisher's postcards is given an identification number. Following the number to the end of each section, or sometimes below the card itself, are explanations of each, including titles, publishers, and complete descriptions. The concluding pages offer a complete Collectors' Checklist of Postcards.

Harrison Fisher is fact-filled and the writing style is interesting, again a Bowers trademark. An excellent and exciting piece of research.

Available from:

> Q. David Bowers
> Box 1224
> Wolfeboro, New Hampshire 03894

What the Postman Saw
Andrew Brooks, Fred Fletcher, and Brian Lund

A favorite pastime for many postcard collectors is reading the messages that have been scrawled on the cards in their collections. In many, if not most, instances, the wording was fairly innocuous: greetings from separated family members; notes between sweethearts—or would-be sweethearts; mundane exchanges of information.

Not all postcard messages are of an ordinary character, however. In a number of instances, the blurbs are either particularly pertinent, quite entertaining or

interesting, or, in not a few cases, more than a little humorous. The authors of *What the Postman Saw* give their readers liberal doses of all of them. Rather than presenting a random selection, they offer the messages under such headings as aviation, sport, work, entertainment, exhibitions, political, transport, and more than ten others.

Historically speaking, the messages with a correlation to significant events and personalities are the most important ones, and a few of this type are reproduced here, but it is obvious that this book is concerned with the more routine communications between "ordinary" folk. This is as it should be, for while many postcard collectors are also historians of one sort or another, even they are emotionally connected with the nostalgia involved in viewing these eighty-year-old and ninety-year-old miniletters. Postcards were, after all, a means of communication for the common man. *What the Postman Saw* gives us another tool for examining our ancestors. It also lets us know how much like us they were—and how unlike.

Available from:

> Reflections of a Bygone Age
> 15 Debdale Lane
> Keyworth
> Nottingham NG12 5HT
> England

Pioneer Postcards
J. R. Burdick

There is no postcard book that cannot be improved upon—including this one—but in the thirty-two years since the first printing of J. R. Burdick's *Pioneer Postcards,* no one has dared tamper with its format.

Oh, sure, there were a few corrections and additions included in later editions by Clark Stevens, and James Lowe presumed to add prices to the cards listed, but these things are cherries on the cake. They don't even represent the icing.

What Jefferson Burdick researched and wrote was nothing less than the best book on pre-1898 postcards that could have been imagined up to that time. Ongoing research has added a number of cards to his listing, and more are being discovered all the time, but Burdick's is the foundation to which all these should be seen as addendums. They are hubcaps on the tires. The pioneer wheel itself was introduced by the author.

Some specifics: After a detailed analysis of early postcard history, replete with black-and-white illustrations on glossy paper, Burdick begins with a section on U.S. expositions. Every card is numbered for identification purposes, further identified by sets or series, where applicable, and granted a brief description. In a book of this nature, dealing as it does with seldom-seen material, one always wishes for more illustrations than what is proffered, but Burdick has been generous in this capacity.

Sections are devoted to U.S. views, Canadian view cards, foreign events, advertising postal cards, greeting cards, and an extensive supplement dated September 1958.

In short, Burdick, with the publication of *Pioneer Postcards,* created the outline into which all that follows may add its individual contribution.

The Military Postcards of the Third Reich
Tom Capparelli

Although military postcards have long been a favored collectible, there were no books about them until Tonie and Valmai Holt's first volume on World War I in the late 1970s. Sadly, only a few have been added since that time.

The Military Postcards of the Third Reich is a welcome addition to this meager list. It contains very little prose, but wording is really unnecessary except for purposes of identification. It is the illustrations that tell the story, and they do a remarkable job. There are almost three hundred of them, more than fifty in color. Reich leaders, character profiles of enlisted men and women, Nazi government postals, medals and flags, battle scenics, propaganda, airplanes, ships, and the obligatory Hitler photographs are among the postcards pictured. Many are identified by artist and are also priced. The values given are open to debate, and it is this writer's opinion that they are on the high side, but many of them are uncommonly encountered items, and the interest in them is as much on the upsurge as it has ever been.

As a visual study of a particular postcard grouping, this book is priceless. As a pictorial representation of the Third Reich, it is in a class by itself.

Available from:

Tom Capparelli
P.O. Box 655
Villa Park, Illinois 60181

The American Postcard Guide to Tuck
Sally Carver

Easily the best known of all postcard publishers was the firm of Raphael Tuck & Sons. It even had a special patent from Her Gracious Majesty, Queen Victoria of England. Tuck produced postcards for several decades and was often the leader in both style and innovation. The firm accepted the whole world as suitable ground for postcard material, and the thousands of Tuck specimens testify to the depth of its commitment.

Sally Carver, postcard dealer and popular article writer, prepared this volume. It is a good one, a very good one. Carver herself would be the first to admit that it is incomplete. It was her desire to offer a work for new to intermediate collectors, and she has done so. The problem thus far is that no one seems willing—perhaps capable is a better choice of wording—to finish the job, and it would be a formidable task. David Pinfold has been writing a monthly article about Tuck's postcards for England's *Picture Postcard Monthly* for years and will probably write for many more, such is the wealth of postcard material.

Carver's book is an admirable start. Her categorical breakdown is appreciated, and so too is her useful numbering system. She discusses artists, both American and foreign, who worked for Tuck. From there, she launches into a dissection of the various postcard categories in which Tuck worked. They include aviation, blacks, comics, expositions, greetings, transportation, patriotic, military, views, Santa Claus, and more. A section on sets and series is also presented. Carver's format has the prose and descriptions on the left while the pages to the right are reserved for the postcard illustrations. Even in black and white, the superiority of much of Tuck's offerings is apparent. Carver also includes information about the firm itself as well as a useful glossary of terms.

Available from:

Sally S. Carver
179 South Street
Chestnut Hill, Massachusetts 02167

Ier Catalogue Cartes Postales Contemporaines, 1975–80
Armande Chivat and Jean-Claude Souyri

Clearly, the French are more serious about modern postcard art than most, if not all, other nations. One of the reasons for this is that some of the best modern postcard artists are French. Because their output is so well received in their native country, this in turn has encouraged them to produce an impressive body of work, impressive both as to its artistic merit and also as regards the huge amount of it.

It is this last fact that makes Armande Chivat's and Jean-Claude Souyri's book welcome and necessary. The additions since 1980 have easily quadrupled what was produced during the five years dealt with here, so another volume, a much larger one, is now needed. This one will serve as an excellent model for it. It lists the precise year-to-year output of all the well-known (and a few of the lesser well-known) French artists in Section I while Section II lists club offerings (artists' work for clubs constituted a large slice of the postcard work that they did; in fact, this amount added to the work done for postcard shows and other events was the bulk of their offerings in those days). Also included are the numbers of postcards printed by each artist, the artist's specialty (for instance, his or her type of workmanship or his or her methodology and style), the issuing price, and the rarity of each specimen.

It may very well have been the French who began the practice of issuing special postcards that related to various club activities or merely as club logos or visual, pictorial identifications. The practice has become a popular one in the United States but is encountered less frequently in Great Britain, especially England proper.

The book's index gives a listing of all French postcard artists, all French postcard clubs, an enumeration of artists from other countries, and a listing of photographers and themes.

Ier Catalogue Cartes Postales Contemporaines, 1975–1980 is both a dictionary and an encyclopedia, combining the finer aspects of each.

Modern Postcards: Postcard Reproductions from the Permanent Collection of the San Francisco Museum of Modern Art
Chronicle Books

Any art lover with an affinity for either Impressionistic or "modern" art will find this book to be a refreshing diversion from the stresses and strains of living in a competitive society. The rest of us may be less enthused or less enthralled with these thirty-two ready-for-mailing postcards reproduced from the paintings, sculptures, and objets d'art at the San Francisco Museum of Modern Art, but even we may experience a few moments of curiosity and interest as we attempt to extract some measure of meaning from the illustrations. A few of them—a few—are pretty pedestrian, straightforward, and may be at least partially interpreted by the less culturally minded. Then again, with modern art, one never really knows.

Perhaps that ambiguity, that built-in absence of concreteness, that lack of resolution is the ultimate appeal for these items.

Ask someone who can adequately define metaphysics to go into this further.

Available from:

> Chronicle Books
> One Hallidie Plaza
> San Francisco, California 94102

Picture Postcards in Australia, 1898–1920
David Cook

David Cook has done a good thing, a very good thing. He has given the postcard collecting world a long-hoped-for item, a book about Australia's antique postcards.

He has also presented any and all future authors who might wish to prepare a similar tome an excellent blueprint to copy. Beginning with a history of postcard collecting, Cook quickly follows with an Australian postcard history. This in turn is followed by a chapter entitled "Thematic Subjects Depicted on Postcards," whose emphasis is correctly on Australian postcards.

But it is the sections that are still ahead that elict the most praise, for author Cook has been more than thoughtful in giving us not merely a listing but also biographical details on the prominent postcard artists and publishers his country has produced. These two chapters are jewels of research, and their value, both to the indigenous population and to postcard collectors everywhere, is incalculable.

Further chapters include "Production Processes," a foray into the various manufacturing and printing methods as they relate to postcards: "How to Collect Postcards," which gives information about purchasing, appraising, and storing postcards as well as introductory remarks about postcard clubs and the business of topic specialization; and a few comments concerning "The Value of Postcards."

Concluding this finely bound, hardcover book is an appendix with an artist's checklist that includes their publishers and the individual card titles. There is also a publisher's checklist, likewise a nice touch though not as extensive or thorough as the artist's checklist. Dozens of postcard illustrations, including some beautiful color specimens, are sprinkled pleasingly throughout.

Picture Postcards in Australia is a marvelous first book on this exciting topic. We may hope that Cook, having increased our appetites, will be pleased to give us more.

Available from:

> Reflections of a Bygone Age
> 15 Debdale Lane
> Keyworth
> Nottingham NG12 5HT
> England

An Album of Old Time Postcards from Houston & Galveston
Corona Publishing

Those without a map at hand may want to know that Houston and Galveston are in South Texas. Houston used to be the place where one went to make the money, and Galveston, with its pretty beaches and pretty women, was where one went to spend it. Some people say times haven't changed.

Some other things have. Changed, that is. Like types of transportation. Like Farmer's Markets (real ones). Like canal and train traffic. Like spacious and lush accommodations. Like beautiful, tree-lined streets.

This album of detachable colored view cards ignites the old images. You might want to do yourself a favor. Buy the book, stare at it a while, then tear out each postcard, one at a time, and mail each one to a friend.

They will thank you for it.

Available from:

> Corona Publishing Company
> 1037 South Alamo
> San Antonio, Texas 78210

An Album of Old Time Texas Postcards
Corona Publishing

If you want to see a series of Texas vignettes before the real estate barons and property developers had turned it into a cement and asphalt wasteland, you might consider purchasing this book.

On second thought, buy three copies. One for you and the other two for a sociologist and an architect. It might be amusing to ask each of them to look at the series of detachable postcards and then write an essay on progress. Nothing too elaborate, mind you. Perhaps something along the lines of how Texas is more esthetically appealing and more dynamic now than it was eighty years ago. Morals, it might be best to leave alone.

Then again, maybe it's safer to make a glass of lemonade, settle back in your rocker/recliner—after turning on the air conditioning—look at the pictures yourself, and think back to the "Good Old Days." Later on, you can watch a rerun of one of those Western movies starring John Wayne or Jimmy Stewart. You know the kind, the ones that tell you how the West was won.

Available from:

> Corona Publishing Company
> 1037 South Alamo
> San Antonio, Texas 78210

How to Price and Sell Old Picture Postcards
Roy Cox

Roy Cox, a man who has certainly done his share toward promoting the hobby of postcard collecting, offers his readers a book designed to inform the uninitiated about the business side of postcards. Step by step, he examines one issue after another. Beginning with a brief historical review of postcard history, he proceeds to a look at the types of postcards, for example, (private mailing cards), undivided backs, and divided backs, then to some general information about a few book titles, and finally to the card that has always been the backbone of the hobby, hometown view cards.

With a couple of personal reminiscences, Cox tells how to acquire postcards. This section is all-too abbreviated and is followed by an "encyclopedia" of postcard categories. Although ten pages are devoted to them, this section is also underdiscussed, and several important categories are not even mentioned. But it is a good beginning, and the information and price guide related to stereo cards are much appreciated.

So much for the book's first half. The second half of this heavy, glossy-stocked volume refers to the selling end of the business, and it is in this area that Cox's expertise shines through in crystal fashion. Apart from a proclivity to treat the reader as if he or she were somewhat mentally unsophisticated by occasionally talking down, the author's comments are well received. Cox clearly knows whereof he speaks and imparts this knowledge and his feelings in no uncertain way. For those interested in becoming a postcard dealer, this part of the book is the most useful.

Sadly, there are no postcard illustrations; instead, Cox offers an interesting group of sketches as a pleasant diversion to staring at page after page of uninterrupted text. *How to Price and Sell Old Picture Postcards* is well worth reading, and though it is incomplete, it does contain much that is unknown to the average collector.

Available from:

Roy Cox
Box 3610
Baltimore, Maryland 21214–0610

The Dictionary of Picture Postcards in Britain, 1894–1939
A. W. Coysh

What we have here is a giant version of George Wolstenholme's *Over 900 Things to Know about Postcard Collecting.* This statement is meant neither to denigrate A. W. Coysh's commendable effort nor to elevate Wolstenholme's book.

Nevertheless, it is obvious that in both cases the emphasis is less on exegesis than it is on introduction

and brief definition. In neither work is the bulk of the entries dealt with in great detail; nor should Coysh be faulted unnecessarily for taking this approach. Had he done the opposite, that is, had he prepared several paragraphs on each entry (which he did do for quite a number of them), the book would have been an impossible 2,500 pages rather than the more easily manageable 310 pages.

It ought to be acknowledged as well that very little is known about some of the entries, and this necessarily forces their brevity. It should be further allowed that the author has included a good deal of information not encountered elsewhere. He has data about publishing firms, artists, categories, famous people, events, and more. There is also information on sets and series. Dozens of illustrations, both black and white and color, are used to dot the pages and are convenient and welcome intervals. It is beyond all reasonable doubt that this book is worth possessing.

Available from:

Antique Collectors' Club
529 Ellis Hollow Creek Road
Ithaca, New York 14850

Collect Modern Postcards
Pete Davies

Those who have read Britain's delightful publication *Picture Postcard Monthly* need no introduction to Pete Davies. They recognize him as an expert in the field of modern postcards. Those who have not read *Picture Postcard Monthly* (for shame) may purchase *Collect Modern Postcards* and be led to the same conclusion regarding Davies's expertise.

It should be noted that Davies's information regarding modern postcards that he has trapped within the pages of his book is not complete. Considering the complexity and size of the modern market, it could hardly be otherwise. There is simply too much to know about too many artists, publishers, and postcards and too many countries from which the information must come. What Davies has done, and done quite well, is cover the British market and to include some information about the situation in a number of other countries. These include Australia, Bahrain, France, Sweden, and the United States. As sketchy as this may be, only another researcher may fully appreciate Davies's difficulties in trying to obtain assistance from dealers, collectors, and publishers outside of one's own country.

As regards the British scene, the book is not only exhaustive but incredibly detailed as well. Loaded with postcard illustrations that are generously scattered throughout the book, *Collect Modern Postcards* is, first of all, a visual treat. Next, it is an educational experience. The modern card, like its earlier counterpart, has devoted itself to almost the whole of human activity and preoccupation, not to mention its pervasiveness, into the natural world of plants, animals, and landscapes. Davies has not been remiss in supplying the reader with examples of this diversity, especially that of the human variety: political cards, movie stars, royalty, sports, transportation, views, shipping, and the military, occupation-related. And yes, there are nature studies for those so inclined.

Of special merit and mention is his section on themes, which is divided into the areas of "Collecting by Theme" and a "Thematic Index," which serves as a sort of abbreviated encyclopedia. The artist listing is likewise a good one and begins with a number of biographies.

Further information relative to sets and series and publishers is offered, making this book a must read even for the nonmodern collector. Knowing of the author's desire for completeness convinces all that future updates and revisions will be even better. We can hardly wait.

While waiting, one would be well served by purchasing this book and reading it, then looking at the illustrations. Then rereading it.

Available from:

> Reflections of a Bygone Age
> 15 Debdale Lane
> Keyworth
> Nottingham NG12 5HT
> England

The Dexter Post Card Story
Thomas Dexter

As a publisher, Dexter Post Card Company fills the years from 1925 to the present with a variety of offerings. United States collectors are quite familiar with the name, especially as it relates to the period since the 1950s.

Thomas Dexter helps put the company in understandable perspective with his eighty-page book of information and illustrations. The one minor flaw is that there are only twelve illustrations, which is something of a disappointment, given the almost innumerable amount of cards Dexter published.

Still, this is a book which every serious or even casual collector of postcards should own. It is packed with history, punctuated by anecdote. Moreover, *The*

Dexter Post Card Story is a substantive book about a fascinating publisher.

Available from:

> Thomas A. Dexter
> 90 Cider Hill
> Upper Saddle River, N.J. 07458

Antique Doll Photo Postcards—
24 Ready-to-Mail Postcards
Dover Publications

There are ugly dolls and pretty dolls, unusual dolls and commonly seen dolls. Then there are exceptional dolls, realistic looking, so well-dressed it is easy to be envious and so gorgeous—or perhaps just cute—that the desire to pinch their ample cheeks is overpowering.

This last type are the ones presented here, obviously lovingly, by Helen Nolan. Words are inadequate to describe the appeal of these postcard representations. One's eyes should do the work. So: Stop, look, and look again.

Available from:

> Dover Publications
> 31 East Second Street
> Mineola, New York 11501

Contemporary American Glass from Steuben
(24 Ready-to-Mail Color Postcards)
Dover Publications

Steuben glass should not be confused with what one casually encounters at discount stores, most glass dealerships, or even at the bulk of antique shows. Not top-class Steuben, that is.

The pieces shown here are top class in every way. These are works of art by every understanding of that term. More than merely beautiful—and they are certainly that—the very appearance of them to the naked eye uplifts and inspires. They touch a responsive chord in the human spirit. It probably has something to do with the desire to achieve perfection. None of us will ever lay claim to it. Not in this life, anyway. But Steuben has come close.

Available from:

> Dover Publications
> 31 East Second Street
> Mineola, New York 11501

Early American Folk Art Masterpieces
(24 Ready-to-Mail Color Postcards)
Dover Publications

If your conception of folk art comes from visits to arts and crafts shows held in shopping malls or from antique shows that occur periodically at city civic centers, this book may come as a surprise.

Oh, there are a couple of quilts and the obligatory stoneware. There are also a few handmade dolls. But even these mundane items are anything but mundane in appearance or pedigree. As for the rest, hold on to your preoccupations. Then let them go. To reveal too much is to destroy the surprise, but perhaps it will not be overly revelatory to indicate that many people's mental images of Indians and certain animals may undergo a change after viewing these colorful cards.

Available from:

> Dover Publications
> 31 East Second Street
> Mineola, New York 11501

Kate Greenaway Postcards
(24 Color Ready-to-Mail Cards)
Dover Publications

Kate Greenaway was an artist who specialized in illustrating children's books. According to the note at the front of this booklet, Greenaway's children are "decorous and carefree, innocent (though sometimes naughty), wide-eyed and wondering." One wonders about this analysis, or at least this analysis as a conclusion, complete in itself.

The children appear to range in age from seven to ten years, and they have the ability to project a psychological precociousness as if they were contemplating the foibles of human nature. Not that Greenaway's children are downhearted. To the contrary. But they certainly appear pensive at times. Even in play, they seem lost in thought.

It is easy to see why Greenaway's young creations attract such attention. Trying to figure out what is going on in all those little minds is a challenge that occasionally serves to bring out the detective in all of us.

Available from:

> Dover Publications
> 31 East Second Street
> Mineola, New York 11501

Collecting Postcards in Color, 1894–1914
William Duval and Valerie Monahan

If there were a list of postcard books whose primary duty was to act as primers for the uninitiated, *Collecting Postcards in Color, 1894–1914* would sit proudly in the ranks. Make no mistake: There are problems with the text. It is too "England"-oriented; its analysis of the various topics is, at best, superficial; and its lack of breadth is a decided drawback.

And yet these problems notwithstanding, this book is filled with useful nuggets of information. From the opening chapter on postcard history to a listing of international postcard dealers (now long outdated) at the end, this tome is a mixture of delightful prose and tidbits of knowledge. As the title suggests, only colored illustrations are used (192 of them). Many are uncommon specimens infrequently encountered. There are stalwart trains of an age now given to memory and history books, beautiful advertising cards, some eye-arresting artist-drawn glamour cards, interesting military cards, early—and wondrously colored—gruss aus views, and much more.

Included is information about publishers, an index of artists with rarity factors, and a description of various categories of postcards.

For an admittedly incomplete book, *Collecting Postcards in Color, 1894–1914* is a remarkable little volume.

The Vanished Splendor III: A Postcard Album
of Oklahoma City
Jim Edwards, Mitchell Oliphant, and Hal Ottaway

Ideally, any book should rise or fall based on its own merits. A poor volume should not be made to appear more appealing by the blurbs on the dust jacket nor by the hyperbole of the author or the media.

This writer is more than willing to permit *The Vanished Splendor III* to stand on its own substantial legs. *Splendor*s I and II sold completely out of their initial printings, and, assuming their quality is the equal of this volume, it is not difficult to understand why. From the leather grain look and feel of the cover with the impressed postcard to the combination black-and-white and color illustrations to the excellently researched captions, this book represents the finest in publishing. It has become the model for several other books of the same type, although all these imitations suffer by comparison with the original.

Knowing that two heads are better than one, the authors have exceeded even this and put their three heads together in a collaborative effort, the results of which are most impressive.

Oklahoma City was part of what we euphemistically refer to as the Wild West (rather than the Wicked West or the Violent West) and was one of the last places to rid itself of the lingering vestiges of that rowdy period in American history.

Jim Edwards, Mitchell Oliphant, and Hal Ottaway use their postcard views wisely to show the old, the emerging, and the new. Churches, schools, hotels, businesses, celebrations, street scenes, entertainers and noted personalities, depots, and aerial views, these and more present an image of a town as complex in its own way as New York City, Chicago, and San Francisco are in theirs.

Corpus Christi, Texas: A Picture Postcard History
Anita Eisenhauer and Gigi Starnes

South Texas is a world unto itself. El Paso, Houston, Brownsville, Austin: all are towns with both proud and infamous histories. But what of that southern jewel on the Gulf of Mexico, Corpus Christi?

Well, if you want to know what it is, go there and do a little digging around, but if you want to know what it was, and how it came to be what it is, you might want to ask historian Anita Eisenhauer and former reporter Gigi Starnes. Better yet, purchase their book *Corpus Christi, Texas—A Picture Postcard History* and let your eyes do the exploration over the pages. They will welcome the diversion, for it is a wondrous excursion into times and lifestyles that were a bit easier to understand than this postatomic age.

It is most difficult to examine the old dirt roads, the pristine beaches, the clapboard habitations, and scenic park areas without being overcome by nostalgia. It is sufficient to make a romantic out of the crustiest of souls (although the old devils probably wouldn't admit it). There was a downside, of course. They didn't have air conditioning nor wall-to-wall carpeting nor microwave ovens into which one might place that delight of the palate, the TV dinner.

There were other things they didn't have as well. They didn't have carbon monoxide, factory fumes, miles of asphalt and concrete, bumper-to-bumper horn-beeping traffic, and deadly contaminates. As the authors' postcards demonstrate, the cost of progress hardly made it a bargain or, in many instances, even worth it.

The postcards illustrated here traverse the years from the first decade of the twentieth century to the 1980s, and they are lessons both in history and sociology. Still, the authors do not make us engage in guesswork, for each of the cards has at least two paragraphs of explanatory prose running alongside it. It's good prose, too, the kind that both entertains and informs.

You may know precious little about Corpus Christi before you pick up this book, but you'll almost feel a part of the town by the time you put it down. This is a truly remarkable piece of visual history. One may not be able to actually go back and rewrite the script of the past, but for as long as books like this continue to be published, we may—perhaps only briefly—relive its better aspects.

Available from:

Anita's Antiques
Word Shop Division
P.O. Box 260056
Corpus Christi, Texas 78426–0056

Trams on Old Picture Postcards
Norman Ellis

Just as many Americans have a fascination, almost a love affair, really, with old cars and trucks, just so a sizable chunk of the British population delights in pictures of antique trams.

For those who don't know, a tram is a motorbus that operated in all of the large cities—and many of the smaller ones as well—during the early part of the twentieth century. It was a convenient method for transporting an increasingly mobile population to jobs, to the stores, or simply to places of visitation.

The author of *Trams on Old Picture Postcards* is Norman Ellis, one of Britain's supreme tram aficionados. Ellis is quick to inform his readers that there is a distinction between British tramways and those in other parts of the civilized world. What he refers to is "the lack of inter-urban systems" peculiar to Britain and also England's "preponderance and variety of double-deck cars."

So much for definitions. In America and elsewhere, this method of transport might be called the electric streetcar, that traction system that operated in the first couple of decades of this century. Both the streetcar and the tram are deserving of more serious attention than either has heretofore received; thus, Ellis's book is welcome all the more. It throws a little light on the matter or, in this case, a lot of light on the tram.

The sixty-four pages of illustrations and accompanying text are neatly arranged to reveal the variety of the vehicles and the manifold locales in which they would have been spotted. Beginning with a section on tramway history, Ellis progresses on to horse trams, steam trams, track laying, deliveries, openings, street scenes, and much more, including a foray into unusual trams. He even shows us some colorful comic tram postcards.

This is one instance in which the color is not really needed; the black-and-white illustrations are sufficiently spellbinding to make their viewer realize that the fascination for a method of conveyance now long gone is a legitimate one.

Available from:

> Reflections of a Bygone Age
> 15 Debdale Lane
> Keyworth
> Nottingham NG12 5HT
> England

Art Nouveau Postcards
Giovanni Fanelli and Ezio Godoli

Anyone who wants to know what postcards and art have in common should see this book. All 375 pages of it. Not only will the experience help the viewer to redefine beauty by placing it on a more elevated plane, but the illustrations will give the reader a more thorough overview of Art Nouveau than he or she is ever likely to get elsewhere.

There are more than 750 full-color illustrations, each one an art lesson in itself. Beginning with Great Britain, the book and its postcard reproductions are divided into geographical sections. Even the United States is included, and though one may argue the appropriateness of placing the names of artists Philip Boileau and Charles Dana Gibson into the category of Art Nouveau, any opportunity to view the works of these gentlemen in color is most welcome.

If the truth were known, it would probably include what is obvious: It is difficult to get unanimity of opinion as to which artist's work fits into the various understandings of what constitutes Art Nouveau. All the experts would agree on placing Kirchner, Jozsa, K. Moser, A. Basch, and Alphonse Mucha squarely in the style's center; but what about A. N. Benois, I. Bilibin, B. Mangold? Always, sometimes, rarely? Is bold, occasionally seductive, use of coloration along with a freedom of line movement to be considered the identifying elements?

Giovanni Fanelli and Ezio Godoli wisely permit the viewers to make the determination for themselves. They are content to furnish the postcard world with a wealth of background information and to let the pictures speak for themselves. They are more than considerate in furnishing biographical sketches of the various artists at the back of the book, and there are dozens of them.

Still, it is to the pictures that the eye returns, and this is as it should be. They are exceptionally well reproduced, and each whets the appetite for more. There may be better postcard books, and those more useful, but none is likely to elicit more appreciation from its readers.

Available from:

> Rizzoli International Publications
> 597 Fifth Avenue
> New York, New York 10017

Old Milwaukee: A Historic Tour in Picture Postcards
Gregory Filardo

Milwaukee, Wisconsin, is a city rich with history and steeped in tradition. Not mired, mind you, but steeped. Milwaukee's citizens are a cultural people, rightfully proud of their town and of its diversity and longevity.

Gregory Filardo, author of *Old Milwaukee: A Historic Tour in Picture Postcards,* knows all of this. A student of architecture and music throughout his life, Filardo has retrieved many pieces of mortar and brick from Old Milwaukee buildings before the ball and chain could demolish their magnificence. He never tires of telling his fellow citizens about their historic city, a habit he carried to its logical conclusion with the preparation of this book. Loaded with postcard illustrations of Milwaukee as it was during the first few decades of the Twentieth Century, the book is visual history at its best.

Filardo does not stop with merely showing us the pictures, but uses them as a backdrop to explain and clarify their places in history. There are street scenes and buildings, offices and businesses, famous locations and cultural institutions. Filardo does not leave one proverbial stone unturned in his quest. His desire and his product are the same, revolving as they do around a commitment to present Milwaukee not only as a city of stability, but also as a place where magic occurs. The magic of growing and learning, of being and doing, of being both reflective and innovative. Milwaukee natives know. And, of course, Gregory Filardo knows. So will purchasers of his book.

Available from:

Vestal Press
P.O. Box 97
320 N. Jensen Rd.
Vestal, New York 13850

Amarillo, Texas II: The First Hundred Years
Ray Franks and Jay Ketelle

It would be difficult not to develop a quick liking for this book. Like the city it presumes to cover, the volume is lavish and inclusive. For those with a poor sense of geography, Amarillo is one of the towns in the flatlands of the Texas Panhandle. In fact, it is the largest town.

Broad and expansive, its location smack in the middle of Interstate 40 (the old "Route 66"), Amarillo is at once both friendly and dominating. Its steakhouses are among the best to be found anywhere, and the typical citizen of Amarillo is reported to be ever-ready with a handshake, an offer of assistance, or a piece of advice. He may not always start with a smile, but that's O.K. You see, he doesn't sell oil leases or pieces of the Brooklyn Bridge for a living. He's more substantial than that.

So is the town. Commanding a view that stretches as far into the horizon as the sinking sun, Amarillo is as real as the stinging winds that race across the Texas landscape. Ray Franks and Jay Ketelle, two Yankees who came to visit and decided to stay, found much to like about the place. Both men were stationed at the local Air Force base. Each recognized a good thing when he saw it. They decided to put their heads—and their postcards—together and came up with two more good things: *Amarillo, Texas I* and *Amarillo, Texas II*. Both are postcard history books.

Only the second one is currently being discussed, and that for a very good reason: The first book has sold out of its original printing. A look at book two explains why.

The postcards tell of a cowtown that progressed from dirt roads and covered wagons—actually, horses and buggies would be more appropriate as Amarillo was not generally recognized as a stop on the road to the West in the early days—to become a center of culture on the plains. It boasts excellent medical centers, educational establishments, first-class hotels, and fine theaters. Along the way to all this finery, Amarillo

endured tornados and other natural disasters. What the citizens of this burg have not done is turn their backs on their western traditions. They still have barrel racing and rodeos, square dances and cattle ranches. And, of course, it's all here in the postcard record.

The postcard on the cover says it best. Beneath the words "Howdy Pardner" is pictured a little girl in western dress, six shooters at her side. To her left is a large suitcase that displays a simple message: AMARILLO TEXAS, THE FRIENDLY CITY.

Available from:

Ray Franks Publishing Ranch
4117 West 49th Street
P.O. Box 7068
Amarillo, Texas 79114

The Topographical Locator for Picture Postcard Collectors
George C. Gibbs

If you collect U.S. view cards, you are going to want this book. After giving preliminary information about real photo postcards and a section on the "Adventures of a Post Card Sleuth," author George C. Gibbs launches into page after page (eighty-four of them in all) of U.S. post offices. The print is quite small, which is something of a distraction, but a good magnifying glass will alleviate this inconvenience. The important thing is that this book allows the viewer to match his postcard postmarks with the locations.

This list is very thorough and exhaustive. This is a book that should be purchased while it is still available. That may not be for long.

Available from:

George C. Gibbs
P.O. Box 614
Syracuse, New York 13201

Calvin Coolidge, A Biography in Picture Postcards
J. R. Greene

J. R. Greene has demonstrated the political utility of the lowly postcard with this book. With their assistance, he has presented the reader with a visual portrait of America's 30th president. This in turn has opened several windows from which Calvin Coolidge may be viewed from different perspectives.

Combined with the obligatory postcards of residences, institutions, and government buildings that form a mosaic surrounding the ex-president's life are many pictures of Coolidge the man. In them, Coolidge is seen as a family man, Massachusetts governor, man of the soil, friend of the famous, and, finally, president. Unfortunately, all the cards are illustrated in black and white. This has the beneficial effect of keeping the price of the book at a modest level, but the worth of such a trade-off might be questionable.

Regardless, *Calvin Coolidge, A Biography in Picture Postcards* is an educational tool for examining a man who was undoubtedly a more complex individual than many people may at first think. Especially helpful in this connection is a section at the end of the book where Greene identifies and analyzes several books that were written either about President Coolidge or that have material about him in their pages. For students of presidential history this section by itself is almost worth the price of the book.

Available from:

> J. R. Greene
> 33 Bearsden Road
> Athol, Massachusetts 01331

The Canadian Patriotic Post Card Handbook: 1900–1914
W. L. Gutzman

No postcard book has ever been the last word on the subject. None ever will be. But W. L. Gutzman's book is an honest effort—and a good one in the bargain—on the topic of Canadian patriotic postcards. More than ninety percent of the almost 120 postcard illustrations are in color. Most are also very close to actual size.

A recognized authority on Canadian postcards, Gutzman gives his readers an in-depth accounting of the various types within this category that he has chosen to illuminate. Under each picture is a listing of the individual cards with each particular set or series. This is itself prefaced by the following information: a) address side type, b) period of use, c) coloring, and d) rarity factor.

There is no guesswork left to the reader's imagination, and though the author may not have covered all the types, he has certainly described the bulk of them and added a much-needed piece of scholarship

to the postcard collecting community.

Available from:

> The Unitrade Press
> P.O. Box 172, Station A
> Toronto, Ontario M5W 1B2
> Canada

The Canadian Picture Post Card Catalogue 1988
W. L. Gutzman

The reason this volume is grouped with the books rather than with the catalogues is because it is a research effort rather than merely a lotting of postcards with estimated values. W. L. Gutzman is too much of a researcher to be satisfied with the latter role.

His first order of business is to list and define seven periods of Canadian postcard manufacture. They bridge the era distance from 1871 to the present. The categories listed and explored include topics from advertising to stamp and coin cards, with a multiplicity of ones in between. A lettered and numbered system precedes the prices, which reflect popularity rather than rarity or availability. Gutzman knows his country's postcards as well, if not better and more thoroughly, than anyone else, and he feels comfortable in discussing and pricing them.

The Canadian Picture Post Card Catalogue 1988 is excellent resource material on a too-little-explored area.

Available from:

> The Unitrade Press
> P.O. Box 172, Station A
> Toronto, Ontario M5W 1B2
> Canada

R & B Stars of 1953
Galen Hart

You may not remember Louis Jordon or The Clovers. You may not have heard of the more famous Johnny Ace or of Earl Bostic. But your knowledge—or lack of it—does not detract from the fact that these folks were very much a part of the 1950s American music scene.

They were black entertainers performing black music, which became in time not black but American music. These thirty-six color postcards show the various artists in their prime, and a listing of their songs is included with each picture. Ever hear "Crawlin' King Snake," "Going To the River," "Crying and Walking"? Maybe you know the singers of these songs: Pee Wee Crayton, John Lee Hooker, and Fats Domino.

These people bridged the gap between Tommy Dorsey and Elvis Presley. They were a bit like both but were in most ways very much their own kind of musicians and entertainers. They entered the American culture and enriched it with their music and their presence. It is easy to be thankful for their contributions, but it is more important to acknowledge them with a bouquet of remembrances from time to time.

That is what this book does.

Available from:

Big Nickel Publications
P.O. Box 157
Milford, New Hampshire 03055

Postmarks on Postcards
Richard W. Helbock

Ever wonder what a "flag cancel" is or how they came into being? Do you know the difference between RPO and RFD? Can you identify a "killer bar design"?

Wonder and muse no more. For these and other—dozens of other—bits of information about postmarks and cancellations are given in Richard Helbock's *Postmarks on Postcards*. A postmark expert of long-standing and much repute, Helbock has written numerous articles and authored several other books on the topic.

Helbock himself would be the first to admit that the book is hardly definitive. That kind of a book would require 2,000 pages, not Helbock's 250. But what the author does do is to illustrate and discuss the major—and some of the minor—types of postmarks that the average collector is certain to encounter with some frequency.

Helbock has divided his book into two major sections, each of which is subdivided into multiple bold-faced-type headings. Section one is entitled "The Postmarks" and goes about the business of simplifying the complex maze of duplexes, doanes, bars, mimics, and the like. Section two has the title "Collecting Postmarks" and explains RFD and RPO markings, armed services postmarks, postmarks related to special occasions, and more.

This is not a book that may be absorbed in one reading, a quality it shares with other good postcard books. What it is is a book that has been long looked for and much needed. No wonder it is in its second printing in less than six months after its original release.

Available from:

La Posta Publications
P.O. Box 135
Lake Oswego, Oregon 97034

Greetings from Southern California
Monica Highland

Monica Highland has been accurately described as a social historian. She has also—just as correctly—been identified as someone who knows the California landscape and something about California traditions. In *Greetings from Southern California,* Highland brings all her talents and knowledge to bear on her favorite state, a California that many people may have only thought they knew.

Highland herself not only knows the state but she communicates that knowledge in an interesting, upbeat style, a style that contains some overtones of the down-home and folksy, too. We are given information about turn-of-the-century California, 1930s California, the war years in California and beyond. We are offered language that tells us of the people: working Californians, relaxing Californians, elegant Californians, and their more pedestrian neighbors and fellow citizens. Talked about are locations and events, people and places.

But the best, as the old carnival pitchman might have intoned, is yet to come, for bolstering and enhancing the prose, enlivening and detailing and defining it are approximately 275 beautiful, full-color picture postcards covering the period circa 1900–1950. They present views of handsome old hotels, some of them with their facades resplendently columned, their terraces and lawns flushed with gorgeous flora of every description.

There are pictures of amusement parks, of panoramic beaches stretching into yellow-orange sunsets. There are horses and buggies and the newfangled horseless carriages meandering down early twentieth century dirt main streets. There are parks and amusement centers, sailing yachts, and battleships. There are bird's-eye views of metropolitan areas, views of coves and caverns that adjoin the picturesque oceanside, each begging to be explored. There are streetcars and trains, ferries and carnival rides. There are scenes of people waterskiing while they wave to overhead cameras; sun lovers on the sand, their unfolded umbrellas protecting them against their own passions. Hot-air balloons float overhead, while underneath, tourists gaze in wonder both up and down as they sail the glass-bottom boats plying the coastal waters.

Not to go unremembered, there are views of California desert cactus and glimpses of inland—and desert—palm trees. There are Catholic missions, each with its distinct identity. There are oranges at a mere fifty cents a box, and there are gigantic watermelons and strawberries. There are fields of onions, the white tops of which salute the mild California breezes. There is oil, or rather, oil wells, their wooden derricks corrupting the otherwise pristine landscape.

Highland concludes, as well she should, with a section entitled "Celebrations and Revelries." California is a state of proud traditions, and it exhibits its pride of those traditions with festivals, fetes, and parades of every imaginable type. It has even sponsored an exposition or two, all with typical California flamboyance and color, thoroughness and beauty. Highland shows that it is relatively simple to wind up when thinking of all that California has to offer—but how does one wind down?

Progress and preservation. The past and the future. *Greetings from Southern California* is not only these things but also an amorphous view of the West Coast. It is a pictorial study of what is right about America, what is great about it. It suggests what needs to be examined and retained, what needs to be adopted and borrowed from.

And you thought California was only fantasy as seen through a Hollywood filmmaker's lens.

For shame.

Available from:

Graphic Arts Center Publishing Company
P.O. Box 10306
Portland, Oregon 97210

Antique Santa Post Cards, Volume I;
Antique Santa Post Cards, Volume II
(27 Detachable Cards, Each Book)
Hobby House Press

Most children have a favorite image of Santa Claus. For many of them in the United States, the overstuffed,

red-suited fellow at Macy's Department Store or in a thousand and one other stores across America is the man they recognize. We all know him. White beard, ready smile, a bag of goodies somewhere close to hand.

Antique Santa Post Cards, volumes I & II give us multiple examples of the fellow—and not just the man described above. There are Santas in black suits and Santa on his sleigh or driving a car. There he is coming down the chimney, riding a hobby horse, bobsledding on a carpet, even descending beneath a helium-filled balloon. Always within sight are toys, toys of every variety for every variety of child.

What's your favorite Santa.

Available from:

Hobby House Press
900 Frederick Street
Cumberland, Maryland 21502

Antique Teddy Bears Post Cards, Volume I;
Antique Teddy Bears Post Cards, Volume II
(27 Detachable Cards, Each Book)
Hobby House Press

No, you are not seeing double. You are just being given more variety. These books use the postcards of Patricia Schoonmaker and those of Beverly Port. Both sets of cards are fanciful, both delightful.

Is teddy at it again? Well, yes. And what a list of roles he/she fulfills. There is teddy cradling a doll; there is papa teddy and teddy friend sleighing down a hillside; momma teddy waving goodbye to hubby as he goes off to make the family's living. There she is again, with umbrella on the beach as she watches junior teddy cavorting in the ocean. There are momma, papa, and junior together examining their empty bowls, unaware that a golden-haired girl slumbers in one of their beds. And—how did that get in there?—a genuine stuffed teddy being read a bedtime story by a pajamad little girl sitting in front of an open fireplace.

Is there more? Sure is.

Available from:

Hobby House Press
900 Frederick Street
Cumberland, Maryland 21502

Old Teddy Bear Post Cards, Volume I;
Old Teddy Bear Post Cards, Volume II
(27 Detachable Cards, Each Book)
Hobby House Press

Teddy bears are cute, little inanimate objects. This is the standard line, and it's true enough. They are likely to be found propped up at a forty-five degree angle against a pillow or carried under the arm of a three-year-old girl, their own limbs stiffly outstanding. Well, if that is your conception of the furry fellow—or female—get set to rearrange the imagination. Just a bit, anyway.

These books show the viewer a slightly different series of vignettes. How about teddy on his knees, proposing marriage to his lady fair? Or a mother teddy preparing the bath for a disgruntled golliwog? Better still is a picture of young teddies roughhousing one another. There's a postal employee teddy delivering the mail; a teddy teacher addressing her bear charges; and even a Piccadilly teddy complete with glass eye.

Available from:

Hobby House Press
900 Frederick Street
Cumberland, Maryland 21502

Victorian Children Post Cards
(35 Detachable Cards, Sepia Toned)
Hobby House Press

These real photo reproductions should be labeled "Victorian Girls and Their Dolls." Yes, there are a couple of boys, almost camouflaged, but they are merely the garnish, the window dressing. Nope, the standard fare here is young girls with long tresses and longer dresses. The range of emotions and feelings portrayed on their adorable faces span the spectrum from pensive and uncertain to proud and pleased. Make no mistake. These are real children captured by a real camera, frozen in time in real settings.

Interestingly, even their dolls are well and fully attired, a concession to the times—and to good taste as well.

A woman might use the word "precious" to describe these pictures. Even a man, crude creature that he is, would know why the term was applied and why

it was appropriate. He might, if caught in secret, agree to its usage.

Available from:

Hobby House Press
900 Frederick Street
Cumberland, Maryland 21502

I'll Be Seeing You: Picture Postcards of
World War II
Tonie and Valmai Holt

Collectors of military postcards are never more pleased than when another book on the topic is added to the few that exist. However, one need not be a collector of militaria to welcome the publication of Tonie and Valmai Holt's new title on the postcards of World War II. The Holts are recognized authorities on both history and postcards, and they bring both these bodies of expertise to bear in *I'll Be Seeing You, Picture Postcards of World War II.*

Measuring a full 9-1/2 × 12″, the hardcover volume has 192 finely papered pages of illustrations and information. Moreover, the Holts have done their homework and know their subject well. Each of the eleven chapters deals with a separate aspect of the war. "Machines in the Air," "Machines on the Land," and "Machines at Sea" are three of them; others include "Patriotism, Propaganda and Sentiment," "The Men," and "The Nazis." There is even a chapter entitled "Humorous," and it, like the others, is most enlightening and rewarding.

Rather than spending time and space on a lot of dry exposition, the authors have used the prose sparingly on chapter introductions and committed the bulk of the wording to detailed descriptions of the hundreds of postcards with which they generously filled the book. Many are in vibrant color, reproduced large enough to elicit the reader's appreciation. Some of the illustrations are outsized, and the effect is striking. The only flaw, a small one, is that the authors' knowledge of American military postcards is less than complete. A few of the cards are valued somewhat higher than one normally sees them priced, and there are a number of U.S. sets and series that are omitted.

But these are minor complaints. The fact is that the Holts have once more presented the postcard community with a volume of undisguised merit. It is exciting, inclusive, well researched, and universal in its scope.

Available from:

Moorland Publishing Company
Moor Farm Road, Airfield Estate
Ashbourne, Derbyshire DE6 1HD
England

Cricket on Old Picture Postcards
Grenville Jennings

Americans adore baseball, Germans love soccer, and Englishmen are passionate about cricket. Or, at least, they were. Now, of course, there are the annual antics at Wimbledon, perhaps the only spot on earth where another British passion, tennis, is seen as more than a game that requires two hours, more or less, to play.

But, then, the British have always been a serious lot, and this attribute is certainly known to carry over into the sporting arena from time to time. In his book *Cricket on Old Picture Postcards,* Grenville Jennings illustrates card after interesting card of cricket teams, cricket champions, and cricket matches. An aesthetically appealing colored section shows a series of artist-drawn cards that poke fun at both the sport and its participants.

Still, it ought to be acknowledged that, during the early decades of this century, cricket was a game of determination, unflagging effort, and a high measure of precision. And, for the most part, this is how it was viewed. It is difficult to view these cards without feeling both the intensity and the pride that the game has engendered among its players. Grammar school teams, college teams, local teams, national teams: all played the game with intensity, if not always with panache and artistry. The captions accompanying Jennings's illustrations offer more than a mere dry recitation of facts but are often worded in such a way as to emphasize the loyalty and dedication that cricket exacts from its participants.

Available from:

Reflections of a Bygone Age
15 Debdale Lane
Keyworth
Nottingham NG12 5HT
England

Mail Memories: Pictorial Guide to Postcard Collecting
John Kaduck

Mail Memories was John Kaduck's first postcard book, and it set the tone for the four more that were to follow. The focus then and later was on the postcards rather than on the prose.

Kaduck is to be commended for using this format since his books are primarily guides for postcard novices or for those who want to know more about the hobby. The author shows them with 1,500 black-and-white illustrations divided into categories, such as political, military, royalty, greetings, pretty women, transportation, ships, advertising, humorous, children, and more. A miscellaneous section concludes the volume, and it is here that one begins to develop an appreciation for the incredible diversity of things revealed on picture postcards.

Mail Memories is a postcard classic from a true pioneer in the field.

Rare and Expensive Postcards, Book I
John Kaduck

Anyone who has ever met John Kaduck can tell you that he is an amusing, agreeable fellow. One supposes that a number of years as a public school teacher, where humor is necessary for warding off the daily frustrations of that particular job, may have something to do with his attitude.

Rare and Expensive Postcards, Book I, is only one of the many books Kaduck has prepared on antiques and collectibles. Though the book makes no pretensions to either scholarship or thoroughness, it is evident that the author has considerable knowledge of his chosen topic. Any collector would be well served by examining it repeatedly. Written more for the novice than the more advanced student of deltiology, the book is also clearly helpful to the latter group of individuals as well. In fact, regardless of how large a body of expertise one garners, the field is much too broad for any one person to master.

Most of us must therefore keep looking and checking and comparing and verifying. The hundreds of illustrations pictured here—including an eight-page color section—are a great resource for this.

The book is also good merely for looking purposes. In true Kaduck style, the author uses his prose sparingly, giving us more delightful illustrations instead. Most of them speak their own language.

Among the categories into which he has divided the book are the following: pioneers, advertising, Art Nouveau, automobiles, exposition, Hitler and company, hold to lights, Indian chiefs, large letters, mechanicals, sports, territorial, and many, many more. Some books are a must read; this one is a must see.

Available from:

Wallace-Homestead Book Co.
Radnor, Pennsylvania 19089

Rare and Expensive Postcards, Book II
John Kaduck

Everything written about John Kaduck's *Rare and Expensive Postcards, Book I,* could be repeated for this volume. One additional comment that might be made is that Kaduck obviously sharpened his already-keen eye for good postcard material.

For *Book II,* besides being—as with *Book I*—a dandy resource for novice and advanced collector's alike, is even superior to its predecessor in the area of specialization. Deserving mention in this regard are the sections on elves, religion, propaganda, patriotic embroidery, fantasy, and dolls.

Access to the postcards of some well-known collectors produced the specimens that grace the pages of the book. It has an eight-page color section in which are reproduced some seldom-seen and gorgeous picture postcards.

Like lightening, Kaduck has struck again.

Transportation Postcards
John Kaduck

Transportation Postcards is out of print. That's the bad news. The next news is even worse: It probably won't be reprinted.

A good suggestion for anyone interested in these types of postcards is to try the secondary market. This is one book certainly worth the effort it takes to locate it. John Kaduck has illustrated several hundred (seven hundred, to be exact) postcards that show almost every kind and type of transport imaginable.

Besides the more conventional automobiles and trucks, there are motorcycles, airplanes, dirigibles and miscellaneous balloon-type aircraft, tractors, farm steam engines and other rural machines, trains, buses, horse-drawn conveyances of all descriptions, fire engines, ships, electric traction cars, buggies, and unusual means of transportation. There are also many views of wrecks.

What Kaduck has omitted is hardly worth mentioning. What he has pictured are vehicles that man has used to take him from where he was to where he wanted to go.

This is quite a book. Ride, anyone?

Wish You Were Here—Post Card Remembrances of a Bygone Day
Jack Kelbaugh

Here are several series of blue-gray view cards of the Chesapeake Bay country. Four hundred, all told. Each is a memory in itself, a story unfolding, with more waiting to be told or perhaps a series of stories waiting to be explored.

Boats, canals, street scenes, amusement parks, famous landmarks, lighthouses, state capitols. The postcards are reproduced full-sized, and that is a plus since the blue-tone images otherwise leave something to be desired. The views themselves are a different matter. It doesn't seem to make much difference how many old postcard views one sees, it's hard not to become nostalgic and at least a bit wistful.

Wish You Were Here not only adds to the storehouse of historical information, it also entertains in the process.

John Bull's Famous Circus
John Killen

The political woes of Ireland have represented an ongoing, centuries-old affair, or so it seems. And, in this case, it seems correctly.

Television sets the world over bring pictures of bombings, shootings, and riot activity taking place on the Emerald Isle. The issues of the antagonists have become much too complex to be treated in less than intelligent fashion. Popular slogans, impromptu songs and chants, and placards carried by street demonstrators are too simplistic, except as gestures of frustration and intense focus, to explain what is going on and why.

Into this chasm of misunderstanding, this black hole of misinformation and prejudice, steps the picture postcard, resolutely proclaiming its message. Actually, its messages. Standing unafraid, the postcard becomes once more what it has ever been: a tool for exploitation and a mirror on the world.

In John Killen's book *John Bull's Famous Circus* (a most significant title), the author has shown the extraordinary political, patriotic, and propagandic use to which the postcard may be put. Subtitled ''Ulster History Through the Postcard, 1905–1985,'' the book is a strong indictment against repressive, oppressive, and violent undertakings, or at least those that take place under the British flag. This, of course, is the crux of the current dilemma: Who is oppressing whom and to what end(s)?

The cards' messages are humorous, anecdotal, quixotic, or given to easy solutions, suggesting that there are no solutions. Cartoons, political candidates and campaigns, street riots, scenics demonstrating unity, pictures that focused on determination, views of consequences: Ireland has been ravaged, and the postcard was there to record the feelings, the disappointments, the frustrations, the never-ending aftermaths. Posterity should be grateful even though it will learn little from the visual lessons.

So here it is, and though there is an accompanying text, and it is a decent one, it seems almost superfluous after viewing the postcards.

The author concludes this most interesting volume with Appendix A, which lists and offers a biographical sketch of each artist and illustration, and Appendix B, which lists all the publishers and their offerings to date.

Is this book likely to change anyone's mind? Doubtful. But it certainly will help define the passions. Even more importantly, *John Bull's Famous Circus* is an excellent book about a specific category of postcards; in a more significant sense, it is a great book as a guide for others who may want to produce a like tome. It is hoped that Killen's format may guide them with their enterprises.

Available from:

Irish Books and Media
2115 Summit Avenue, Box 5026
Saint Paul, Minnesota 55105

The World's Tackiest Postcards
Klutz Press

Whew.

I mean, well . . .

Let me put it this way: Those who do not believe that a book's title says all there is to say about the book's contents have never examined *The World's Tackiest Postcards*.

Real photos of rabbits with antlers and a picture of a cowboy biting his horse are a few of the more innocuous postcards illustrated in this book. No text is given, and none, absolutely none, is needed. Klutz Press must have spent a considerable amount of time coming up with this jewel. Pigs diving in perfect form; a smiling family preparing to consume their TV dinners; a giant fish about to take a bite out of a fisherman bent over in his boat—and all this in glorious living color.

The news gets better: *Son of Tacky* is reported to be on its way. Keep those _____ and letters coming.

Available from:

Klutz Press
2170 Staunton Court
Palo Alto, California 94306

Picture Postcards of Cyprus 1899–1930
Stavros Lazarides

Tipping one's hat as a sign of deference and respect was one of man's finer practices. This writer wishes to reinstitute it, at least for this occasion, as it is tipped in the direction of Stavros G. Lazarides.

What Lazarides has done that deserves such special meritorious treatment is to undertake the considerable effort and time that was needed to produce this book. The volume does have its shortcomings, mind you. It has no color illustrations, contains no index, and does not have a table of contents. This last is the most difficult problem initially as it forces the reader to discover for himself or herself just how the text is organized and presented.

Yet these are really minor distractions, for the truth is that the author has given his readers in particular and the postcard community in general an excellent research work in a little-known area of postcard concentration: the postcards of Cyprus. Besides the many postcard illustrations all reproduced actual size is a lengthy section on Cypriot postcard publishers, each one of the gentlemen photographed and discussed at length. This is a first in postcard research. The section that follows is entitled "Selected Postcards," and it is clear that Lazarides knew exactly which cards to select. Close-up city views, museums, monasteries, points of interest, the Cypriot countryside, the citizenry of various localities, views from the Mediterranean, hotels: one cannot examine them without learning a good deal about the country and in some sense almost having a feeling of being there.

The text is printed in both Greek and English, a concession that is certainly welcome to the non-Greek speaking world. The final section illustrates page after page of postcard backs, and each is described and lengthy lists are provided where necessary.

Picture Postcards of Cyprus represents years of exhaustive research, and it should not go unnoticed that the author has presented the results of this research in highly readable, entertaining prose.

Available from:

Stavros G. Lazarides
P.O. Box 75107
Kallithea
Greece 9354439

Postcard Collecting, a Beginner's Guide
Brian Lund

Purchasing this book will be the wisest dollar any postcard collector has ever spent. First, what this book is not. It is not thorough, not comprehensive, not voluminous. Now, what it is. It is a quick, practical examination of why postcard collecting is so popular, how someone may choose what to collect from the wide variety of categories and types available, how to start, and where to buy.

There are paragraphs about postcard condition, about how to win at fairs, how to get a good deal from approvals, how to house your collection, how to extend your contacts, how to keep a checklist on them, and much more. Brian Lund concludes with a glossary of postcard terms, samples of recent issues, and a section entitled "How Much Should You Pay for Picture Postcards?" which is a brief analysis of several card categories. In between are enough examples to illustrate the many kinds of cards under examination.

What more may one reasonably expect for a dollar?

Available from:

Reflections of a Bygone Age
15 Debdale Lane
Keyworth
Nottingham NG12 5HT
England

Edwardian Childhood on Old Picture Postcards
Brian Lund and Mary Lund

As a rule, most reviewers do not openly endorse the purchase of a book they are reviewing. Their professional integrity and objectivity are said to be at risk should they do otherwise.

This writer would like to break out of that artificially created mold, at least insofar as this book is concerned. The reasons for this action are essentially twofold. First—and perhaps most importantly—the proceeds from *Edwardian Childhood on Old Picture Postcards* is being donated to children's charities: the first two thousand pounds sterling to "Smile, Don't Stare," which helps the disabled children in Nottingham, England; the rest to the British Broadcasting Corporation's "Children in Need" appeal.

This is enough reason by itself for the emptying of the pockets, but there is another fact that must be considered and that is embodied between the pages: this book is, beyond doubt, the best postcard volume ever to be devoted to the subject of children. There are others in which children are the focal point, but in them they are portrayed as either whimsical or humorous.

Edwardian Childhood is more sobering and ultimately more in touch with reality. Does this mean that the book is somber and depressing? Hardly. But it is a nice-sized slice of the real world, accurately portraying England's youth during the first decade of the twentieth century.

There are children in school and children at play; children riding trams and children as part of the montage making up a busy street scene; there are children in parades and children at the circus. There are scouting children and singing children. There are also children at work, a not uncommon scene the world over during the early to middle part of this century, when all able bodies, especially poor ones, were required to help support the family.

In the main, these are postcard views of innocence, the uncrustiness of not knowing what life held in store. Tomorrow they will be soldiers and coal workers, civil servants and shop owners.

For today, or rather the today of long ago, they are children, young people whose dreams and aspirations make even our hearts hurt. At least a little.

Buy the book.

Available from:

Reflections of a Bygone Age
15 Debdale Lane
Keyworth
Nottingham NG12 5HT
England

Greetings from Jamestown, Rhode Island
Sue Maden

Local historian and author Sue Maden knows more than a little about the town in which she lives. To her credit and our delight, Maden has sought to share her knowledge in this book, which both tells and shows its readers what Jamestown, Rhode Island, was and is all about.

Subtitled *Picture Post Card Views 1900–1950*, the book is easy, interesting reading and has informative pictorial comment. The postcards are all printed in sepia tone, outlined in such a way as to present an eye-catching three-dimensional effect. The cover is laminated and the paper used is acid free, alum free and rosin free. In short, this book was created to be a lasting showpiece.

Maden's prose accompanies the postcard illustrations and it is here that the reader will notice the book's only defect, which is a minor one. Although there is a wealth of detail offered with some of the illustrations, many others do not enjoy similar elaboration, which would further enhance what is unquestionably a historically significant book. That aside, it is the viewer who is the real winner. Readers will treat themselves as often as they like to views of a New England town which is at once both old and new, quaint and progressive, loaded with tradition yet preparing for tomorrow.

The views, while seemingly frozen in time, also represent a transition from one era to another, from one mindset to a different one. Maden shows the reader that the past may haunt and entertain us simultaneously. There is a wistfulness at work here, a wistfulness which indicates that—at least in part—we can be, and are, what we were.

Available from:

Sue Maden
West Ferry Press
P.O. Box 154
Jamestown, Rhode Island 02835

A Book of Postcards from a Century of Illustrations, 1880–1910
Madison Square Press

What we have here are thirty-two detachable postcard reproductions of the work of some of America's greatest illustrators. If you don't recognize a good many of these illustrators, at least by name, you've probably never been to an art museum.

Here in lavishly realistic color are the works of Gibson and Remington, Farny and Pyle, Bradley and Nast. And more. It's said that America is a land "from sea to shining sea." These postcards show what lies between these waters: the people, the customs, the events. That's a decent achievement for an art book.

Available from:

Madison Square Press
10 East 23rd Street
New York, New York 10010

Liberty, A Centennial History of the Statue of Liberty in Post Cards
Madison Square Press

Whatever is said about this book probably won't be enough. Not if you're an American, anyway. Of course, one need not be an American to revel in the beautiful artwork or get lost in the unashamed symbolism. Thirty-two detachable cards, but where is the uncultured buffoon who would mail these lovelies? Perhaps that should be phrased a little differently: The mailee would have to be a very close friend to justify the sender taking leave of these specimens.

Let us begin a casual checklist. There are cards of the statue's construction, scrolls and certificates related to it, magazine covers displaying it, scenes of it by night with fireworks going off in its background, representations of it as defender, as provider, as a seller of products; views of what it purports to represent, of the visions it offers, of its future; postcards of its commanding presence. What these cards tell us is that the Statue of Liberty was designed to be the physical embodiment of Freedom, Opportunity, Justice, and Peace. Many think it still stands for these things and that the country in which it rests strives to perpetuate them.

She's a grand lady.

Available from:

Madison Square Press
10 East 23rd Street
New York, New York 10010

40 Antique Postcards of Santa Claus
Madison Square Press

This book of postcard facsimilies, ready for detaching and mailing, is subtitled "His Life and Legend." And well it should be.

One would have to be very eclectic not to find every image of Santa Claus found in this book to be fascinating by itself. There are American Santas and German Santas, East European Santas, and even Russian Santas. Each is colored, embossed, and finely detailed. Obviously, the world has come a long way from commemorating Christmas as the birth of Christ to Christmas as commercial holiday. There may be blame laid here and there for this greed and nonsense, but little of it, at least in the primary sense, may be laid at Santa's doorstep. The white beard and the kindly, crinkled eyes have always stood for giving and for sharing.

Madison Square Press offers us a book that re-creates the simple credo, "It is better to give than to receive." Nice message.

Available from:

Madison Square Press
10 East 23rd Street
New York, New York 10010

A Pennsylvania Album: Picture Postcards, 1900–1930
George Miller

George Miller is less a man with a point of view than he is a man with several of them. Points of view, that is. Or perhaps they are just views, as in picture postcards.

A Pennsylvania Album is proof of the thesis. The word evocative may be an overused one, but it certainly applies here. From the postcard portraits, it is obvious that Pennsylvania could be Anyplace, America. The views are all such familiar ones while at the same time being so very rare. Railroad engines, once luxurious hotels, metal-encased cars and trucks, deserted small-town street scenes, dirt roads, glimpses of wooden sidewalks.

Pictures like these should not be limited to only a thousand words.

Miller shows us Gramps in his prime; ankle-length dresses that were more than fashionable—they were elegant; he gives us old theaters, days at the beach, substantial church facades, ballparks, restaurants, celebrations, and special occasions. He pictures men at work when work was not a four-letter word.

What Miller has not given us is a series of meaningless vignettes. Instead, he offers bread at five cents a loaf and ten cents a pound beefsteak. Baggy pants and fedoras. Idyllic Sunday afternoons with a picnic basket.

Franklin Roosevelt's New Deal put us back on our feet.

George Miller takes us back to a time before we fell off of them.

Available from:

The Pennsylvania State University Press
University Park, Pa.

Collecting Postcards in Color, 1914–1930
Valerie Monahan

The coauthor with William Duval of *Collecting Postcards in Color, 1894–1914*, Valerie Monahan wrote this volume entirely on her own. In some ways, it is superior to the earlier book; in other ways, it suffers by comparison.

It ought to be noted in the beginning that the words "in color" are a bit disingenuous as a good many of the postcards are reproduced in black and white. It should also be observed that some of the features of the previous volume are omitted here. The book is also in paperback rather than hardcover, as was its predecessor.

But the book does have pluses. The biographies on a number of postcard artists are a commendable addition. So too is the implementation of prices to accompany the illustration descriptions. There is a most interesting year-by-year accounting of important events during the decade of the 1920s. This is a particularly pertinent feature as numerous postcards were produced that related to a number of these events.

The descriptions themselves reveal that such categories as advertising, humor, military, glamour, views, Art Deco, and much more are presented for inspection. Their handsomeness almost dispels the fact that the emphasis is primarily on British material.

Postcard clubs and dealers and even an American source of postcards are among the listings.

Prairie Fires and Paper Moons: The American Photographic Postcard, 1902–1920
Hal Morgan and Andreas Brown

It's time to pick up the thesaurus and brush the dust off the accolades. Seldom has this writer been so excited about a postcard book—not that he hasn't seen some good ones in his time and not that he won't see more.

But *Prairie Fires and Paper Moons* is something special, something on the order of an ice-cold glass of tea after a hard day of laboring in the fields. A little description is called for.

Hal Morgan and Andreas Brown (of Gotham Book Mart fame) have put their heads together to good effect here. Not one of the dozens of photographic postcards that they display are less than interesting. Most are more; some are absolutely striking. What they represent is what they present: the diversity of America, its sanity, its absurdity, its pithiness, its humor, its celebrations, its preoccupations and fascinations, its workers, its individuality, its entertainment and foibles, its sense of community. These are views of this and that in the days when this and that was worth more and more.

Prairie Fires and Paper Moons is America as it was and occasionally—although rarely—still is. We're a good people and strange. We're a mixture of the best that humanity has to offer and are tainted with a bit of

the terminally ugly from time to time. So what? You can't see this book without being proud to be an American. It also makes you wonder about the ingredients that are necessary to make an American.

Who said you had to go to a museum to see pictures that make you think?

Teddy Bears on Paper
Susan Brown Nicholson

Ever since their invention, teddy bears have always been immensely popular. They have been made into stuffed animals, portrayed in cartoon strips, represented on postcards, become part of valentine designs, used in advertisements, and used in cutouts.

Susan Nicholson, well-known postcard researcher, has shown all these and more in *Teddy Bears on Paper*. This 127-page, hardcovered, finely papered volume contains one exciting picture after another. Beginning with a history lesson on the teddy bear and the story of Theodore Roosevelt, sometime ''Rough Rider'' and U.S. president, Nicholson proceeds to illustrate and define the paper reminders of these wondrous creatures. She covers all the items listed above and also includes paper dolls, sheet music, and other paper ''teddies.''

The illustrations are about evenly divided between black and white and color, but all are reproduced with attention to detail. For the postcard enthusiast, there is information about artists, publishers, sets, and series. The chapter on novelty postcards was particularly enlightening and intriguing. So also was the section dealing with valentines.

Actually, none of the book is less than interesting. Be warned: Reading one page leads to reading another.

Available from:

Taylor Publishing Company
1550 West Mockingbird Lane
Dallas, Texas 75221

The Opera House Album
Charles Osborne

Were the postcards themselves to be illustrated without comment or explanation, *The Opera House Album* would still be a book worth possessing. Reminders of a world rapidly disappearing (for all intents and purposes, already gone), the pictures of these old European theaters serve as pleasant history lessons. Even in sepia tone, the memories are there to be felt. Among the images are visual representations of Vienna's old Cafe Society, views that relate to the Old World generally.

Each card is illustrated on the page to the right and the descriptive information covers the page to the left. Looking at the pictures puts the viewer in the frame of mind in which he or she may imagine being present during the ballets, the operas, and the dramas. But there was an array of delights. In some of the houses, dancing was standard fare; in others, symphony music suitable for sitting and listening to was commonplace.

Charles Osborne has both a feel for the subject and no small amount of knowledge about it. In *The Opera House Album,* he shares a bit of both.

Fantasy Postcards
William Ouellette

William Ouellette, an aficionado of things strange and peculiar (he was one of the original "faces" with the Ugly Model Agency), has decided to share part of his mesmerizing postcard collection in this book.

Fantasy Postcards is both a book title and an umbrella designation. Under its canopy, Ouellette has placed and illustrated puzzle-type cards, animals in human clothing, ladies' faces in bubbles, babies in large letters, city views in pickles or sausages, installment cards, beautiful women emerging from eggs, rabbits driving automobiles, multiple babies in unusual settings taking part in sometimes strange activities, flying fish with humans atop them, human freaks and oddities.

Some of these cards are considered to represent categories of their own: metamorphics, humorous, romantic, posed silliness, and others. But no matter. Ouellette has given the postcards a chance to feed his imagination, and ours as well. Strange little things they are. Amusing, too. Once you take the time to figure them out—if such a thing is possible—you may not be sure whether they are entertaining or if they are suggestive or if they are irritating.

They're all three.

Landmark Hawaii, Favorite Postcard Views of the Islands
Douglas Peebles

If it's all you can do to resist the urge to go on a Hawaiian vacation after seeing the television commercials promoting America's fiftieth state, then please be advised to avoid this book at all costs. If you are leaning, it will certainly push you over the edge and deep into the azure waters of the Hawaiian Islands.

Two minutes alone with the modern picture postcards in this book will satisfy any lingering doubts concerning Hawaii's appeal. No wonder Hawaii was granted statehood. America wanted a paradise that only a loving God could have created for His children.

Hawaii has it all, the postcards scream.

They are probably right. Now, if they can just get rid of all those hotels.

Available from:

Mutual Publishing of Honolulu
2055 North King Street, Suite 201
Honolulu, Hawaii 96819

World War II Military Comics
Gilbert Pittman and Roberta Greiner

Whereas the postcards of World War I were devoted to propaganda, patriotism, destruction views, and battle scenics—with a fair-sized selection of humorous issues—the postcards of World War II were weighted heavily in favor of the comic element. This was especially the case with the American postcards. The Germans and Italians took a different tact; they were kept busy churning out one propaganda and patriotic card after another, which is not to be surprised as this type of activity always seems to be the prevailing situation with aggressor nations who never tire of glorifying themselves in the eyes of their citizenry.

But America is the land of Huck Finn and Tom Sawyer, a nation peopled with the sort of folk who can manufacture a bit of homespun humor even in the worst of predicaments. Is it any wonder that America produced both Samuel Clemens and Will Rogers? Could either of them have been raised anywhere else?

Gilbert Pittman and Roberta Greiner have joined their efforts to produce this checklist of the publishers and titles of America's World War II comic postcards. The list is not a complete one but is a commendable effort nonetheless. Certainly all the major sets and series are recorded here, and, in fact, those omitted are only a fraction in comparison to what is included.

They have recorded the issues of E. C. Kropp, Graycraft, Tichnor, the Asheville Post Card Company, and of Mr. Postcard himself, Curt Teich. There are also several entries by little-known publishers. Future updates will eventually make this an exhaustive work.

Available from:

Gilbert Pittman
1903 High Street
Wichita, Kansas 67203

American Advertising Postcards Sets and Series, 1890–1920
The Postcard Lovers

Some books on postcards may be identified and described in a few words. *American Advertising Postcards* is not one of them. Frederic and Mary Megson, who have chosen the pseudonym "The Postcard Lovers" as their mark of identification, have produced a volume without which no postcard library in the world would be complete. Authoritative and factual, the book is terse, wasting little space on unnecessary prose.

That their readers might wish to read a bit of descriptive, perhaps even lively, prose and entertaining text seems to have escaped the Megsons, and it must be observed that the book is the poorer for the omission, but this is merely "window dressing" criticism. The fact is that *American Advertising Postcards* is a deltiological treasure chest. Eighteen hundred different sets of postcards are numbered, lettered, listed, and priced. Each page has several illustrations, and though the postcards are greatly reduced in size, they are still easy to identify—well, relatively easy—and are extremely helpful.

It is to be appreciated that the Megsons do not restrict themselves to easily recognized advertising cards but include those infrequently encountered and some that the more pedestrian collector may never encounter. All the illustrations are in black and white—with the exception of those on the cover—but this is not altogether unpleasant and no doubt served to hold the book's cost to a minimum, as does the small print.

As the book's structure is so well laid out, it would be best to list the sections according to its own format. They include products (by categories), products—department stores (by states), services—entertainment (by categories), services—hotels and restaurants (by states), services—transportation (by categories), and other services (by categories).

Each of the larger designations is broken down by turn into areas, subjects, and geographical regions. Clearly, *American Advertising Postcards* represents many years of research. The appendix seeks to simplify matters further by offering sections with the following headings: abbreviations, glossary, index of publishers, references, arrangement of the data in the entries, and a general index.

The sixteen-page publisher's identification guide is an appreciated informational source that illustrates dozens of publishers' colophons. It is to be hoped that a future edition would be larger and contain bigger illustrations—with many in color—but it must be admitted that this is a book of decided merit and unimpeachable distinction. Agree or disagree with the values given, all are obliged to concur with the judgment that the Megsons have given the postcard world a much-needed volume on a very popular topic.

Available from:

The Postcard Lovers
Box 482
Martinsville, New Jersey 08836

Postcards from Old Kansas City
Mrs. Sam Ray

Mrs. Sam Ray is two things: an historian and a lover of Kansas City. She combines both these aspects of her personhood with her wondrous collection of old picture postcards and creates a little magic.

The magic is this book, fifty-four colored postcards that tell the story of Kansas City during the first two decades of the twentieth century. Close-up views of busy street scenes, luxurious train terminal interiors, fashionable department store exteriors, famous landmarks, hotels, and more. These are pictures of a Kansas City spreading out and growing up, quaint yet becoming modern, old-world charm and new architecture.

These are pictures of the "good old days." Kansas City style, that is.

Postcards from Old Kansas City II
Mrs. Sam Ray

Book I wasn't enough, not by half. Not by more than half. The citizens of Kansas City saw it and clamored for another book. Who can blame them?

The only drawback to this book is that all the cards are not illustrated in color as was the case with Book I. But this is small potatoes as complaints go. Everything else is pluses, the first being the ninety-five postcards, almost double the number of its predecessor. Then there is the extensive fact-filled text. Then the index of illustrations, which is also quite a nice touch.

The center of attention, however, is what it should be: the postcards. For variety and to cover as many areas of early Kansas City life and institutions as possible, the viewer is presented with a divergent range of images. They include Lindbergh standing in front of the Spirit of St. Louis, military monuments, church facades, important personages, sports-related scenics, more main streets, and famous locations.

The best news is that, unlike Book I, this book is still available.

Available from:

> Historic Kansas City Foundation
> 20 West Ninth Street
> Kansas City, Missouri 64105

The Old Raging Erie: A Postcard History of the Erie and Other New York State Canals, 1895–1915
Harry Rinker

If you like canals, this book is for you. If you like picture postcards and are ambivalent about canals, you will discover that this book is still worth a look-see.

Many of the black-and-white postcard illustrations used in *The Old Raging Erie* are reproduced almost double-sized, and the effect is as the author would want it. Locks, canals, busy street scenes running alongside the waterfront are brought into close-up focus, giving the viewer the sense that he or she is eavesdropping on reality rather than merely glancing at a series of picture postcards, however otherwise tantilizing that might be.

The author himself is uniquely qualified to prepare this volume. Founder and past president of the Pennsylvania Canal Society and publisher of Canal Press from 1972 to 1977, Harry L. Rinker is a man with a fascination. Combining that interest with a wealth of knowledge, he created the necessary ingredients for producing *The Old Raging Erie*.

The book is about more than the Erie Canal, though that topic has been a central theme of both songs and literature. It is also about other New York state canals. It is about the towns through which these canals flow. It is also about the times, especially those from 1895 to 1915. It is also about one hundred pages (ninety-six, to be precise).

It is a trip backward, or is it forward, forward to the paradise of yesterday?

Available from:

> Canal Captain's Press
> 103 Dogwood Lane
> Berkeley Heights, New Jersey 07922

Cornell & Ithaca in Postcards
Harvey Roehl

Anyone who has ever been to Ithaca, New York, wants one thing out of life: to go back and see it again.

The highway that leads into the town reveals the rural New York countryside, and it is beautiful. No doubt about that. Dotted with small farms and quaint towns, upstate New York is unsurpassed in natural splendor. Watkins Glen, Seneca Falls, Auburn, the entire Finger Lakes area.

And on and on it goes. In some places and in some ways, parts of it seem untouched—or perhaps the word is uncontaminated—by the ravages of urbanity. It is here that the rustic flavor remains intact, almost aromatic.

Then the road takes a turn to the left, and sharply ahead lies the town of Ithaca, sprawled gloriously in front and then on both sides of the road, the hill cascading down in grandeur to the town or rising in prominence to that bastion of learning, Cornell University. It is the heart and soul of an overused term: panoramic, which means, of course, that it is also breathtaking and exhilarating. The natural waterfall just outside of town, the haughty Victorian-style houses planted along the steep incline at whose top, and to the left, is presented a mixture of old and new. Stores and shops, one atop the other, feed the eyes until the buildings of Cornell come into view.

The town of Ithaca is down the hill, way down the hill, in fact, planted on the hill like a giant nugget adorning a gold mine.

But this goes on too much. The same may not be said of Harvey Roehl's book, *Cornell & Ithaca in Postcards*. Like a master painter at work on his canvas, Roehl offers glimpses, postcard glimpses, of this once and forever beautiful location. Unlike the painter, however, who presents us at last with a completed view and a finished product, Roehl's postcard portraits serve only to tantalize and excite our senses. He knows what anyone who has ever been to Ithaca knows: Ithaca may be shown on postcards, but the essence of what it is must be captured firsthand, on the spot.

When one gets there, he or she should have Roehl's book ready to hand, making comparisons and checking landmarks. In a very real way, *Cornell & Ithaca in Postcards* is less a book about postcards than it is a tribute to what these particular ones portray. Thanks, Harvey. Thanks for the memories.

Available from:

Harvey Roehl
The Vestal Press
P.O. Box 97
Vestal, N.Y. 13850

A Picture Postcard History of New York's Broome County Area
Vestal Press

The first in what is hoped to be a long list of such titles, *A Picture Postcard History of New York's Broome County Area* is a splendid postcard view of early twentieth-century America.

Every one of the black-and-white illustrations are reproduced full-size. The accompanying captions are detailed, informative, and interestingly written. The author knows his subject and depicts the various towns with a loving selection of representative views. Binghamton, Johnson City, Owego, Endicott, and Union, New York, are among the communities thus described and illustrated. Main streets with early forms of transportation, rushing pedestrians, and marvelously quaint old business fronts; school buildings, solid and four-square; magnificent churches with their steeples and spires; elegant hotels where breakfasts worth eating were often served; train stations, post offices, important residences, and much more.

The author has given more than old pictures of old towns. He has shown vignettes of history, views of our ancestry and our roots. Books like this deserve a second look. A long, hard one.

Available from:

The Vestal Press
P.O. Box 97
Vestal, New York 13850

Peerless Princess of the Plains, Postcard Views of Early Wichita
Hal Ross, Hal Ottaway, and Jack Stewart

This book has it all: a quality hardcover with impressive postcards, fine art paper, and detailed descriptions. These are the trademarks of excellence. They are also the description of this book. More than ninety percent of the postcard illustrations are in color, another slice of pleasure.

The topic of the book itself is a fascinating one. Wichita, Kansas, has always been one of the few American towns whose name, as it rolls deliberately off the tongue, does so with the flavor of adventure and more than a little sense of romanticism. Wichita is a cliché for multiple images: wild and untamed, it is thought about as a place where a man might experience the full measure of his manhood—if he is able to assert himself. The postcards give hints of this as all the early buildings project solidity, permanence, ruggedness. Not a dainty or a petunia in the bunch.

Of course, there were opera houses and popular entertainments, but it's easy to think that Wichita's men had muscles under their dresscoats and hardheaded sensibilities under their top hats. Look at the churches, schoolhouses, depots, restaurants and hotels, and other postcard illustrations of which this book is composed. Again, solidness, but the authors of *Peerless Princess of the Plains* also went about the business of gathering information about the town and passing it on to us. Each view (only three postcard illustrations per page) is accompanied by at least one descriptive paragraph. This is another one of the out-of-print postcard books that should be reissued.

Picture Postcards in the United States, 1893–1918
Dorothy Ryan

When this book was first published in 1976, it attracted a lot of media attention. It was reviewed by the *New York Times,* touted by certain of the literati, and discussed on the "Today" program on American television.

It is not hard to figure out what all the hoopla was about. *Picture Postcards in the United States* is as good a piece of research on postcards as one is likely to find. It is not, of course, complete, but given the ubiquitous character of the subject matter, it is a monumental achievement. The author's informational sources are one of the many pluses that the book has going for it. Dorothy Ryan is also to be commended for her logical division of chapters into those headings most pertinent and most easily recognized.

From pioneer view cards to novelties, she includes sections devoted to expositions, advertising, political and social history, views, sets, signed artists, patriotics, and greetings. Each chapter is filled with prose tightened to the point where each sentence is useful and offered in terse fashion. It would not be possible to list all American postcards or all the publishers or all the artists, but Ryan, with considerable assistance, has given her readers an amazingly large number of separate pieces of information.

So much so, in fact, that this volume will take several readings in order to assimilate most of the facts. Then it must be examined again and again and mental notes made. Even then, one will not easily retain all the data.

The one complaint is that there are so few illustrations, but each is used effectively and appropriately to interact with the text. A separate sixteen-page color section is especially helpful, and each postcard is exquisitely reproduced. A price guide in the rear is useful both for the types and categories of cards that may be encountered and for the values offered, which are still fairly accurate.

A truly great book.

The Scherer-Silman Bamforth Postcard Catalog
Robert W. Scherer

Some men are willing to spend a sizable chunk of their time and energy for projects that they deem to be worthwhile. Whether their efforts are to be rewarded with acknowledgment and appreciation is known mostly to posterity. It is a truism, but often true nonetheless, that the verdict of history is not always what the past had expected.

That verdict has been rendered in the positive for the work of Robert Scherer. His passion was a straightforward one. He wanted to search for, examine, and record all the postcards of the Bamforth Company, one of the most prolific of all publishers of picture postcards. Humor, children, greetings, pretty women, song cards, religious, military, romance, all were grist for their decades-old postcard mill. Bamforth produced them, and collectors bought them all. They even saved many, although many more were undoubtedly tossed into garbage bins.

Many years ago, Scherer began the tedious, time-consuming job of listing them. The result is *The Scherer-Silman Bamforth Postcard Catalog,* a 150-page book that identifies thousands of cards by type, series, and wording. Looked at purely from a numerical point of view, this text is the most comprehensive volume of its type produced in the entire history of postcard collecting. Scherer and Silman clearly took their task seriously.

Does this mean that the list is a complete one? Sadly, no. The word sadly is used because Scherer died while engaged in adding to the list. The three hundred illustrations that accompany the groupings are instrumental in helping to identify the variety of Bamforth's postcard offerings. This book has been well researched. It has also been very well received. The pity is that Robert Scherer is not here to take a much-deserved bow.

Available from:

Bertram Silman
3500 Pineland Drive
Birmingham, Alabama 35243

Horatio Nelson, A Catalogue of Picture Postcards
David Shannon

One of the most popular military heroes is that sailor's sailor, Lord Horatio Nelson. His body may have been British, but his soul was of a kind with every dedicated soldier and sailor in every army and navy the world over.

It is the English who most highly revere him, and this is as it should be. Just as it should be true that dozens of British publishers produced hundreds of postcards related to the man. In his book *Horatio Nelson, A Catalogue of Picture Postcards,* author David Shannon has provided the world with a listing of them all, identified by publisher and heading. This must have been a daunting task, if not a thankless one, but the results of this labor are gratefully accepted not only by Nelson collectors but by all students of deltiology.

The thirty-two black-and-white cards that end the book are a representative sampling, and though one may lament the fact that there are not more illustrations and that a text is unprovided, it ought to be admitted that these are secondary complaints. For the truth is that *Horatio Nelson* is just what it set out to be, a catalogue and a compilation. All postcard books should be so true to their intentions and purposes.

Available from:

> D. J. Shannon
> 12 Wroxham Gardens
> Potters Bar
> Hertfordshire, EN6 3HD
> England

Military Postcards 1870–1945
Jack Smith

It has been claimed that the first picture postcards were a series of military specimens produced by both the French and the Germans during the Franco-Prussian War (1870–71) that were related to that conflict.

From that point forward, the postcard has been pressed into service during war after war, right through to that greatest of cataclysms, World World II. Author/historian Jack Smith somewhat presumptuously, and certainly ambitiously, takes the entire realm of military postcards as his domain in this volume, and he attempts to explain, examine, and illustrate all the major conflicts during the period 1870–1945.

The results are mixed. To have produced a book that approached completion, the author would have needed a tome on the order of 1,500 to 2,000 pages and containing possibly that many illustrations. What the reader is given instead is about three hundred pages and eight hundred illustrations, of which one hundred are in color. Nor is every set or type of card identified or pictured, but with these provisos in mind, it must be admitted that Smith has done a pretty fair job. In addition to some interesting—if occasionally controversial—text to enliven the facts, he offers the reader a listing of the major commanders and incidences plus a series of chronologies, those for World Wars I and II being quite extensive.

For the Spanish-American War, the author even lists the naval vessels while his World War I analysis includes casualty figures, economic costs of the war, and a listing of the aerial aces and their numerical successes. The postcards themselves are all identified and rated according to a rarity scale. At the end of each chapter, space is devoted to the names of artists, publishers, and categories of cards, with each designation being given a rarity number.

Military Postcards 1870–1945 is not a perfect book, but it is more than acceptable, given its limitations. To find all the related information that Smith presents here is both refreshing and time saving. Smith's training as an historian is apparent in this as in other areas. The overall effect is not only such as to elicit the reader's attention but to overwhelm his or her senses, at least until repeated readings and examinations offer an opportunity to absorb some of the material. This is a book no serious student of history or of militaria—or of both—can afford to overlook or be without.

Available from:

> Wallace-Homestead
> Chilton Book Company
> Radnor, Pa 19089

Royal Postcards
Jack Smith

Since antiquity, mankind has had an ongoing fascination with royal personages. In those earlier times, royal figures were often viewed as partaking of deity and sometimes—few, to be sure—as visible manifestations of God. Though we in the modern world enjoy a bit more sophistication than our ancestors, even we tend to see royalty as a class apart. An intriguing class apart.

In his book *Royal Postcards,* Jack Smith examines these august folk from several perspectives. From military leaders to political figureheads to symbols of national identity, kings, queens, and the like are placed under the postcard microscope and scrutinized. Nor are their private personas ignored. The four hundred postcards that illustrate the book show their majesties in settings ranging from the pomp of fully attired regalia to informal attire while relaxing at home.

A special eight-page color section is a welcome addition, and these one hundred cards are strikingly rendered. Reduced to easily identified chapter headings, the topics include early cards, royal families, royalty around the world, special occasion cards, categories of interest, and more. Further inclusions embrace sections on postcard publishers and one on sets and series. Of special interest is a chapter entitled "Artist Drawn and Royalty Signed Cards," in which the author offers compelling reasons for not lumping together all cards that might otherwise seem to be the same.

For those with an historical inclination, *Royal Postcards* will serve as a delightful opportunity for fruitful reading. A special encyclopedic-type listing of various royal activities and occurrences from 1888 to 1925 is both revealing and time-saving in matching postcard with event. The book concludes with a list and value guide for world royalty from Abyssinia to Zanzibar plus a valuation for both sets and series and types. The author includes a rarity scale to offer the collector an idea as to a particular card's scarcity. It is to be hoped that *Royal Postcards* is an archetype of postcard books to come.

Available from:

Wallace-Homestead
Chilton Book Company
Radnor, Pa 19089

Coney Island: A Postcard Journey to the City of Fire
Richard Snow

For those of us too young to remember New York's Coney Island during its years of grandeur—and, of course, that means most of us—a book like this comes wrapped in fascination, the picture postcards viewed with a mixture of delight and wistfulness. Most of the almost one hundred cards are illustrated in color; not a few of them are outsized and detail-laden, a treat for both eye and imagination.

Coney Island itself was a combination of architectural styles and a visual blend of textures. Art Nouveau stood alongside Romanesque, flamboyant carnival rides coexisted with beautiful oil paintings and well-lit castles. Both Luna Park and Dreamland beckoned to the more than 300,000 visitors who toured Coney on any given Sunday during the first decade of the twentieth century. All came for the single purpose of being amused. Few went away disappointed although many were "shook by the rides, burned by the sun or disposed to indigestion after sampling the Park's various culinary offerings along the way."

Richard Snow's postcards bring it all back, this being no small feat considering that we were never actually there to begin with, but we may suppose that we were as we juxtapose images of Disneyland, King's Island, and Six Flags over Texas with the pictures presented here.

Snow is thorough as well as kind enough to share his postcard images with us, for he also provides text running alongside and beneath the postcard illustrations. The summation of the book and the culminating effect of the pictures may be found in a paradoxical position, for there in the book's beginning are to be found the quintessential statement made by Richard Le Galliene in 1905:

Perhaps Coney Island is the most human thing that God ever made, or permitted the devil to make.

Indeed.

Available from:

Brightwaters Press
235 Park Avenue South
New York, New York 10003

Postcard Collecting: A Fun Investment
Bernard Stadtmiller

One of the true giants in the reemergence of America's interest in postcard collecting during the 1960s and 1970s was Bernard Stadtmiller. His *Postcard Collector's* magazine, which was begun in 1976, helped create an atmosphere conducive to both scholarship and to a rise of interest in the hobby. The book *Postcard Collecting* was actually published personally by Bernard in 1973 and served much the same function. Conveniently divided into informative sections, each of which is profusely illustrated with both black-and-white and colored postcard reproductions, the book is a visual and informational delight.

The cards are all illustrated full-size and are captioned with useful prose. Included are sections on advertising cards, early postal cards, what to collect, pricing of cards, and collecting for profit. Stadtmiller discusses the various categories and is not averse to making recommendations. A few of them have even exceeded what must have been the author's expectations for them.

Subtitled "A Fun Investment," Stadtmiller's book easily manages to breathe life in his descriptions of the hobby. His reminiscences provide interesting sidelights, taking the reader to a world that may now only be examined with wistfulness.

The book has one shortcoming: its brevity. With his obvious relish for deltiology and his knowledge of it, Stadtmiller should have furnished posterity with a much larger volume. Only in this way are we cheated. This is of course compensated for by all the informative articles included in his magazine a few years later.

Postcard Collecting is, without doubt, one of the most enjoyable seventy-eight-page books ever written on any topic. It is a colorful and delightful introductory text.

Available from:

Mrs. Martha Walton (Stadtmiller's sister)
707 Collegewood Drive
Ypsilanti, Michigan 48197

Ryan II and Horina, Too
Kathryn Stansbury

This book, short as it is, has a lot going for it, more even than its catchy title. Amateur historian and a delightfully refreshing lady, Kathryn Stansbury puts her considerable talent to work on the book and gives the reader a detailed checklist of the postcards of artists E. Ryan and H. Horina.

Both of them use a number of themes, but Horina seems to stick closer to the broad umbrella of humor than may be said of Ryan. Little is known of either artist though both are obviously avidly collected. The illustrations Stansbury uses throughout the book are useful both for showing the artists' variety and for demonstrating their command of the brush and the drawing pencil.

The book itself is necessarily short, although the checklists are lengthy, given that these are artists about which little is known. The only problem with *Ryan II and Horina, Too* is that Stansbury gives the reader all too little of her prose. It's a shame because she has a refreshing way of using the language.

Available from:

Kathryn Stansbury
P.O. Box 34
Mulhall, Oklahoma 73063

Old Knoxville
Chattanooga Album
Memphis Memories
University of Tennessee Press

Each of these three books contains thirty-two historic, antique postcards of the cities named. Each of these sepia-toned reproductions is taken from an original real photo postcard that dates to the first two decades of the twentieth century. They depict early transportation, busy street scenes, social customs, and local points of interest. These are all rare cards, all historically significant. All are links that unite our grandparents to us and us to posterity. They are views of where we, as a civilization, have been and also of what we have been. They are mirrors, important ones, and whether they may or may not serve to help us prepare for an uncertain future is not as important as is the fact that they offer us roots with which we may trace the adventure of the human journey.

Available from:

University of Tennessee Press
Knoxville, TN

Varga, The Esquire Years
Alfred van der Marck

Breathes there a soul so pure as not to know the name of Alberto Varga or, more appropriately perhaps, not to have seen the "Varga Girl"?

The background information is presented directly and simply by the publisher in the following way:

On October 15, 1940, *Esquire* magazine introduced Alberto Varga's Varga Girl to the world. By the end of World War II, troops in every part of the world were attesting to the Varga Girl's unique importance as a motivator. A combination of barely concealed sexuality and wholesome domestic virtue, she had come to represent everything American soldiers were fighting to defend. By 1947 the Varga Girl was finished (because of) her close connection to the war.

One may question the clause "wholesome domestic virtue," but almost everyone would agree with the part about her "barely concealed sexuality." Ah, hmm. Just think allure and you have the idea that Varga wanted to impress on your mind.

The only Varga postcards are a set of twelve outsized Esky cards of the artist's paintings. They are illustrated in color, as are all of the images reproduced in this book. It is the perfection that entrances: perfection of anatomy, of facial detail, of hair, turn of leg, fingertip, eyes.

Varga Girls were what men wanted but couldn't have. They were—and probably always will be—the manifestation of man's erotic dreams.

Look at the pictures, then nothing more will be necessary in the way of explanation.

Available from:

Alfred van der Marck
1133 Broadway, Suite 1301
New York, New York 10010

Border Fury: A Picture Postcard Record of Mexico's Revolution and U.S. War Preparedness, 1900–1917
Paul J. Vanderwood and Frank N. Samponaro

A serious book deserves serious treatment, and *Border Fury* is, among other things, a serious book. The authors are Paul J. Vanderwood and Frank J. Samponaro, professors of history at San Diego State University and the University of Texas of the Permian Basin, Odessa, respectively.

Vanderwood and Samponaro discovered something that postcard collectors have known for a very long time. What they found out is that postcards are an excellent tool for historical reconstruction. In this instance, they were used to analyze the conflict that became known as the Mexican Revolution (actually, it was only the last of Mexico's revolutions).

The postcards illustrated here are intriguing slices of the various realities surrounding these hostilities. Most are real photographic types that document mindsets of soldiers, lifestyles of refugees, maneuvering activities, battles, executions, the goings on of Mexican and American citizens, and military and political leaders. The messages on many of them are indispensable to a fuller understanding of that skirmish and its participants/victims.

It is easy to determine that this wealth of photographs and printed material came from a number of sources. Besides the types already mentioned, there are views of military vehicles, including aircraft, troops in training, troops relaxing and entertaining themselves, decomposing bodies, humorous cartoon types, patriotic cards, and more.

One may not always agree with the authors' conclusions, but it must be acknowledged that their bibliography is an impressive one and that their scholarly approach is beyond criticism. They have used their postcards wisely and by so doing proved the historical and sociological value of them.

Available from:

University of New Mexico Press
Albuquerque, New Mexico 87131

Horsham in Old Picture Postcards
Tony Wales

One need not be an Englishman to appreciate this book. In fact, as much as anything else, *Horsham in Old Picture Postcards* is a volume of universal flavor. Whether British, German, French, Italian, or American, the early years of the twentieth century presented many parallels.

Bicycles were everywhere in evidence; delivery trucks (lorries to the English) were seen in town squares and residential neighborhoods; glass-framed shop fronts boasted of everything from sumptuous chocolates to barrels of nails; family business establishments proudly stood alongside heavily trafficked main thoroughfares; and post offices, town markets, hotels, tobacco shops, and railway stations were familiar landmarks.

Life was, as the old cliché would have it, simpler then and, one suspects, more rewarding, too. Tony Wales shows us all this and then some. His illustrations of all the above are comments, statements of the type worthy of examination and remembrance.

Available from:

Tony Wales
31 Hurst Avenue, Horsham
West Sussex RH12 2EL
England

Mommy, It's a Renoir
Aline D. Wolf

Just when we thought no one could come up with another use for that recorder of all things human, the picture postcard, along comes Aline D. Wolf to show us the shallowness of our thinking.

By reproducing the paintings of such art masters as Van Gogh, Goya, Chagall, and Renoir in postcard format, Wolf has demonstrated the postcard's use as a tool for instructing the young. The book contains thirty-six full-color specimens dotted on their backs for easy cutting removal. By a series of "Easy Travel Steps," the child is taught to match the paintings, to pair them, and to lot the cards of individual artists in groups of four. The business of matching is geared to become progressively more difficult as the child/student advances to higher levels until similarities of style and technique are understood and an appreciation of them has begun to be developed within the mind of each child.

Clearly, this is a welcome combination of art, postcard, and education, and it should not go unnoticed that this approach has the added benefit of focusing on the finer qualities of each of them.

Available from:

Parent Child Press
P.O. Box 767
Altoona, Pennsylvania 16603

A B C of Postcard Collecting:
Peeps into the Postcard Past
George Wolstenholme

George Wolstenholme, who died recently, produced this and the following informative booklets. Both and each are worth having. They contain fairly basic information, but it's also true that primer material is necessary for the promotion of postcard collecting. No one, after all, starts out as an expert. Both of these have a dictionary-type approach with definitions of postcard categories, publishers, and the like.

Over 900 Things to Know about
Postcard Collecting
George Wolstenholme

This book offers from one sentence to a paragraph on topics that range from aerial post to C. Zirker. The information given is little, but it covers so large an area.

Then again, there is either little or much provided, depending on one's level of deltiological expertise or awareness. Can you answer the following questions: What is the Clay Cross series? Who is B. Cobbe? What

is a faciograph? What is a laxey wheel? Who is Vivien Mansell?

These questions and more than 895 others are answered in this "little" book.

Reflections from Kansas 1900–1930:
A Prairie Postcard Album
Frank Wood and Scott Daymond

Images of Kansas often include visions of broad, flat lands dotted with grain elevators, blowing fields of wheat, miles of corn and farmhouses with large expanses of land surrounding them. The authors of *Reflections from Kansas* both tell and show their readers that a state known for its sunflowers is, well, much more than sunflowers. With the assistance of 312 postcard illustrations which are, according to the publisher, "exhilarating and touching views," and a readable prose style that is informative without being stuffy, the book certainly brings old Kansas to life.

The stories abound: avid Prohibitionist Myra McHenry crusading for wholesome living, cities springing to life on the prairie almost overnight; a people tough and determined, yet tenderhearted main streets and businesses.

Wood and Daymond have more than a passing acquaintance with the state and both are proud of its sometimes colorful, sometimes sobering human interest background. "Every part of Kansas is here" says the advertisement. It might have added "and much of America as well."

Available from:

Daywood Publishing Company
P.O. Box 9547
Wichita, Kansas 67277–0547

POST CARD.

Post Card

6
Modern
Postcard
Publishers

ST

РАҒІД

ARD.

ONLY TO BE
IN HERE.

E.

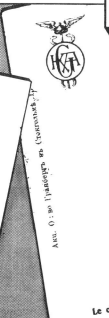

АКЦ. О: ВО ГраверЪ въ СтокгольмЪ, Ш

THE ROYAL FAMI

Raphael Tuck & Sons'"REAL PHOTOGRAPH" Postcard No. 36

ART PUBLISHERS TO THEIR MAJESTIES THE KING & QUEEN.

AND TO H.R.H. THE PRINCE OF WALES.

Copyright. London.
Printed in England

TUCK'S POST CARD

By Appointment

CARTE

H.M. KING GEORGE V., born 3rd June,
1865; ascended the Throne 6th May,
1910.
H.M. QUEEN MARY, born 26th May,
1867.
H.R.H. PRINCESS MARY (Countess of Hare-
wood) born 25th April, 1897.
And from left to right of picture:— born
H.R.H. THE PRINCE OF WALES,
23rd June, 1894.
H.R.H. PRINCE HENRY, born 31st March, 1900.
H.R.H. THE DUKE OF YORK, born 14th
December, 1895.
H.R.H. PRINCE GEORGE, born 20th December,
1902.

THE WORLD'S ART SERVICE
RAPHAEL TUCK & SONS

POSTALE

For Address Only

By Appointment

Le chemin militaire Grousien. Le pont de
et la rivière Terok.   Vues de

6
Modern Postcard Publishers

Although interest in postcard collecting experienced a decline during the 1920s, 1930s, and 1940s, it would be incorrect to assume that all, or even most, postcard activity had ceased at that time. In fact, some of today's most avidly collected postcards were produced during those decades, mute testimony to their fruitfulness. It was during the early part of this period that the beautiful (some might say gaudy or pretentious) Art Deco style in everything from furniture to bric-a-brac to basic concepts of architecture began to make its presence felt.

Even postcards reflected the rage, with paintings of glamorous women and brightly colored greetings with perhaps a touch of chrome, but certainly a wealth of patterns reflecting acute right angles was in evidence.

Also introduced during this era was a group of effervescent and mischievous animal characters, including Bonzo, Mickey Mouse, and a host of others. Accompanying them into comic strip, celluloid, and postcard popularity were the likes of Popeye, Dick Tracy, Little Orphan Annie, and more. What these styles and proliferation of character personalities might symbolize is perhaps best left to the devices of sociologists and students of modern archaeology. It is sufficient for our purposes to recognize that, once more, postcard publishers were part and parcel of all the current trends.

They still are. Since the 1950s (1950 is generally recognized as the beginning of the modern era in postcard collecting), the world has witnessed many alterations of mind set, of national temperament, of scientific fascinations, and so forth. Armed conflicts, improvements in medicine, advances in biological studies, more mobile societies, faster means of both transportation and communication, an improved standard of living, space explorations, to name a few—always there to record and immortalize was the postcard. One of the ways that our present generation will be studied by posterity must certainly be through the medium of the postcard, for it's all there.

More importantly, the story is still being recorded. The following list is only a fraction of the postcard publishers who are currently supplying our need for greetings, for information, and for analysis of the world in which we live. We must hope that their views and messages continue to offer insight.

Listing of Current Publishers

Helen O. Ackert (De Kalb, Illinois)
Adfactor Postcards (Toronto, Canada)
Alliance Party (Ireland)
American Greetings Corporation (Cleveland, Ohio)
American Post Card Company (New York, New York)
Aqua Ink (Washington, D.C.)
Argonaut Press (Madison, Wisconsin)
Argus Communications (Allen, Texas)
Art Unlimited (Amsterdam, the Netherlands)
Athena International (London, England)

Baloo Chimera Publishers (West Lafayette, Indiana)
Baxtone (Amarillo, Texas)
Biri Publishers (Amsterdam, the Netherlands)
Blue Mountain Printmakers (New Sharon, Maine)
Rita Booth Studios (Freewater, Oregon)

California Dreamers (Chicago, Illinois)
Camden Graphics (Berkeley, California)
The Card Works (Bedford, New Hampshire)
Chance of a Lifetime—Black Ice Publishers (Worcester, Massachusetts)
City Sights (Ontario, Canada)
Classico (San Francisco, California)
Coastal Photo Scenics (Southwest Harbor, Maine)
Colour Tech Productions (Canberra, Australia)

Colourpicture (Boston, Massachusetts)
Columbus Street Press (Toronto Canada)
Contemporary Designs (Ames, Iowa)
Coral Lee (Rancho Cordova, California)
Crane Creek Graphics (Wilson, Wyoming)
H. S. Crocker (San Francisco, California)
Current (Colorado Springs, Colorado)
Curteich & Company (Chicago, Illinois)

Dalkeith (Britain)
E. Danielson AB (Geneva, Sweden)
Democratic Unionist Party (Ireland)
Design 4 (Newtownards, North Ireland)
Dexter Press (New York)
Diana's Cards (Providence, Rhode Island)
Dover Publications (Mineola, New York)
Drawing Room Cards (Dallas, Texas)

Editions Cartes D'Art (New York, New York)
Editions Nugeron (France)
Kristin Elliot (Beverly, Massachusetts)
Enthusiastic Enterprises Maine Line Company
    (Rockport, Maine)
Ephemera (San Francisco, California)

Fast, Cheap & Easy Graphics (San Francisco,
    California)
Fischgrund (Mexico)
Flashcards (Fort Lauderdale, Florida)
Foreign Cards (Guilford, Connecticut)
Foto Folio (Canal Station, New York)
Freezz Frame (San Bruno, California)

Hubert Gassner (Vaduz, Liechtenstein)
Gee Whiz (Seal Beach, California)
Gronlund Publishers (Copenhagen, Denmark)
Guffoz (Kansas City, Missouri)

H. & L. (San Diego, California)
Jim Haberman (Arlington, Massachusetts)
Hallmark Cards (Kansas City, Missouri)
Hold the Mustard (Oakland, California)
Harvey Hutter & Company (New York)

Images & Editions (Britain)
Impact (Concord, California)
Independent (Ireland)

J.V. Postcards (Britain)
Joli Greeting Card Company (Chicago, Illinois)
Just Books (Belfast, Ireland)

Klein P.C. Service (Hyde Park, Massachusetts)

M. Lab (Bethel, Ohio)
Ludlow Sales (Chelsea Station, New York)

Molloy Postcard Services (Covington, Kentucky)

New Boundary Designs (Chanhassen, Minnesota)
Numismatic Card Company (Lansing, Michigan)

One World Artist Cooperative (New Haven,
    Connecticut)
Out of the West Publishers (Sacramento, California)

Paper Moon Graphics (Los Angeles, California)
Paper Peddler (Richmond, California)
Paula Company (Cincinnati, Ohio)
Postcard Factory (Toronto, Canada)

Quantity Post Cards (San Francisco, California)

Recycled Paper Products (Chicago, Illinois)
Red Farm Studios (Pawtucket, Rhode Island)
Renaissance Greeting Cards (Springvale, Maine)
Mike Roberts (New York, New York)
Rykovoorlichtingsdienst (The Netherlands)

Seashore Studios (Ponce Inlet, Florida)
Shoot That Tiger (Britain)
Smith Western (Portland, Oregon)
Southern Postcard Company (Tennessee)
Souvenirs Australia (Glynde, Australia)
Stenders (Sweden)
Suzy's Zoo (San Diego, California)

Texas Post Card Company (Plano, Texas)
Three Star Press (Masonville, Iowa)
TNT Designs (New York, New York)
Tyler Publishers (Augusta, Maine)

Ultraforlaget AB (Stockholm, Sweden)

Erella Vent (Toronto, Canada)
Visual Vacations (Salem, Oregon)

This partial listing of some of the more well-known publishers offers a hint of the geographical diversity that these companies represent and also correctly indicates the postcard's current popularity, even among those who may know nothing of antique cards. Special thanks are herewith extended to Joan Carlson, who was instrumental in supplying many of the names on this list. Carlson writes period articles for *Barr's Post Card News* in which she offers information on artists, publishers, and, of course, some of the newer postcards that have come on the market. The attention her articles receive is another indication that the modern card is finding a comfortable place for itself within the deltiological community.

This popularity extends to several points on the globe other than the United States, however. In fact, the enthusiasm is even greater in Great Britain, where Pete Davies's column on modern cards in *Picture Postcard Monthly* is greeted with such excitement that Davies found it necessary to compose a book on the topic, *"Collect Modern Postcards,"* which was reviewed in Chapter 5.

A few of the publishers who have been gracious enough to supply examples of their postcard output are described briefly below. For more information about publishers or offerings, the reader is advised to contact Dave Long in the United States or Pete Davies in England. Both men are dealers in modern postcards, and their addresses are supplied in Chapter 9, "Postcard Dealers." Please send a self-addressed, stamped envelope with this type of correspondence; also, check Chapter 9 for the names and addresses of others who deal in modern postcards.

Coral Lee

Publisher Profiles

Coral Lee (Coralie Dixon Sparre)

When Coral Lee first discontinued her postcard publishing in the early 1980s, the outcry, led and focused in large measure by the efforts of postcard dealer and researcher Roy Nuhn, was loud and prolonged. So she returned. However, within a short period of time, Coral Lee was forced by age and economics to turn her valuable storehouse of political and social postcards to others.

Why all the fuss? That question might best be answered by beginning with a look at the lady herself.

Coralie Sparre was raised in Dixon, Illinois, which was also the town in which President Ronald Reagan grew up. Coralie remembers Reagan from those days, although the president's memory is such that he cannot return the favor. "I remember the last time I saw him in Dixon. He was in front of Meisenheimer's Dry Goods store in a cut down Ford coupe," she told a reporter for the *Washington Post.*

Coralie was to remeet Reagan in the White House, and she carries a personally autographed photo of the occasion as a souvenir. Clearly, though, their lives had followed dissimilar roads. While the president went into sportscasting and acting before settling at last on public service, Mrs. Sparre chose the less financially rewarding career of a teacher. It was her experiences while in the classroom that led eventually to her postcard publishing.

Discovering that too many schoolchildren had, at best, a superficial knowledge of history and geography, Coralie hit upon the idea of using postcards to record contemporary history. She correctly assumed that they

Coral Lee

would make excellent visual aids. Her entire life savings, all $50,000, was placed in the project. Lowering her expectations a bit, Coralie decided to use her full-color cards to teach her young wards about the presidency. This she did by making postcards of the significant events—and some merely humorous as well—of the presidencies and the lives of Jimmy Carter and Ronald Reagan.

In an effort to raise funds and to reach an audience not restricted to her students, Coralie branched out into reproducing in postcard form the images of some of the more well-known American entertainment figures. Later, she included British royalty to the list, but her venture failed and though the sting of disappointment was keenly felt, the lady has remained philosophical about her enterprise.

But what a body of work she has produced. The total figure approaches three million, and each of the hundreds of individual cards are bites from the reel of history, be they political or social or humorous—or all three in one package. Some of the cards are artist-drawn specimens by the excellent caricaturist Art

Coral Lee

Coral Lee

Coral Lee

Strader. Many of these are quite thought-invoking, not far removed from satire and political comment, but the largest number are of the photographic variety, and anyone even remotely familiar with the politics of the last dozen years will find them most revealing and assuredly pertinent. Again, visual history.

Coralie should serve as a role model for every teacher and postcard dealer in America. That her dream was shattered because of lack of attention and respect on our part tells us less about Coralie Sparre than it does about us. Her sole desire was to acquaint, at her own expense, if necessary, the students of today with their world. Not a bad dream. Too bad we could not share it with her.

Curt Teich

Easily the largest and most popular of modern postcard publishers was the firm of Curt Teich (also Curteich). Among the categories of postcards it produced during its seventy-six years of business (1898–1974) were military, street scenes, animals, advertising, social customs, humorous, famous people, children, political, sports, map cards, bathing beauties, art, presidential, large letter, transportation, Indians, blacks, special occasion, exaggerations, and an unbroken string of others.

Texas Cowboy Riding a Jack Rabbit

Curteich

Curteich

260

Curteich

Curteich

Whatever one's collecting interest, he or she had a better than fair chance to find it represented on a Curt Teich card. In some instances, Teich itself was both publisher and printer, but in most cases the firm printed the artwork or photographs of others for a fee. Over the years, Teich also adopted other designations, among them Tichnor Brothers, Tichnor Art Company, C.T. Art Colourtone, and others.

Postcard collectors of every stripe and inclination will be pleased to learn that the entire individual output of Curt Teich has been preserved and retained in the Curt Teich Postcard Collection of the Lake County Museum in Lake County, Illinois. This facility and its contents are unmatched anywhere on earth (although it is recognized that England's Bamforth Museum is also a rightfully proud institution and repository). There is a collection supervisor, Katherine Hamilton-Smith, the museum's curator, and an assistant, Christine Pyle. Together, they perform and conduct research and outreach activities, including preparing and issuing a quar-

terly newsletter, *Postcard Journal,* devoted to information about Curt Teich and the collection.

Membership is offered in the Curt Teich Postcard Collection, and a trip to the museum will provide an unparalleled opportunity to view the results of Teich's seven-plus decades of postcard production. Membership in the collection will go a long way toward ensuring its continuation and preservation of priceless archival material.

Available from:

The Curt Teich Postcard Collection
Lake County Museum
Lakewood Forest Preserve
Wauconda, Illinois 60084

Faga

Arguably the most well known, if not the best, of all British artists is the man who goes by the pseudonym "Faga." Doubling as a publisher, his postcard art includes ships, royalty, special occasion, political, military and much more; he has always been popular and in demand.

There is good reason for this. Faga's part calligraphy, part add-on, and part original artwork is a treat for the eye. Even those not done in color are appealing. Since 1961, Faga has labored in the postcard medium and that without an appreciable amount of financial remuneration. Although not overly embittered by his lack of economic success with his postcard output, it is certainly possible that the bulk of Faga's work is in the past. If this is true, all postcard collectors are the poorer.

Molloy Postcard Services

It is a well-known axiom among consumers that businesses are judged by the quality of the product they produce. Using this as the sole criterion, it must be observed that Ruth Molloy of Molloy Postcard Services operates a business well worth patronizing.

The photographic images she reproduces are no clearer or more detailed than the original photographs. That, in effect, is her only restriction. If the photographic artwork is first-class, the postcard will be no less so. Most of Molloy's clients are the sort of people who demand perfection. That she is still in business indicates that she meets this specification. It is also

261

Molloy Postcard Services

Molloy Postcard Services

Molloy Postcard Services

not to be wondered how she has expanded her base of operations to include Cincinnati and Columbus in Ohio and Louisville, Lexington, and the whole of northern Kentucky, but the orders she receives come from a lot farther away than that and include several overseas customers. Seeing her work firsthand and up close will convince even the most critical.

Available from:

Molloy Postcard Services
1100 Pike Street
Covington, Kentucky 41011

Visual Vacations

Paul McGehee has a good idea. Some might call it a great idea. McGehee has decided not to take the world too seriously, neither it nor its inhabitants nor its occasional proclivity for war nor its other various forms of organized and structured nonsense.

The further news is even better. McGehee wants us to laugh at our idiosyncrasies and to poke fun at our conventions. He does his part through his postcards. All are in brightly divergent colors, and most

Molloy Postcard Services

Visual Vacations

Numismatic Card Company

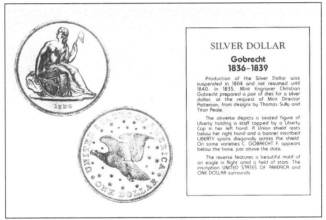

Numismatic Card Company

Visual Vacations

appear to be of the "greetings from" genre. There are greetings from each of the nine planets, from the moon and the sun, from Halley's Comet, from the Asteroid Belt, and one from Hades. There is even one from nowhere, a most interesting place about which most of us have at least a passing knowledge.

Each of the cards contains information within the large-letter format that McGehee uses. There must be multiple messages therein, but it is enough for the time being to take part in the escapism.

Available from:

Paul McGehee
Box 7384
Salem, Oregon 97303

Numismatic Card Company

In the beginning, reports co-owner Craig Whitford, his partner Rocky Jennings was skeptical about the whole idea.

The idea Whitford was talking about was the plan to produce postcards related to U.S. coinage and paper money. What he did produce were postcards of the first order, postcards that won over his partner—but not before thousands had been sold to fascinated collectors. It's easy to determine what all the excitement is about. The quality of the reproductions as well as the topics themselves are both deserving of attention and examination.

Among the sets the firm has offered for sale are an eight-card U.S. silver dollar grouping, a set of eight U.S. large cent reproductions, a four-card set of Civil War numismatics, and a twelve-card set related to the U.S. Mint at Philadelphia, with vignettes from early days to modern.

Numismatic Card Company

Adfactor

This is just the beginning. There are sets on paper money, fractional currency, a twelve-card set on Civil War currency, individual coinage, and mint-related issues. Most are in black and white, but even they are exceptionally well produced while the colored cards are brightly and clearly rendered.

The latest release is a set of forty-five Continental-size postcards, which features every president since George Washington, and includes Confederate States of America President Jefferson Davis and President for a Day, David Rice Atchinson. Printed in red, white and blue, with portrait and signature in black, these ''Presidential Portraits'' are an excellent example of combining modern postcards with history and aesthetics. (Inquire at: American Images, Box 19231, Lansing, Michigan 48901).

Most of the cards contain useful information, another reason that the owners of these specimens—or, rather, the smart owners of them—have decided to frame many of them. The few illustrated here are insufficient to do justice to the product line. A catalogue is also available.

Available from:

Numismatic Card Company
P.O. Box 14225
Lansing, Michigan 48901-4225

Adfactor

The word has spread in Toronto, and it has spread outside Toronto as well. What word? The word that Adfactor Postcards does excellent work and does it at an inexpensive price. Its commitment to producing a

Adfactor

quality postcard at a reasonable price is evident in the postcards illustrated, but this Canadian firm is not content to rest on past accomplishments.

Although the postcards reproduced here are black and white, the originals are printed in full four-color. The subject matter may only be imagined as Adfactor dislikes restrictions. The firm has already produced more than seven hundred designs and is considering putting on a show in Toronto to illuminate all of them in the near future. Illuminate or illustrate? Well, both.

Available from:

Adfactor Postcards
984 Queen Street West
Toronto, Ontario M6J 1H1
Canada

Columbus Street Press

Columbus Street Press

No one ever accused George Walker of having a lack of imagination. If anything, his creative, imaginative side works overtime doing double duty. The two linocut cards shown here are pretty pedestrian stuff compared to what Walker has produced. It may not be everyone's cup of tea, but Walker is secure enough not to lose much sleep over a little disapproval.

Walker, a native Canadian, is founder and proprietor of Columbus Street Press, a company dedicated to producing quality books and individual, original art, including postcards. His list of credits and honors is a lengthy one, and it is beyond doubt that both Toronto and Walker are committed to a serious examination and perusal of the type of art that reflects individualistic perceptions.

Available from:

Columbus Street Press

Columbus Street Press
563 Gladstone Avenue
Toronto, Ontario
Canada

Suzy's Zoo

It is sometimes the case that postcard artists become postcard publishers. Not only do such people draw and paint the designs that are produced in their own fertile imaginations, but they also do the advertising and promotion and even market the material themselves. In short, they do everything but the actual printing (and a few even do this).

Suzy Spafford, founder and chief architect/presiding officer of Suzy's Zoo, a company created

to produce, market, and distribute Spafford's many paper offerings, was and is a most talented lady. Having drawn cartoon-like animal characters from her early childhood, Spafford had strong feelings concerning the direction she wanted her life to take. She had the good fortune to be spotted at a local art show by a man who was to become her benefactor. The rest, as they say, is history. What they don't say is that Suzy Spafford has worked her way into even more good fortune.

Tirelessly devoted to her craft, she has ranged far afield from her original beginnings. Her many products (postcards, greeting cards, invitations and announcements, stickers and stationery, coloring books, and more) are all parts of Suzy, the artist. Her business acumen is worthy of emulation, and the lady will do nothing without much thought and a fair amount of research. The results of this careful, studied approach has been steady growth of the kind that will probably continue into at least the foreseeable future.

Suzy's Zoo

Suzy's Zoo

Suzy's Zoo

The artwork shown here is a first-rate example of attention to detail. That sounds like an accurate description of Spafford as well. Add a concern for people and a desire to make them smile and the artist's portrait is near completion.

Available from:

Suzy's Zoo
9541 Ridgehaven Court
San Diego, California, 92123-1624

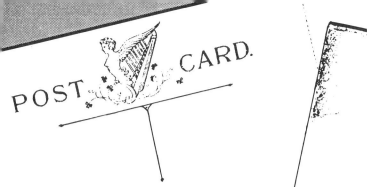

7
Modern
Postcard
Artists

7
Modern Postcard Artists

The old masters of the postcard art form are gone, the cards themselves performing duty as their lasting testament. Though our debt to them is immeasurable, we must not let this deter our attention from the new generation of postcard artists who have arisen from the common clay of humanity during the last two decades. Coming slowly—but certainly—into prominence with the reemergence of interest in the postcard itself, these are men and women who dare to offer us their artwork for our perusal.

It is clear that not all of their work is uniformly good or even passable, but, as someone observed a number of years ago, most of what passes for art—whether in music, video, painting or sculpture, even architecture—is either mediocre or less than aesthetically appealing. On the other hand, some of these artists are remarkably talented. It ought also to be noted that most of them do postcard artwork either recreationally or as an adjunct to more "respectable" art forms.

The profiles presented here represent a mere fraction of the artists currently producing postcard artwork. More significantly, additional names are added to the list on a regular basis.

Overall, they are a decent group and true, dedicated to their profession and jealous of maintaining their artistic integrity. Twelve of them have generously furnished original artwork that is being seen here for the first and only time. Each of these twelve have a few introductory paragraphs devoted to them by way of furnishing a backdrop for their work, and the addresses are given for those who may be willing to work on commission.

The postcard sketches and minipaintings of several others are also illustrated, and it is easy to determine that they represent a disparate lot in terms of themes and artistic approaches. One thing is certain: The postcard world has much for which to be thankful, not least the cadre of talented postcard artists.

Artist Profiles

Richard Blake

Richard Blake is another of those artists who backed into working in the postcard medium. Previously, he had been in advertising and promotions, designing album covers, placards, and scenic flats. He eventually rose to the exalted position of art director, but the time he spent behind the wheel in London traffic proved too distracting and Blake decided to work out of his own home on a commission basis as a freelance artist.

His favorite topic, and that by far, is old British mail coaches. The National Postal Museum shared his fascination and commissioned him to paint five of the mail coach designs in postcard form. The fact that the bicentennial of the British mail coach was that year proved to be a fortunate happenstance.

Blake has since branched out to perform postcard work both for the larger dealers, such as J. H. D. Smith of International Postcard Market, and also for individual collectors. As with many other good artists, there are simply not enough hours in the day to execute his growing list of commissions.

The piece of original artwork displayed (see color section) demonstrates both the imaginative ability of Blake and also his technical expertise. It is no overstatement to claim that Blake's work leaves little to be desired. It's all there: creativity, attention to detail, focus.

What Blake needs is a little rest. His chances of getting it are pretty slim, at least as long as the quality of his art remains constant.

Richard Blake
The Mardens, Tupwood Lane
Caterham, Surrey
England

Richard Blake

1862. *Central Overland California & Pike's Peak Express Company Passenger Wagon*

Richard Blake

Jean Boccacino

Jean Boccacino

Jean Boccacino

Born in Angers, France, in 1946, Jean Boccacino is a teacher who works with mentally disturbed children. He is also an artist whose paintings and drawings are much appreciated and highly received. Putting these bits of information together helps to create the outline of a man very much worth getting to know.

As for postcard artwork, Boccacino is known to publish two sorts. The first is reproductions of his paintings. These paintings (see color section) are al-ways popular at art shows, and he occasionally has them reproduced into invitations sent out for his art exhibits as well as putting them in postcard form.

Rick Geary

Rick Geary

Rick Geary

The second group is in black and gold—or black and white—and are graphic-like sketches. These are done for card collectors and are shown and sold at fairs, postcard clubs, and cultural exchanges. They are not offered for sale to the general public but strictly to collectors on a first-come, first-served basis. They are all limited editions and contain a facsimile signature. Selling out very quickly, they soon become rare items on the secondary market.

The French are often more serious about art in general and their own artists in particular. In the case of Jean Boccacino, who is a special favorite of the French people, it is easy to understand the appeal.

Jean Boccacino
14 Rue du Clos du Pin
49130 Les Ponts de Ce
France

Rick Geary

Rick Geary is a man with a portfolio. An impressive portfolio. His artwork has graced the pages of *Rolling Stone, Los Angeles Magazine, and National Lampoon,* to name but a few out of many. He has been a cartoonist and illustrator for local newspapers and has authored several books.

Geary has also been a postcard artist, although the demands on his time are such that his postcard work is primarily recreational—and, lately, very limited. Born in 1946 in Kansas City, Missouri, the multitalented Geary was a former native of Wichita, Kansas, where he attended public schools. He later graduated from the University of Kansas. He wasted little time putting his commercial art degree to work for him and has been active ever since.

It is universally acknowledged that Geary is a nice fellow, quick of smile, pleasant, and enjoyable company. This is nice to know, but it is his art that sets him apart. Primarily a caricaturist and sketcher, Geary's drawings need take a secondary position to no one working in the field today, and that, as everyone knows, covers quite some territory. His lines are straight and true, yet they have a gracefulness about them that, though hard to define, is clearly present. His keen artist's eye translates well onto sketch book or art board, and his drawings contain all the necessary ingredients. Geary does; Geary does not overdo. Pictures are messages, and artist Geary is distinct.

Whether presidential portraiture (see color section, scenics that display an active, healthy imagination at work, or humorous cartoon figures, Geary has proven time and again that he can draw with the best of them. He is a man with a vision or visions. His delightful drawings make us want to share it—or them—with him.

Fred Gonzalez. The Mountain Man, a Vanished Breed.

Fred Gonzalez

The best words to use when describing some people are their own. That is certainly the case here, and this short biographic sketch—which should be called an autobiographic sketch—will make ample use of the artist's basic, unadorned, and unpretentious prose.

His letter of introduction begins and proceeds as follows:

My name is Fred M. Gonzalez. I am thirty years old and married to Laura. Going into a brief history of myself, I was raised in Newton, Kansas, and my parents are Fred and Ramona Gonzalez. I come from a family of five boys. My thoughts of pursuing a career in commercial art began when I was twelve. I didn't fully understand what it was all about so I

would go to the library and read books about careers in commercial art. I began meeting people that were in the business and I tried to learn as much about it from them as I could.

After graduating from high school I went aimlessly from job to job. I had the desire to be a commercial artist but I was obviously lacking the necessary ambition. Finally, after six years had gone by, I forced myself to enroll in an art correspondence course. Two years later I had completed it and though I was pleased with my sense of accomplishment, it still did not seem to be enough to satisfy me. By this time Laura and I had already been married for two years and we were living in Salina, Kansas. While there I completed two years of training at the Salina Tech in the commercial art program.

Following graduation I began my journey into the world, my portfolio close at hand. I had undertaken several art-related projects for local merchants in Salina and the experience was to prove invaluable. Now I was pursuing my dream.

My search ended in Kansas City where I am now employed as a graphic artist. But I still freelance in my free time. At this point I think that freelancing as a designer and illustrator is very self gratifying because of the freedom from working in the structured environment of the traditional job.

Patrick Hamm

So much for the artist's self-description. What this autobiography does not tell us—among other things— is that Gonzalez sincerely desires to share his creations with the world. It also does not indicate his religious base, a base from which he draws guidance, strength, and direction. One of his creations, the one that this writer thinks is headed for success, is what Gonzalez calls his ''Cassie Kids'' (see color section). One of them is illustrated here, but for some background information we will turn once more to the artist's words:

Cassie Kids are fictitious childlike characters designed from the images of my niece Cassie and also from remembrances of me as a child. Laura and I don't have any children yet but we expect to have them someday. In the meantime, the Cassie Kids are our children. I love the innocence of children, they are the closest thing that we have to God. Children are so beautiful and I strive to capture that beauty and innocence in all of my little Cassie creations. Currently, I am illustrating Cassie Kids for custom birth announcements and for children's birthday invitations.

Who can add anything to that?

Fred Gonzalez
217 Northwest 62nd Terrace
Kansas City, Missouri 64118

Patrick Hamm

Patrick Hamm

Patrick Hamm is one of only a few postcard artists whose work is not only popular but avidly sought on both sides of the Atlantic Ocean. One of the 300 postcards produced from his first design realized almost $240 in auction in 1987, further proof of his ascent up the ladder of desirability.

A young man of but twenty-eight years, Hamm's rise has been sudden. If what he has done thus far is any indication of his potential, his popularity is clearly based on the substantial grounds of artistic merit. Hamm's style and use of subject matter is eclectic. Art Nouveau seems to be a favorite of his (see color section), and he can paint a pretty face indeed, but his choice of topics also includes transportation, views, and special occasion. Hamm's use of color is daring and innovative, throwing yet more light on the various motifs that constitute his pictures.

Hamm is no one-dimensional person, however. When his father died, Patrick was only eighteen years old, but he was already man enough to cease his art studies and shoulder the responsibilities of supporting his family. This type of dedication coupled with his ever-present smile—even if only a hint of one sometimes—are qualities with which he should be able to make his way successfully through life.

As for his art? Do us all a favor, Patrick: Keep those postcards coming.

Patrick Hamm
23 Route Burkel
67400 Illkirch
Graffenstaden
France

Patrick Hamm

Sherry Kemp

Sherry Kemp

Sherry Kemp

It's a big world, and in it there may be people who can draw or paint a better picture than Sherry Kemp. But be advised: Don't go looking for art that is superior to hers without first packing a lunch because the journey will take you pretty far afield.

"I've been drawing since I was three or four," Kemp says, and continues, "I'm completely self-taught." What the rest of us want to know is when this delightful—and that word is used advisedly—creature will open a studio of her own and take in students. After examining some of the stuff that passes for art these days, one would think that Kemp's days *and* nights would be filled with the questions coming from an ever-increasing throng of students wanting to know how she so vividly captures reality on canvas and paper.

Why she ever wasted her time on anything other than art is beyond the comprehension of this writer, but she did. After graduation from Hood College (where she was told that her doodling was "anything but art") in 1973, where she obtained a degree in English literature, Kemp pursued such diverse occupations as an office gofer (for lack of a better term, she explains), a caterer's assistant, a post office letter carrier, an antiques dealer, and a supervisor for the Dairy Herd Improvement Association. The last job was the one she enjoyed most, but it was the one that paid the least.

Sherry Kemp

Marc Lenzi

Marc Lenzi

That does it for the résumé. Those of us who would rather stare at her art (see color section) than look at her credentials will leave that latter pastime to personnel officers. We've better things to do: Like Roy Rogers, who commissioned her to do a portrait of him, Dale Evans, Gabby Hayes, and their horses; the judges in five states who awarded her best-of-show ribbons; Governor Pete Dupont of Delaware, who has commissioned her talent; and even the U.S. government that has sought her artwork as gifts to foreign dignitaries. Like them all, the only thing we need to do is examine one single piece of her creativity to be hooked, hooked beyond any unhooking.

Good art sometimes has that effect. Great art, Sherry Kemp's art, always does.

Sherry Kemp
1319 East Patrick Street
Frederick, Maryland 21701

Marc Lenzi

At this writing, very little in the way of biographical data are available on Marc Lenzi. In fact, his French nationality, his many art showings, his amiability, and his artistic creativity are all that is known by this writer.

On the other hand, perhaps these things tell us all that is really important. Clearly, Lenzi is a man with strong social sensibilities. All of his thoughts may not be important or significant ones (whose are?), but, as indicated by his postcard images (see color section), many of them are.

Marc Lenzi would make a good character study. In the meantime, we should examine his art—and enjoy it.

Marc Lenzi
8, Rue du Pont-Vieux
06300 Nice
France

Daniel Mennebeuf

France is culture, France is art. In fact, those two words—culture and art—sum up the universal understanding with which much of the world regards the French nation. And, while it is true that not all Frenchmen are artists nor are all the women walking examples of fashion, it is also true that the French have often led the world in defining and exhibiting some of the more elevated aspects of human aesthetics.

Daniel Mennebeuf

Daniel Mennebeuf, artist and social thinker, is a man for whom art and culture are avenues for exploring the world about him and expressing the multifacetedness of his personality and his talent. The work shown here, ''Love is Blind,'' is simple in design yet loaded with meaning and lending itself to multiple interpretations. This is the way that artist/caricaturist Mennebeuf would want it.

Like the poet, the artist uses his art to make a statement or to suggest alternatives. When this is ac-

Ed Pfau. Cincinnati: From Frontier Settlement to Metropolis.

complished through insightful humor of the type Mennebeuf utilizes, the effect is enhanced and driven home with added force. The impact is, at the least, doubled.

The best news is that Mennebeuf is still a very young man. Born on March 26, 1956, at Chalon/Saône, France, Mennebeuf has been quite active during his short span of years. Among his clients have been the press, industry, the medical community and the banking business. His art has been represented at French galleries and expos, in addition to various other types of showings. He was also honored to have his illustrations presented at the International Cartoon Festival in Edinburgh. Daniel Mennebeuf is a busy, much-sought-after explainer of what we are pleased to call the human condition. His art reports on the ever-changing social and political situation as well. Is he Don Quixote?

Treat yourself by contacting him to find out. He may even be available for some freelance work.

Daniel Mennebeuf
4, Rue Des Poulets
71100 Chalon Sur-Saône
France

Ed Pfau

Ed Pfau is the sort of person who it is hard to dislike. In fact, the only people who would have any problem relating to Pfau are the phonies of this world. Pfau, you see, is a man totally devoid of guile and subterfuge. Deception is as alien to his nature as frowning, another

Don Preziosi

Don Preziosi

Don Preziosi

practice he attempts to avoid. Whether Pfau acquired his optimistic disposition while working on a cattle breeding dairy farm in Minnesota as a child or developed it in high school where he received the American Legion Award bronze medal for ''Boy Most Likely to Succeed'' is unknown.

One thing is for sure: Pfau has never been a second-rater at anything he puts his hands and mind to. Being the naturally inquisitive fellow he is, that has included a number of things. The correspondence schools he has profited from include the following: I.C.S. Architecture and the Building Trades; Commercial Art Institute in Minnesota; and the Alexander Hamilton Institute in which he studied business. During his brief naval career (1944–46), Pfau was on the aircraft carrier Intrepid and was ship artist, a not unlikely vocation for a man with his abilities.

To earn his living, Pfau has labored since 1947 in store planning design. Since 1981, he has been self-employed in this line of work, and Pfau will be the first to tell you that he is not lacking for gainful employment.

The truth is, Pfau is just too bursting with enthusiasm, intellectual curiosity, and artistic ideas to sit still even for a moment. One of his favorite activities is etching intricate designs on wooden eggs. Among the artistic topics rendered in this fashion has been an entire set devoted to the American presidents while numerous larger (goose-size) eggs illustrate Russian and Byzantine items, duplicating their delicate colors

to precision. Never a stingy person, Pfau has arranged displays for local libraries where he shares his craftsmanship with the public.

He is a newcomer to the postcard field, (see color section), but it is clear that he can continue in the medium as long as he wishes.

Ed Pfau
1640 Rockhurst Lane
Cincinnati, Ohio 45255

Don Preziosi

Like Fred Gonzalez, the language Don Preziosi uses to describe himself is simple and direct. Also like Gonzalez's, it bears repeating:

I was born October 18, 1947, and raised in New Jersey. I graduated in 1969 from Syracuse University with a B.F.A. in advertising design. I went to New York City to pursue a career as an art director. I learned a lot about advertising and realized that I was not interested in spending my lifetime as a ''skilled professional liar.'' I did, however, meet my future wife, Newly, and in 1975–76 we took a year leave of absence from our jobs to backpack around the world. We returned, determined to escape from corporate control. A few more years in advertising enabled us to buy a loft in New York City. In the meantime, we used our interest and enthusiasm for antique photography and for collectibles to develop a part-time business. This led to the discovery of old postcards.

Original Art by Postcard Artists

Anthony Quartuccio. *Peaceful Evening, Yosemite Indians in California*, 1988.

Sherry Kemp. Caring, *1988*.

Sherry Kemp. Reconnoitering, 1988.

Ann Rusnak. Postcard Queen, *another example of the artist's creativity.*

Patrick Hamm. Alsace, *colorful Art Nouveau design.*

Don Preziosi. El Presidente, *one artist's impression of the Reagan persona.*

Don Preziosi. Buckle Up . . . , *even Nixon is watching.*

Ed Pfau. Harry Truman: A Man for All Seasons.

Ed Pfau. Smuggler, *among the most famous of horses.*

Ed Pfau. Steven Newman: The Worldwalker.

Marc Lenzi. The Statue of Liberty, with symbolism intact.

Richard Blake. A testimony to the postcard's durability—or is it longevity?

Rick Geary. Only one title is suitable for this original caricature of Roosevelt: Bully.

Fred Gonzalez. From the Cassie Kids collection.

Jean Boccacino. Scene reflecting on the bittersweetness of life.

Postcards

Luxembourg embossed stamp card (novelty). Ottmar Zieher

Texas state Capitol with inset of Stephen Austin (state capitols). Curt Teich

German soldier reminiscing, World War I (military). Anonymous

Who Wouldn't Be a Forester? (romance). Ullman Manufacturing Co.

Washington crossing the Delaware (military/Washington). Anonymous

Chinese Sunday school children (Sunday school-related). Pacific Novelty. Co.

"Yo'all cain't go an' two-time me" (blacks). C.T. Art

American Broadcasting Co., Hollywood, California (television related) Western Publishing & Novelty Co.

Turkey being attacked by Balkan leaders (military). Bruder Kohn.

Memorial Day motifs (greetings). Anonymous

Entertaining the kitties (animals/humorous). Anonymous

Museum of the Sovereigns, Franz Joseph (Art Nouveau/royalty). Le Rire

Museum of the Sovereigns, Princess Wilhelmina of the Netherlands (Art Nouveau/royalty). Le Rire

Erin Go Bragh, St. Patrick's Day salutation (greetings). International Art Publishing Co.

Hymns and prayers at Christmas (greetings). Anonymous

The original Christmas image (greetings). Anonymous

A joyful Christmas (greetings). Anonymous

Winter scene (Art Deco). Anonymous

A beautiful embroidered card (novelty). Anonymous

Wilhelm II in lunatic asylum, World War I-related (military/ royalty). Anonymous

Kaiser Wilhelm II (royalty). Stengel & Co.

Wedding commemorative of German crown prince (royalty/special occasion). Anonymous

President John Tyler (presidential). Raphael Tuck

A colorful Fourth of July card (greetings) Anonymous

Temple of Jupiter, Athens (antiquity, ruins). Anonymous

The panorama of Niagara Falls (famous locations). Buffalo Stationery Co.

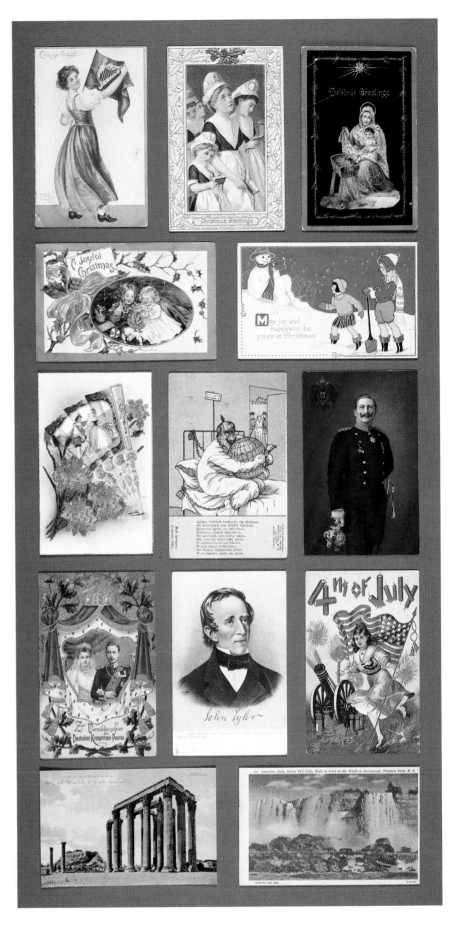

General Joffre (French), World War I (military). Vise

"Alexander's Ragtime Band": Wilhelm II and the Central Powers (military). Anonymous

America's Capitol with inset of the Great Seal (capitols). C. E. Wheelock & Co.

The basic message (romance). Anonymous

George V's Coronation commemorative (roylaty/special occasion). Raphael Tuck

"Our Next President," William Howard Taft (presidential). Anonymous

An embossed Memorial Day card (greetings). Anonymous

The elves at New Year's (greetings). Anonymous

Another colorful New Year's offering (greetings). Anonymous

Animal symbols of Easter (greetings). Anonymous

Thanksgiving Day souvenir card (greetings). Anonymous

Drinkers of Red Bird Coffee (advertising). Red Bird Coffee

Buffalo Bill (cowboys). Sanborn Souvenir Co.

The Home of Shredded Wheat, Niagara Falls, New York (advertising). Shredded Wheat

Message from Winston Churchill, World War II-related (famous people/military). Valentine's

A Happy Crowd. Eskay's Foods (advertising). Eskay's Foods

A new 1959 Chevrolet (advertising). Anonymous

"Curley," General Custer's scout (Indians). Illustrated Postal Card Co.

Happy Go Lucky (blacks). Edward Mitchell

Choctaw Indian princess, Oklahoma (Indians). Oklahoma News Co.

Winnebago Indians, Wisconsin (Indians). Curteich.

Cherokee Indians in full native costume, North Carolina (Indians). Curteich.

Tijuana, Old Mexico (large letter). Curteich

Suspension bridge, Cincinnati, Ohio (bridges). Kraemer Art Co.

We were so enamored of them that in a matter of two years our part-time business was almost exclusively in old postcards. In January of 1980 we became full-time postcard dealers. As an artist/designer, I was always dazzled by the beauty, graphics and subject matter of the cards. I was inspired to do my own cards and from 1978 forwards was making personal postcards for Christmas and other occasions.

In 1983 I produced my first "commercial" card and have made many since then. Most have utilized socio-political themes. As I've gotten older I have become increasingly concerned about social justice, immoral foreign policy, environmental concerns and et cetera. My postcards enable me to make a statement(s) on a variety of issues. I also feel that postcards are an artform that is affordable to almost everyone fortunate enough to be employed.

As for the old postcards, we are still full-time dealers, and I have been writing a monthly column for *Postcard Collector* magazine primarily about cards from the 1930s through the 1960s.

I live in an old house in Mendham, New Jersey, with my wife and two children.

Don Preziosi is obviously an interesting person, but he is more, including being that rare breed to whom age has not proved detrimental to their politics. Many of us start out our lives with something of a liberal orientation, that is, concern for the underdog, for those less fortunate generally, for civil rights, educational mobility for the poor, and so forth. But as time wears on and we get older, becoming taxpayers, parents, and home owners, a strong taint of conservatism begins to color our perceptions. This has not happened to Don Preziosi, and though one may disagree with him politically (see color artwork) or philosophically, one must, at the same time, admire the strength and dedication that he brings on a persistent basis to his ideals and beliefs.

Don Preziosi
Box 498
Mendham, New Jersey 07945

Anthony Quartuccio

The epitaph left on Will Rogers's grave expresses the humorist's mind-set: "I never met a man I didn't like." Will Rogers may have been the only man to make that statement and keep a straight face at the same time. The problem with the rest of us is that everybody is not Anthony Quartuccio, who it is impossible not to like.

An artist from his youth, Quartuccio has painted pictures of his beloved Santa Clara Valley in California since he was thirteen years old. Born in Sicily, which he left with his parents at the age of seven, he lived at

Anthony Quartuccio

Anthony Quartuccio

first in Akron, Ohio, before moving to San Jose, California, in 1936. It was love at first "site" for young Anthony. Looking at his sketches and paintings, it is simple enough to see what it was that so fascinated him.

The topics he has illustrated include mountains, valleys and streams, vegetation-filled landscapes, Indians (see color section), maps, rock formations, and his two favorite subjects, missions and Catholic saints. So prodigious has been Quartuccio's output that he has had three books devoted to his renditions, *Rambling Through Baja, California, with Pen and Brush; Saints of the California Landscape;* and *Santa Clara*

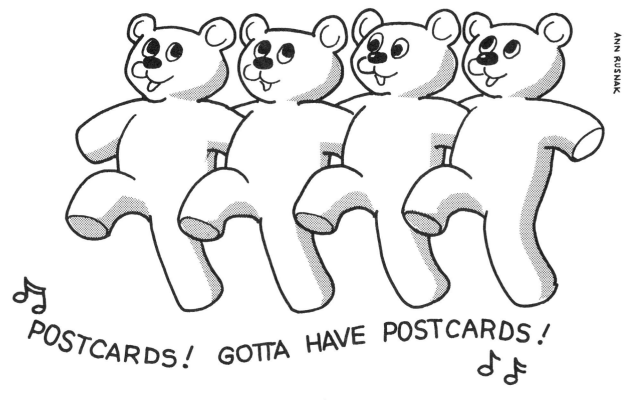

Ann Rusnak

Valley, Today and Yesterday. These are in addition to his first publishing effort, *Tony's Guide to Better Painting.*

He has exhibited at art shows as well as putting on shows of his own. He has also generously given of his time and talent to the San Jose Postcard Club, of which he is a member.

Quartuccio's art, like the man who creates it, has a living, breathing quality about it, at once uplifting and refreshing. It is said that Anthony Quartuccio smiles a lot.

So does his art.

Anthony Quartuccio
4819 Kingdale Drive
San Jose, California 95214

Ann Rusnak

Busy, helpful, vital. These are the three words that often come to mind when the name Ann Rusnak appears. She is all three, and just listening to her outline her upcoming activities is sufficient to tire we lesser souls.

Artist, article writer, lecturer, postcard newsletter editor, wife, homemaker, correspondent to letter writing friends the world over: These are some of the many hats Rusnak wears, and she wears them with grace and taste. One measure of her artistic achievement is to be found in the fact that she is one American who is well respected by the French. Her biography lists one honor and position after another: A Press and Union League Club scholarship helped her pay her way through college (San Jose State College and the University of Nevada); she was editor for the Nevada Artists Association newsletter and later secretary of its executive board; and she has been exhibit chairperson for the Carson Valley Art Association and its vice president for publicity.

The list goes on.

Her postcard art (see color section) has been featured in the following publications: *Barr's Post Card News; Comic Buyer's Guide; Gardnerville Record-Courier; Nevada Nurses Association Rnformation; Postcard Examiner; Linn's Stamp News; Scott's Stamp Monthly; The Stamp Wholesaler;* and *Reno Impact.*

In 1984, Rusnak was given the "Writer of the Year" award from *Barr's Post Card News.* Her vitality is demonstrated by the fact that, year in and year out,

Ann Rusnak

Ann Rusnak

It is this writer's pleasure to acknowledge Rusnak's contributions to deltiology and to express appreciation for her kindnesses to so many.

Thank you, Ann. Thank you.

Ann Rusnak
PO Box 1417
Gardnerville, Nevada 89410

Other Artists

American

Angela Beadell
Jennifer Berman
Rita Booth
Doris Jean Bray
Ken Brown
Kate Gawf
Joan Klepac
Harry and Betty McCallion
Marge Mayes
Anne Petitjean
Lucy Rigg
Del Schuler
Jack Smith
Laura Tarantino
Richard Watherwax

Ann Rusnak

she produces more cards for National Postcard Week than any other artist. She's a personable lady, this Ann Rusnak.

British

Douglas Anderson
Glen Baxter
Steve Bell
Molly Brett
Frank Burridge
Graham Dean
Maggi Hambling
John Mac
Ken Sprague
Jake Sutton

Canadian

Stephen Andrews
Carlo Cesta
Andy Fabo
Adly Gawad
Oliver Girling
Alan Glicksman
Sybil Goldstein

Doug Guilford
Dennice Hall
Matt Harley
Tim Jocelyn (deceased)
Rae Johnson
Barbara Klunder
Michael Merrill
Carol Moisewitch
Lisa Neighbor
Runt
Tom Slaughter
Fiona Smyth
Kurt Swinghammer
Erella Vent
Julie Voyce
George A. Walker
Ben Walmsley

French

Charles Berg

Jean Claval
Filipandre
Gerard-Louis Gautier
Pierre Jeudy
Pierre Marquer
Jean Michael-Cristo
Yannick Moure
J. M. Petrey
Etienne Quentin
Pat Thiebault
Albert Thinlot

Others

Willy Bohm (West German)
Jack Clafferty (Irish)
Cormac (Irish)
Erich Johner (West German)
Peter Kennard (Irish)
Christine Spengler (Irish)

Angela Beadell

Angela Beadell

Jennifer Berman

Doris Jean Bray

Doris Jean Bray

Ken Brown

Ken Brown

Jennifer Berman

Joan Klepac

Joan Klepac

Marge Mayes

Marge Mayes

Anne Petitjean

Anne Petitjean

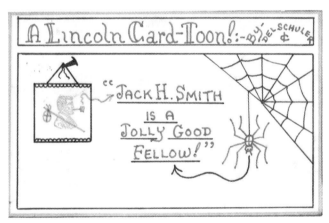

Del Schuler

Del Schuler

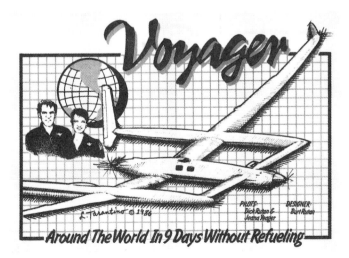

Laura Tarantino

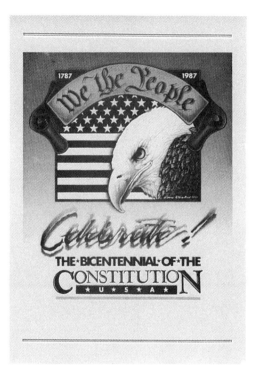

Laura Tarantino

Jean Claval

Jean Claval

Alan Glicksman

Doug Guilford

Matt Harley

Tim Jocelyn

Barbara Klunder

Michael Merrill

Sixteen cards in "Small Wonder, Small World" series, published by Droplit Books

Runt

Tom Slaughter

Kurt Swinghammer

George A. Walker

Erella Vent

Adly Gawad

Sixteen cards in "Small Wonder, Small World" series, published by Droplit Books

Oliver Girling

Julie Voyce

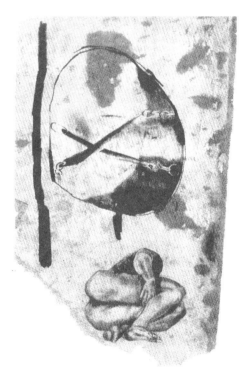

Stephen Andrews

Andy Fabo

Sixteen cards in ''Small Wonder, Small World'' series, published by Droplit Books

Gerard-Louis Gautier

Gerard-Louis Gautier

Pierre Jeudy

Pierre Jeudy

Pierre Marquer

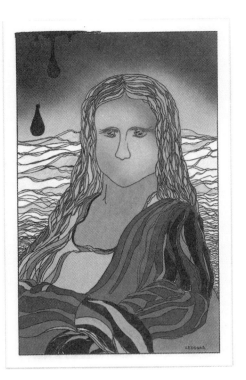

Marc Ledogar

Jean Michael-Cristo

Jean Michael-Cristo

Yannick Moure

Yannick Moure

Etienne Quentin

Entienne Quentin

Albert Thinlot

Albert Thinlot

8
Postcard Publications

8
Postcard Publications

One of the many ways in which the postcard collecting community has been blessed and enriched is through the many postcard publications that have been devoted to it. Moreover, this has been true not only in our postatomic era, with its proliferation of magazines, newspapers, club newsletters, and the like, but this was equally the case during and since the earlier "craze period" (1894–1914).

Much research is still needed in the area of early postcard literature, but enough has been undertaken and unearthed to show the variety and multitude of these former publications. Some of them, like some of today's, were mediocre at best, both as regarded the writing and the research.

The fact that the number of these publications is increasing and that their readership ranks are swelling augurs of a healthy hobby. Further, the expertise and knowledge that they generate through the articles and checklists that they print add not only to the storehouse of deltiological information but also encourages others to engage in yet more research.

Essentially, the categories of postcard publications may be grouped under the following headings: 1) postcard periodicals, 2) postcard price catalogues, and 3) postcard auction catalogues. Some are more well known than others and consequently enjoy a wider readership, but even the less well-traveled ones partake in information dispersal. Interestingly enough, a few of the smaller ones are among those that are the most well written and detail packed.

Periodicals

Picture Postcard Monthly
(Nottingham, England)

It has long been accepted that *Picture Postcard Monthly (PPM)* reaches a wider international audience than any of the other periodicals. Offered in magazine format, *PPM* has a glossy, colorful cover that reproduces two of the postcards discussed in the articles inside. These articles by themselves are well worth the price of purchase and are the major reason for *PPM*'s popularity beyond its British shores.

In most cases, the articles are written by individuals who are recognized authorities in the specific areas to which they lend their expository prose. David Pinfold contributes a monthly article on the postcards of Raphael Tuck; Peter Davies lends his knowledge to a regular article on modern cards; and Jack Sammons frequently writes about the well-known publisher, Bamforth. Other contributors include David Cook, an authority on Australian postcards; Tom Hutchinson, focusing on topographical material; Jack Smith, specializing on the royalty and military; and Ian McDonald, whose research crosses into several areas.

Yet another feature of *PPM* that deserves mention is its "Round the Clubs" section in which special activities or articles from postcard club newsletters are mentioned. Often accompanied by photographs, these news reports are often significant, relaying necessary information in a way that suggests that the British are as serious-minded with their pleasures as they are with their more mundane affairs. These last comments apply as well to the advertising found in *PPM*, much of which is both professionally presented and attractively designed in addition to containing all necessary information. Aware of their public responsibilities, the *PPM* publishers, Brian and Mary Lund, are careful to leave column space for an analysis of new postcard book titles. The books are reviewed with a critical eye, their strengths and weaknesses illuminated in a refreshingly candid style.

Perhaps the most delightful—and instructional—parts of the magazine are the columns by J. H. D. Smith (not to be confused with the author of this volume) and his archnemesis, an occasionally sharp-penned and always quick-witted writer who offers his opinions under the pseudonym "Questor." Both Smith and Questor have relative, valid, and interesting points of view. Like Tevye from the famous play and movie "Fiddler on the Roof," who listens to two points of view and is forced to conclude that both are correct, the reader of these columns walks away with his or her head freshly filled with facts, figures, and liberal doses of common sense. In few cases is either party exclusively and completely correct. Indeed, it seems that each takes turns being only marginally correct, but from topic to topic, this business of rightness or wrongness is not only open to interpretations but is subject to the force of any given argument on any given issue.

One final note is in order. By keeping mail auctions to a minimum (not more than a few a year are included annually), *PPM* has performed an invaluable service to its readership. Some publications would intimate that their running of mail auctions is a "necessary evil" that offsets costs and that they are a reader service in the same way that articles, advertisements, and postcard club news are. These may be valid arguments, but the simple fact is that many of the letters from readers of the various publications lament the shortage of good articles while this writer has yet to see the first letter requesting more auctions. *PPM* has kept itself above the fray by offering an infrequent auction but using the bulk of its space on useful information.

PPM's overworked but personable publishers are the husband and wife team of the aforementioned Brian and Mary Lund. Brian, who has collected postcards since 1974, is a former teacher of history, English, and physical education. His other interests include rugby, cricket, tennis, and sunbathing. Mary was also a former teacher, and her interests are tennis, swimming, and netball.

The Lunds were asked to give their opinions regarding *PPM* and the hobby of postcard collecting generally. They consider the functions of *PPM* as the dispensing of information, the offering of entertainment, and enlightenment. They also want it to serve as a vehicle for the expression of opinions. These functions are performed with news items, research articles, background articles, "viewpoint" articles, checklists, humorous items, and advertising. Brian Lund's further comments, offered in the sort of shorthand that indicates his efficient use of time, are worth repeating:

We hope *PPM* achieves its aims as fully as we can make it [do so]. We try to make it of international interest but its basis must be the Great Britain collecting scene in order to cater for readers here. There is, however, a fair proportion of articles in any given year featuring several cards/events/personalities.

Our aim for the future is to continue producing *PPM* to give it maximum interest. The possibility of a separate magazine dealing with modern cards is in the pipeline. We believe that the hobby is still in its infancy and that there is massive potential for research and expansion in number of collectors. The one primary way in which the hobby could be improved would be for it to receive more TV/radio exposure.

Picture Postcard Monthly
Reflections of a Bygone Age
15 Debdale Lane
Keyworth
Nottingham NG12 5HT
England

Postcard Collector
(Iola, Wisconsin)

Another magazine. Although *Postcard (PC) Collector* does not sell as many international copies nor reach as many diverse geographical areas as *Picture Postcard Monthly*, it is to be understood that the United States is a very large country and that it requires the best, unflagging efforts of any publication to keep apprized of its domestic readership.

This is not a job for the faint of heart nor the weak spirited. *PC Collector* may be thankful, as may we all, that its publisher is neither of the above. If anything, Diane Allmen is the classic workaholic, attempting to stay squarely atop every situation and determined to be in control of every detail. She in turn may be thankful that her monthly magazine is owned by Krause Publications, the largest literary marketplace for collectibles in America. Many of Krause's other publications have a comfortable history of longevity and growth, and it is to be hoped that *PC Collector* may follow in that tradition.

Concerning the magazine itself, *PC Collector* does have a select group of writers—plus many others who are featured from time to time—who turn out, on a regular basis, many fine articles and informational columns. To begin with, there is a university professor, George Miller, a postcard devotee and author of considerable standing. Then there is Susan Brown Nicholson, another author and noted collector. There are others: Dave Long, the well-known dealer in modern postcards; the always refreshing Don Preziosi (qv), with his monthly offering "Linens and Beyond"; and Sally Carver, author of *The American Guide to Tuck*, is available to answer questions.

PC Collector has an excellent feature written by Allmen herself entitled "Greetings from Iola," in which the publisher relates events and market trends as well as providing some timely and pertinent tips on this topic or that. It is good reporting but altogether too brief.

As with all of the best postcard publications, *PC Collector* has a "Letters to the Editor" section. Some of these letters have been exceptional little miniarticles that either inform, challenge, or merely question in a very lucid, entertaining manner. A "Show Calendar" section that lists upcoming events is also included, along with occasional impromptu inserts where questions are posed or information is tendered. Many of the advertisements represent a pleasing combination of good graphics and clear prose, true not only of the larger ads but some of the smaller ones, as well. Allmen is thoughtful enough to include information on new postcard releases from a few of the bigger publishers. She also offers several book reports each year, although these numbers could surely be increased.

Another interesting column is the infrequent "Collector's Showcase," which may spotlight a new book, an intriguing collecting type or category, or an information-packed piece that relates to any of a number of areas, all worth investigating.

There are a couple of minor flaws, however, which this analysis draws attention to in the hopes that a good periodical may become an even better one. The first involves the paper used. If *PC Collector* were the sort of magazine whose worth was confined to a single reading then off to the garbage bin or the bird cage, perhaps it might be appropriate to use the sort of paper that is acid-filled and seeks its own destruction even as it comes off the press. But it is not. This is a magazine that deserves to be kept for future reference, and thus its producers should use the kind of paper that lends itself to lengthy preservation.

The other minor flaw is in the area of mail auctions. This has already been mentioned, but it is a significant area of concern. It is obvious that a large percentage of *PC Collector*'s income is generated through advertisements and mail auctions. It surely must be admitted as well that auctions do perform a reader service, especially for those folk who may live in a rural or isolated area with few dealers or for those collectors whose tastes are somewhat more sophisticated and who seek material that may more easily be found in this format, but this should be balanced against the needs and wants of the bulk of the readership that, if their letters are to be believed, desires more articles and information rather than more auctions.

When all is tallied, *PC Collector* must be viewed as the premier postcard periodical in America. Under the guiding influence of Allmen, its layout is first-rate, the articles are interestingly and clearly presented, and the overall appearance of the magazine is one of seriousness and professionalism. Its desire to expand and

to discover new vistas for research is unparalleled. Its future looks promising, which means that American postcard collectors will have the opportunity to grow and learn with them.

When asked to tell something about both *PC Collector* and herself, Allmen graciously consented with what follows, printed in its entirety:

What Function Does *Postcard Collector* Serve?

Postcard Collector is a monthly publication designed to provide timely and useful information for the American collector and to offer the largest mail marketplace for buying, selling, and trading postcards.

Does *Postcard Collector* Fulfill this Function?

Yes, *Postcard Collector* is the leading American publication about postcards, providing monthly auctions and other advertising in a format filled with news and information about postcards of all ages, on all topics, and in all price ranges.

The flexible advertising options provide opportunities for collectors at all levels of involvement in the hobby: from casual to serious collector; collector/researcher to collector/investor; and trades-only collector/dealer to full-time postcard dealer. Repeated testimonials from satisfied advertisers and buyers prove the effectiveness of postcard auctions and fixed price sales; display advertising for all postcard-related products and activities; classified word ads; and economical miniads designed especially for the small and beginning publisher.

Fact-filled, intelligently written articles and lavish illustrations cover all ages, topics, and price ranges of postcards, from pioneers and exposition cards to modern, personal, and National Postcard Week postcards. Special annual features include the Roster of American Postcard Clubs (published in November); the Supplies Buyers Guide (published in February); and the list for Buying Moderns Off the Rack (published in May). Monthly columns by experts Dave Long (on chromes), Don Preziosi (on linens), Terry Johnson (on moderns), Susan Nicholson and Sally Carver (on rare older cards and sets), and features by all-around expert George Miller (pioneers, expositions, artists, the postcard industry, and other topics) all have avid readership. Announcement briefs in the "News Up Front," "Letters," "Where Is It?," "From PC's Mailbag," and "Show Calendar" departments are always popular.

What Are *Postcard Collector*'s Plans for the Future?

We will continue to be sensitive and responsive to reader and advertiser interests.

Where Is the Postcard Hobby Headed? How Can it Be Improved?

In the thirty years I have collected contemporary postcards, I can remember no more dynamic activity nor better quality of contemporary postcards than the present. In the ten years I have collected antique postcards, I have seen a remarkable change in dealers' understanding and appreciation of the rarity and value of antique postcards. As this awareness of the value of postcards as unique historical visual documents continues to increase both in the collector community and among the public, we should expect a bright future for postcards and for collectors.

Biography

Diane Allmen was born in Detroit, Michigan, in 1944. She gained a bachelor of science degree in microbiology from the University of Michigan in 1967 and a master of business administration degree in finance and marketing from the University of Chicago in 1979. She served in a number of technical and information management positions in Chicago-area publishing and research organizations from 1967 to 1983. As a member of the Windy City Postcard Club, she served as editor of the *Club Bulletin* in 1982 and 1983. In February 1983, she founded the bimonthly *Post Card Collectors Bulletin*. In September 1983, she sold the publication to Krause Publications of Iola, Wisconsin, and moved to Iola as editor of the new *Postcard Collector*. Allmen continues to live in Iola and is currently publisher, with overall responsibility for *Postcard Collector*. Her postcard collection consists of many topics, from the 1890s to the present, including American suffrage and real photos of Deer Creek and Cohoctah, Michigan.

Postcard Collector
700 East State Street
Iola, Wisconsin 54990

Barr's Post Card News
(Lansing, Iowa)

In order to maintain itself in business, every periodical must have a loyal following. For a number of very good reasons, *Barr's Post Card News* has its share of admirers and devotees.

Barr's provides a forum for opinions in its "Letter" (to the editor) section, it maintains a cadre of interesting writers, and it has some old-fashioned human interest elements that may be lacking in the two periodicals just described.

Examples of this abound. *Barr's* has encouraged its readers to get involved with the sick and less fortunate by printing addresses where postcards—as symbols of condolence and human compassion—may be dispatched. It has attempted to add real human dimensions to both dealers and collectors by its "Know Your Dealers" and "Collector of the Month" inserts. It provides considerable coverage of postcard shows and any other postcard-related activities.

Not given to extravagance, *Barr's* is a meat-and-potatoes type of operation. It has a decided country flavor and a sort of Midwestern integrity that prevents it from becoming pretentious. Like the *Reader's Digest, Barr's* can become a comfortable, familiar publication to have lying around the house. Sadly, it is

these very homespun qualities that may have created a few problems of the minor variety. Although most of its article writers are obviously well-educated people—and all are clearly well meaning—a few of the more infrequent ones could use a couple of lessons in syntax and grammar. It is the job of the editor to check the prose before it is put to print, but unfortunately all of the problems are not confined to the "Letters" section. This is all the more lamentable because some of the worst offenders are people with the most interesting stories to tell or significant information to relate.

Most of *Barr's* regular contributors are about as good a group as one is likely to find anywhere. Roy Nuhn, (qv), a well-known figure in deltiology, has at least one article in most of *Barr's* weekly issues. Nuhn writes in essay style, and his wording is crisp and succinct. Joan Carlson, one of the most fascinating and lovable people in or out of postcard collecting, offers articles on modern postcards, both listing and illustrating examples of the new deltiological arrivals. Historian Charles Burns contributes some interesting and well-written material to *Barr's*. There are others, as well, gracious folk who add to the sum of postcard knowledge and should be applauded for their efforts.

Barr's has much more to commend it. The aforementioned Nuhn is ever available to answer questions in a special section created with that purpose in mind. Marilyn Link prepares a delightful weekly piece entitled "As Time Goes By," where she demonstrates the historical utility of postcards by combining them with events and people of the past.

Unfortunately, there are all two few book reports in *Barr's*. As it occurs, the reason has to do with economics. To begin with, it must be understood that *Barr's* publishes a weekly periodical in newspaper format. Common sense dictates that the expenses it incurs in staff work hours, postage costs, and other items of overhead are proportionally greater than those incurred by less frequently produced publications. Therefore, *Barr's* has more auctions and advertising than both *PPM* and *PC Collector;* in fact, in any given month probably from three to four times as much. Watching the budget and thus the print space has made *Barr's* conclude that book reviews may not be printed unless the author or reviewer first purchases advertising space for the book. *Barr's* considers a book review to be a book endorsement, thus, a book advertisement, and as other advertisers have to pay for the privilege, *Barr's* has concluded that book reviewers must do the same.

Thankfully, these are not monumental problems, and it is expected that *Barr's* may find a system that works both to its benefit and to the readership it wants to serve. There is always room for accommodation. With a publication this well-received, one always wants the best.

Barr's Post Card News
70 South Sixth Street
Lansing, Iowa 52151

A Note About "The Big Three"

The three publications just described are the largest of the postcard periodicals, and each is well-worth subscribing to. In fact, it would not be possible to have an adequate understanding of the dynamics in the market without subscribing to and reading all three. All and each are excellent, with much to commend them, and though a few complaints have been registered, these have merely been offered in the hopes of improving what are already very good products.

However, before taking leave of "The Big Three" and moving on to an examination of a few other periodicals, it might be a positive idea to make one observation that involves all three. That is this: Each of these periodicals—*Barr's, PPM*, and *PC Collector*—has the problem of being too regional in nature and flavor. Both *PPM* and *PC Collector* make an effort at encouraging a bit of internationalism, but the attempts, though admirable, fall short of the desired goal. *PPM* is clearly the leader in this field of endeavor, but even it could stand some enhancement in this all-important area.

The standard argument that is presented by the editors and publishers regarding this issue is often a shoulder shrug followed by wording to the effect that their readership, or the bulk of it, anyway, is confined to their own country. Thus, they feel compelled to present, almost entirely, news, views, and articles on issues about which Britons or Americans (or Germans, Australians, French, Italians) are interested, and this, or so we are told, deals only or primarily with their own country and people.

This thesis is a valid one and should not be lightly or easily dismissed. It also seems to make good sense, on its face, without the seeming necessity of further scrutiny. There, as Shakespeare would say, is the rub, for such facile thinking, even when accurate, omits other significant parts of the equation. What these publications' owners and editors are inculcating in their readers with this type of isolationist policy is a mindset that encourages separation from fellow collectors

in different countries. This in turn creates what are often petty differences of opinion: in America a postcard collector is called a deltiologist while the British collectors refer to themselves as cartologists. It would be to the benefit of both if each realized that the two words are invented terms that do not alter the fact that the activity is the same and is practiced in much the same way the world over.

There is one piece of evidence to suggest that each member of "The Big Three" could learn from one another. *PPM*, for example, is a most professional journal, but it does not permit this elevated position to prevent its writers from disagreeing with each other in print, in some instances belaboring their points and complaints both loud and long. While true invective seldom arises, the verbal brickbats that are hurled (as in the minor linguistic assaults on one another by J. H. D. Smith and Questor) add much to the storehouse of knowledge, this in addition to giving the reader an opportunity to rethink his or her own position on the various issues that are dealt with. The Americans especially could profit from this example, as too much of American postcard opinion is one-dimensional, a situation exacerbated by the American tendency to avoid confrontational discussions. This could lead to the presentation of individual points of views that takes little cognizance of divergent opinions. It is as if each position existed in some sort of vacuum. To debate and examine in an open environment is the basis for growth in postcard collecting, as in other areas of life. The British have learned this lesson. Perhaps Americans may yet develop along these lines.

Conversely, the British, French, Germans, and others could benefit from the exuberance and camaraderie that many American collectors exhibit both toward the hobby and other collectors. Other countries might also learn something from the American desire to share the results of their findings. With the exceptions of the postcard titles of local interest published through the European Library Series, more than fifty percent of the postcard books published in the last ten years are of American origin. Most of these are printed in limited edition, which suggests that profit was not the overriding motive for writing them.

Both the Americans and the British—and certainly the Germans—could profit from the French preoccupation with their postcard artists. This encouragement has resulted not only in there being up to ten times more postcard artists in France than elsewhere but also tends to stimulate competition because of the increased number of artists. This in turn promotes the creation of more artistic, professional-looking postcards. To be sure, one must not lose sight of the fact that England has its Fagas, Whites, and Blakes while America boasts the likes of Geary, Rusnak, Kemp, and others, but the French take not only pride and interest in their postcard artists, they offer them several outlets and purchase much of the material as quickly as it is made available. Moreover, the French collectors and their artists are paving new roads in the experimental usages of color, design, and photography, and all this primarily because they are encouraged and supported by an appreciative public.

The implication inherent in all this should be clear: There is room for growth, maturation, and diversity for the world of postcard collecting. This realization is both exciting and challenging. The rewards that await are not for those who lag behind. For the collector and for the newspaper publisher, the time to demonstrate excellence and dedication is when it has always been: Now!

At this point, let's continue our examination of some of the more well-known postcard periodicals.

Gruss Aus
(Munich, West Germany)

You will need to understand the German language in order to read this magazine, but all you require in order to develop an appreciation of it are a set of eyes and a liking for quality. Full-color covers with gorgeous and seldom-seen postcard reproductions on them, glossy art paper, and finely detailed illustrations combine to make *Gruss Aus* an optical delight.

The problem is not that the prose is in German—that difficulty may be overcome—the disappointment comes instead with having to accept the fact that *Gruss Aus* is only printed bimonthly. German research in this periodical, as in so many other areas of endeavor, is second to none, nor is the prose dry or pedantic, which only makes one wish there was more of it as well as more types of features to the magazine generally.

There is an average of three articles per issue, not nearly enough by the standards of "The Big Three." The improvement to be desired is in quantity, and the hope is that the quality will remain constant, for this is a slick publication. Though it is lacking in some of the features of some other magazines (for example, in club news, book reviews, and the like), it is to be

acknowledged that *Gruss Aus* represents a brilliant beginning. The publishers make us want more—and more.

Gruss Aus Verlag
Birkenhainstrabe 4
8000 Munchen 70
West Germany

British Postcard Collector's Magazine
(Hertfordshire, England)

Ron Griffiths, who accepts the title "King of the Mods" because of his connection with modern—primarily British and American—postcards, is a fellow devoted to research and its dissemination. The result is the *British Postcard Collector's Magazine* (*BPCM*), which he issues periodically at his discretion. Griffiths also passes along, or rather, he used to pass along, information on the modern scene to J. H. D. Smith for inclusion in Smith's *I.P.M.* catalogue.

The *BPCM* is not a slick, showpiece sort of magazine nor was it ever intended to serve that function. What it does do in its black-and-white, small-scale format is to inform the postcard collecting world of this and that: this new postcard issue, that new artist; this style of postcard preservation, that manner of organization; this category of postcards, that personality. There are reviews, the results of original research, articles about artists, opinions on various subjects, advice, and a snippets section, again about this and that.

Altogether, *BPCM* is an excellent tool for learning.

British Postcard Collector's Magazine
47 Long Arrotts
Hemel Hempstead
Hertfordshire. HP1 3EX
England

Forum Cartes et Collections
(Paris, France)

It is easy to understand, especially after examining a few issues of *Forum Cartes et Collections*, why the French have always been among the top fashion designers, since the days of Louis XIV, anyway, which takes us back three centuries and more.

Striking colors and fine art paper are only two reasons among many why this bimonthly magazine is a first-class offering. Articles about antique postcards are printed alongside reproductions of modern cards and information about their authors. After a bit of looking, the seeming incongruity begins to disappear, especially in light of the fact that some of the themes utilized by the new generations of postcard artists are not themselves new: beautiful maidens, special occasions, children. The French love going into detail, and, whether writing about old artists or new ones, they include much information. Sets and series are described and illustrated with such color and clarity of reproduction that they seem to leap from the page and pleasantly massage the eyes, sending sometimes soothing and sometimes contemplative messages to the brain.

But make no mistake: *Forum Cartes et Collections* is not merely fluff and fashion with an occasional accompanying list of one sort or another. It is also scholarship and the aforementioned attention to detail, both of which are afforded opportunity for expression. Beautiful and welcome as the graphics are, it must be remembered that one of their functions, if not always the main function, is to draw attention to the prose that complements and fulfills the pictures themselves. A "Calendar of Events" and "Special Announcements" sections are good barometers of French postcard activities and of *Forum*'s desire to be a repository and dispenser of useful information to its readers. Like *Gruss Aus, Forum* still has a ways to go and should include more features, but it is clear that the publishers are people dedicated to obtaining and presenting a quality publication. They don't need this writer to tell them that they have succeeded.

Forum Cartes et Collections
42, rue Legendre
75 017 Paris
France

De Prentbriefkaart—A.P.C. Magazine
(Antwerp, the Netherlands)

This publication is the official organ of the Antwerp Postcard Club (A.P.C.) and is included here because it could serve as an excellent model for all other postcard clubs that are wondering how they might improve

their own newsletters or bulletins. Ron Griffiths of *BPCM* has described this monthly Dutch publication as being much like his own in format and printing. He is correct, but the similarities do not end there (also, to be totally honest, it might profitably be maintained that the graphics in *De Prentbriefkaart* are superior to those in *BPCM* both as to clarity and aesthetic appeal).

Both periodicals are small in size but are packed with useful information. Both include data about postcard artists, sets and series, book and magazine reviews, and, in general, the significant events and forces that are shaping, and have shaped, the hobby. Because of space limitations, much that might have been added or included is omitted, but the format works admirably well given its size. It still manages to find the space for in-depth coverage on some of its articles, which is a great foundation for what is hoped to be more coverage and more diversity as the Dutch market expands.

E. Demey
J. F. Van de Gaerstraat 76
2020 Antwerpen
The Netherlands

La Cartolina
(Rome, Italy)

The Italians have the reputation for being energetic pursuers of all their activities. Whether this is a valid statement or merely one of those stereotypical views one is always encountering is the subject for a debate best not entered into here.

But if *La Cartolina* is any indication of the mindset of the Italian postcard collector and the Italian postcard market, it would be safe to assume that both are healthy and vibrant, which is not to say that the magazine is trouble free. It is not. Clearly, this bimonthly magazine would be better serving its readership with the addition of a few color illustrations and the inclusion of some in-depth articles. These are not minor complaints, but neither are they of the sort that cannot be remedied.

These criticisms aside, it is to be observed that *La Cartolina* does a good job of increasing deltiological information in its own fashion. And a good one it is. It chooses a topic, such as artist, publisher, or type of card, and begins to explore it either chronologically, categorically, or in any other way in which it may offer a detailed body of information. The effect is a positive one, and it is hoped that the publishers may eventually put much of this into book form at a later date.

Although reproduced in black and white, the illustrations are sharp and clear and are great enhancers of the subject matter, proving beneficially instructive. Also useful is a thorough ''Calendar of Events.''

La Cartolina
35 via A. G. Barrili
00152 Roma
Italy

Other Postcard Periodicals

Postcard Journal (United States)

A magazine issued quarterly by the Lake County Museum, where the Curt Teich collection is housed, *Postcard Journal* is devoted to researching this particular grouping of cards and has become a useful vehicle for doing so. As indicated previously, this is a very worthwhile project.

Postcard Classics (United States)

James Lewis Lowe, editor and publisher of the now-defunct publication *Deltiology* (qv), has recently begun this magazine. As only one issue has been produced at this writing, it is not possible to offer a comprehensive evaluation. What *Postcard Classics* will be, if Lowe's past performance and efforts are to be accepted as an indicator, is an attempt to increase postcard knowledge through the printing of checklists, the use of various kinds of articles, and an occasional book review.

C.P.M. (France)

This is another of the glossy, slick publications of the type for which the French are becoming world renowned. *C.P.M.* is devoted to modern postcards and modern postcard artists. The French, who love much that is stylish and artistic, are well served by this publication, which combines sharp graphics, information about new offerings—and artists—and other sorts of useful checklists.

Et Cetera

C.P.C. (Cartes Postales et Collections), France; *Cart' Postales,* France; *Collector's Mart,* Isle of Wright; and *Catalogo Delle Cartoline Italiane,* Italy; *Stamps* Magazine, a highly recommended British publication with international circulation.

Former Publications

It would probably be all but impossible to know the titles of all the postcard periodicals that have existed since the postcard was first issued in 1861. On the other hand, there are a few former publications that should not go unmentioned. Among the best and most instructional were the following.

American Postcard Journal

It is to be doubted that any living person has written more words about postcards than Roy Nuhn. For the past several years, Nuhn has been the composer of articles on postcards for *Barr's, PC Collector, Grit, Reader's Digest,* and a number of other publications. Previous to this, he was the editor, publisher, and chief writer for the *American Postcard Journal (APJ)*. Nuhn used the *APJ* both to gather information from various sources and to disseminate it. The subjects of his expositions included postcard publishers, artists, sets and series, categories, and types. Nuhn was never a slouch in the gathering of information, nor was he stingy—or lazy—in the sharing and dissemination of it. *APJ* was his child, his brainchild, and he treated it and his readers with high regard.

Postcard Dealer and Collector

John McClintock has been one of the most productive individuals ever to become involved with deltiology. He founded the International Federation of Postcard Dealers and has been the most active person in it to promote the association and to keep it a legitimate, well-received enterprise. He has helped to start postcard clubs, other publications, and has held postcard shows in locations far and wide. McClintock has freely given of his time to adjudicate complaints between collectors and dealers. He has generously offered advice of the sort worth listening to, and, somehow, between all these activities, he found the time to be the editor and publisher of the *Postcard Dealer and Collector,* one of the finest publications of its type.

His article contributors in the periodical included Bert Silman, Roy Nuhn, Edward Sobol, Roy Cox, Richard Novick, and others, counting McClintock himself. The editorials he wrote for the bimonthly publication are what people in the trade call "keepers," meaning that the information or opinions expressed in them are of sufficient merit to make them worth retaining for future rereading and reference. McClintock's "honesty policy" was an admirable one that he held to firmly. If he couldn't tell the truth for fear of lawsuit or reprisal, he wouldn't say anything at all—or at least as little as possible.

For the most part, McClintock had few problems in speaking with conviction, and anyone with even a modicum of common sense found him worth listening to. As for the articles, the topics were generally universal in collector interest, although there were a few articles on topics with more limited appeal. Even this move shows McClintock's character as a man who thought that even these areas deserved some exposure and research. Though this was an American publication and much of the reporting concerned itself with American postcard clubs, artists, publishers, and the like, McClintock encouraged his writers to cover areas of interest the world over; the pages of his magazine were the better for it as they reflected this cosmopolitan approach.

Postcard Collector's Guide and News (England, 1958–1968)

To British postcard collectors, the name of A. James Butland stands out in landmark fashion. He was one of the true pioneers who reintroduced the collecting of picture postcards to a world that had all but forgotten its earlier obsession with them. This was especially the case in Britain, where interest in the postcard as a collectible was minimal at best. But like the cavalry putting in its appearance at the most propitious moment—if one may be allowed the use of an American metaphor—Butland came upon the scene and gave his unstinting efforts to reviving interest in what had once been the most popular hobby ever known to man.

Butland communicated his own social and historical fascination with the postcard in his publication, *Postcard Collector's Guide and News.* The subjects he touched upon were many and varied; those he ignored were few. This comprehensiveness was really remarkable when one considers that Butland had no models to follow. Indeed, the next generation of writers and researchers was to use him as their prototype. Butland died several years ago and, like James Burdick, a fellow researcher and pioneer on this side of the Atlantic, both his enthusiasm and his dedication will be sorely missed.

Deltiology

James Lewis Lowe, who currently publishes *Postcard Classics,* has not always been interested in postcards. As a young child, he probably couldn't have cared less about signed artists, military postcards, Art Nouveau, advertising cards, and the like. But he has been involved with deltiology for so long that it is hard for today's collectors to imagine a time when Lowe was not an integral part of the hobby.

His former publication, *Deltiology,* was the official organ of the organization Deltiologists of America (D.O.A.). Lowe founded both. D.O.A. itself was described in the literature as "an international society for postcard collectors and dealers," and its membership was, indeed, universal. So too was the format of *Deltiology,* which dealt with postcard topics the world over: Stengel in Germany, Tuck in England, reviews of books published both in America and Europe, articles on artists from many countries, and more. It also covered postcard clubs, offered information about upcoming events, and information related to philatelics. Further, the magazine and the organization became personally involved with people and activities as evidenced by the several postcard titles that they published.

Postcard Collector's Magazine (United States)

The late Bernard Stadtmiller was a man given to research and promotion, two areas in which he excelled. One need look no further for proof of this than at the pages of his fine periodical, *Post Card Collector's Magazine*. In conjunction with the efforts of John Mc-Clintock, publisher of *Postcard Dealer and Collector,* Stadtmiller successfully went about the business of producing the sort of postcard publication that was collector-oriented rather than strictly dealer-oriented. Responding to readers' requests, Stadtmiller, along with his readers—whose assistance was always welcomed and gratefully received—would pursue information about an artist, a publisher, or other topic into several issues in order to be as complete as possible. One example was the space devoted to children's artist Maud Humphrey, the mother of Actor Humphrey Bogart.

The paper used in the production of the magazine was of enduring quality, and the illustrations were always sharp. During its first year of operation (1976), *Post Card Collector's Magazine*'s cover and other illustrations were in full color, and it was issued monthly. From 1977–79, economic considerations forced Stadtmiller to revert to black and white and issue the magazine bimonthly. Fortunately, the paper quality and the content of the publication remained consistently superior until its demise after the third annual edition of 1982. Fortunately also, the entire stock of *Post Card Collector's Magazine* can be obtained—along with Stadtmiller's book (see Chapter 5 for review)—from his sister as long as supplies last.

Available from:

> Mrs. Martha Walton
> 707 Collegewood Drive
> Ypsilanti, Michigan 48197

Et Cetera

The Picture Postcard and Collector's Chronicle (England); *The Deltiologist* (Ridley Park, Pa.); *The Picture Postcard Collector's Gazette* (London, England).

Postcard Price Catalogues/Annuals

The explosion of postcard knowledge that has occurred during the last fifteen years has created a climate where annual, information-filled catalogues have found a ready, receptive audience. Many of them are constructed with the collector in mind and are, therefore, useful tools.

Some of the more prominent catalogues are profiled below.

I.P.M. Catalogue of Picture Postcards & Year Book
(England)

J.H.D. Smith is not only a well-known postcard dealer but is a very busy one as well. In addition to producing quarterly auction catalogues, he sells postcards at shows, by private treaty, and in other manners. He also writes a monthly column for *Picture Postcard Monthly*. All this, mind you, on top of preparing the *I.P.M. Catalogue.*

This is a good book. It contains thematic information, a listing of postcard artists, a modern postcard section, a most welcome grouping of dealers' advertisements, several pages of postmarks, information on British auction houses, a directory of postcard dealers, accessory supplies, a listing of world postcard catalogues, and a fourteen-year price survey (1975–1988).

Smith's analysis and price quotes are his own, but this does not mean that they are arbitrary since his connection with the market is both widespread and immediate. Likewise, his opinions and expertise, subject to modification by other knowledgeable individuals, are to be respectfully considered as coming from a significant source: himself.

As with all these publications, the major flaw is that their appeal is too parochial due to the regional nature of the information contained in them. Someday, a truly international publication will be prepared. Until then—and even after that time—Smith's catalogue will be worth subscribing to.

> International Postcard Market
> P.O. Box 190
> Lewes
> Sussex BN7 1HF
> England

Catalogo delle Cartoline Italiane
(Italy)

The only copy of this Italian annual catalogue that was available for review at the time this book went to print was one dealing with Italian postcard artists and categories. But what an issue it is.

Assuming it to be representative of Furio Arrasich's offerings (a safe assumption given the thoroughness of his other publications such as *La Cartolina*), it is clear that Arrasich is the man to ask if any question about Italian postcards needs to be answered. Though it is to be regretted that the focus of attention is so very narrow, it is to be appreciated that the thoroughness is the result of such informational constriction. Almost every page has helpful illustrations, fully twenty-five percent of them in bright, vibrant color.

After each artist's name are the categories of cards he or she produced and their general price value range. The same system is applied to the category section, where everything is simplified into distinguishable units and priced.

La Cartolina
35 via A. G. Barreli
00152 Roma
Italy

Stanley Gibbons Postcard Catalogue
(England)

Few people, if any, know more about postcards than the husband and wife team of Tonie and Valmai Holt. Their specialty, as attested by the books they have authored on the topic, is military postcards. In this connection, their expertise is not limited to postcards only as the Holts conduct several yearly tours of great historical battle areas.

This same enthusiasm and the dedication to detail that accompanies it are apparent in all the yearly *Stanley Gibbons Postcard Catalogues* that they have prepared since 1980. Each of these annual offerings is noteworthy in itself, not merely a reproduction of the ones preceding it. Although each must, by nature of the way they are constructed, reproduce some of the same information, there always seems to be additions, expansions, and inclusions. Further, each of these annuals has created its own place in history with its additional coverage on some topic or theme.

The second edition in 1981 is a prime example. The generous artist section in it includes a giant listing of the works of the popular English artist, Reginald Phillimore. The same annual also prints an interesting chronology of events related to royalty from the years 1888 to 1981.

The typical catalogue features an impressive artist section in which many of the entries have added biographical information, an explanatory grouping of postcards into categories with price ranges, and a modern section (of perhaps less merit than *I.P.M.*). Missing are listings of postcard clubs, dealers, and auction houses. Though this information, if included, might be considered duplication (since *I.P.M.* and *P.P.M.* annually list these things), the fact is that their omission makes *Stanley Gibbons Postcard Catalogue* incomplete and of less value than would be the case or should be the case. Still, it is an excellent catalogue, and the room it has for improvement only offers anticipation to all future potential buyers.

Stanley Gibbons
399 Strand
London WC2R OLX
England

Neudin (Joelle Neudin)
(France)

Neudin is considered by many to be the best of all the annual postcard publications. One look at the catalogue offers some measure of support for this contention. Without a wasted inch of space, Neudin stacks page after page of useful information into his publication.

The 1987 issue contains thousands of artist entries, with types of postcard produced by each artist and a price valuation for each of them. There are sections on postcard history, postcard categories and types, postcard clubs, modern postcard artists (with multiple examples of their work and biographical data about each), pages of advertisements, dealer information, and more. The flavor and slant are decidedly French, but the inclusion of much foreign information, such as postcard artists and clubs, is a pleasant change of pace from the fare offered by similar publications.

Conversely, it must be acknowledged that ninety percent of the illustrations and most of the textual material are oriented to the French collector and the French market. This is, as they say, to be expected. What is a bit more difficult to comprehend is how a book that is universally sold is printed only in French. Ultimately, this is the magazine's most unattractive feature given its obvious utility and appeal to those who speak other tongues. Had the printing been in English only, there would have been less cause for lament since English has been accepted as the universal language for more than a quarter of a century.

Everything, it seems, has room for improvement, even a marvelously conceived and constructed magazine such as this.

Picture Post Card Catalogue, 1870–1945
(Germany)

Some names are universally known and respected in postcard circles: Jefferson Burdick of America; J. H. D. Smith of Great Britain; Joelle Neudin of France; and—last but not least—Willi Bernhard of Germany.

A researcher of long-standing, Bernhard has continued to upgrade and update his postcard knowledge, being sure in the process to place this knowledge into the hands of collectors the world over. He does this with the issuance of catalogues relating strictly to German postcards. All of these catalogues are worthy efforts, unpretentiously supplying information as their illustrations present a visual treat for the eyes.

His first book was titled simply *Picture Postcard Catalogue, Germany 1870–1945*. Like the books that followed, it is more than commendable. What it set out to do, it did. Just what that was was to examine, illustrate, and price many of the various categories of German postcards that span the years from 1870 to 1945. The question: Is it total and comprehensive? The answer: Of course not.

But it does show, and that in wondrous fashion, the incredible diversity of German picture postcards that were produced over the decades. Bernhard wastes no time and little space with prose, letting the terse descriptions and the illustrations speak for themselves. Not one of the hundreds of illustrations are in color, yet the texture and grade of paper used complement the crisp clarity of the reproductions to create a series of pictures that suffer little from their black-and-white presentation.

Beginning with the predecessors of the picture postcard, Bernhard proceeds through the early gruss aus specimens and special occasion material to dozens of other categories; all are legitimately well represented in the hundreds of illustrations. The author leads his readers through the maze of categories, spellbinding them at the same time with a wealth of pictures, pictures, and pictures.

Better still, Bernhard gives the captions and prices in German, French, and English. A wise man, this. His later issues are even more accomplished, but, like the good architect he is, Bernhard knows that a solid building begins with a firm, substantial foundation. That, in effect, is the definition of this catalogue.

Other Publishers Catalogues
(Preparers in Parentheses)

Australian Postcard Catalogue (P. Kornan): *Catalogue International* (M. and J. Rostenne), Belgium; *Catalogue des Cartes Postales Anciennes* (A. Fildier), France; *Bildpostkarten Spezial-Katalog Automobile* (Bernhard), Germany; *Bildpostkarten Spezial-Katalog Nation-Sozialismus, 1933–45* (Bernhard), Germany; Bildpostkarten Spezial-Katalog Weihnachten (Bernhard), Germany; *Travemude Bildpostkarten-Katalog, 1892–1940* (Bernhard), Germany; *Ansichtskarten Katalog* (Ahland), Germany; *R. F. Picture Postcard Catalogue* (Ron Mead and Joan Venman), Britain; *Postais Antigos Portugeses*, Portugal; *Cartoline d'Epoca e Gli Illustratori Italiani* (B. Federico), Italy; *Catalago Italiano delle Cartoline d'Epoca* (Gaibazzi), Italy; *Standard Postcard Catalog* (James Lowe), U.S.A.; and *Bamforth Postcard Catalog* (Bert Silman and R. Scherer), U.S.A.

Special Mention: former publication, *Picton's Priced Postcard Catalogue & Handbook* (Ron Mead and Joan Venman), Britain.

Postcard Auction Catalogues

One way in which the vitality of any specific collectible may be determined is by counting the number of auction catalogues devoted to it. By this measurement, the hobby of collecting picture postcards is clearly healthy. In fact, it is not only growing but expanding into what was once the exclusive domain of other collectibles. Thus, postcards may be seen offered for sale in fixed price lists and auction catalogues that were originally designed to promote items other than postcards. As with auctions in general, some of the ones listed below are of more worth than others.

The Nuhns' Postcard Auction Fair
(U.S.A.)

Roy Nuhn has been commented on elsewhere, but it is difficult to overstate the case regarding his deltiological contributions. His auction catalogue, which is issued at periodic intervals, is but one way he keeps his fingers on the pulse of the market. Generally, he offers about one thousand lots per catalogue, approximately twenty-five percent of them being illustrated. Listed on the cover in alphabetical order are the various categories presented inside and the corresponding page numbers where each category is to be located. As a working rule, Nuhn offers advertising cards, blacks, cats, coins and stamp cards, presidential, royalty, famous people, hometown views, mechanicals, hold-to-lights, Santa Claus, children, quality foreign, sets, signed artists, and greetings. Interwoven through the catalogue is information about artists, sets, publishers, and categories that Nuhn includes as an unsolicited but much appreciated reader service. Nuhn himself is a walking compendium of postcard knowledge, and he finds himself hard-pressed to bottle up that information. Instead, he shares it, enriching us all. Another appealing feature of Nuhn's catalogue is the addition of prices realized from former auctions. This is a service that all producers of auction catalogues should include.

Roy Nuhn
RR 2, Box 638
Stagecoach Road
Durham, Connecticut 06422

Sally Carver Auctions
(U.S.A.)

No one can accuse author and postcard dealer Sally Carver of producing a second-rate postcard catalogue. Like Roy Nuhn, Carver has devoted many years of her life to postcards, and the knowledge she has gathered along the way is evident in her annual catalogues. The March 1987 edition, which was submitted for review, contains more than 1,200 lots, almost half of which are pictured. These illustrations are first-rate, sharp images on quality paper.

Carver includes a table of contents that, like Nuhn's, lists the categorical offerings and their various locations in the catalogue. There are advertising cards, alligator borders, artist-signed cards, expositions, Art Nouveau, greetings, pioneers, royalty, transportation, novelties, and more. Again like Nuhn, price estimates are furnished for each card. As with all auctions where these estimates are furnished, the bidder should be guided first and last by his or her own desire for the card. Valuations tend to vary from dealer to dealer and from location to location, and Carver would be the first to indicate that all potential buyers should be more attuned to their own feelings about what a card is worth than the arbitrariness of a number placed in front of them. Conversely, the dealer is presumed to have some measure of expertise about the market, and his or her opinions are therefore worth considering.

What postcard auctions offer—and Carver's is one of the better ones in the United States—is a convenient outlet for collectors, one that permits them to examine the material (at least vicariously) in the ease and comfort of their own home. Carver's auctions take the business a step further by ensuring that the cards thus presented for sale are scarce to rare. She takes care to select a spectrum of cards that have broad appeal and enough variety to satisfy the tastes of collectors all over the United States and abroad.

Sally S. Carver
179 South Street
Chestnut Hill, Massachusetts 02167

Other American Auction Dealers

The Phi Shop, Box 1136, La Mesa, California 92041 (stamps, covers, postcards); Harig, 12 Owen Avenue, Glen Falls, New York 12801 (postcards, other paper items); Cherryland Postcard Auction Company, P.O. Box 485, Frankfort, Michigan 49635 (postcards); H. J. W. Daugherty, P.O. Box 1146, Eastham, Maine

02642 (postcards); The Antique Paper Guild Auctions, P.O. Box 5742, Bellevue, Washington 98006 (postcards); Southern Tier Antiquities, 198 Main Street, Hornell, New York 14843 (postcards); Randy Treadway, P.O. Box 90741, Long Beach, California 90809 (postcards); John McClintock, P.O. Box 1765, Manassas, Virginia 22110 (postcards).

Neales of Nottingham
(Britain)

For Americans, the pursuit of their hobbies presupposes enthusiasm and dedication. For the British, sophistication and seriousness are the trademarks by which they are recognized, and that both in business and pleasure. Thus, although the return of interest in postcard collecting in America preceded the same phenomenon in Britain by a decade, the English have generally treated the hobby in a very professional and reserved manner. Until, that is, some disagreement appears.

Nowhere is this professionalism more evident than in their auction catalogues. This is not to state that all British catalogues are superior to all American catalogues. In fact, a couple of the English publications are inferior by comparison to the American ones. But in those instances when the British go about the business of producing a first-rate publication, they are the models to follow. Neales of Nottingham is one such model.

Starting with the full-color covers and continuing through the fine art paper, Neales has proven itself, time and again, to be among the leaders in producing quality publications. The reason for this is probably related to the fact that it has been in the business of auctioning fine art and collectibles since 1840. Its postcard catalogues often combine desirable autographic material and cigarette cards along with the postcards. A decent percentage of the material is photographed and made into clear illustrations.

Gorgeous Art Nouveau and rare political/ military/social postcards are offered along with autographed pictures of Boris Karloff, Vivien Leigh, and Princess Grace of Monaco. As regards the postcards, most of them are bulk lotted (that is, several cards offered as one grouping) and estimated at fractions of

what they would be valued at in the United States. This sight alone is worth the price of the Neales catalogues, which are, among other things, collectors' items themselves.

Neales of Nottingham
192 Mansfield Road
Nottingham NG1 3HX
England

I.P.M. Auctions
(Britain)

There are more colorful auction catalogues than those produced by J. H. D. Smith. There are also more thorough ones containing more descriptive prose. But— and pay close attention here—there are few, if any, other ones that illustrate every single card offered for bidding upon. Smith is not to be commended for this effort: He is to be applauded for it, applauded and cheered loudly. His example in this should be a clarion call for all his competitors to follow.

Smith is not one-dimensional, with only this achievement to the credit of his I.P.M. catalogue. Also recommending it is his practice of lotting the postcards under area headings (for example, Middlesex, Oxfordshire, and London). Again, this practice cannot be praised too highly as it saves much time, especially for those collectors of only one area of topographical postcards.

British-oriented, there is still much here to catch the fancy of collectors in other parts of the world. Who can resist a close-up view of a shipwreck? Or of a tram or horse-drawn conveyance? Who is immune to real photographic cards of store interiors displaying products that have not been available for sixty years or more? Who doesn't want to see airships and trains?

No, Smith has not given us a slick publication, but he has given us a substantial one that bears examination—close examination.

International Postcard Market
P.O. Box 190
Lewes
Sussex BN7 1HF
England

Phillips
(Britain)

Phillips is yet another English auctioning firm that produces a quality product. Like Neales, the emphasis should be placed on the word quality, for, also like Neales, its catalogues have full-color covers and often utilize fine art paper. Its list of auction material includes postcards, cigarette cards, autographic material, and paper memorabilia. The February 28, 1988, issue has reproductions of Art Nouveau postcards while the November 1987 catalogue illustrated some colorful cigarette cards on its cover.

The inside illustrations are all clear images that faithfully reproduce the necessary details. One is struck with the variety of scarce and desirable material that is presented for sale. There are, as regards the postcards, artist-signed cards, trains, street scenes, military, silks, shipping, and on and on. The estimated values are another bonus, being pleasingly modest. The autographic material may seem a little expensive to many Americans (especially that related to movie stars), but the British have a keen appreciation for those items they find desirable and are willing to pay for them.

Then again—and this is also the same with Neales— a number of Phillips's catalogues find their way into American (and European) hands, thus reflecting the fact that some items have a universal popularity and are pursued with greater or lesser vigor all over the world.

Phillips
Blenstock House
7 Blenheim Street
New Bond Street W1Y OAS
England

Acorn Philatelic Auctions
(Britain)

Though not as colorful as Neales or Phillips, and though they do not reproduce their illustrations with quite the same clarity, Acorn Philatelic Auction catalogues are certainly worth a look. Small in size, their offerings include some seldom-seen postcards, original artwork, covers with special postmarks and cancellations, rare

stamps, and all sorts of other paper ephemera. It is easy to see why their clientele circles the globe.

Acorn Philatelic Auctions
27 Pine Road, Didsbury
Manchester M20 OUZ
England

Specialized Postcard Auction
(Britain)

This is also a small catalogue that is small in size but long on content. The best news is that postcards are the primary sale item, not merely one among many. The number of illustrations range from 50 to 120 of the 600-plus lots. They are sharp pictures on glossy paper, similar to Neales and Phillips. Among the categories of cards included are artist-signed, entertainment figures, Art Nouveau, transportation, royalty, advertising, political, social history, and much more. Also useful are the prices realized from former auctions that the preparers have thoughtfully included.

Specialized Postcard Auction
Corinium Galleries
25 Gloucester Street
Cirencester, Gloucester GL7 2DJ
England

Other British Mail Auction Firms

Barum Auctions, The Old Glove Factory, Pilton, Barnstaple, North Devon EX31 1QS, England; James of Norwich, 33 Timberhill, Norwich, Norfolk NR1 3LA, England; Nostalgia Auctions Ltd., 17 Market Buildings Arcade, Maidstone, Kent ME14 1HP, England; Sotheby's, Booth Mansion, 28 Watergate Street, Chester CH1 2NA, England; Suffolk Stamp & Postcard Auctions, 3 Lexton Road, West Bergholt, Colchester, Essex, C06, 3BT, England; Taviner's, Prewett Street, Redcliffe, Bristol BS1 6PB, England; and Murray Cards Ltd., 51 Watford Way, Hendon Central, London NW4 3JH, England.

Helmut Labahn's Auktions
(Germany)

Helmut Labahn has taken the auction catalogue to a new height. Two minutes alone with one of his catalogues will prove the point, just two minutes of idle thumbing through any one of them. More than seven thousand illustrations grace the more than four hundred pages of a typical catalogue. The first eight pages are in color, a color that must be seen to be appreciated. All the other illustrations are also well reproduced, even though up to twenty of them are on each 6 1/2 × 9 1/2″ page.

The postcard categories presented are incredibly varied: military, royalty, stamp and coin cards, entertainment figures, early chromolithic views, street scenes, artist-drawn cards, social history, shipping, animals, greetings, children, famous people, historical, fantasy, Art Nouveau, advertising, floral designs, sports, and political. The list is near endless. Moreover, each of these catalogues is an excellent resource source to add to any deltiologist's library, especially on European cards.

Helmut Labahn
Ziehtenstrabe 5a—2000
Hamburg 70
West Germany

9
Postcard Dealers

9
Postcard Dealers

In the modern world the business of commerce is transacted between those who need specific goods or services (the customers) and those who possess the goods or services (the dealers). The word "need" is probably too strong a term, as Henry David Thoreau in his now-immortal *Walden's Pond* has been quite forthright in outlining the difference between a need and a want. Nevertheless, the people who supply what it is that we require are every bit as necessary as any other group for continuance of society along the lines it is now constituted.

For the postcard collector, such people are essential since one soon exhausts the offerings from his or her local clubs and geographic areas and must look farther and farther for the material the collector is seeking. This is especially the case for those with highly specialized want lists, but it is also valid—if somewhat less so—for those seeking relatively common material as well. In both cases, the point is soon reached where either advertising or direct recourse to dealers becomes the prevailing reality. Even in advertising, it must be admitted that a fair amount of one's respondents are dealers, so . . .

Those who are just entering the fascinating occupation of postcard collecting may be unaware of who the dealers are or of what sort of material they handle. For such folk, the following list may prove helpful. It should also be of some use to the seasoned collector as well since the proliferation of dealers has made it almost impossible to maintain a list of them all. As with all such transactions, it would be wise to include a self-addressed, stamped envelope when corresponding with these individuals.

The following list has been confined to American dealers, and there is a very good reason for this. The British, French, Germans, Canadians, Australians, Italians, and many others generally have at least one periodical that annually updates the dealers in their areas and commonly accepts advertising from them. Moreover, in most cases, there are, in addition to these annuals, at least one monthly publication that also accepts dealers' advertising and, sometimes, auctions as well.

The American market is a bit different. Although there are a number of periodicals devoted to the postcard, and most of these accept advertising and auctions from dealers, there is no annual publication that acts as a central clearinghouse of information. John McClintock offers a listing of the dealers who belong to his postcard dealers' association, but this represents only a fraction of the dealers who maintain postcards in their stock. It is to be hoped that some sort of annual publication for the American market may be shortly forthcoming. In the meantime, this listing is offered with the expectation that more complete ones will soon follow it.

Before the list is provided, there should be some understanding about the various services that postcard dealers may supply. Some of them perform several while most tend to specialize and perform only a few of the services. These services include the following.

Services Defined

Approvals: The dealer is willing to send postcards on approval, with the collector paying postage both ways. The collector selects what he or she wants and returns the remainder with payment.

Mail Auction: Specifically, these are dealer auctions in postcard periodicals. These include *Barr's Post Card News, Postcard Collector,* and, less frequently, *Picture Postcard Monthly.* Thirty to forty-five days is the usual period of time that the auction is open to receive bids. Upon notification of lots successfully won, the bidder is given five to ten days in which to send payment before a late payment fee is assessed.

Mail Auction (catalogue): The dealer sends out a specified number of catalogues (usually limited to former bidders and those who have purchased the catalogue, although there are still a minority of dealers who will send catalogues gratis upon request) that are filled with pictures and descriptions of his or her offerings.

Mail Service: The dealer will send cards that he or she has advertised for sale after first receiving payment.

Mail Service (price lists): The dealer sends out fixed price lists of postcards upon request.

Other: Shows (a dealer transacts business either at postcard shows or antique shows); postcard suppliers (dealers who sell everything from postcard sleeves to albums, mailing bags, and frames for showcasing one's cards); and postcard books.

Addresses and Services of Postcard Dealers

John and Matt Abbott
P.O. Box 374
Birmingham, Michigan 48011

(approval service)

Abraham's Corner
2708 ''Y'' Street
Lincoln, Nebraska 68503

(mail auctions; postcard supplies)

Ackert Enterprises
521 South Seventh Street
De Kalb, Illinois 60115

(mail service—price lists; books)

Bernard Aclin
P.O. Box 330
Bronx, New York 10475

(mail service; shows)

Barbara Agranoff
P.O. Box 6501
Cincinnati, Ohio 45206

(mail service; shows)

Aladin Postcards
Douglas and Jeanne Acheson
2801 East Kessler Boulevard
Indianapolis, Indiana 46220

(shop owner)

Joan C. Angier
6365 West Lost Canyon Drive
Tucson, Arizona 85745

(mail auction)

Annapolis Oldies
P.O. Box 454
Arnold, Maryland 21012

(shop owner)

Antique & Art Search Service
P.O. Box 40407
Cincinnati, Ohio 45240-0407

(shows)

The Antique Freaque
P.O. Box 875
Cambria, California 93428

(approval service)

Antique Paper Guild
P.O. Box 5742
Bellevue, Washington 98006

(mail auction—catalogue)

Sam Armao
35887 Mildred Street
North Ridgeville, Ohio 44039

(shows)

Carl D. Arnott
132 Cambridge Street
Holbrook, New York 11741

(mail service)

The Artist's Daughter
242 Tubac Road
Box 4098
Tubac, Arizona 85646

(postcard supplies)

Artvue Post Card Company
160 Fifth Avenue
New York, New York 10010

(shop owner; approval service)

Avis Post Card Company
P.O. Box 5053-PC
Albany, New York 12205

(mail service—price list)

The Bag Man
P.O. Box 858
Vernon, New Jersey 07462

(postcard supplies)

Ball Four Cards
2844 West Forest Home Avenue
Milwaukee, Wisconsin 53215

(postcard supplies)

J. C. Ballentine
Hatcher Point Mall
P.O. Box 761
Waycross, Georgia 31501

(shop owner; mail service)

Don and Pam Barnes
48 Milbern Avenue
Hampton, New Hampshire 03842

(shop owner; mail service)

Ann R. Bartlett
P.O. Box 47
Horseheads, New York 14845

(mail auction)

Keneth Bay
101 Gedney Street 1-G
Nyack, New York 10960

(shows)

Edward J. Beiderbecke
P.O. Box 155
Williamson, New York 14589

(mail service; shows)

Gilbert R. Beliveau
P.O. Box 76, South Station
Fall River, Massachusetts 02724

(mail auction)

Robert Bernstein
4079 Huerfano, No. 202
San Diego, California 92117

(approval service)

Jim and Vera Berry
200 Pleasant Boulevard
Riverview, Florida 33569

(shows)

Henry Betz
294 Briar Lane
Chambersburg, Pennsylvania 17201

(shows)

V. G. Block
1900 South Ocean Boulevard
Pompano Beach, Florida 33062
(approval service; mail auctions)

Peter Bosse
23 Orange Street
Lewiston, Maine 04240
(approval service; mail auction)

Ken Bower
2902 Ontario Avenue
Baltimore, Maryland 21234
(shows)

A. C. Boxell
Box 224
Holden, Massachusetts 01520
(Cape Cod postcards—price list)

Thomas Boyd
140 Andover Lane
Williamsville, New York 14221
(mail service; shows)

Neal and Tillie Boyle
11305 Commonwealth Drive
Rockville, Maryland 20852
(shows)

Jeff Bradfield
745 Hillview Drive
Dayton, Virginia 22821
(mail service; shows)

Norm and Barry Brauer
114 West Main Street
Dalton, Pennsylvania 18414
(mail auction)

Paul Brenner
P.O. Box 402
South Orange, New Jersey 07079
(blacks only)

Carol Brockfield
P.O. Box 7115
Napa, California 94558
(mail service; shows)

Andreas Brown
Gotham Book Mart
41 West 47th Street
New York, New York 10036
(shows; postcard books)

G. R. Brown
Post Card Company
Rt. 5, 2329 Kane Road
Eau Claire, Wisconsin 54703
(mail service)

Lee Brown
P.O. Box 92
Sunland, California 91040
(mail service)

Margaret Bukin
P.O. Box 716
North Dighton, Massachusetts 02764
(shows)

David Burke
26418 South New Town Drive
Sun Lakes, Arizona 85248
(mail service)

William Burt
P.O. Box 24690
Kansas City, Missouri 64110
(mail service)

Kenneth Butts
97 Fairhaven Drive
Cheektowaga, New York 14225
(mail service; shows)

Cameo Creations
2912 Lakeview Cove
Hastings, Nebraska 68901
(postcard supplies)

Carlton's Modern Postcards
P.O. Box 111
Bogata, New Jersey 07603
(mail service—price lists of linens and chromes)

Carousel Cards
Ann Bartlett
P.O. Box 47
Horseheads, New York 14845

(mail auctions)

Sally S. Carver
179 South Street
Chestnut Hill, Massachusetts 02617

(mail auction—periodic catalogues)

The Cat's Paw
P.O. Box 16
Lahaska, Pennsylvania 18931

(shop owner; mail service; shows)

Agnes Cavalari
RD 2, Bethlehem Road
New Windsor, New York 12550

(shop owner; mail service; shows)

Cayuga Lake Postcards
R. L. Hungerford
RD 2, Box 263
Interlaken, New York 14847

(mail auctions)

Gloria and Rudy Cazanjian
26920 Alamaden Court
Los Altos Hills, California 94022

(shop owner; mail service)

Cherryland Postcard Auction Company
P.O. Box 485
Frankfort, Michigan 49635

(mail auctions—catalogues; shows)

Alan and Mary Christmas
P.O. Box 143
Lynnville, Indiana 47619

(shows)

Chuck's Cards
Chuck Haywood
P.O. Box 13664
Spokane, Washington, 99213

(mail auctions)

Ronald W. Clark
P.O. Box 2723
Manassas, Virginia 22110

(mail service; shows)

Bill Cole Enterprises
P.O. Box 60
Randolph, Massachusetts 02368-0060

(postcard supplies)

Collector's Cabinet
P.O. Box 17305
Mesa, Arizona 85212

(mail auction)

Collector's Gallery
725 South Adams
Birmingham, Michigan 48011

(mail auctions; postcard supplies)

Colonial Antiques
661 West Market
Lima, Ohio 45801

(shop owner; shows)

The Constantian Society
123 Orr Road
Pittsburgh, Pennsylvania 15241

(mail service—price lists of modern royalty
    postcards only)

Roy Cox
Box 3610
Baltimore, Maryland 21214

(postcard supplies; shows)

Victor L. Cox
P.O. Box 66
Keymar, Maryland 21757

(mail service)

Maxine Cozzetto
2228 Northeast Gilsan
Portland, Oregon 97232

(shop owner; mail service)

Donald Craig
163 New Boston Road
Fall River, Massachusetts 02720

(shop owner; shows)

Anne Cunningham
P.O. Box 270
Effort, Pennsylvania 18330
(mail auctions)

BeBe Curry
418 South Elm
Henderson, Kentucky 42420
(mail service; shows)

Danny and Kathy Danielson
P.O. Box 630
O'Fallon, Illinois 62269
(shows)

Anne A. Darrah
528 West Baumstown Road
Birdboro, Pennsylvania 19805
(shows)

H. J. W. Daugherty
P.O. Box 1146
Eastham, Massachusetts 02642
(mail service—catalogues; shows)

Hank and Coby DeBoer
2 Aviles Street
St. Augustine, Florida 32084
(shop owner; shows)

Robert and Jean DeChiara
P.O. Box 2365
Ogunquit, Maine 03907
(mail service; shows)

Jay Dee
Box 574
Wilkes-Barre, Pennsylvania 18703
(mail service—price lists)

Thomas Dekle
9 Farmington Boulevard
Hampton, Virginia 23666
(mail service; books)

Robin Delphin
1616 North Fort Harrison
Clearwater, Florida 33515
(shop owner)

Diana's Cards
23 North Fair Street
Warwick, Rhode Island 02888
(mail service—moderns)

Thomas Digenti
P.O. Box 781
Lawrence, Massachusetts 01842
(mail auctions)

Sheldon Dobres
P.O. Box 1855
Baltimore, Maryland 21203-1855
(mail service—primarily moderns; auctions—older
    cards)

Pam and Paul Donath
P.O. Box 16
Lahaska, Pennsylvania 18931
(shop owner)

John F. Doneilo Enterprises
P.O. Box 2450
Menlo Park, California 94026
(mail service—moderns)

Wolford Dow
P.O. Box 8705
Jacksonville, Florida 32211
(mail service; shows)

Dragon Cards
Lloyd A. de Vries
Box 145C
Dumont, New Jersey 07628
(price lists—maximum cards)

Dave Drake's Timesearch Auction
5431 Rt 53
Naples, New York 14512
(mail auctions)

Harry S. Drake
5108 Laurel Lane
Fort Worth, Texas 78160
(mail service—price lists)

Daniel Duffy
20 Lennox Avenue
Yardville, New Jersey 08620

(shows)

E. & S. Antiques
P.O. Box 514
Huntington Station
New York, New York 11746

(mail auctions)

Frank D. Ely
19 North Street
Livonia, New York 14487

(mail service; shows)

The Evans Boxes
Majorstamps
P.O. Box 808
Columbus, Ohio 43216-0808

(postcard supplies)

Michael Fairley
17430 Ballinger Way Northeast
Seattle, Washington 98155

(mail service; shows)

John and Lynne Farr
P.O. Box 6086
Omaha, Nebraska 68106

(mail service)

Erv Felix
P.O. Box 3953
North Las Vegas, Nevada 89030

(mail auctions; approval service)

Feslers Auctions
Box 19665
St. Paul, Minnesota 55119

(mail auctions; approval service)

Wes Finch
152 Oakdale Road
Johnson City, New York 13790

(shows)

Nancy Foutz
P.O. Box 459
Rosendale, New York 12472

(mail service; shows)

Frank Fox
2131 East Yandell
El Paso, Texas 79903

(mail auction)

Fox Valley Coin Mail Auction
103 East Kimberly
Kimberly, Wisconsin 54136

(mail auctions)

Michael Freid
P.O. Box 817
San Leandro, California 94577

(mail service; shows)

Marian Frye
P.O. Box 11529
Memphis, Tennessee 38111

(mail service; shows)

Veronica Gabossy
8610 Rayburn Road
Bethesda, Maryland 20817

(mail auctions)

Chris Gallagher
816 North Foote Street
Olympia, Washington 98502

(mail auctions)

George Gibbs
P.O. Box 614
Syracuse, New York 13201

(mail service; mail auctions)

Gosnell's Postcards & Collectables
Ray Gosnell
P.O. Box 34782
Los Angeles, California 90034-9998

(mail auctions)

Marilyn Gottlieb
P.O. Box 35
Rockhill, New York 12775
(shows)

Grab Bag Antiques
39 Main Street
Sabattus, Maine 04280
(approval service)

Edward Gralnik
251 Warren Avenue
Kenmore, New York 14217
(mail service)

Gisela Granstrom
4418 Dean Drive
Ventura, California 93003
(mail auctions)

Jayne Gray
Box 535
Brookfield, Massachusetts 01506

(approval service)

Great Western Mails
P.O. Box 31510
Tucson, Arizona 85751
(mail auctions; approval service)

J. R. Greene
33 Bearsden Road
Athol, Massachusetts 01331
(buying/selling Calvin Coolidge and Massachusetts
     views)

Sondra Gregory
13029 Scarlet Oak Drive
Gaithersburg, Maryland 20878
(mail auctions)

Clay Griffin
1100 Merriman Road
Akron, Ohio 44303
(mail service; shows)

Charles Griffiths
15 Circle Road
Millersville, Pennsylvania 17551
(mail service)

John D. Grubbs
6088 Eagles Nest Drive
Jupiter, Florida 33458
(shows)

Hamilton House Antiques
Howard Dreasler
209 South 12th Street
Fort Dodge, Iowa 50501
(mail auctions; approval service)

Happy Collector Auction
Don Sartwell
P.O. Box 4856
Mesa, Arizona 85201
(mail auctions)

Harig
12 Owen Avenue
Glen Falls, New York 12801
(mail auctions)

Don Hatfield
Box 706
Webberville, Michigan 48892
(mail auctions)

Dan Herzog
645 Irvington Avenue
Newark, New Jersey 07106
(mail service; shows)

Allam Hillesheim
441 Ridgewood Avenue Apt. 3
Minneapolis, Minnesota 55403
(mail auctions)

Houde's Auction House
Frank Houde
Box 2577
Missoula, Montana 59806
(mail auctions)

Frank E. Howard
856 Charlotte Street
Macon, Georgia 31206
(mail service; shows)

J. & B. Postcards
Robert Rau
RD 2, Box 223-28
Kingston, New York 12401
(mail auctions)

Hobbs W. Jackson
P.O. Box 116
Lafayette, Alabama 36862
(shows)

Fran Jay
10 Church Street
Lambertville, New Jersey 08530
(shop owner)

Joan L. Jay
142 Palfrey Street
Watertown, Massachusetts 02172
(approval service)

Jim's Cards
Jim O'Brien
193 Indian Field Road
Bridgeport, Connecticut 06606
(shows)

John Jones
P.O. Box 574
Wilkes-Barre, Pennsylvania 18703
(mail service; shows)

Joselyn Postcards
Joselyn Howell
1948 South 50th Street
Orem, Utah 84058-7830
(mail service)

K. & E. Postcards
144-19 1/2 Avenue North
St. Cloud, Minnesota 56301
(mail service—price lists)

Daniel P. Kabza
P.O. Box 1686
Grand Island, Nebraska 68802
(mail auctions)

William Katsker
3000 Southwest 83rd Court
Miami, Florida 33155
(mail service; shows)

Bernice Kaufman
1239 South Tamiami Trail
Sarasota, Florida 33579
(mail service)

Kay's Goodie Shoppe
Rt. 28
Poland, New York 13431
(shop owner; mail service—price lists; approval
    service)

Clayton and Evelyn Keehn
2117 Barcelona Drive
Clearwater, Florida 34624
(shows)

Toey Kelly
P.O. Box 537
Postville, Iowa 52162
(mail auctions)

Kempfs Kards
Adele Kempf
13048 West Watson Road
St. Louis, Missouri 63127
(mail auctions; mail service—price lists)

Susan R. Kennedy
RD 2, Box 181
Zionsville, Pennsylvania 18092
(mail auctions)

Kenrich Company
9418-N Las Tunas Drive
Temple City, California 91780
(shop owner)

R. D. Kisch
P.O. Box 281
West Bend, Iowa 50597
(mail auctions)

Reg R. Koehn
Box 121
Exeter, Nebraska 68351
(mail service—price lists on maximum cards)

Robert J. Kurey
585 Overbrook Road
Johnson City, New York 13790
(mail service)

L. & M. Enterprises
Laura Shinkman
P.O. Box 5524
Sherman Oaks, California 91413
(mail auctions)

George Lass
RR 1
Hardwick, Minnesota 56134
(mail auctions)

Alan Lavendier
139 East Clinton Street
New Bedford, Massachusetts 02740
(mail service)

Fred Lego
6506 Kipling Parkway
Forestville, Maryland 20747
(mail auctions; shows)

Hazel Leler
2212 Bellefontaine
Houston, Texas 77030
(shows)

Roger LeRoque
P.O. Box 217
Temple City, California 91708
(mail service; shows)

The Lion Shop
P.O. Box 231
Hudson, Massachusetts 01749
(mail auctions)

Dave Long
P.O. Box 644
Elkhart, Indiana 46515
(mail service—price lists of moderns; shows)

Looking Glass Products
Victor Cox
Box 35
Keymar, Maryland 21757
(postcard supplies)

Walter Lozoski
910 Fourth Avenue North
Apt. 102
Seattle, Washington 98155
(mail service)

Paul and Peg Lytle
7197-D Holyoke Court
Ocala, Florida 32672
(mail service; shows)

Ed McAllister
3413 West Jefferson
Joliet, Illinois 60435
(mail service; shows)

Harry and Betty McCallion
P.O. Box 151
Bedford, Pennsylvania 15522
(shows)

John McClintock
P.O. Box 1765
Manassas, Virginia 22110
(shows)

James McMillin
P.O. Box 50124
Fort Worth, Texas 76106
(mail service; shows)

Malcolm Postcards
Box 403
Monroe, Georgia 30655

(shop owner)

Audrey Malone
Lot D-410
3586 Northwest 41st Street
Miami, Florida 33142

(approval service)

Mary L. Martin
231 Rock Ridge Road
Millersville, Maryland 21108

(approval service; postcard supplies)

Ronald Marzlock
P.O. Box N
Kew Gardens, New York 11415

(mail service)

Mashburn Cards
P.O. Box 609
Enka, North Carolina 28728

(mail auction)

Mayhew-Reece
P.O. Box 20081
Greensboro, North Carolina 27420

(mail service—price lists)

Carol Rae Maynard
47 1/2 Columbia Avenue
Greenville, Pennsylvania 16125

(mail auctions)

Fred and Mary Megson
P.O. Box 482
Martinsville, New Jersey 08836

(shows)

Tom and Sara Mertens
3605 Dunkeld Drive
North Little Rock, Arkansas 72116

(postcard supplies; shows)

Ronald Millard
P.O. Box 485
Frankfort, Michigan 49635

(mail auctions; mail service; shows)

Millns Postcards
40 North Third Street
Waterville, Ohio 43566

(approval service; shows)

Charles M. Moler
4235 East McDowell Road
Apt. 104
Phoenix, Arizona 85008

(mail service; shows)

Alton Morgan
117 Granby Road
South Portland, Maine 04106

(mail service; shows)

S. R. Nelms
Box 633
Hicksville, New York 11802

(mail auctions)

Marie Nemeth
35 Inglis Avenue
P.O. Drawer 579
Inglis, Florida 32649

(mail service)

The Nickel Trader
P.O. Box 176-P
Venetia, Pennsylvania 15367

(approval service)

Nippon Philatelics
Drawer 7300
Carmel, California 93921

(mail service—both regular postcards and
    maximums, primarily Japanese cards)

Nostalgia Enterprises
Box 300
Lockport, New York 14094

(mail service)

Richard Novick Products
P.O. Box 206, Department PCD
Uniondale, New York 11553

(postcard supplies)

Roy Nuhn
RR 2, Box 638
Stagecoach Road
Durham, Connecticut 06422

(mail auctions—periodic catalogues)

Lucy O'Brien
Red Horse at Ybor Square
1901 North 13th Street
Tampa, Florida 33600

(shop owner)

Michael O'Brien
35 Bulfinch Street
North Attleboro, Massachusetts 02760

(mail auctions; shows)

The Old Barn Antiques
2513 Nelson Road
Traverse City, Michigan 49684

(shop owner; mail service—price lists)

Oldtyme Collector
920 Chambers Road
St. Louis, Missouri 63137

(mail auctions)

Hal Ottaway
P.O. Box 780282
Wichita, Kansas 67278

(mail service; shows)

Ted Pardee
3604 Dunkeld Drive
North Little Rock, Arkansas 72116

(mail service; shows)

Parker's Hobby Shop
P.O. Box 74
Mishawaka, Indiana 46544

(mail auctions)

Parlour Memories
Carlo Sisters
P.O. Box 13561
St. Louis, Missouri 63138

(mail auctions)

Terry Pavey
Verde Mail Auction
P.O. Box 6202
Phoenix, Arizona 85005

(mail auctions)

Peg's Treasures
P.O. Box 6182
South Bend, Indiana 46660

(mail auctions)

Stan and Jane Pepper
3048 Doddridge Avenue
Maryland Heights, Missouri 63043

(mail service)

Robert J. Pereira
1771 Sternwheel Drive
Jacksonville, Florida 32223

(mail service)

Dean Petersen
4232 Orleans
Sioux City, Iowa 51106

(mail auctions)

V. Petersen
928 Dellapenna Drive
Johnson City, New York 13790

(approval service)

William H. Petersen
P.O. Box 398
Plainfield, Connecticut 06374-0398

(mail auctions; shows)

James Petit
P.O. Box 4097
North Myrtle Beach, South Carolina 29597

(mail service)

Petrella's Paper Collectibles
P.O. Box 2588
North Canton, Ohio 44720

(mail auctions)

Charles Pitts
P.O. Box 29151
Sumter, South Carolina 29151

(mail service; shows)

Post Cards for Posterity
N. & I. Obradovits
1225 Fain Drive
St. Louis, Missouri 63125

(mail auctions)

Postcards, Etc.
Rita Nadler
P.O. Box 4318
Thousand Oaks, California 91359

(mail service; shows)

The Postscript
Pat Snyder
P.O. Box 75
Mascoutah, Illinois 62258

(mail auctions)

Ken Prag
P.O. Box 531
Burlingame, California 94011

(shop owner; mail service; shows)

Previously Owned Postcards
John Corliss
P.O. Box 20899
Baltimore, Maryland 21209

(mail auctions)

Don Preziosi
P.O. Box 498
Mendham, New Jersey 07945

(approval service; shows)

Michael G. Price
P.O. Box 7071
Ann Arbor, Michigan 48107

(mail service; shows)

Arlene Raskin
3196 Bedford Avenue
Brooklyn, New York 11210

(mail service)

Mike Rasmussen
P.O. Box 726
Marina, California 93933

(shop owner; mail auctions)

Larry Roberts
P.O. Box 4
Micanopy, Florida 32667

(shop owner)

Rock Aires Collectibles
P.O. Box 2301
Loves Park, Illinois 61131

(mail auctions; postcard supplies)

Jose and Aida Rodriquez
P.O. Box 903
Cheshire, Connecticut 06410

(mail service; shows)

Gordon I. Root
RFD 1, Box 93
Lancaster, New Hampshire 03584

(mail auction; mail service—price lists)

Theo Rosenbrand
P.O. Box 101
Rutherland, California 94573

(mail service—price list of maximum cards)

Murray and Joanne Ruggiero
359 Silver Sands Road
East Haven, Connecticut 06512

(shows)

Rustco
P.O. Box 580 PC4
Lima, Ohio 45802
(mail service—price lists)

Don Sartwell
P.O. Box 4856
Mesa, Arizona 85211
(mail auctions)

Scene Again
11958 Glen Alden Road
Fairfax, Virginia 22030
(mail auctions)

Fred and Gail Schiffman
2907 Morgan Avenue North
Minneapolis, Minnesota 55411
(mail auctions)

Ben Schiffrin
16-08 212th Street
Bayside, New York 11360
(mail service—Jewish cards)

Stephen Schmale
448 Tanglewood Court
Santa Rosa, California 95405
(mail service)

Leah Schnall
67-00 192nd Street
Flushing, New York 11365
(shows)

Jane Schryver
226 Main Street
Dansville, New York 14437
(mail service—price lists)

Edward Schultz
1905 Sherwood Street
Allentown, Pennsylvania 18103
(mail service; shows)

Larry and Anne Sell
P.O. Box 604
Hornell, New York 14843
(mail auctions—catalogues)

Jonah and Rita Shapiro
P.O. Box 2930
New Haven, Connecticut 06515
(mail auctions)

Shiloh Postcards
Jack Leach
225 Third Street
P.O. Box 886
Macon, Georgia 31202
(mail service—price lists; postcard supplies; shows)

Betty Sidle
444 Heather
Powell, Ohio 43065
(approval service)

Don Skillman
6646 Shiloh Road
Goshen, Ohio 45122
(shows)

Eva Slater
400 East Fifth Street
Dayton, Ohio 45402
(shows)

C. Michael Smith
P.O. Box 12092
Huntsville, Alabama 35802
(mail service)

Pat Snyder
P.O. Box 75
Mascoutah, Illinois 62258
(mail auctions)

S. R. and Nancy Snyder
Rt. 1, Box 28868
Middleport, Ohio 45760
(approval service)

Delores Sobojda
2630 Co. Rd. 24
Gibsonburg, Ohio 43431
(shows)

Edward Sobol
427 King Street
Woodbury, New Jersey 08096
(mail service)

Richard Spedding
22 Tanglewood Road
Sterling, Massachusetts 01564
(approval service)

E. K. Springston
1610 Park Avenue West
Mansfield, Ohio 44906
(mail service—price lists)

Staub's Postcards
Herb and Mary Staub
P.O. Box 5233
Coralville, Iowa 52241
(mail auctions)

Edward Stefanik
P.O. Box 2558
Fall River, Massachusetts 02722
(shop owner; shows)

Jim Stovall
P.O. Box 8182
Springfield, Missouri 65801
(mail auctions)

Joseph Stransky
P.O. Box 1672
Madison, Wisconsin 53701
(mail service; shows)

Alan E. Stricker
P.O. Box 176
Venetia, Pennsylvania 15367
(shop owner; shows)

Thompson
1220 Chickasaw
Paris, Tennessee 38242
(mail service—price lists)

Three Star Press
Box 57
Masonville, Iowa 50654
(mail service—price lists)

Tippett
P.O. Box 49257
Sarasota, Florida 34230
(mail auctions)

Randy Treadway
P.O. Box 90741
Long Beach, California 90809
(mail auctions—catalogue)

University Products
P.O. Box 101, Department 11
Holyoke, Massachusetts 01041
(postcard supplies)

Edward Valladoa
P.O. Box 484
Mattapoisett, Massachusetts 02739
(shop owner; shows)

Fox Valley
103 East Kimberly
Kimberly, Wisconsin 54136
(mail auctions)

JoAnn Van Scotter
208 East Lincoln Street
Mt. Morris, Illinois 61054
(mail auctions; mail service)

Van's Card Sales
2616 Ferdon Road
Kalamazoo, Michigan 49008
(mail auctions)

Harry A. Victor
1408 18th Avenue
San Francisco, California 94122

(mail service—price lists of moderns; shows)

Donald Wachter
5713 Main Street
Frederick, Maryland 21701

(mail service; shows)

Doug Walberg
Rt. 1, Box 428
Brandon, Oregon 97411

(approval service)

Martha Walton
707 Collegewood Drive
Ypsilanti, Michigan 48197

(shop owner; approval service; books, magazines)

Michael Wasserberg
1025 Country Club Drive
Margate, Florida 33063

(shop owner; mail service)

Arretta Wetzel
1325 45th Street
Rock Island, Illinois 61201

(shows)

Shirley Williams
2005 North Linwood Avenue
Indianapolis, Indiana 46218

(shows)

Florence K. Witt
120 Paumanake Avenue
Babylon, New York 11702

(mail auctions)

Frank Wood
P.O. Box 9524
Wichita, Kansas

(mail auctions; shows)

World Hunger Relief Postcard Auctions
Warren and Barbara Andrews
628 20th
Ames, Iowa 50010

(mail auctions)

World Postcards
Jerry S. Riley
111 First Street
Suite 15-978
Calexico, California 92231

(approval service; shows)

The Wright Place
1460 Northwest 138th Avenue
Portland, Oregon 97229

(mail auctions)

M. J. Yegge
P.O. Box 669
Bettendorf, Iowa 52722

(approval service; shows)

Dorothy E. Young
P.O. Box 1231
Estes Park, Colorado 80517

(mail auctions)

Thomas Zollinger
1023 Markle Avenue
Elkhart, Indiana 46514

(mail service; shows)

Michael Zwerdling
P.O. Box 240
Boston, Massachusetts 02130

(approval service; mail auctions; shows)

Postcard Supply Dealers

The longevity of coin collecting, with its more than two thousand-year history, is ample testimony to the fact that hobbies have survived, if not prospered, in both good times and ill. However, since the early days, man has also been presented with the problems of both housing and showcasing his collections. In modern times, that task has been rendered somewhat less bothersome by the increasing presence of dealers who specialize in holders of every type, albums of every description, special wallets, tubes, and many other useful devices.

Since the first decade of the twentieth century, a period that represents the time when the fascination for collecting picture postcards was at its apogee, beautiful postcard albums, some made with luxurious leather and inlaid with mother-of-pearl, were offered by supply dealers. There were, of course, always those of an inferior but cheaper variety, and they too were purchased by the multiple thousands. During the last ten years, this supply business has become quite sophisticated. The number of dealers so occupied is an expanding one, but only a select group of them handle what might be termed top-of-the-line products. Many of those so far identified fall into this grouping.

A few of the dealers deserve special mention. In this connection, Cameo Creations of Hastings, Nebraska, is certainly among the best. Its specialty is a series of freestanding frames that come in two sizes: 4 × 6″ (horizontal) and 5 × 7″ (of this size, both horizontal and vertical are available). Both sizes come either unadorned or with a blue-and-gold border. Similar to the clear acrylic frames used for photographs, these items are excellent for the long-term viewing enjoyment and preservation of those special cards most worth displaying and preserving.

Other dealers who merit attention are Bill Cole of Randolph, Massachusetts; Mary L. Martin of Millersville, Maryland; Lee Cox of Keymar, Maryland; Vera Trinder of London, England; Roycroft of Eltham, Australia; M. & E. Clarke of West Germany; and Stanley Gibbons of London.

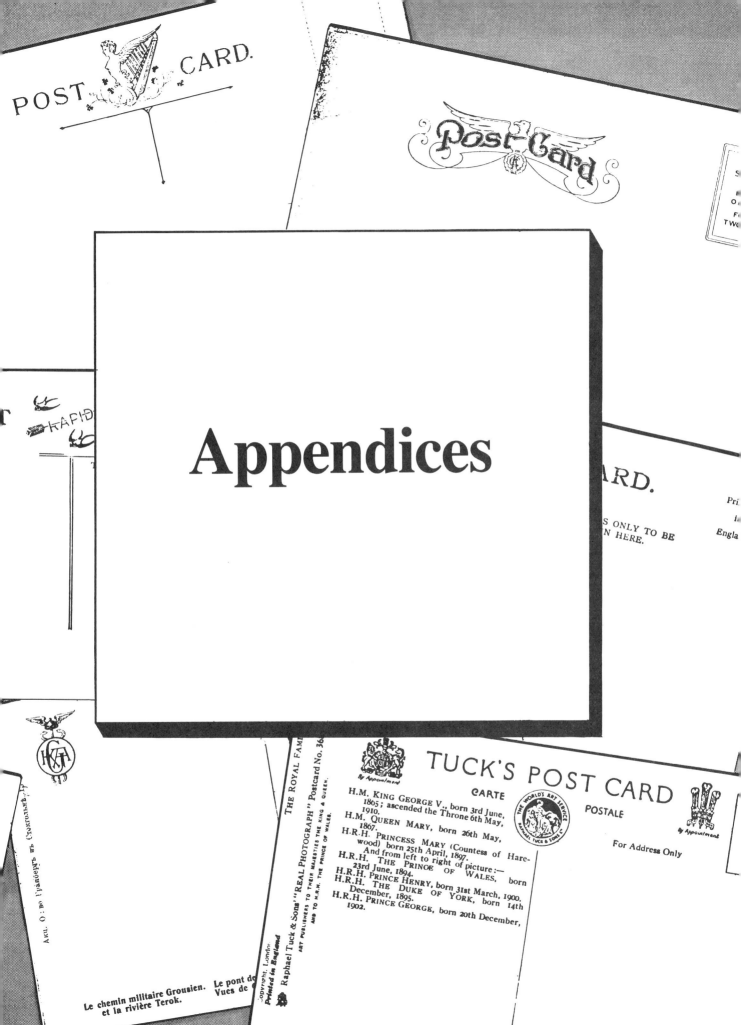

Appendices

Appendix A
Everything You Wanted to Know About Postcards: Questions and Answers

One of the most basic pieces of sage advice that is given to people who have just started to become aficionados of any collectible is to "buy the book first." What this advice refers to is for the new collector to learn as much as possible about his or her new hobby BEFORE he or she spends too much money on purchases. The recommendation is a good, solid one, and this appendix will attempt to provide information about deltiology to all those interested in it, both the novice and the advanced collector alike. The first order of business will be to examine some of the more frequently asked questions that one continually encounters at postcard shows and club meetings.

Q. Is it post card or postcard?

A. This question has been debated since the time of the earliest cards. Even then, both forms were used. This being the case, all arguments in favor of one usage over another are in reality little more than matters of preference. Perhaps, as with the general diversity of the hobby itself, this is the way it should remain. The half-filled glass is also half-empty.

Q. What factors should be borne in mind when examining a postcard for possible purchase?

A. 1. Is it undamaged by tears, bends, delamination, dirt, cracks, and the like?
2. Are the corners rounded?
3. Are the colors or photographic details unaltered by heat, direct sunlight, or other exposure?
4. If it is a pioneer card, is there unsightly writing on the face?

5. Is the cancellation or postmark appropriate to the picture? Are either the cancellation or postmark rare?
6. Is the message politically or socially significant?
7. Does the card contain the signature of an important person?
8. Have you comparison shopped on similar cards to see if the price asked is a reasonable one?
9. Finally, and for some people most importantly, how much do you want the card?

Q. What is the difference between deltiology and cartology?

A. "A rose by any other name . . ." In essence, the only difference in the names arises from location. Deltiology is the American term for postcard collecting and study while the British—or many of them, anyway—prefer the word cartology. Some American dictionaries—but not all—contain the word deltiology, and it is presumed that some English dictionaries list cartology among the terms defined. So, it literally depends on where one is at any given time. To quote another cliché, "When in Rome, do as the Romans do."

Q. What is an English court card?

A. In 1894, the British Post Office retired its monopoly on the printing of postcards, thus giving private publishers an inroad into the market; private firms promptly began to issue postcards. The one provision by the postal authorities was that the cards had to adhere to a size requirement of 4-3/4 × 3-1/2″. The shape imposed by this restriction led to them being called "court cards." The size restriction was relaxed in November 1899, and the standard dimensions of 5-1/2 × 3-1/2″, which was in use elsewhere, was quickly patterned. The English court cards are highly prized both for their scarcity and their unusual shape and are collected worldwide.

Q. Are artist-signed cards worth the sums of money that are sometimes asked for them?

A. There may not be a "safe" answer to this question as this is an issue around which many opinions accumulate. Depending on one's personal perspective, the rationales that are developed for these varying points of view are either valid ones or they are lacking in credibility.

Certainly, some artist-drawn and artist-signed cards are more difficult to find than others. In fact, some are very infrequently located. However, it ought to be remembered that, as a general rule, the elevation of prices for certain cards is frequently followed by increasing numbers of them being offered for sale. As with coins, stamps, and other collectibles, the business of hoarding is sometimes a reality in the hobby of postcard collecting as well. Still, there are a number of artists whose work in postcard form is genuinely scarce, if not rare.

It is also true that art has a unique, universal appeal to man, the only creature under the sun who has developed an appreciation of it. Postcard art furnishes many of us an opportunity to pursue and purchase art at prices far below what is asked at art galleries and antique shops, for the most part, that is.

That aside, there are a few other considerations that should be examined. In the first place, "artist-signed" is a misnomer, as none of these cards is actually signed by the artist. All are facsimile signatures on reproductions. Thus, they are thought to be of considerably less value than limited edition prints, which are frequently numbered and sometimes signed as well. Also to be entered in the equation is the fact that many artist-signed postcards were not drawn for postcards in the first instance but are copies of posters or handbills.

The motive that seems to be operating here as in other fields is that of popularity. Thus, many Art Nouveau cards are fetching very high sums indeed while some of the scarcer cards by artists like Robert Robinson and Howard Chandler Christie bring a pittance by comparison. It is interesting to observe that the British do not share the fascination of Art Nouveau postcards with their American collecting counterparts and therefore have priced them considerably lower.

The proper solution for the pricing dilemma might be found in more research into the artists. To date, less than a dozen books have been devoted to postcard artists, sure evidence that more room is certainly available in this area. Until more is undertaken, we may have to live with the up-and-down vagaries of pricing artist-signed postcards almost solely on the basis of popularity.

Q. What ways are there to sell postcards?

A. 1. To a dealer;
   2. To a collector;
   3. By auction (mail or on site); or
   4. In a fixed price list.

Q. What are sets and series?

A. These are groups of cards, either numbered or unnumbered, that are produced by a single publisher and deal with a specific item, event, personality, or theme. Sets and series have been manufactured on almost every topic that one may imagine. These include religious, military, political, special occasion, humorous, informational, historical, and a host of other themes. The fact that there were so many of them made and that they were produced for so long a time testifies to their popularity. From as few as two to forty or more, sets and series continue to be sought in order to satisfy the completion mania of their owners and seekers.

Q. What is the most expensive postcard?

A. This is an impossible question to answer although many have tried. It is possible that up to a dozen different answers might be given depending upon who was asked. The main problem in answering this question lies in the fact that the published figures for cards at auctions are often unreliable numbers. To be sure, the price paid for a specific card might have been very large indeed, but this is not always an accurate barometer of what the same card might fetch in a dealer's stock, far removed from the sometimes frantic bidding activity that some auctions have been known to generate. In such an atmosphere, it is hard to determine when impulse was the governing factor taking precedence over the common sense approach, which most of us recognize as our more normal routine.

But just as there is no denying that these numbers are real ones, they must be quoted in the attempt at resolving the question before us. By looking at them, we are quickly made to realize that some categories of postcards have been the recipients of some very generous bids. One of the Art Nouveau cards by artist Alphonse Mucha realized in excess of $4,000, a figure that is hard to best. Nevertheless, it is entirely conceivable that the excessively rare postcards produced during the Franco-Prussian War will top this amount in the near future, if they are ever offered for sale, that is. The rising valuations placed upon a few of the early exposition cards have exceeded several hundred dollars, and there is every reason to believe that they too will rise in both price and popularity. Early cards postmarked prior to 1880 are also continuing an upward spiral.

Yet another card in the supervaluable category is the so-called "garbage postcard," of which only five hundred are thought to exist. It is a U.S. government postal (Scott UX-17) and is keenly sought by both stamp and government postal card collectors as well as picture postcard collectors. The rarity of the card is related to the fact that it was never intended for circulation. The card's design originally had a full-face inset of President William McKinley, the twenty-fifth president, but a side view of the president was preferred, and the earlier full-faced specimens were ordered destroyed. By one means or another (perhaps surreptitiously, like the rare 1913 "Liberty Head" nickel), five hundred of them were thought to have been preserved after being rescued from the government furnace. To date, they have been variously valued at between $600 to $2,000.

Q. Is there one category of postcards that may be said to be the backbone of the hobby, a category that has always been in demand?

A. Yes, the hometown or local view card has consistently been the one card to be requested at shows and bid on in auctions the world over. It has been suggested that the French, who are often the trend-setters in postcard collecting (at least for the rest of Europe), have increased their fascination for French street scenes and local view cards to the point where interest in most other material pales by comparison. The British have long been avid collectors of local views, and they show no sign of changing their preferences. If anything, the appeal is stronger and is including linens and some chromes as the topography of city landscapes is changing before their eyes. To their way of thinking, these cards represent not only nostalgia but a bit of permanence in an otherwise changing world.

In America, the hometown view card had lost some of its popularity several years ago to artist-signed cards, early exposition material, Art Nouveau cards, and others, but for the past five or six years, local street scenes have come back with a vengeance. The best-selling postcard books during this period—and that by a considerable margin—have been tomes directed toward local history and that use local view cards to punctuate the lessons.

The "greetings from" series by Graphic Arts Publishing have been monumental successes, and more are planned for the future. The story is the same with the "Vanished Splendor" books on Oklahoma City as well as the local view books on Wichita, Kansas, and Amarillo and Corpus Christi, Texas. The 1,500 titles that will eventually be published on most of the towns in Europe should be testimony enough of their appeal.

The only problem that has tended to diminish interest in a few of the local view cards is the sometimes astronomical figures that have been asked for the real photo cards. It is becoming more common with the passage of time to see these specimens routinely bringing $10 to $25 each. Though they may be worth that sort of money, their jump to these prices in such a brief period of time (during the last three years) has considerably dampened enthusiasm for them among some collectors (see the questionnaire results in Appendix B).

Q. Are modern postcards worth collecting?

A. First, let us understand what a modern postcard is. It is a card produced after World War II or, according to many dealers, since 1950.

It might be best to consider the opinion of modern postcard dealer Pete Davies in attempting to answer this question. Davies' book, *Collect Modern Postcards,* was released last year, and though sales were limited for the most part to Great Britain, he has managed to sell in excess of two thousand copies. Given that England proper has (or so it has been conjectured by more than one source) less than five thousand active postcard collectors, this is a very surprising number.

In France, two of its postcard publications are devoted almost exclusively to modern postcards, and their readerships are said to be increasing. The proliferation during the past ten years of postcard publishers indicates a demand that is hard to deny. When a question about the modern postcard's viability was put on a questionnaire addressed to collectors and dealers (see Appendix B) from all over the United States and England, they responded in large numbers (forty percent) with an affirmation of the modern card's potential.

Unlike the world of a few centuries ago, this one is rapidly changing. The postcard, since 1870, has been there to record the transitions, and it is still performing the same function. The modern cards of the 1950s, even of the 1960s, show us views of a world that no longer exists. In time, the postcard will be recognized as one of our most accurate mirrors to those times, but only if specimens of them remain.

It has been argued, and with some validity, one must quickly add, that all too many of the modern cards are tasteless and uninspiring compared to those of the "Golden Age." This was true but is becoming less so as more and more publishers begin to take both themselves and their product more seriously. Some of the modern artist-drawn cards are, in fact, quite nice, and a bevy of collectors is pushing the prices on them ever higher.

A more direct answer to the question would apply not only to modern cards but to the earlier ones as well. Not all are deserving of respect, not all are significant, not all are equally well rendered, but those that do merit attention and whose prices are not prohibitive ought to be considered worthwhile collectibles: good to look at and good to pass on to posterity.

Q. How do postcards compare with other collectibles as investments?

A. Only time will really tell, but the small track record for them (twenty years) would indicate that they compare quite favorably with many other collectible items. Cards that might be purchased for a few pennies a few decades ago are now priced in multiple dollars. In fact, about the only postcards not to increase many times in value have been the common greetings and the common views. A few examples might better make the point. In 1968, a good pre-1920 street scene showing a fair amount of activity and the name of a business or two on the sides of buildings might fetch twenty-five cents, and that was top price. If it showed a close-up view of a streetcar or tram, perhaps fifty cents would be asked. Today, dealers routinely price the first card at $3 to $5 and the second one at $5 to $10.

Other figures are even more astounding. Ethnic cards (blacks, Indians, Jewish) could be purchased for from ten to twenty-five cents apiece. Today, some of them bring $10 and more (some of the Jewish cards $25 and more). Early close-up transportation cards were realizing $1 each, and collectors were crying foul! at such prices. Such cards now sell from $5 to $25 for the rare ones. Art Nouveau cards could be had for a couple of dollars, which is some distance removed from the $100 plus asked for many of them from today's dealers.

Interestingly, many collectors (see the questionnaire in Appendix B) believe that prices will continue to rise. As one man put it, "They're not making any more of the stuff." As regards the early material, he is right. Even today, postcard prices are cheap compared to the values placed on the more-established collectibles.

Yet another fact should be considered and that is that many picture postcards are bona fide works of art while others stimulate feelings of nostalgia for those days now gone forever. This nostalgia appeal, coming in the face of increasing technology, skyscraper buildings, industrial pollution, and a highly structured, impersonal world, should not be underrated. People are looking to return to simpler times and simpler pleasures; postcards remind them of those times.

Finally, the pre-1920 postcards are undeniable antiques whose link to our past is a personal one. Note what has happened in the areas of similar types of items with a personal flavor, such as Shirley Temple dolls and Mickey Mouse watches, and it becomes plausible to think that picture postcards face a bright economic future.

Q. Should postcards be purchased on impulse?

A. The obvious answer to this question would seem to be a simple one: No. But "no" is not always the right answer all the time, although most everyone would agree that it is the correct response most of the time. All one really need do is ask how many times his or her refusal to purchase an item in haste has been a wrong decision.

Still, there are times, few to be sure, when an opportunity to purchase an item is presented for a short time then withdrawn. Some of the wisest decisions in all of human history—as well as some of the most foolhardy ones—were made in an impromptu fashion. So . . .

The decision in any event is a personal one and should be decided by each individual after deliberation.

Q. What is the difference between a postcard and a postal card?

A. A postal card is a card manufactured by the government that has an imprinted stamp on it. A postcard is a privately produced card. The standard size for either type is 3-1/2 × 5″, although private producers may make cards as large as they please as long as the appropriate postage is attached. (Continental postcards, those used on the European mainland and occasionally elsewhere, are 4-1/8 × 5-7/8″).

Q. Is there a uniform grading scale?

A. No, nor is there likely to be one in the foreseeable future. There are two sides to this issue, and both should be examined. In the one instance, the lack of uniformity has created some problems that many collectors find most unpalatable. Examples of differences among dealers include the appropriateness of using certain designations at specific times or under certain conditions. Some dealers find no problem in defining a card as "mint," even if there is writing on it, while others consider that to be a disreputable practice. Some dealers move one slot from mint to very good while other dealers have graduations in between (excellent, very fine, fine). Some dealers discount for a faded appearance, and others do not. Some discount for too-heavy postmarks while others ignore this in their descriptions. In short, each dealer appears to have his or her own measurements and criteria to determine what constitutes what.

For years, similar problems existed in the coin collecting community. At last, a numerical grading system was devised and put into place to alleviate the many complaints. Instead, the grading system complicated them, as each dealer considered himself or herself the best judge of a coin's grade. This in turn led to the creation of an independent board being set up to be the final arbiter of grade. Even here, trouble crept into paradise as both dealers and collectors would quibble about the validity of a specific examiner's grade. The situation was exacerbated when the coin was returned and regraded by a different examiner, whose determination was frequently different than that of the first grader.

Clearly, the same sort of problems and dissentions should not be allowed to infect the deltiological community. Ultimately, the best course of action is to purchase cards from those dealers whose grading scale and practices match one's own. Of course, this is not always practical since all the cards one is seeking will not come from one source, but it does answer part of the problem. For the rest, it is recommended that the dealer first be questioned as to his or her refund practices before any purchases are made. Most dealers are willing to listen to reasonable complaints, which is really all one can logically expect.

Appendix B
Questionnaire Results

In an effort to bring some measure of understanding about where the hobby of postcard collecting is now and where it may be headed, two questionnaires were developed and sent to dealers and collectors. The first was devised for the dealers in the United States and England while the second was geared for the collectors in these countries. The six hundred questionnaires were not meant to be a scientific survey but were intended instead to represent the views of a cross section of dealers and collectors in the hope that the answers might prove useful for those who are seeking firsthand information. Since multiple answers are possible on many of the questions, the responses frequently exceed 100%.

In most cases, the responses expressed opinions that are already relatively well known by many who have been involved with deltiology for several years' or more. Yet this is the first such attempt at putting on paper the inclinations, thoughts, and feelings of dealers and collectors. There are a few instances where the answers are at least mildly surprising. Again, it is the anticipation that these answers may add to the storehouse of knowledge and be useful as tools to give both dealers and collectors a better understanding of one another.

Dealers' Questionnaire

1. Are modern postcards the collectible of the future or are collectors only deluding themselves and engaging their time and money with a speculative bubble that is sure to burst?

a) Collectible of future   40%
b) Speculative bubble   15%
c) Some will/some won't   10%
d) Don't know/no response   35%

2. Should there be a standardized grading scale?

a) Yes   40%
b) No   40%
c) No response   20%

3. What are the most important postcard books you have read?

a) *Picture Postcards in U.S., 1898–1917*   64%
b) Neudin's catalogue   27%
c) *American Guide to Tuck*   23%
d) *Picture PC & Its Origins*   25%
e) *Pioneer Postcards*   21%
f) Bernhard's catalogue   15%
g) No response   19%

4. The practice of listing estimated values or price ranges with auction lots is:

a) A good policy   76%
b) A poor policy   11%
c) Other/no response   13%

5. *To what postcard periodicals do you presently sub-scribe?*

a)	*Postcard Collector*	82%
b)	*Barr's Post Card News*	70%
c)	*Picture Postcard Monthly*	32%
d)	Club/other	63%

6. *Which postcard periodical is your favorite?*

a)	*Postcard Collector*	19%
b)	*Barr's*	16%
c)	*Picture Postcard Monthly*	10%
d)	*Neudin*	10%
e)	All are good	14%
f)	No response	31%

7. *In what particular area(s) do you think more schol-arship is needed?*

a)	Card types	19%
b)	Publishers	11%
c)	Everything	9%
d)	Checklists	6%
e)	Postal history	4%
f)	No response	51%

8. *What categories and types of postcards are cur-rently undervalued?*

a)	Pre-1920 artist-drawn	16%
b)	All postcards	14%
c)	Early litho types	11%
d)	Good real photos	11%
e)	No response	48%

9. *Which postcards are overvalued?*

a)	Pioneers	11%
b)	Most/all of them	10%
c)	Linens	5%
d)	Real photos	4%
e)	Greetings	5%
f)	Expos and advertising	4%
g)	Glamour	6%
h)	Santas	5%
i)	Common views	6%
j)	Railroad depots	4%
k)	Auction material	4%
l)	No response	36%

10. *Do you feel that the hobby is healthy and vibrant or is it in a state of decline?*

a)	Healthy/vibrant	59%
b)	In decline	26%
c)	No response	15%

11. *Identify one or more ways in which postcard col-lecting may be improved.*

a)	More publicity	29%
b)	More professionalism	11%
c)	More books	11%
d)	No response	49%

12. *Do you feel that prices have peaked or do you think they will continue to increase?*

a)	Increase	60%
b)	Peaked	31%
c)	No response	9%

13. *Do you feel there are too many or too few postcard shows each year?*

a)	Too many	10%
b)	Too few	21%
c)	Just right	59%
d)	No response	10%

14. *What category(ies) of cards do you expect to ex-perience the greatest growth during the next decade?*

a)	Linens	14%
b)	Chromes	14%
c)	Views	9%
d)	Don't know	6%
e)	All of them	12%
f)	Real photos	11%
g)	Pioneers	6%
h)	Topicals	4%
i)	No response	24%

Collectors' Questionnaire

1. List your three favorite categories of postcards.

   a) Local views   35%
   b) Greetings   14%
   c) Artist-signed   14%
   d) Real photo   11%
   e) Advertising   4%
   f) Other   13%
   g) No response   9%

2. What is your least favorite?

   a) Local views   13%
   b) Humorous   10%
   c) Chromes   10%
   d) Greetings   9%
   e) Linens   7%
   f) Animals   5%
   g) Other   30%
   h) No response   16%

3. Are modern postcards the collectible of the future or are collectors of them only deluding themselves and engaging their time and money with a speculative bubble that is sure to burst?

   a) Collectible of future   41%
   b) Speculative bubble   13%
   c) Don't know/no response   46%

4. Do you collect modern cards?

   a) Yes   71%
   b) No   29%

5. What type of modern cards do you collect?

   a) View cards   20%
   b) Animals   12%
   c) Special occasion   10%
   d) Other   28%
   e) No response   30%

6. What is the best way to protect postcards?

   a) Plastic sleeves   51%
   b) In albums   40%
   c) Keep cool and dry   17%

7. Do you find that the auction lots you win are as described?

   a) Most of the time   49%
   b) Half of the time   13%
   c) Less than half of the time   34%
   d) No response   44%

8. What is your favorite type of postcard?

   a) Real photo   40%
   b) Hold-to-light   8%
   c) Mechanicals   5%
   d) Silks   4%
   e) Other   4%
   f) No response   39%

9. What do you consider the three most important postcard books you have read?

   a) *Picture Postcards in U.S., 1898–1917*   20%
   b) Kaduck (Rare I & II)   7%
   c) *Standard Postcard Catalog*   6%
   d) *Royal Postcards*   3%
   e) *American Guide to Tuck*   3%
   f) No response   61%

10. The practice of listing estimated values or price ranges with postcards in auctions is:

   a) A good policy   73%
   b) A poor policy   11%
   c) No response   16%

11. What postcard periodicals do you presently subscribe to?

   a) *Postcard Collector*   35%
   b) *Barr's Post Card News*   33%
   c) *Picture Postcard Monthly*   3%
   d) No response   56%

12. Which is your favorite?

   a) *Postcard Collector*   24%
   b) *Barr's Post Card News*   20%
   c) *Picture Postcard Monthly*   19%
   d) No response   37%

13. Is your postcard club an active one, sincerely promoting the betterment of the hobby?

   a) Yes   92%
   b) No   6%
   c) No response   2%

14. *Is your postcard club more interested in buying, selling, and trading than in socializing, having guest speakers and lecturers, and giving slide shows?*

    a) Yes   48%
    b) No   45%
    c) No response 7%

15. *What postcards are currently undervalued?*

    a) None   11%
    b) Greetings   7%
    c) Foreign   8%
    d) Artist-drawn 8%
    e) Other   12%
    f) No response 54%

16. *What cards are currently overvalued?*

    a) Real photos   12%
    b) Greetings   9%
    c) Modern   5%
    d) Foreign   3%
    e) All or most   9%
    f) Tuck   7%
    g) Other   17%
    h) Don't know/no response 38%

17. *Is the hobby healthy and vibrant or do you think it is stagnant or declining?*

    a) Healthy/vibrant 78%
    b) Declining   6%
    c) No response   16%

18. *Do you think that prices have peaked or will they continue to increase?*

    a) Continue to increase 61%
    b) Peaked   27%
    c) No response   12%

19. *In which ways do you make most of your postcard purchases? (Some respondents made more than one choice.)*

    a) Postcard shows   61%
    b) Flea markets   39%
    c) Antique shows   28%
    d) Approvals   12%
    e) Trades   21%
    f) Mail auctions   10%
    g) Other/no response 6%

Appendix C
Annual Postcard Shows

The list of annual or, in some cases, periodic postcard and collectible shows below gives an idea as to the postcard's popularity among collectors. In many cases, the names of the people to contact for further information are provided, but in all cases, a wise precaution would be to contact the postcard club nearest to the event. U.S. shows are arranged in alphabetical order by state.

American Shows

Arizona

Arizona Post Card Club Show (Scottsdale, Arizona).
Fall show. Contact: Bob Phelan, P.O. Box 15005, Phoenix, Arizona 85060.

California

California's Capital Show, Postcards and Paper Collectibles (Sacramento, California).
Summer show. Admission $3. Contact: Rudy and Natalie Schafer, 2820 Echo Way, Sacramento, California 95821.

Orange County Postcard and Paper Collectibles Show (Garden Grove, California).
Fall show.

San Bernardino Coin/Hobby Show.
Winter show. Contact: Al Hall, P.O. Box 1028, Colton, California 92324.

San Diego Post Card Shows.
Two shows: winter/summer. Contact: Grace Watts, P.O. Box 886, Valley Center, California 92082.

Connecticut

Connecticut Postcard Show.
Spring show. Admission $1.50. Contact: Peter Maronn, 180 Goodwin Street, Bristol, Connecticut 06010.

Florida

Paper Collectibles and Postcard Show and Sale (St. Petersburg, Florida).
Winter show. Contact: Evans Events, 31 West Fifth Street, Pottstown, Pennsylvania 19464.

Tropobex (Boynton Beach, Florida).
Winter show. Admission $1. Contact: Tropical Post Card Club.

Georgia

Annual Savannah Postcard Show (Savannah, Georgia).
Fall show. Contact: Clifford Burgess, P.O. Box 13277, Savannah, Georgia 31406.

Georgia State Postcard Show (Atlanta, Georgia).
Fall show. Contact: Georgia Postcard Dealer's Association, P.O. Box 886, Macon, Georgia 31202.

Illinois

Annual Collectibles Exposition (Chicago, Illinois).
Fall show. Admission $3. Contact: Howard Rossen, 1370 Ontario Street, Suite 410, Cleveland, Ohio 44113.

Cornpex—Corn Belt Philatelic Society's Annual Show (Bloomington, Illinois).
Fall show. Admission free.

Evanston Postcard and Paper Collectibles Show (Evanston, Illinois).
Contact: Louis Berman, 2115 Washington, Wilmette, Illinois 60091.

Homewood Flossmoor Postcard Club Exhibit (Homewood, Illinois).
Fall show. Admission free.

Windy City Post Card Club Show (Hillside, Illinois).
Spring show. Admission $1.

Indiana

Indianapolis Postcard Club Annual Show.
Spring show.

Midwest Postcard Exposition (South Bend, Indiana).
Summer show. Admission $1.

Twinbridges Postcard Club Show (Evansville, Indiana).
Spring show. Admission free.

Iowa

Black Hawk Post Card Show (Bettendorf, Iowa).
Winter show. Admission free.

Kentucky

Kentucky Postcard Club Show and Sale (Louisville, Kentucky).
Summer show. Admission fifty cents.

Maine

Maine Antique Paper Show (Portland, Maine).
Summer show. Contact: Richard Bunker, HCR 33, Box 78, South Thomaston, Maine.

Maryland

Greater Baltimore Collectors Mart (Pikesville, Maryland).
Fall show.

Pikpost—Monumental Postcard Club of Baltimore Postcard Show and Sale (Timonium, Maryland).
Fall show. Admission $1. Contact: Perry Judelson, Box 7675, Baltimore, Maryland 21207.

Washington Collector's Market (Gaithersburg, Maryland).
Summer show.

Massachusetts

Baseball and Postcard Show (Hyannis/Cape Cod, Massachusetts).
Spring show. Admission $1. Contact: E. F. Stefanik & Associates, Box 2558, Fall River, Massachusetts 02722.

Cape Cod Post Card Collectors Club Annual Show and Sale (Dennis, Massachusetts).
Contact: Ed Robinson, P.O. Box 104, Cataumet, Massachusetts 02534.

Central Massachusetts Postcard Club Annual Show (South Barre, Massachusetts).
Fall show.

Collectorama's Fall Baseball, Postcard and Paper Show (Fall River, Massachusetts).
Fall show. Admission $1. Contact: E. Stefanik, P.O. Box 2558, Fall River, Massachusetts 02722.

Michigan

Michigan Antiquarian Book and Paper Show (Lansing, Michigan).
Fall show. Contact: Curious Book Shop, 307 East Grand River, East Lansing, Michigan 48823.

Southwest Michigan Post Card Club Bourse (Kalamazoo, Michigan).
Spring show. Admission free. Contact: Sue Hodapp, 1415 Seminole, Kalamazoo, Michigan 49007.

Missouri

Gateway Postcard Club Annual Show and Sale (St. Louis, Missouri).
Summer show.

Nebraska

Lincoln Postcard Club Show (Lincoln, Nebraska).
Summer show. Contact: Lincoln Postcard Club, 7100 Hook Drive, Lincoln, Nebraska 68507.

New Jersey

Garden State Postcard Show (Somerville, New Jersey).
Fall show. Contact: Mrs. Delores Kirchgessimer, 421 Washington Street, Hoboken, New Jersey 07030.

Jersey Shore Annual Postcard Show (Belmar, New Jersey).
Fall show. Admission free. Contact: John McGrath, 95 Newbury Road, Howell, New Jersey 07731.

Pocax—Annual Exhibition of the South Jersey Postcard Club.
Spring show. Admission $1.50. Contact: South Jersey Postcard Club, Alex F. Antal, No. 4 Plymouth Drive, Marlton, New Jersey 08053.

New York

Buffalo Postcard Club Show and Sale (Cheektowaga, New York).
Winter show. Admission $1.

International Post Card Bourse (New York, New York).
Contact: Leah Schnall, 67-00 192nd Street, Flushing, New York 11365.

Long Island Postcard Club Show (Lindenhurst, New York).
Spring show.

Thousand Islands Stamp, Coin, Postcard and Collectibles Show (Clayton, New York).
Summer show. Contact: P.O. Box 316, Clayton, New York 13624.

Ohio

Annual Postcard and Paper Show (Ashland, Ohio).
Spring show. Admission $1. Contact: Johnny Appleseed Postcard Club, P.O. Box 132, Ashland, Ohio 44805.

Cincinnati Postcard Show.
Summer show. Admission $1. Contact: Don Skillman, 6646 Shiloh Road, Goshen, Ohio 45122.

Heart of Ohio (Columbus, Ohio).
Fall show. Admission $1.50. Contact: Betty Sidle, 444 Heather Lane, Powell, Ohio 43065.

Pennsylvania

Great Eastern U.S. Book, Paper, Advertising and Collectibles Show (Allentown, Pennsylvania).
Spring show.

King of Prussia Postcard Show and Sale.
Summer show. Admission $2. Contact: John McClintock, Box 1765, Manassas, Virginia 22110.

Morlatton Post Card Club Show (Lancaster, Pennsylvania).
Fall show. Admission $1.

Ohio Valley Postcard Club Show (Pittsburgh, Pennsylvania).
Spring show. Admission free. Contact: Mary Martin.

Paper Americana Show (Pittsburgh, Pennsylvania).
Spring show. Admission $1. Contact: Crown Antiques, 2301 Murray Avenue, Pittsburgh, Pennsylvania 15217.

Suburban Philadelphia Spring Postcard Show.
Spring show. Admission $1.25. Contact: K. & K. Shows, P.O. Box 1031, Roslyn, Pennsylvania 19001.

South Carolina

Heart of Dixie Postcard Show (Fort Mill, South Carolina).
Fall show.

Texas

Cowtown Postcard Club Annual Show and Sale (Fort Worth, Texas).
Summer show. Contact: Ruth Scott, 1615 Bluebonnet Drive, Fort Worth, Texas 76111.

Wisconsin

Four Lakes Post Card Show (Madison, Wisconsin).
Summer show. Contact: Lois Heft, 1305 Debra Lane, Madison, Wisconsin 53704.

Madpex—Stamps, Coins, Postcards (Madison, Wisconsin).
Fall show. Contact: Lois Heft, 1305 Debra Lane, Madison, Wisconsin 53704.

British Shows

Any of the British annual publications (with perhaps *Picture Postcard Monthly*'s annual being the most complete for this purpose) are ideal sources for a listing of British postcard dealers and postcard shows, or "fairs," as they prefer to call them. A couple of the more well known are included below for those who may be planning a trip to England.

Bipex—British International Postcard Exhibition (Kensington Town Hall, London).
Summer show. Admission £2.50. Contact: Mrs. Vera Hughes, 6 Chute Close, Rainham, Kent ME8 9RW, England.

I.P.M. Promotions.
Several shows annually. Contact: J. H. D. Smith, P.O. Box 190, Lewes, Sussex BN7 1HF, England.

R.F. Postcards.
Postcard shows at London, Birmingham, and elsewhere. Contact: Joan Venman, 17 Hilary Crescent, Rayleigh, Essex SS6 8NB, England.

Reflections of a Bygone Age—Postcard, Cigarette Card Fairs (Nottingham, England).
Contact: Mary Lund, 15 Debdale Lane, Keyworth, Nottingham NG12 6HT, England.

Appendix D
Postcard Clubs

It is difficult for any hobby to survive without its dedicated coterie forming themselves into associations, unions, and clubs. Deltiology is no different and has, in fact, grown in giant leaps in postcard club formations during the last twenty years. Perhaps the most complete listing of the clubs in America and Canada is the one provided as a service to its readers by *Barr's Post Card News*. Unfortunately, club presidents, corresponding secretaries, and the like often have a way of changing, sometimes on an annual basis. For that reason, the listing provided below will include only the names and addresses of clubs known to the author. All other clubs are cordially invited to contact the author with information to be included in future volumes. The postcard clubs are in alphabetical order by country and state.

American Clubs

Alabama

Birmingham Postcard Club (Birmingham, Alabama)
Contact:
Louise Griffies
Corresponding Secretary
309 Running Brook Road
Birmingham, Alabama 35226

California

San Jose Post Card Club (San Jose, California)
Contact:
Peggy Nash
Treasurer
P.O. Box 21429
San Jose, California 95151

Torrance-South Bay Post Card Collectors (Torrance, California)
Contact:
Art and Carolyn Lee
Secretary/Treasurer
P.O. Box 1403
Lomita, California 90717

Connecticut

Garfield Gang Post Card and Fan Club
Contact:
Joan Carlson
905 Rt. 163
Oakdale, Connecticut 06370

Florida

Tropical Postcard Club
Contact:
Marvin Shapiro
Secretary
P.O. Box 431131
South Miami, Florida 33143

Illinois

Black Hawk Post Card Club
Contact:
Arretta Wetzel
Secretary
1325 45 Street
Rock Island, Illinois 61201

Windy City Post Card Club (Chicago, Illinois)
Contact:
Windy City Club
P.O. Box 8118
Chicago, Illinois 60680

Indiana

Indianapolis Post Card Club (Indianapolis, Indiana)
Contact:
Jeanne Acheson
Secretary
2801 East Kessler Boulevard
Indianapolis, Indiana 46220

Kansas

Wichita Postcard Club (Wichita, Kansas)
Contact:
Wichita Postcard Club
P.O. Box 780282
Wichita, Kansas 67278-0282

Maine

Pine Tree Post Card Club (Portland, Maine)
Contact:
Jon Stokes
Secretary
P.O. Box 5106, Station A
Portland, Maine 04101

Massachusetts

Cape Cod Post Card Collectors Club
Contact:
Helen Angell
Corresponding Secretary
Short Neck Road
South Dennis, Massachusetts 02660

Michigan

Wolverine Post Card Club
Contact:
Laura Goldberg
Corresponding Secretary
1313 East Harry
Hazel Park, Michigan 48030

Missouri

Gateway Post Card Club of St. Louis (St. Louis, Missouri)
Contact:
Kathy Danielson
Corresponding Secretary
P.O. Box 630
O'Fallon, Illinois 62269

Montana

Montana Post Card Club
Contact:
Tom Mulvaney
Box 814
East Helena, Montana 59635

New Jersey

Garden State Post Card Collectors Club
Contact:
Dolores Kirchgessner
Corresponding Secretary
421 Washington Street
Hoboken, New Jersey 07030

South Jersey Post Card Club
Contact:
Alex Antal
Corresponding Secretary
No. 4 Plymouth Drive
Marlton, New Jersey 08053

New York

Maximum Card Study Unit
Contact:
Andrew DiComo
5 Taurgo Lane
Centereach, New York 11720

Metropolitan Post Card Club (New York City, New York)
Contact:
Ben Papell
146-17 Delaware Ave.
Flushing, New York 11355

The Upstate New York Post Card Club
Contact:
Dorothy Baron
1832 Fiero Avenue
Schenectady, New York 12303

Ohio

Greater Cincinnati Post Card Club (Cincinnati, Ohio)
Contact:
Al Wettstein
900 American Building
30 East Central Parkway
Cincinnati, Ohio 45202

Heart of Ohio Post Card Club (Columbus, Ohio)
Contact:
Elbert Sidle
444 Heather Lane
Powell, Ohio 43065

Western Reserve Post Card Society (Cleveland, Ohio)
Contact:
Marie Hajma
Secretary
24800 Emery Road
Warrensville Heights, Ohio 44128

Oklahoma

T-Town Postcard Club (Tulsa, Oklahoma)
Contact:
Beverly Jenkins
Corresponding Secretary
P.O. Box 700334
Tulsa, Oklahoma 74170

Oregon

Webfooters Post Card Club (Portland, Oregon)
Contact:
Alan Patera
Secretary
5155 Southwest Firwood
Lake Oswego, Oregon 97034

Rhode Island

Rhode Island Post Card Club
Contact:
Evelyn Marshall
Corresponding Secretary
37 Ryder Ave, Apt. 2
Cranston, Rhode Island 02920

Tennessee

Mid-South Post Card Club of Memphis (Memphis, Tennessee)
Contact:
Angela Beadell
5575 Walnut Grove Road
Memphis, Tennessee 38119-1960

Texas

Dallas Metroplex Postcard Club
Contact:
Larry Seymour
822 Southeast Eighth Street
Grand Prairie, Texas 75051

Virginia

Postcard History Society
Contact:
John McClintock
Box 1765
Manassas, Virginia 22110

Australian Clubs

New South Wales Postcard Collectors Society
Contact:
Michael Cousens
Secretary
P.O. Box 123
Cougee 2034
New South Wales
Australia

Queensland Cartophilic Society
Contact:
Roy Pugh
Secretary
60 Binowee Street
Aspley, Queensland 4034
Australia

British Clubs

Canal Card Collectors Circle
Contact:
David Clough
12 Wellstead Gardens
Westcliff-on-Sea
Essex SS0 0AY
England

Norfolk Postcard Club
Contact:
Janet Harrison
68 Nasmith Road
Norwich NR4 7BJ
England

The Postcard Club of Great Britain
Contact:
Mrs. Drene Brennan
Secretary
34 Harper House
St. James's Cresct.
London SW9
England

Red Rose Postcard Club
Contact:
Bob Charnley
99 Liverpool Old Road
Much Hoole
Preston PR4 4GA
England

Wealden Postcard Club
Contact:
Charles Kay
2 North Court
Hassocks
West Sussex BN6 8JS
England

Canadian Clubs

Toronto Postcard Club (Toronto, Ontario, Canada)
Contact:
Bob Atkinson
P.O. Box 6184, Station A
Toronto, Ontario M5W 1P6
Canada

French Clubs

Club International de la Carte Postale Contemporaine
Contact:
J. C. Souyri
Centre Culturel
81000 Albi
France

Norwegian Clubs

Postkortsamlere i Vest
Contact:
Tone Sandmo
P.O. Box 965
5001 Bergen
Norway

South African Clubs

Southern Africa Postcard Research Group
Contact:
Archie Atkinson
46 The Crofts
Castletown
Isle of Man

Analysis of a Few Clubs

Windy City Postcard Club (Chicago, Illinois)

Well, it now has forty years under its belt, and though its current president, Joseph May, sometimes despairs even with all his efforts to keep the club churning along, it is obvious that he is the right man for the job.

Keenly interested in postcards and dedicated to promoting the hobby, May typifies the type of individual who is critical to the success of any organization. Also serving duty as editor of the club newsletter, May has set as a goal for the 1988–89 club year the formation of a complete checklist of postcards from the 1933–34 Century of Progress Exhibition that was held in Chicago. This seems to be an altogether fitting theme as it will presumably combine scholarship with the natural inclination for people to become involved with their own area.

The May 1988 newsletter includes the usual requests—pleas, actually—for members to give more of their time to the club, either serving as elected officers or as volunteers. These types of requests are pretty standard fare in many postcard clubs, necessitated by the fact that most people would rather be a free roaming member than a tied-in-place officer or assistant of some sort. The treasurer's report for May indicates that the Chicago club is economically healthy, and the list of activities shows that the area's collectors have a good number of shows to keep them occupied. There also appears to be a series of bourses and other activities sponsored by the club or the ones it promotes.

It is nice to see that enthusiasm can still remain high even after forty years.

The Toronto Postcard Club (Toronto, Ontario, Canada)

The largest deltiological association in Canada is the Toronto Postcard Club. It is also the most active, as club meetings are held every two weeks rather than the standard monthly routine. Like most clubs, it has annual auctions to raise funds, but the reports suggest that these and other club activities fail to turn out the number of collectors that one might expect.

353

The numbers they produce indicate that less than ten percent of the membership are actively involved with the club by offering their services. This figure is not as dismal as it may seem and closely parallels what is happening in most other clubs. For the Toronto club, the good news is that its membership is sufficiently large that even five percent participation represents almost as many people as belong to many other clubs in toto.

The club's publication, *Card Talk,* is well produced and gives its pages to the dissemination of useful facts, announcements, and pertinent information. Sadly, it is only printed quarterly. The future of the Toronto club may be bright with promise; only time will tell.

San Jose Postcard Club (San Jose, California)

It is a pleasure to report that there are some decent, well-intentioned, and well-produced clubs within the deltiological community. The San Jose club, with its grass roots support by the membership, is one of them. It is a small but determined and dedicated group of strugglers, groaning and thrusting, pushing and demanding, laboring and persevering, always striving for more. And for better, too. Sure, the club has had its problems, and not everyone pulls his or her weight, but this is small potatoes as complaints go for these people are decided achievers.

This is too general; specifics are required. Let us examine a few concrete items. A good place to start is the club newsletter. Coedited by Walter Kransky and Peggy Nash, the bimonthly publication includes articles on postcard artists, postcard sets and series, postcard publishers, postcard categories, and more. There is also information about the club's activities, both past and future, and all sorts of other interesting items, far too many to mention in this brief review. It should be included that the San Jose club is not remiss in printing checklists as they become available, a service that will prove even more invaluable to future postcard historians than it already does to today's collectors. It should also be mentioned that one of its members, Anthony Quartuccio, (q.v.) has given of his time and talent in order to promote the club. We could all learn something from his unselfish example.

In summation, it is perhaps fitting for each of us who is sincerely concerned with the direction that deltiology should take to give support to the San Jose club. We may even wish to join it and discover its joys for ourselves. Better still that we would join and do a little contributing of our own.

Rhode Island Post Card Club

Although a decade younger than the Windy City Postcard Club, the Rhode Island organization is easily one of the oldest postcard clubs on earth (founded in 1958). Since its inception, it has operated continuously, trying to improve with the passage of time, progressing comfortably and productively into the future. One of the primary reasons for the club's success has been—and is—Evelyn Marshall, who has labored tirelessly for many of those years as the Rhode Island club's corresponding secretary.

Marshall has acted as a liaison between members—or prospective members—and the club's executive officers. She has mailed information, sent and completed forms, dispatched the newsletter, and written for it herself. She is, in short, the Rhode Island Post Card Club's number one asset.

The publication, *What Cheer News,* titled after an early American Indian greeting, is first-rate. It always begins with news and notes about what's happening with the club. This information sometimes contains a humanitarian dimension: snippets concerning reinstatements, changes of address, in memoriams, and hospitalizations. Then there are original articles on various topics and also reprints of significant articles that have appeared in other publications. All is geared toward enrichment, enjoyment, and plain, old-fashioned camaraderie. Sure to be seen are lots of illustrations, treating the eyes and informing the mind. There are checklists and a plethora of other fascinating tidbits. This would be a fine organization to join regardless of where one lived.

Clearly, as hundreds of collectors have discovered through the years, the Rhode Island Post Card Club is an organization well worth exploring.

The Wichita Postcard Club (Wichita, Kansas)

See Hal Ottaway. See Hal run. See Hal run to write an article. See Hal run to answer the voluminous correspondence. See Hal run to fill the club's newsletter with useful information, requests, and announcements. See Hal writing books about deltiology. See Hal too busy to take a much-deserved bow. And at the end of another crazy, active day, fraught with this and replete with that, see Hal collapse gratefully into bed, his mind pursuing the activities and possibilities for the morrow.

Ho, hum.

Of course, it would be both incorrect and unfair to conclude that the Wichita Postcard Club revolves around the life and works of Hal Ottaway. Nope, that is one assertion we cannot make, not as long as there are the willing postcard offerings of master caricaturist Rick Geary to grace and enrich the club. A busy, talented, and much-sought-after man himself, Geary manages to find time for the club. Then there is the youthful, exuberant and helpful Frank Wood. In years past, Wood has assisted not only the Wichita club but has offered his energies and expertise as well to the T-Town Postcard Club in Tulsa, Oklahoma, among others. There is the smiling John Pittman, and there is historian Margaret Tharp, treasurer Hal Ross, and . . .

One complaint of a minor nature is that the club newsletter, *Wichita Postcard Club News,* is too abbreviated. Were it a second-class piece of journalistic endeavor, no one would care about its lack of length, but it has the potential to be a real leader. Reproduc-

tions of new postcard releases, book reviews, information about artists, announcements, miniarticles, and a section entitled "Member's Marketplace" help to make the club a very popular one with an international membership.

Even here, however, the shadow of Ottaway may be easily discerned for, as editor of the newsletter, his imprint may be detected everywhere. In this way, as in others, Ottaway symbolizes what is best about this club. With his spirit of generosity and willingness to expend his energies and talents, he illustrates the unselfishness and desire to serve that should characterize all postcard clubs. Because of his additions—and those of the others already mentioned—the Wichita club has prospered. With its prospering, postcard collectors everywhere have been made the richer.

355

Appendix E
Publishers' Colophons

Ever since the early days of postcard manufacturing, collecting by publisher has been popular. The reasons for this are varied, but the two most prominent ones are related to artistry and to the completion of sets and series. As regards the artistry, it is obvious that some publishers went to extremes to ensure that their cards were both aesthetically pleasing and artistically rendered. The results of these efforts were postcards which have lost none of their desirability with the passage of time. Modern collectors are every bit as enthused about owning them as were their early twentieth-century counterparts.

The second reason was a less-than-subtle ploy by not a few publishers to print postcards in sets of four, six, eight or more specimens. More often than not, the cards had to be purchased separately, as they were released. So common did this practice become that there were only a minority of publishers who did not use it. And, of course, it was successful: collectors both then and now rushed to purchase the latest offering to add to their set.

So sophisticated has the practice of collecting postcards by publishers become that many dealers have included at least one, if not several, groupings of their material by publisher. The colophons or trademarks presented in this section are only the smallest representation of the publishers who have produced postcards. They are offered as an additional insight into what is rapidly becoming one of the more fascinating ways of gathering and preserving picture postcards.

M. Abrams (Roxbury, Massachusetts)

Acmegraph Co. (Chicago, Illinois)

American News Co., Polychrome (New York; Leipzig; Dresden)

Anonymous (Japan)

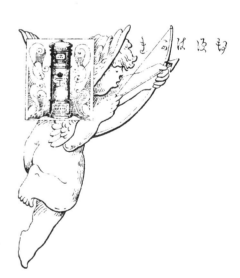

Anonymous

Copyright

Anonymous (Japan)

Anonymous (United States)

Anonymous (Russia)

Art Institute of Chicago (Chicago, Illinois)

Barkalow Bros. (Omaha, Nebraska)

J. Beagles (London, England)

Aristophot (New York, New York)

Bamforth (England; United States)

B. H. Publications, Post Card Collectors Club of America (Los Angeles, California)

J. Beagles (London, England)

Berger Bros. Publishers (Providence, Rhode Island)

B.K.W.I.—Bruder Kohn (Vienna, Austria)

Julius Bien (New York, New York)

Birn Bros. (London, England)

Boots Cash Chemist (Nottingham, England)

B. H. C. (Germany)

Cardinell-Vincent Co. (San Francisco, California)

Bryant Union Publisher (New York)

A. R. P. deLord (Zanzibar)

359

Detroit News Co., (Division of American News Co.), Americhrom (Detroit, Michigan)

G. D. & D. L. (London, England)

Detroit Photographic Co. (Detroit, Michigan)

G. T. Co. (United States)

Gale & Polden (London, Aldershot, England)

Emil Engel (Vienna, Austria)

Gale & Polden, Wellington Series (London, Aldershot, England)

Giesen Bros. & Co. (London, England)

P. J. Flion (Brussels, Belgium)

Gibson Art Co. (Cincinnati, Ohio)

Gloria-Viktoria (Vienna, Austria)

R. Goodrich (England)

C. P. I (Paris, France)

Kanda (Tokyo, Japan)

A. H. (American)

Alex. Inglis (Edinburgh, Scotland)

Kraemer Art Co. (Cincinnati, Ohio)

International Art Publishing Co. (New York; Berlin)

M. Kashover Co. (Los Angeles, California)

V. O. Hammon Publishing Co. (Chicago, Illinois)

Louis Kaufmann & Sons (Baltimore, Maryland)

William Jubb Co. (Syracuse, New York)

F. Hartmann (London, England)

Kyle Co. (Louisville, Kentucky)

Lowman & Hanford (Seattle, Washington)

Manhattan Post Card Publishing Co. (New York, New York)

L. L. (Paris, France)

T. Watson Lythe (England)

Manson News Agency (Rochester, New York)

Hugh C. Leighton (Portland, Maine)

N. R. M. (Italy)

Metropolitan News Co. (Boston, Massachusetts; Germany)

Majestic Publishing Co. (American)

Miller Brewing Co. (Milwaukee, Wisconsin)

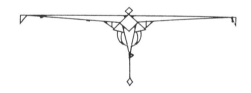

F. P. LeSueur (Toledo, Ohio)

I. L. Maduro (Panama)

J. M. P. (American)

W. B. Perkins (Black Hills, South Dakota)

Philadelphia Post Card Co. (Philadelphia, Pennsylvania)

Bob Petley (Phoenix, Arizona)

Philco Pub. Co. (London, England)

Philadelphia Post Card Co. (Philadelphia, Pennsylvania)

Photogelatine Engraving Co. (Ottawa, Canada)

Pacific Novelty Co. (San Francisco, California)

Pictorial Stationery Co. (London)

Rapid Photo Printing Co. (London, England)

Sackett & Wilhelms (New York and Brooklyn, New York)

B. S. Reynolds (Washington, D. C.)

Portland Post Card Co. (Portland, Oregon)

Prince Publishing Co. (Buffalo, New York)

Richmond News Co. (Richmond Virginia)

St. Joseph Calendar & Novelty Co. (St. Joseph, Missouri)

Rapid Photo (London, England)

Rotophot (London, England)

Rochester News Co. (Rochester, New York)

J. Salmon (Seven Oaks, Kent, England).

P. Sander (Philadelphia, Pennsylvania)

H. H. Stratton (Chattanooga, Tennessee)

A. & G. Taylor (London, England)

Scenic View Card Co. (San Francisco, California)

H. H. T. (American)

Ern Thill (Brussels, Belgium)

Arthur Schurer & Co. (Schonberg, Germany)

E. A. Seeman (Leipzig, Germany)

Raphael Tuck (London, England)

A. Sorocchi (Milan, Italy)

T. P. & Co. (United States)

Curt Teich (Chicago, Illinois)

U. S. A. Post Card (United States)

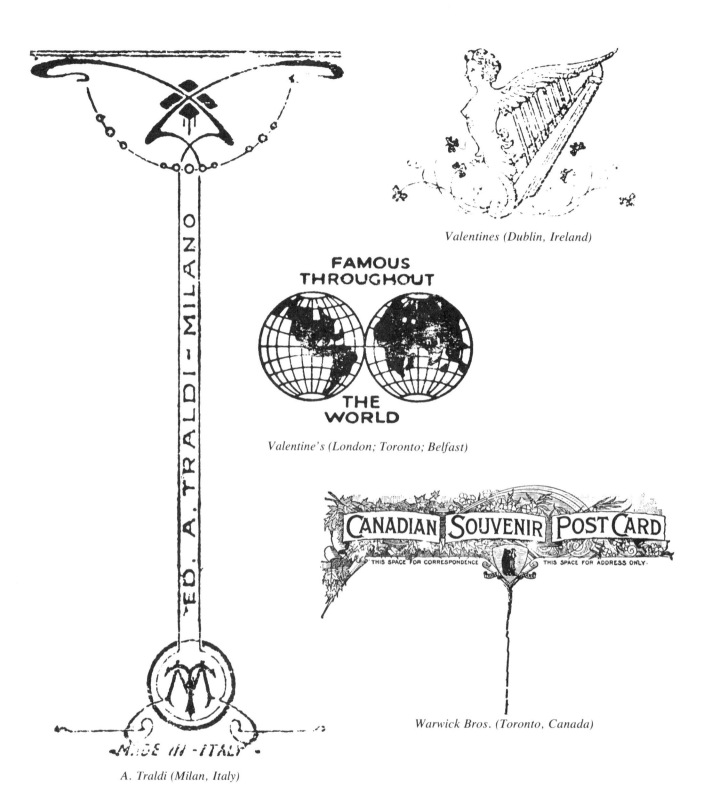

Valentines (Dublin, Ireland)

FAMOUS THROUGHOUT

THE WORLD

Valentine's (London; Toronto; Belfast)

CANADIAN SOUVENIR POST CARD

THIS SPACE FOR CORRESPONDENCE   THIS SPACE FOR ADDRESS ONLY.

Warwick Bros. (Toronto, Canada)

ED. A. TRALDI - MILANO

MADE IN - ITALY

A. Traldi (Milan, Italy)

Washington News Co., Colorchrome (Washington, D. C.)

C. E. Wheelock (Peoria, Illinois)

Wohlfahrts-Karte (Berlin, Germany)

Wholesale Post Card Co. (Dallas, Texas)

Woolstone Bros. (London, England)

Wohlfahrts-Postkarte (Berlin, Germany)

Y. M. C. A. (United States)

Glossary of Foreign Terms

French

Amitres: Greetings, felicitations, salutations
Annee: Year
Bonne Annee: Happy New Year
Bonjour: Good day
Bonne Nuit: Good night
Bonne Chance: Good luck
Bon Soir: Good evening
Bon Souhaits: Best wishes
Carte Postale: Postcard
Cote Reserve a L'Adresse: This side reserved for address
Ducal(e): Duke/duchess
Depose: Lay foundation; also deposit
Etat Unis: United States
Expediteur: Sender, shipper
Fete: Feast, party, festival, holiday
Heureuse Annee: Happy New Year
Imprime: Printed matter
Joyeux: Joyful, happy, merry
Joyeux Paques: Happy Easter
Rendez-vous: Date, appointment
Reproduction Interdite: Reproduction forbidden
Souvenir de: Souvenir from or souvenir of
Salut: Salutations, greetings
Union Postale Universelle: Universal Postal Union or Association

German

Anstalt: Institution, establishment
Auf Ewig: Always, ever, forever
Austellung: Celebration. festival, fair
Bitte Gegen Das Licht zu Halten: Please hold to the light
Bitte zu Wahlen: Please, you choose
Druksache: Printed matter
DRMG: Patent pending (registered with the German Empire)
Dein: Yours
Frohfichne Ostern: Happy Easter
Gerichtlich: Legal(ly); also forensic medicine

GMBH: United with, together, incorporated
Gruss Aus: Greetings from
Gruss Vom: Greetings from
Jagd: Hunting, sports, sportsman
Jagdschloss: Hunting lodge or castle
Konig: King
Konigin: Queen
Kunstler: Artist
Kunst Verlag: Art publisher
Nur Fur Die Adresse: This side for address
Nachdruck Verboten: Strictly forbidden
Postkarte: Postcard
Prosit Noujahr: Happy New Year
Rund: Round; frank or plain
Schloss: Castle
Um: Round about; repeatedly; in another way; down; over
Verlag: Publisher
Viele Grusse: Many thoughts, many good wishes
Veir Gluck im Neuen Jahre: Good Wishes for the New Year
Wird: Emerging, growing, developing
Weltpostverein: World Postal Union

Other Languages

Brefkort (Swedish): Postcard
Boktryckare (Swedish): Printer
Briefkaart (Dutch): Postcard
Cartolina Postala (Italian): Picture postcard
Casa de Correos (Spanish): Post office
Cartao Postal (Portuguese): Postcard
Carte Postala (Romanian): Postcard
Correspondenz Karte (Austrian): Postcard, writing card
Memorias de (Spanish): In memory of, anniversary of
Naam (Dutch): Name
OTKPbITOE NCbMO (Russian): Postcard
Postikortti (Finnish): Postcard
Ricordi di (Italian): Souvenir of or remembrance of
Salutari Din (Romanian): Greetings/salutations of or from
Saluti da(i) (Italian): Greetings of or from

Bibliography

Astolat, John. *Phillimore: The Postcard Art of R. P. Phillimore*. London: Greenfriar Press, 1985.

Bernhard, Willi. *Picture Postcard Catalogue, 1870–1945 (Bildpostkartenkatlog)*. Hamburg: Willi Bernhard, 1972.

Bowers, Q. David, and Christine Bowers. *Robert Robinson: American Illustrator*. Vestal, N.Y.: Vestal Press, 1981.

Bowers, Q. David, George M. Budd, and Ellen H. Budd. *Harrison Fisher*. Q. David Bowers, 1984.

Brooks, Andrew, Fred Fletcher, and Brian Lund. *What the Postman Saw*. Nottingham, Eng.: Reflections of a Bygone Age, 1982.

Burdick, J. R. *Pioneer Postcards*. Franklin Square, N.Y.: Nostalgia Press, 1957.

Cook, David. *Picture Postcards in Australia, 1898–1920*. Victoria, Aust.: Pioneer Design Studio, 1986.

Coysh, A. W. *The Dictionary of Picture Postcards in Britain, 1894–1939*. Woodbridge, Suffolk, Eng.: Antique Collectors' Club, 1984.

Davies, Pete. *Collect Modern Postcards*. Nottingham, Eng.: Reflections of a Bygone Age, 1987.

Duval, William, and Valerie Monahan. *Collecting Postcards in Color, 1894–1914*. Dorset, Eng.: Blandford Press, 1978.

Fanelli, Giovanni, and Ezio Godoli. *Art Nouveau Postcards*. New York, N.Y.: Rizzoli International Publications, 1987.

Gibbons, Stanley. *Postcard Catalogue* (5th ed., 2nd ed.). London: Stanley Gibbons Publications, 1982, 1987.

Gutzman, W. L. *The Canadian Patriotic Post Card Handbook: 1900–1914*. Toronto: Unitrade Press, 1985.

———. *The Canadian Picture Post Card Catalogue 1988*. Toronto: Unitrade Press, 1987.

Holt, Tonie, and Valmai Holt. *I'll Be Seeing You: Picture Postcards of World War II*. Derbyshire, Eng.: Moorland Publishing Co., 1987.

———. *Till the Boys Come Home*. Ridley Park, Penn.: Deltiologists of America, 1978.

Killen, John. *John Bull's Famous Circus*. Dublin, Ire.: O'Brien Press, 1985.

Kornan, Paul. *Australian Post Card Catalogue 1984*. West Melbourne, Australia, 1983.

Lund, Brian. *Postcard Collecting, A Beginner's Guide*. Nottingham, Eng.: Reflections of a Bygone Age, 1985.

Monahan, Valerie. *Collecting Postcards in Color, 1914–1930*. Poole, Dorset, Eng.: Blandford Press, 1980.

Nicholson, Susan Brown. *Teddy Bears on Paper*. Dallas, Tex.: Taylor Publishing Co., 1985.

Ouellette, William. *Fantasy Postcards*. Garden City, N.Y.: Doubleday & Co., 1975.

Ryan, Dorothy. *Picture Postcards in the United States, 1893–1918*. New York, N.Y.: Clarkson Potter, 1982.

Smith, J. H. D. *I. P. M. Catalogue of Picture Postcards and Year Book 1988* (14th ed.). Brighton, Eng.: J. H. D. Smith, 1988.

Smith, Jack. *Military Postcards*. Lombard, Ill.: Wallace-Homestead, 1988.

Smith, Jack. *Royal Postcards*. Lombard, Ill.: Wallace-Homestead, 1987.

Stadtmiller, Bernard. *Postcard Collecting: A Fun Investment*. Palm Bay, Fla.: Bernard Stadtmiller, 1973.

Wolstenholme, George. *Over 900 Things to Know about Postcard Collecting*. U.K.: George Wolstenholme.

Subject Index

A B C of Postcard Collecting
(Wolstenholme), 251
Acorn Philatelic Auctions, 309
Adfactor, 262-263
advertising, 241, 243, 246, 248
*Album of Old Time Postcards from
Houston and Galveston*, 224
*Album of Old Time Texas
Postcards*, 224
albums, 329
Allmen, Diane, 296, 298
*Amarillo, Texas II: The First
Hundred Years* (Franks and
Ketelle), 230
*American Advertising Postcards
Sets and Series, 1890-1920*,
243
American Postcard Guide to Tuck
(Carver), 222
American Postcard Journal, 302
Antique Doll Photo Postcards, 226
Antique Santa Post Cards, 233
Antique Teddy Bears Post Cards,
233
Antwerp Postcard Club, 301
approvals, 314
Arrasich, Furio, 305
art, 250-251
Art Deco, 241, 255
Art Nouveau, 7, 220, 229, 236,
308, 309, 334, 335
value of, 336
Art Nouveau (Barilli), 218
Art Nouveau Postcards (Fanelli
and Godoli), 229
Arthur Schurer & Co., 363
artists, 55-134, 222, 267-291
Australian, 224
French, 223
signed cards by, 334
Asheville Post Card Co., 243
auction catalogues, 307-310
Australia, 223-224, 225
Austrian Postal authority, 3, 12
automobiles, 236
aviation, 222

Bahrain, 225
balloon cards, 7
Bamforth Company, 246
Barr's Post Card News, 256,
298-299
Bernhard, Willi, 306
Besnardeau, M. Leon, 6, 12
blacks, 222
as musicians, 231-232
Blake, Richard, 267
Boccacino, Jean, 268-269
*Book of Postcards from a Century
of Illustrations, 1880-1910*,
239
books, 209-251
Border Fury (Vanderwood and
Samponaro), 250
Britain, 9, 225, 250
children in, 238-239
first postcards in, 3
postal system in, 5
British Post Office, 333
*British Postcard Collector's
Magazine*, 300
Brown, Andreas, 209
business, postal use by, 6

Butland, A. James, 303

C.P.M., 302
C.T. Art Colourton, 259
California, Southern, 232-233
*Calvin Coolidge, A Biography in
Picture Postcards* (Greene),
230-231
Cameo Creations, 329
Canada, 231
*Canadian Patriotic Post Card
Handbook: 1900-1914*
(Gutzman), 231
*Canadian Picture Post Card
Catalogue, 1988* (Gutzman),
231
canals, 244
cancellations, 232
Carlson, Joan, 256
Carter, Jimmy, 257
Cartolina, 301-302
Cartolina Militari 1900 (Arrasich),
218
cartology, vs. deltiology, 333
Carver, Sally, 307
Catalogo delle Cartoline Italiane,
305
catalogues, 304-306
auction, 307-310
Charlton, John P., 3, 12
Chattanooga Album, 249
Chesapeake Bay, 236
Chicago World's Fair, 12
children, 238-239, 246
Victorian, 234
children's books, illustrations
from, 227
Christie, Howard Chandler, 334
Chrome Era, 13
chronology, 12-13
clubs, 11, 223, 347-353
coins, 261
Collect Modern Postcards (Davies),
225-226
collectibles, postcards as, 11
collecting, 235, 238, 248-249, 251
*Collecting Postcards in Color,
1894-1914* (Duval and
Monahan), 227
*Collecting Postcards in Color,
1914-1930* (Monahan),
240-241
collectors, questionnaire to,
341-342
colleges, 244-245
colophons, of publishers, 355-365
Columbian Exposition (Chicago,
1892-1893), 9, 12
Columbus Street Press, 262
comics, 222
communication, postcards as, 9
Coney Island (Snow), 248
*Contemporary American Glass
from Steuben*, 226
Continental postcards, 337
Coolidge, Calvin, 230-231
copyrights, 3, 12
Cornell & Ithaca in Postcards
(Roehl), 244-245
*Corpus Christi, Texas: A Picture
Postcard History* (Eisenhauer
& Starnes), 228

Correspondenz Kartes, 3
"court cards", 9, 13, 334
Cricket on Old Picture Postcards
(Jennings), 235
Curteich. See Teich, Curt
Cyprus, 237-238

dealers, 313-328
questionnaire to, 339-340
definitions, 147-149
Deltiologists of America, 303
deltiology, 11
vs. cartology, 333
Deltiology, 302, 303
Dexter Post Card Company, 226
Dexter Post Card Story (Dexter),
226
*Dictionary of Picture Postcards in
Britain, 1894-1939* (Coysh),
225
divided back cards, 13
dolls, 226, 236

*Early American Folk Art
Masterpieces*, 227
education, 4
*Edwardian Childhood on Old
Picture Postcards* (Lund),
238-239
Eiffel Tower, 12
elves, 236
England, Bamforth Museum, 259
English court card, 333-334
ethnic cards, value of, 336
European Library in Zaltbommel,
209
expositions, 222, 236, 246

Factory Act, 4
Faga, 259
fantasy, 236
Fantasy Postcards (Ouellette), 242
Fisher, Harrison, 221
folk art, 227
*40 Antique Postcards of Santa
Claus*, 240
Forum Cartes et Collections,
300-301
France, 225
first postcards in, 3
Franco-Prussian War, 6-7, 335
French artists, 223
French Exposition (Paris, 1889),
12

Galveston, Texas, 224
"garbage postcard", 335
Geary, Rick, 269
German Army Corps Society, 6
Germany, 9
glass, Steuben, 226
Gonzalez, Fred, 290-291
Gotham Book Mart, 209
government postal, 12
grading scale, uniformity in, 337
Graphic Arts Publishing, 335
Graycraft, 243
Greenaway, Kate, 227
greetings cards, 7, 222, 246, 261,
335
*Greetings from Jamestown, Rhode
Island* (Maden), 239
Greetings from Oregon (Bosker
and Nicholas), 219
*Greetings from Southern
California* (Highland), 232-233
Gruss Aus, 300
"gruss aus" cards, 7, 12

Hamm, Patrick, 291
Harrison Fisher (Bowers, Budd,
and Budd), 221
Hawaii, 242
Helmut Labahn's Auktions, 310
Hermann, Emmanuel, 12, 13
history, 222
Hitler, Adolf, 222, 236
hoarding, 334
Holt, Tonie and Valmai, 305
hometown cards, 335
*Horatio Nelson, a Catalogue of
Picture Postcards* (Shannon),
246-247
Horina, H., 249
Horsham in Old Picture Postcards
(Wales), 250
House of Oberthur de Rennes, 6-7
Houston, Texas, 224
*How to Price and Sell Old Picture
Postcards* (Cox), 224-225
humor, 241, 242, 246

I.P.M. Auctions, 308
*I.P.M. Catalogue of Picture
Postcards & Year Book*, 304
*I'll Be Seeing You: Picture
Postcards of World War II*
(Holt), 234-235
*Ier Catalogue Cartes Postales
Contemporaines, 1975-80*
(Chivat and Souyri), 223
illustrators, 239
Impressionistic art, 223
Indians, 236
Industrial Exposition (Chicago,
1873), 9, 12
Industrial Revolution, 4
International Federation of
Postcard Dealers, 302
International Postal Service, 5
International Postcard Market,
267
Ireland, 236-237
Ithaca, New York, 244-245

Jamestown, Rhode Island, 239
Japan, 9
Jennings, Rocky, 261
John Bull's Famous Circus,
236-237

Kansas, 251
Kansas City, 243, 244
Kate Greenaway Postcards, 227
Kemp, Sherry, 272-273
Krause Publications, 296
Kropp, E.C., 243

Labahn, Helmut, 310
Lake County, Illinois, Museum,
259
Landmark Hawaii (Peebles), 242
Lee, Coral, 257-258
Lenzi, Marc, 273
*Liberty, A Centennial History of
the Statue of Liberty in Post
Cards*, 239-240
lighthouses, 236
linen cards, 13
Lipman, H.L., 3, 12
lithography, 9
local view cards, 335
Louis XI of France, 5
Lowe, James Lewis, 302, 303

mail auctions, 296, 297, 314

Mail Memories: Pictorial Guide to Postcard Collecting (Kaduck), 235
mail service, 314
McClintock, John, 302
McGehee, Paul, 260
McKinley, William, on government postal, 335
Memphis Memories, 249
Mennebeuf, Daniel, 273-275
messages, 221
Mexican Revolution, 250
military cards, 305
Military Postcards 1870-1945, 247
Military Postcards of the Third Reich (Capparelli), 222
military, 6, 218, 222, 234-235, 241, 242, 246, 247
Milwaukee, Wisconsin, 229
modern art, 223
Modern Postcards (San Francisco Museum of Modern Art), 223
modern postcards, collecting, 336
Molloy Post Card Services, 259-260
Mommy, It's a Renoir (Wolf), 250-251
money, 261
Mucha, Alphonse, 220, 335
musicians, 231-232

National Postal Museum, 267
National Postcard Week, 279
Nazi postals, 222
Neales of Nottingham, 308
Nelson, Lord Horatio, 246-247
Neudin, 305-306
New York
   Broom County, 245
   Coney Island, 248
   Statue of Liberty, 239-240
Nickelodeon Theatres and Their Music (Bowers), 219-220
North German Confederation, 3, 12
novelty postcards, 145-146, 241
Nuhn, Roy, 302, 307
Nuhns' Postcard Auction Fair, 307
Numismatic Card Company, 261-262

Oklahoma City, 227-228
Old Knoxville, 249
Old Milwaukee: A Historic Tour in Picture Postcards (Filardo), 229-230
Old Raging Erie (Rinker), 244
Old Teddy Bear Post Cards, 234
Opera House Album (Osborne), 241-242
Oregon, 219
Over 900 Things to Know about Postcard Collecting (Wolstenholm), 251

"par ballon nom monte", 7
patriotic cards, 222, 246
Peerless Princess of the Plains (Ross, Ottaway and Stewart), 245
Pennsylvania, 240
Pennsylvania Album: Picture Postcards, 1900-1930 (Miller), 240
periodicals, 295-304
Perkins, W.B., 361
Pfau, Ed, 275-276
Phillimore, Reginald, 305

Phillimore: The Postcard Art of R.P. Phillimore (Astolat), 218
Phillips auctioning firm, 309
photographic postcards, 241
Picture Post Card Catalogue, 1870-1945, 306
Picture Postcard History of New York's Broome County Area, 245
Picture Postcard Monthly, 225, 256, 295-296
Picture Postcards in Australia (Cook), 223-224
Picture Postcards in the United States, 1893-1918 (Ryan), 246
Picture Postcards of Cyprus 1899-1930 (Lazarides), 237-238
Pioneer Era, 13
Pioneer Postcards (Burdick), 221-222
post cards, vs. postcards, 333
post offices, 230
postal cards, vs. postcards, 337
Postcard Classics, 302
postcard clubs, 11
Postcard Collecting; A Beginner's Guide (Lund), 238
Postcard Collecting: A Fun Investment (Stadtmiller), 248-249
Postcard Collector, 296-298
Postcard Collector's Guide and News, 303
Postcard Collector's Magazine, 303
Postcard Dealer and Collector, 302-303
Postcard Journal, 259, 302
postcards
   artist-signed, 334
   beginnings of, 3
   business aspects of, 224-225
   chronology of, 12-13
   collecting modern, 336
   as communication, 9
   decline of interest in, 11
   grading scale for, 337
   most expensive, 334-335
   novelty, 145-146
   popular category of, 335
   pre-1898, 221-222
   selecting for purchase, 333
   selling, 334
   types of, 137-144
   vs. other collectibles, 336-337
   vs. post cards, 333
   vs. postal cards, 337
Postcards from Old Kansas City (Ray), 243, 244
Postcards of Alphonse Mucha (Bowers and Martin), 220
postmarks, and card value, 335
Postmarks on Postcards (Helbock), 232
postmen, 5
Prairie Fires and Paper Moons (Morgan and Brown), 241
Prentbriefkaart – A.P.C. Magazine, 301
"Presidential Portraits", 262
Preziosi, Don, 276-277
price catalogues, 304-306
prices, 55, 241, 246, 248
   Canadian postcards, 231
printers, 17
propaganda, 236
publications, 295-310
publishers, 17-52, 255-264

Australian, 224
colophons of, 355-365
puzzle cards, 242

Quartuccio, Anthony, 277-278

R & B Stars of 1953 (Hart), 231-232
Raikes, Robert, 4
Raphael Tuck & Sons, 222, 363
Rare and Expensive Postcards (Kaduck), 235-236
rarity scale, 55
reading, importance of, 4
Reagan, Ronald, 257
Reflections from Kansas 1900-1930 (Wood and Daymond), 251
Reflections of a Bygone Age, 209
religion, 236
Robert Robinson: American Illustrator (Bowers and Bowers), 220
Robinson, Robert, 220, 334
Royal Postcards (Smith), 247-248
royalty, 247-248
Rusnak, Ann, 278-279
Ryan, E., 249
Ryan II and Horina, Too (Stansbury), 249

St. Joseph Calendar & Novelty Co., 362
Sally Carver Auctions, 307
Salmon, J., 362
San Francisco, California, Museum of Modern Art, 223
Santa Claus, 222, 233, 240
Scenic View Card Co., 363
Scherer-Silman Bamforth Postcard Catalog, 246
Schwartz, A., 7, 12
Seeman, E.A., 363
series, 243, 334
sets, 243, 334
shows, 343-346
Smith, J.H.D., 267, 304, 308
song cards, 246
Sorocchi, A., 363
Spafford, Suzy, 263
Spanish-American War, 247
Sparre, Coralie Dixon, 257-258
Specialized Postcard Auction, 309
sports, 235, 236
Stadtmiller, Bernard, 303
Stanley Gibbons Postcard Catalogue, 305
Statue of Liberty, 239-240
stereo cards, 225
Steuben glass, 226
Strader, Art, 257-258
street scenes, value of, 336
subjects, on postcards, 137-144
Sunday School, 4
supply dealers, 329
Suzy's Zoo, 263-264
Sweden, 225

teddy bears, 233, 234, 241
Teddy Bears on Paper (Nicholson), 241
Teich, Curt, 243, 258-259
Texas, 224
Thill, Ern, 363
Third Reich, 222
Tichnor, 243
Tichnor Art Company, 259
Tichnor Brothers, 259

Topographical Locator for Picture Postcard Collectors (Gibbs), 230
toys, 233, 234
Trams on Old Picture Postcards (Ellis), 228-229
transportation cards, 222, 228-229, 236
   value of, 336
Transportation Postcards (Kaduck), 236
Tuck, Raphael, 222, 363

United States, 225
   early picture postcards in, 9
   first postcards in, 3
   government postal of, 335
Universal Postal Union, 5, 12

Vanished Splendor III (Edwards, Oliphant, & Ottaway), 227-228
Varga, Alberto, 249
Varga, The Esquire Years (van der Marck), 249-250
Victorian Children Post Cards, 234
Vienna Cafe Society, 10
views, 222
Visual Vacations, 260-261

Walker, George, 262
What the Postman Saw (Brooks, Fletcher, and Lund), 221
white border cards, 13
Whitford, Craig, 261
Wichita, Kansas, 245
Wish You Were Here (Kelbaugh), 236
World War I, 10, 247
World War II, 234-235, 242, 247
World War II Military Comics (Pittman and Greiner), 242
World's Tackiest Postcards, 237

Zaltbommel, European Library, 209

Index to Illustrations

A.H., 359
A.K., 97
A.R.P. de Lord, 357
Aberdeen, Maryland, Richard's
    Restaurant, 167
Abrams, M., 355
Acacia Card Co., 152
Acmegraph Co., 355
Acoma Indian Brave, 161
Adamson, C.R., 189
Adfactor, 262
Adolph Selige Publishing Co., 180
advertising, 156, 167-169
airplanes, 185
airports, 186
Akron, Ohio, greetings from, 157
Albert I of Belgium, 196
Alex, Inglis, 359
Alexandra, Queen of England, 198
Alfred E. Newman and sister, 173
Allied Printing, 150
Allmann, R., 56
Amalia, Queen of Portugal, 198
American News Co., 160, 355
Amorozo, 57
Andrews, Stephen, 284
Andrews, Wesley, 193
animals, 178-180
Apache Ghost Dancers, 161
Appalachian handicrafts, 163
Aristophot, 356
Arizona, buffalo, 180
Art Deco, 175
Art Institute of Chicago, 356
Art Nouveau, 175
Art View Card Distributors, 169
Ashe, Oscar, 203
Asheville Post Card Co., 162, 163,
    191
Athens
    Parthenon, 172
    Temple of Theseus, 172
Atlantic City, New Jersey,
    Boardwalk, 151
Auburn Post Card Manufacturing
    Co., 187
Austen, J.I., 206
Austria, emperor, 187
Austrian Correspondenz Karte, 3

B.H.C., 357
Bairnsfather, Bruce, 59
Baltimore, Maryland, Johns
    Hopkins Hospital, 206
Bamforth, 356
Barbados, sugar weighing, 163
Barbier, Paul, 60
Barkalow Bros., 193, 356
Bartow, Florida, Wonder House,
    171
Bastien, A., 61
Batey, Robert, 61
Bavaria
    1884 postal, 6
    Richard Wagner Theatre, 170
Beadell, Angela, 280
Beagles, J., 356
Becker, C., 62
Behrendt, Richard, 160
Berger, Georg, 64
Berger Bros., 356
Bergman, S., 182, 183, 184

Berlin, Germany, 154
Berman, Jennifer, 280-281
Bernstein, Max, 186
Berstein, Max, 194
Bertiglia, A., 64
Betanzos, 65
Bible Institute Colportage
    Association, 192
Bieber, Ernest, 65
Bien, Julius, 357
Bill's Gay Nineties, 167
Billings, Montana, Range Rider,
    175
Billings News Agency, 175
Billy the Kid, 175
birds, 178, 188
Birn Bros., 357
birthday cards, 181
Bismarck, Count von, 201
blacks, 162
Blackwell Wielandy, 194
Blake, Richard, 268
Blarney Stone, 206
Boccacino, Jean, 269
Boer War, 201
Boileau, Phillip, 66
Bonneville Salt Flats, 189
Boots Cash Chemist, 357
Bosselman (A.C.) & Co., 154
Boucher, J.F., 67
Braun & Cie, 165
Bray, Doris Jean, 281
Brayton, Lily, 203
Breger, Dave, 68
bridges, 155-156, 177
Britain, Ann Hathaway's Cottage,
    169
Brown, Ken, 281
Brown, Tom, 69
Bruch, O., 69
Bruder Kohn, 198, 199, 357
Brundage, Francis, 69
Brussels, Belgium, Hotel
    Metropole, 168
Bryant Union Publisher, 357
buffalo, 180
bus depots, 205

C.B., 59
C.P.I., 359
C.T. American Art, 165
C.T. Art, 150, 156, 157, 158, 161,
    162, 167, 188, 190
Cairo, Illinois, Safford Memorial
    Library, 159
California, Alligator Farm, 177
Capitol News Co., 193
Carcedo, P., 72
Cardinell-Vincent Co., 357
Carlos, King of Portugal, 198
Catalina Island, Flying Fish, 180
cats, 178
Cavi, R., 73
Cennia, A., 73
Centerville, Iowa, post office, 151
Century of Progress (Chicago,
    1933), 151
Chaffee & Co., 163
Chaplin, Charles, 204
Chapman, 74
Charles M. Monroe Co., 196
Charleston, South Carolina, Old
    Slave Market, 170

Charlotte, Queen of Wurttemberg,
    Germany, 199
Cherokee Indians doing Corn
    Dance, 162
Cheyenne, Wyoming, Union Pacific
    Station, 193
Chicago
    double deck buses, 176
    public libraries, 159
    Women's Building, Moody Bible
        Institute, 192
    Wrigley Field, 188
Chicago World's Fair, Intra Mural
    Bus, 176
Chickasha, Oklahoma, Oklahoma
    College for Women, 207
Chief Iron Tail, 161
China Clipper, 186
Christmas, 182
Christoph Reisser's Sohne, 198
Christy, F. Earl, 75
Chrysler Corporation, 163
churches, 158-159
Cincinnati, Ohio, tornado (1915),
    160
circus train wreck (1915), 160-161
city halls, 195
City News Agency, 157
Clapsaddle, 75
Clark, P.G., 157
Claval, Jean, 287
Clifford, Camille, 203
Cline, W.M., 161
Cline Photo Co., 169
Cockington Village, Torquay
    (pre-1920), 153
colleges, 189-190, 207
Columbus Street Press, 262
Cooper, Frank E., 155, 156
Corbin, Kentucky, Sanders Court
    and Cafe, 169
Cork, Ireland
    Kissing the Blarney Stone, 206
    Patrick Street (pre-1920), 152
    St. Patrick's Bridge, 155
courthouses, 187
Crocker, H.S., 207
Cuba, 10
Cunningham Post Card, 161
Curteich, 207, 258-259

Dallas Post Card Co., 179
Dare, Phyllis, 204
death condolence, 204
De Lesseps, Ferdinand, 164
De Longpre, Paul, 79, 167
De Queen, Arkansas, Business
    district (1950s), 152
Dermbach, 11
Des Moines, Iowa, Old Dutch Mill,
    190
Deseret Book Co., 173, 186, 189
Detering, Osc., 81
Detroit News Co., 358
Detroit Photographic Co., 358
Dexter Press, 167
Dickens, Charles, Old Curiosity
    Shop, 204
disasters, 159-161
divided back card, 12
Dodd, Francis, 80
Dollfuss, 165
Downe, Charles Darwin's house,
    171
Drake, Sir Francis, 166
Dreger, T., 81
Droplit Books, 284, 286-287
Druco-Optus Drug Stores, 195

Dunlap Henline Distributors, 165
Dutch Royal Family (1909), 197
Duval News, 187, 205

E.L.D., 202
E.P. Charlton & Co., 193
Earle, 171
Easter, 182
Eastern National Park &
    Monument Association, 192
Egypt, 4
El Reno, Oklahoma, Fort Reno,
    207
Elizabeth, Queen of England,
    coronation, 196, 197
Endacott, Sidney, 83
Engel, Emil, 358
Enid, Oklahoma, First
    Presbyterian Church, 158
Ern Thill, 170
Essanay, 204
ethnic humor, misplaced, 162
exaggerations, 157-158
Eyre & Spottiswoode, 176

Fabo, Andy, 284
famous people, 164-167
Fisher, Harrison, 84
flags, 187, 203
Flion, P.J., 358
Florida, Royal Poinciana Tree, 174
Fort Lauderdale, Florida, banyon
    tree, 205
Founder's Day, 12th annual
    celebration (Lawton,
    Oklahoma, 1912), 151
Founder's Week, 225th
    Anniversary (Philadelphia,
    1908), 151
Four Horsemen, 174
Fox, Craig, 85
Francken, B.V., 86
Franco-British Exhibition (1908),
    150
Franz Ferdinand and Sophie
    Chotek, crown prince of
    Austria, 199
Franz Joseph, 198, 199
Frashers, 161
Free (The), 168
Fuilford, Doug, 285

G.D. & D.L., 358
G.E.S., 118
G.T. Co., 358
Gable, Clark, 203
Gale & Polden, 170, 171, 358
Galveston, Texas, Union Station,
    194
Galveston Wholesale News Co.,
    194
Gannett, W.H., 181
Garland, Judy, 203
Gautier, Gerard-Louis, 288
Gawad, Adly, 286
Geary, Rick, 269
George VI of England, 197
Germany
    advertising card, 8
    1890 card, 4
    emperor, 187
Gerson Bros., 151
Gerstenhauer, I.A., 87
Gibson Art Co., 182, 358
Giesen Bros. & Co., 358
Giessel, Carl, 170
Gilbert, Sir Humphrey, 165
Girling, Oliver, 287

Glaser, Louis, 196
Glasglow, Kentucky, Dutch Mill Village, 190
Glicksman, Alan, 285
Gloria-Viktoria, 358
Goodrich, R., 359
Gopher News Co., 162
Greenville, South Carolina, Main Street (1920s), 153
greetings, 157, 183, 205
Griggs, H.B., 90
Gruss Aus Hall, 8
Gruss Aus Steinau, 7
Gruss Aus Verchau, 7
Gutjahr, Erich, 200

H.H., 90
H.H.T., 363
H.S.B., 175
H.W., 129
Hackley News, 190
Halloween, 183
Hamilton, Ohio, Great Flood (1913), 160
Hamm, Patrick, 291, 292
Hammon Publishing Co., 359
Hannibal News Co., 166
Harley, Matt, 285
Harriman, George, 160
Harris News Agency, 166
Harrop's, 177
Hartmann, F., 359
Hassell, John, 92
Havana, Cuba
  delivery wagon, 176
  funeral car, 179
  San Rafael Street, 154
headgear, 205
Healing Cup, 149
Henry Ford Factory, 170
Hiawatha and Minnehaha (Minneapolis, Minnesota), 162
high schools, 193
Hillsboro New Co., 204
Hochstetter & Vischer, 199
Hofatelier Kosel, 199
Hoffmann, Anton, 94
Holdup on the Road, 176
holidays, 181-184
Holland, Michigan, windmill, 190
Holloway, Edgar A., 94
Hollywood, California, Hollywood and Vine (1940s), 152
Hollywood, Florida, dog track judge's stand, 189
Hondo, Texas, Courthouse and jail, 187
hotels, 207
Huld, Franz, 162
Humbard, Rex, 167
humorous cards, 173-174

Ibbetson, Ernest, 95
Ibsen, Henrik, 165
Independence, Missouri, City Hall, 195
Independence Day, 184
Indian Country, greetings from, 157
Indianapolis, Indiana, Speedway, 188
Indians, 161-162
International Art Publishing Co., 359
International Post Card Co., 164
Italy, postal card, 8

J. Beagles & Co., 197, 198, 203, 204
J.B. Pound Hotels, 156
J.M.P., 360
J.O. Stoll Co., 159
J.S. Broadbent & Co., 195
Jacksonville, Florida
  Hotel George Washington, 168
  Union Bus Station, 205
jails, 205
Jamaica News & Post Card Supplies, 158
Japan, Philander Smith Biblical Institute, 149
Jeudy, Pierre, 288
Jobber-Bradford News Co., 166
Jocelyn, Tim, 285
Jordi, 154
Joshua Trees in desert, 174
Juarez, Mexico, Jail, 205

Kanda, 359
Kansas City, Missouri
  Municipal airport, 186
  Union Station and Sky Line, 194
Karl I, Austrian emperor, 198
Kashover Co., 359
Kaskeline, 97
Keller, Don, 98
Kellern, Morris, 98
Kemp, Sherry, 272
Kingston, Jamaica, Catholic Church, 158
Kitchener, Lord, 202
Klepac, Joan, 282
Klunder, Barbara, 285
Kirksville, Missouri, State Normal School, 190
Kraemer Art Co., 160, 359
Kropp, E.C., 152, 159, 168, 194, 207
Kruis, Ferdinand, 100
Kuroki, General, 202
Kyle Co., 179, 360

L.L., 153, 177, 204, 360
Lakeland News Co., 171
Laplanders, 204
Larsen, L.H. ("Dude"), 101
Lawrence, 153
Lawton, Oklahoma, Lawton State Bank, 168
Leap Year, 182
Lebanon, Ohio, Bible Church of God, 159
Lebrun, Albert, 165
Lee, Coral, 257-258
Lee, Robert E., 200
Leighton, Hugh C., 359
Lenzi, Marc, 273
Leslie, F.H., 156
LeSueur, F.P., 360
Lewis and Clark Exposition, 150
libraries, 159
Liersch, Gustav, 197, 200
Lincoln, Abraham, 191
linen card, 13
Liszt, Franz von, 167
lithography, 11
Liverpool, double deck tram on Lord Street, 177
Lollesgard Specialty Co., 175, 180
London
  bus, 176
  Cheapside, 155, 177
  First Avenue Hotel, 169

Gunn Carriage, Tower of London, 171
London Bridge, 155
Ludgate Circus (pre-1920), 154
Oxford Circus, 177
Prisoner's walk, Tower of London, 170
Rotten Row, 154
Royal Exchange, 153
St. Ermins Hotel, 169
Westminster Bridge, 155
Long, Huey P. "Catfish", 166
Longpue, Paul, 79
Longshaw Card Co., 203
Los Angeles, California
  Ostrich Farm, 178
  Union Depot, 194
Louis Kaufmann & Sons, 359
Louise, Queen of Prussia, 199
Lowman & Hanford, 360
Luxembourg postal, 5
Lythe, T. Watson, 360

M.P.G., 87
MacFarlane, W.G., 181
Mackain, F., 104
Maduro, I.L., 360
Majestic Publishing Co., 360
Man of War, 179
Manhattan Post Card Publishing Co., 360
Manning, Reg, 105
Manson News Agency, 360
Marci, G., 168
Marquer, Pierre, 288
Mary, Princess of Wales, 197
Marysville, California, City Hall and Fire Department, 195
Mater, 106
Max, German prince, 198
May, Edna, 203
Mayes, Marge, 282
McCleery, Dr., 166
McLaughlin & Barkhart, 193
Megaree, Lon, 107
Merrill, Michael, 285
Metrocraft, 170
Metropolitan News Co., 360
Mexico, 9, 180
  Juarez, 10
Miami, Florida, Sausage Tree, 174
Michael-Cristo, Jean, 288
Mid-Continent News Co., 157
military, 200-202
Miller, Joaquin ("Poet of the Sierras"), 206
Miller Art Co., 150
Miller Brewing Co., 360
Minsky Bros., 189, 194
Mitchell, Edward, 163, 206
Mitchell, South Dakota, City Hall, 195
Molloy Post Card Services, 260
Monroe, James, 191
Montreal, Canada, Canadian Pacific Railway Station, 193
Mooi, Holland, windmill, 190
Moscow, Russia, bird's-eye view, 155
Moses Tabernacle in the Wilderness, 158
Mother's Day, 184
Moure, Yannick, 289
Munson, Walt, 109

N.R.M., 360
Napoleon I, Emperor, 201, 202

Nashville, Tennessee, Union Station, 193
native costumes, 204
New Orleans, Louisiana, Morning Call, 168
New Year, 182, 183
New York City, 156
  Brooklyn Bridge, 155
  Cleopatra's Needle, 170
  George Washington Bridge, 156
  Times Square (1950s), 152
New York World's Fair (1939), 150, 207
Niagara Falls, New York, Shredded Wheat Plant, 168
nickel, Indian on, 161
Niles, Michigan, Main Street (1940s), 152
Niles Office Supply, 152
Nimy, Buck, 110
Nixon, President and Mrs. Richard, 191
Nogales, Mexico, Cavern Cafe, 167
North American Post Card Co., 157, 158
Northampton, The Drapery (pre-1920), 154
Norwich Flood, 159
Notre Dame, 157
Novelti-Craft Co., 174
Numismatic Card Company, 261-262
Nunes, E.H., 110
Nuremberg, Germany, flood (1909), 160

Oberammergauer Passion Play, 149
occupations, 163-164
Ocean Comfort Co., 196
Ohnet, Georges, 164
Oklahoma
  cotton picking in, 164
  greetings from, 157
Oklahoma News Co., 159
"Old Ironsides", 201
Olson, H.A., 186
Omaha, Nebraska, Central High School, 193
Oregon, Columbia River, 163
Orr, E.M., 110
Ottenheimer, I.& M., 196
Outcault, Richard F., 112

P.H., 91
Pacific Novelty Co., 150, 178, 361
Pallis (A.) & Cie., 172
Pallis & Cotzias, 205
Pallolio, A., 112
Pan American Airways, 186
Pan-Pacific Exposition (1915), 150
Paris, France
  Opera, 171
  Paix Street (pre-1920), 153
  traffic, 177
Partridge, Bernard, 113
patriotic cards, 188
Payne, Harry, 114
Peace Bridge connecting Fort Erie and Buffalo from Canada, 156
Pearse, Alfred, 114
Pennsylvania, anthracite coal loading, 163
Peoria, Illinois, Bradley Polytechnic Institute, 189
Perry, Commodore, 202
Petitjean, Anne, 283

Petley, Bob, 361
Pfau, Ed, 275
Philadelphia, Pennsylvania
  Betsy Ross House, 169
  Carpenter's Hall, 192
  City Hall, 195
  Home of William Penn, 207
Philadelphia Post Card Co., 361
Philander Smith Biblical Institute
  (Japan), 149
Philco Pub. Co., 361
Photoceler, 204
Photogelatine Engraving Co., 361
Pictorial Stationery Co., 169, 362
Piltz, Stanley A., 186
Pittsburgh, Pennsylvania
  Allegheny County Courthouse,
    187
  Carnegie Institute of
    Technology, 189
  Dusquesne University, 189
  Pennsylvania Railroad Station,
    194
Pompeii, 191
Pope Leo X, 164
Portland Post Card Co., 362
Portugal, 178
post offices, 151
Poulbot, 115
Presser, T., 167
Preziosi, Don, 276
Prince Publishing Co., 362
prisons, 205
Prosdocimi, A., 115

Quartuccio, Anthony, 277
Quebec, Canada, riding buggy, 178
Quentin, Etienne, 289

R.L.S., 119
railroad stations, 193-194
Raleigh, Sir Walter, 164
Rapid Photo Printing Co., 362
Ravenhill, Leonard, 116
Reichard & Lindner, 199
Reichner Bros, 201
religious cards, 149
Remscheid, 7
Renatus, O.H., 116
Reno, Nevada, 186
Reynolds, B.S., 193, 362
Rhiptchu, L.R., 117
Riccardi, 164
Richmond, Virginia
  Edgar Allan Poe Shrine, 169
  White House of the Confederacy,
    171
Richmond News Co., 169, 171, 362
Rigot, Max, 176
Roberts, British field marshal
  Earl, 201
Rochester News Co., 362
Rockne, Knute, 165
Rogers, Will, memorial card to,
  165
romance, 172
Romer, G.W., 174
Roosevelt, Franklin, 191
Roosevelt, Theodore, and family,
  191
Rotary, 196, 197, 198
Rotograph Co., 191, 202
Rotophot, 362
Rotterdam, Holland, windmill, 190
Roy, Tony, 118
royalty, 196-201
Rusnak, Ann, 278-279

Russia, undivided back card from,
  10
Russo-Japanese War, 202
RUWA, 165

S.H. Kress Co., 164
S.I.P., 201
S.V.D., 198
Sabinal, Texas, Sabinal Christian
  College, 189
Sackett & Wilhelms, 362
Safford Memorial Library, 159
St. Augustine, Florida, oldest
  schoolhouse, 187
St. John, 119
St. Joseph, Missouri, 177
  Pony Express Barn, 170
St. Joseph Calendar & Novelty
  Co., 177
St. Louis, Missouri
  City Hall, 206
  riverboat race, 188
  Union Station and Post Office,
    194
  Union Station at Night, 194
St. Louis World's Fair (1904), 151
St. Patrick's Day, 184, 185
St. Paul, Minnesota, Holman
  Municipal Airport, 186
Salina, Kansas, City Hall, 195
Salt Lake City, Utah, Main Street
  (pre-1920), 152
Samuel Cupples Envelope Co., 151
San Antonia Card Co., 174
San Francisco, California
  Cooking in streets after
    earthquake (1906), 160
  Dutch windmill, Golden Gate
    Park, 190
  Golden Gate Bridge, 156
  Golden Gate International
    Exposition, 207
Sandborn Souvenir Co., 175
Sander, P., 207, 363
Sandoval News Service, 174, 205
Sarasota, Florida, business section
  (1940s), 153
Scandanavia, 4
Scenic South Card Co., 191
Scenic View Card Co., 156
Schaefers, J.H., 197
Schever, Mann, Willi, 120
Schuler, Del, 283
Schwormstadt, Felix, 121
Scranton News Co., 163
Searle, R., 121
Shaw News Agency, 190
Sheahan, M.T., 178
Shearer, 122
ships, 196
Slaughter, Tom, 286
Slimgo, 122
"Small Wonder, Small World",
  284, 286-287
Smith, F.V., 123
Smith, Harvey Partridge, 123
Smith, Larry, 124
Smokey Mountains Park, 191
Socrates, prison, 205
Southern Post Card Co., 153
Souvenir Athenes, 11
Souvenir d' Egypte, 8
Souvenir of Zante, 11
sports, 188
stage stars, 203-204
Standard Sales Co., 188-189
Standing, William, 124
Stanley A. Piltz Co., 190

steamboats, 196
Stengel & Co., 164
Stilwell, Oklahoma, 157
  greetings, 192
  Indians in, 161
Stimson, 125
Stockton, California, Hotel
  Stockton, 207
Stollberg, 12
Stratton, H.H., 363
street scenes, 151-155
superlatives, 186-187
Suzy's Zoo, 264
swastika, 205
Swinghammer, Kurt, 286

T.P. & Co., 363
T.R.G., 151
Tampa, Florida, Gasparilla
  carnival, 204
Tarantino, Laura, 283-284
Taylor, A. & G., 363
Teich, Curt, 151, 152, 170, 180,
  190, 195, 207, 363
Tempest, D., 126
Tex, 126
Texas, 186
  cactus, 174
  Centennial Celebration (1945),
    150
Texas Longhorn, 179
Thanksgiving, 181
Thinlot, Albert, 289
Thomas, J., 172
Three Rogues, 178
Tichnor Bros., 151, 159, 188, 192
Times Square (New York, 1950s),
  152
Torggler, H., 127
Toronto, Canada, City Hall, 195
Tourist Development Bureau, 185
trains, 177, 180-181
Traldi, A., 364
transportation, 176-179
trees, 174-175, 205
Trouche, Paul E, 170
Tuck, Raphael, 177, 187, 191, 196,
  201
Tulsa, Oklahoma
  Boston Avenue Methodist
    Church, 159
  Main Street looking south
    (1940s), 152
Twain, Mark, 166
Twin Falls, Idaho, High School,
  193
Tyrrell, E.R., 128

U.S.A. Post Card, 363
United Art Publishing Co., 183
United States
  1898 card for private use, 5
  government postal, 3
  National Birds, 188
  private mailing card (1898-
    1901), 8
University of Notre Dame, 157
Utah
  first house built in, 186
  State Capital at night, 173

Valentine-Black Co., 195
Valentine cards, 183, 184
Valentine's, 150, 155, 159, 197,
  364
Valentine's XL Series, 192
Van Ornum Colorprint Co., 167
Venice, Italy, 154

Vent, Erella, 286
Veteran's Day, 184
Vicksburg, Mississippi, 164
Victor Emmanuel III of Italy, 197
Victoria, Queen of England, 197
Villa, General Francisco "Pancho",
  202
Visual Vacations, 261
Voigt, Hugo, 128
von Haesler, German General in
  World War I, 200
von Schneider, Rud., 129
Voyce, Julie, 287

Walker, George A., 286
Wall, B., 130
Warwick Bros., 364
Warwick Bros. & Rutter, 178
Wasatch News Service, 166
Washington, George, 192
  mansion, 193
Washington, D.C., Blair House,
  171
Washington News Co., 364
Washington Novelty, 191
Wellington Hippodrome, 170
Wellman, Walter, 130
Weltstadt, 154
Wessler, H., 131
Western Publishing & Novelty Co.,
  152, 174, 194
Wheelock, C.E., 364
white-bordered card, 13
Wholesale Post Card Co., 364
Wilhelm II, 198, 199, 200, 201
  marriage commemorative of
    daughter (1913), 197
Wilhelmina, Queen of Holland, 200
Wilkie & Son, 163
William Jubb Co., 359
Willis, J.R., 132, 157, 186
windmills, 190
Witt, 132
Wohlfahrts-Karte, 364
Wohlfahrts-Postkarte, 365
Wolfe, P.A., 132
Woodgifts, 170
Woolstone Bros., 364
World War I, 187
World War II, 200
Worth & Co., 164, 165, 166
Wurttemburg, Germany
  governmental postal, 5

Y.M.C.A., 365
Yankee Clipper, 185
Young, A.J., 202
Young, Brigham, 166

Zimmerman, 134
Zita, Empress of Austria-Hungary,
  199